Key To Gracious Living
Wine and Spirits

Peter J. and

Gracious Living

Wine and Spirits

Frances D. Robotti

Prentice-Hall, Inc.
Englewood Cliffs, New Jersey

2936

Key to Gracious Living: Wine and Spirits
by Peter J. and Frances D. Robotti
Copyright © 1972 by Peter J. and
Frances D. Robotti

ISBN: 0-13-514869-3
Library of Congress Catalog Card
Number: 76-167626
Printed in the United States of
America   3
Prentice-Hall International, Inc.,
London
Prentice-Hall of Australia, Pty. Ltd.,
North Sydney
Prentice-Hall of Canada, Ltd., Toronto
Prentice-Hall of India Private Ltd.,
New Delhi
Prentice-Hall of Japan, Inc., Tokyo
CREDITS:
Illustrations for Chapters 1, 3, 5, 11:
Sketches by John Groth © 1965 by
Esquire, Inc.
For Chapters 4, 7, 8: Woodcuts of
Spiro, 1493. Courtesy Jean Hugel,
Mayor of Riquewihr (Haut-Rhin),
France.
For Chapter 6: Bacchus, by Jonas
Silber. Courtesy Metropolitan Museum
of Art, Harris Brisbane Dick Fund,
1936.
For Chapters 9, 10: Sketches by
Theodore R. Davis from *Harper's
Weekly,* May 11,1872. Courtesy
Pleasant Valley Wine Company,
Hammondsport, N.Y.

Dedication To
Raymond L. Vaudard,
President, L'Académie
Culinaire de France,
founder of the American
Group of the
Commanderies des
Cordons Bleus, Chevalier
and Companion of the
wine and food societies of
France and of the United
States, contributor and
correspondent to the
foremost French-language
culinary magazines and
newspaper food and wine
columns. . .for his tireless
crusade in behalf of the
perpetuation of the
ancient traditions of wine
and spirits in the world of
gastronomy, and for his
warm personal friendship.

Authors' Previous Books

PETER J. ROBOTTI
French Cooking in the New World
Much Depends on Dinner: The Tablecloth Game

FRANCES D. ROBOTTI
French Cooking in the New World
Key to New York: Empire City
Whaling and Old Salem: A Chronicle of the Sea
Chronicles of Old Salem: An Epic of New England

Introduction   America is fast becoming a nation of wine lovers. There are an estimated 87 million consumers of wine, ranging from young adults who begin by drinking sweet, fruity and sometimes sparkling "pop" wines to sophisticated connoisseurs who have graduated to delight in the pedigree as well as the taste of continental wines. And, in spite of the fact that but 300 million gallons of wine are consumed here annually compared to 3.5 billion gallons in France and Italy together (with about half of our population), curiosity, interest and even knowledge in wine is much greater on these shores. Wine is taken for granted and consumed as part of the basic diet in Europe. The average European drinker knows his favorite table wine from his town or region, but he concerns himself with the greats of the wine world only on exceptional occasions.

The 1970's may well go down in history as the decade when wine came of age in America. Its popularity is growing at such a phenomenal rate that experts predict total annual consumption will match that of all distilled spirits by 1980 (including such favorites as scotch, bourbon, vodka and gin).

Peter and Frances Robotti have written an impressive book that can serve as a complete guide to the joys of wine—both as a delightful beverage and as an ingredient in haute cuisine— for a new generation of aficionados. They bring to these pages impeccable credentials that enable them to blend the creation of gourmet food with the service of fine wines. For years they have pleased discerning palates in their New York restaurant, Le Chateau Richelieu, named for the crafty French cardinal who was so expert in matters gustatory. The restaurant's well-chosen wine cellar and finely appointed bar reflect the taste and knowledge of true connoisseurs.

Mr. and Mrs. Robotti have captured the spirit of the times in their new book. They present the reader—whether he be a novice or an amateur in the true sense of the word—with an easily understandable compendium of information on the complexities of wine. But this is not all—their new book is also an exhaustive source of information on whiskies, brandies, liqueurs and the entire gamut of mixed drinks concocted for their use, plus dissertations and recipes for enjoyable eating along with the potables.

Home entertainment has great appeal today, and the Robottis bring the skilled experience from their distinguished restaurant into the home kitchen and dining room to help one play the perfect host. They appeal to the adventuresome inquisitiveness about wines, spirits and food that has captivated increasing numbers of Americans who have been exposed to more travel, more education, more leisure time and more affluence than ever before in our nation's history.

This consummate guide will enable the reader to recreate the pleasures of Le Chateau Richelieu in his own home.

Julius Wile

Julius Wile Sons & Co., Inc.

Foreword This book was conceived in 1961 after the publication of *Much Depends on Dinner,* covering three decades of haute cuisine at Le Chateau Richelieu. So much interest was aroused, and so many questions asked, that we were determined in due course to enlarge upon the theme of wine and spirits in their association with gastronomy.

With a fresh viewpoint gained in the intervening decade, we believe that since gastronomy and oenology are social arts, evolved through ages of mankind's history, they will continue to be more and more necessary components of our lives, as people turn toward the basic and enduring truths of what constitutes well-being.

Herein, then, is revealed the marvelous world of wine and spirits in relation to hospitality and to gastronomy, to which we have devoted more than a lifetime of enthusiastic and dedicated interest. Through these pages, all may participate according to their individual tastes and inclinations.

This book offers a basic understanding of the subject of wine and spirits without becoming entangled in the specialized world of the true wine connoisseur. It is easily comprehensible and personal in order to bring pleasure through the printed word to old friends and new.

We have tried to point out how the pleasures of the table affect people in every phase of their existence. Our purpose has been to show that the enjoyment of wine and spirits derives not only from consumption of rare and expensive bottles, but to illuminate the vast area of enjoyment open in the ways and byways of the world of wine and spirits.

Above all, wine and spirits are honest, have integrity and character. They stand or fall on their own merits after their entry into the world. In our own way, we have tried to convey their story, and point out some concrete ways in which wine and spirits may add a more lustrous facet to our lives, for they are truly the gracious touch.

Acknowledgments   We acknowledge with gratitude assistance received from many sources in the compilation of this volume: The Wine Institute of San Francisco, Greyton Taylor, Walter S. Taylor, Brace B. Foster and David J. Reagen of the Taylor Wine Company; Allan Moskowitz and E. Otto Sichel of Fromm & Sichel and the Brothers of The Christian Brothers; Schieffelin & Co; Julius Wile for his perceptive introduction; the authors of the books consulted and the food writers for their wonderful, timely articles in magazines and newspapers; the staff of Le Chateau Richelieu, particularly Michel Ratte for his letters to picture sources in France; Peter Zuliani, Maître d', and Joseph Humes for invaluable assistance on the cocktail section; Mrs. Rose P. Portugal, Director of Fountainhead Publishers, for her inspired interest and valuable suggestions; Raymond L. Vaudard for his counsel on the culinary section; Mrs. Carmel Balser for help on pagination; Michael Baritelli, American Blueprint, for reproducing prints for the illustrations with such artistic skill and unfaltering acumen; Miss Carol Cartaino of Prentice-Hall for her unfailing faith in us and wise counseling and others of the Prentice-Hall staff who worked in behalf of the book; the encouragement and interest of our friends and Richelieu clientele and of our son, Armando, who spurred us on and often accompanied his mother on library trips for research.

Proprietors of Le Chateau Richelieu

CONTENTS

OF WINE

*There is no other liquid
that flows more intimately
and incessantly through the
labyrinth of symbols we
have conceived to mark our
status as human beings
from the rudest peasant
festival to the mystery of
the Eucharist. To take wine
into our mouths is to savor
a droplet of the river of
human history.*

Clifton Fadiman

OF SPIRITS

*The water of life was given
to us to make us see for a
while that we are more
nearly men and women,
more nearly kind and gentle
and generous, pleasanter
and stronger than without
its vision there is any
evidence we are. It is the
healer, the weaver of
forgiveness and
reconciliation, the justifier
of us to ourselves and to
one another. One more,
and then with a spirit made
whole again in a cleansed
world. . .to dinner.*

Bernard De Voto in
The Hour

The main dining room of Le Chateau Richelieu.

Comrades, pour the wine tonight
For the parting is with dawn.
Oh, the clinks of cup together,
With the daylight coming on.

RICHARD HOVEY (1864–1900)

Chapter 1   Wine And Spirits In A Changing World

FIRST came fire, then the miracle of fermentation. According to anthropologists, these two events mark the beginning of civilization: the history of wine and spirits is the history of the world and the history of art has preserved it. Across the stretches of time, human-kind has turned to fermented juices and distilled spirits as one of life's abiding comforts and, at times, the best medicine under God's firmament for the natural ills of mind and body. Used in moderation, alcoholic drinks stimulate the appetite, aid digestion and have a good effect upon health. The enjoyment of wine and spirits is one of the few private pleasures still reserved to people in a world where scintil-latingly rapid changes are becoming more and more difficult to un-derstand and to tolerate.

Thus, it is useful for everyone to know something about the ab-sorbing subject of absorbing alcohol. The great mistake is that every-one knows too little or too much. Those who know too little either do not admit their lack of knowledge and make an enemy of alcohol by abusing it, or are so terrified of it that they regard it as something

1

unnatural and Satanic. Those who know too much become intolerant of every form of liquid other than the one about which they consider themselves expert. Surely there is a need for a happy medium.

The service of food and wine has been recognized as the eighth art since the Middle Ages (the other arts in that era were classed as grammer, dialectic, rhetoric, music, arithmetic, geometry and astronomy—the liberal arts as distinguished from the mechanical arts and professions). Even in our present age of instantaneous communication and jet flight, there is much to be said for the special firsthand contact between persons that takes place in the sharing of food and wine. Life in a civilized city embraces everything from good food, wine and spirits to good theater, from floral cultivation to intellectual pursuits. Paris, Rome, Vienna, Berlin, London and other great cities beyond the European continent have recognized this for centuries. As travel widens, people become more aware of the nuances of the culinary art and its natural accompaniment—wine and spirits.

Drinking is a vital part of dining out. It is part of a restaurant's function to offer good drinks and good service and to provide the right atmosphere for a pleasant afternoon or evening. The diner will enjoy the experience even more if he is knowledgeable about the fundamentals of wine and spirits. The greater his knowledge, the greater his enjoyment in the participation of the ritual and in hosting his party. Understanding basic rules for choice and service of wine and spirits lends an enviable mastery to a truly social skill, applicable to at-home or restaurant entertainment, travel or even to stocking a home bar or cellar.

As Lucius Annaeus Seneca, the Roman philosopher (3 B.C.–65 A.D.), asked as he sat down to his well-appointed dinner table: "When shall we live if not now?" The sociability of partaking of good food and wine introduces opportunities for love, friendship, business speculation, influence, solicitations, patronage, ambition and intrigue. Conviviality affects practically everything of importance in our lives and deserves the constant pursuit of excellence in strategy and execution.

Our book is offered in a spirit of sharing with the reader, the best of what has been culled from the Old World's beautiful traditions and from our experience in the continuous operation of elegance in the hub of the great gastronomic universe, right in mid-Manhattan, New York City, at our Le Chateau Richelieu. The ideal we have cherished is to perpetuate the symbolism of the gracious approach to life.

To a large extent this book reflects the Peter Robotti philosophy of wine and spirits. Just as our previous book, *Much Depends on Dinner,* concerns the appreciation of gracious dining in and out of the home, it is intended that this volume be a guide to a zestful and intelligent appreciation of wine and spirits relevant to a concept of gracious modern living. There are sparks of graciousness, of unhurried unordinary pleasure, that even the most scheduled and budget-bound person can profitably incorporate into his life.

This work is not intended to be encyclopedic, but observations and information are offered from the vantage point of decades of restaurateurship, traveling and close living within the world of wine and spirits, and with the subject of extending hospitality to the public.

To answer every possible question about when and what to drink and what is proper on a given occasion would be an overwhelming task. Our principal aim is to provide a common-sense understanding of alcoholic beverages as a basis for using your own judgment as to their uses, governed by individual preferences and taste. While the inexperienced will find many answers to their natural questions, the seasoned host or hostess will also find information useful for entertaining. Too many people miss out on the adventure of wine and spirits by limiting themselves to one or two particular wines or drinks. A rich field lies before you, ready to add a touch of exuberance and graciousness, a new and different type of pleasure to highlight a moment or a meal.

The Changing Tastes of Americans

In some respects, one would think that wine and spirits were, of all things, among the least subject to rapid change. There are vineyards in Italy, Germany and France that were first planted by the Romans and are still producing grapes for wine production after 1800 years. While many venerable vineyards survive, many succumb to changing times—as is apparent in California where some vineyards have given way to shopping centers.

Drinking, however, has always been part of the American scene. Our American forefathers of all classes were a groggy lot. Every day before breakfast, John Adams, who had wine for dinner, worked through a tankard or two of hard cider. The Justices of the Supreme Court under John Marshall established a firm rule not to drink on the bench except on rainy days. With clever logic, the Justices promptly decided that their jurisdiction covered the whole country, where it must rain every day in some place. Old records tell of a joyous ordination at which 80 guests honored a 1787 seminary graduate by consuming many delicious victuals accompanied by four huge bowls of spiked punch. John Hancock liked a good party. At a dinner in his home in 1792, the famed signer of the Declaration of Independence provided his 200 guests with 136 bowls of punch, 300 bottles of wine and—for those still standing—Sherry and Brandy after supper.

The American colonists welcomed any occasion for drinking: holidays, proclamation signings, weddings, baptisms, funerals. And drinking helped both the Army and Navy during the Revolutionary years. When the U.S.S. *Constitution* set sail from Boston (August 23,

1779), she carried 475 officers and men, 48,600 gallons of fresh water, 74,000 cannon shot and 79,400 gallons of Rum. The ship's mission was to destroy and harass English shipping. When the *Constitution* reached Jamaica (October 6), she took on 826 pounds of flour and 68,300 gallons of Rum. Three weeks later, reaching the Azores, the *Constitution* garnered 550 pounds of beef and 64,300 gallons of Portuguese wine. The officers and crew rested until November 18, then set sail for England. The records say the *Constitution* crew captured and scuttled 12 English merchantmen before running out of shot and making her way safely up the Firth of Clyde for a night raid. A landing party took a distillery and brought aboard 40,000 gallons of Whiskey. Thus well-stocked, the ship set out for America, arriving in Boston on February 20, 1780. When she docked, there was no cannon shot, no powder, no food, no Rum, no Whiskey —but there were 48,600 gallons of stagnant water.

In America's colonial days and during the first decades of the Republic, Madeira Wine was a great favorite. Ships used the trade-wind route on their way back from Europe, and Madeira was a convenient stopping place to stock up on water, food and wine. "My manner of living is plain," wrote George Washington. "A glass of wine and a bit of mutton are always ready, and such as are content to partake of that are always welcome."

The initial institutions established with the colonization of America were places for refreshment. The first person issued a license to operate a place of food and drink in the Massachusetts Bay Colony was Samuel Coles, Deacon of Boston's First Church. His establishment was called Cole's Ordinary, and Mr. Cole became a leading businessman (he was appointed steward of the newly established Harvard University in 1632). In New York, the Stadts Herrberg, or City Tavern, was licensed by Governor Wilhelm Von Kieft. After serving for some 10 years as a place of refreshment, it became City Hall in 1653 when New Amsterdam became a city.

Wine Drinking in America Before World War I, in the days of the legendary private fortunes, there existed in this country a certain aristocracy for whom wine drinking was part of the traditions inherited from Great Britain, France and Portugal. When the Italians immigrated here, they brought a taste for table wine, but Prohibition put a stop to these pleasures. In retrospect, it succeeded in removing a gracious note and gave Americans a taste for the strong spirits in which the tradition of refinement in the consumption of wine was destroyed.

After the 20 years of Prohibition, a new generation came on the scene. It had no wine culture at all, but accepted strong drinks neat (straight). To be lamented by connoisseurs is what a strong cocktail does to the palate before a meal. The difficult post-World War II years brought many changes in America's wine-drinking habits. Travel was more extensive, cultural provincialism diminished and a more pronounced taste evolved for the good things of life: a more sophisticated cuisine, a more refined way of living and . . . wine.

Wine is gradually becoming a part of the American way of life. Americans are drinking more table and sparkling wine each year, with total consumption doubling every nine years. Wine has what no other beverage possesses: glamor. Therefore it has unique appeal to women as well as to men.

More Americans are becoming familiar with the whole subject of wine, its history and use. Wine-tasting parties serving both American and imported wine are becoming more numerous. (A glossary of terms pertaining to wine tasting is included in this book, page 320, plus aspects of wine and spirits that should be noted, pages 321-323.) France exported 3.6 percent of the wine consumed in the U. S. in 1969. Americans do not buy as much French wine as the Germans or the Scandinavians, but they do buy a superior brand.

Never has the printed advice been so precise as to the wine to be served, and never have the ingredients in cooking recipes published in magazines and newspapers included so much wine and spirits. It is now well-known that cooking with wine and spirits steps up the flavor of old-time favorite dishes; the fine flavoring brings out the natural goodness of foods and adds subtle rich savoriness.

Younger wine is becoming more popular in America and all over the world. This certainly is a revolutionary change. While noble vintages are still venerated, wine bottled for only one or two years is offered. Some German wine is bottled at the age of eight months, but most wine cannot be brought forward so quickly. The great red Bordeaux and the California Cabernets, the French Burgundies and Pinot Noirs from the North Coast counties, require time as always.

The manner in which wine is produced today is vastly different than at the turn of the century, and many wines are ready for the table in a few years rather than a few decades. This is in keeping with changes in attitudes toward food. Our affluent forefathers dedicated themselves to the consumption of seven-course dinners with five different qualities of wine. Today our courses are curtailed and desserts are less elaborate. Dryer table wine is favored, and many prefer fruity wine. An example of this trend is the Almadén Grenache Rosé; Americans are enthusiastically drinking more than a million bottles a year since it was introduced three decades ago.

The opportunity to drink a truly great wine is rare. However, it is good to know about the pleasant Rosés that are not too expensive and are readily available. When Rosé first appeared, many people accustomed to either white or red wine regarded it as an intruder. They believed it a blend of red and white wine, which it is not. Today most people are aware that all good Vins Rosé, wherever they come from in the world, belong in a special category, produced in a special way from black grapes that usually have white juice and pigment in their skins.

It is important in America for restaurants and hotels to suggest wine with meals. Unlike Europeans, many Americans do not automatically ask for a wine list.

Changing Tastes in Spirits Innovation and a continual reshaping of tastes are the result of a greatly increased number of young people entering the market for items ranging from alcoholic beverages to new homes. The large number in the over-20 under-30 age bracket results from the soaring birthrate that followed the end of World War II. More than at any other time in the post-Repeal history of the wine and spirits industry, consumer preferences are more definitely colored by youthful tastes —a fact brought about by millions of new purchasers (granted, of course, that there is a disparity between the average purchasing power of young people in their early twenties and their elders who enjoy higher income).

Who in the beverage field in the late 1940s would have predicted the tremendous growth in public favor for Vodka, for instance, or the popularity of imported Gin and the near tripling of Scotch consumption, which took place in the 1960s? Youthful partakers who prefer a light taste have leaned to the so-called "white" Liquors, Gin and Vodka. There was almost no national consumption of Vodka in 1949, but by 1970 it accounted for almost 13 percent of all distilled spirits consumed that year. While the rate has slowed, it finally surpassed the popularity of Gin. Imported Scotch and Canadian Whisky have increased noticeably in sales, much of it imported in bulk and bottled in the United States.

Aperitifs are being used more widely than previously as an ingredient in mixed drinks with a spirits base. An example of this is the Negroni, made with equal amounts of Campari, Gin and Italian Vermouth, shaken well with ice and strained into a cocktail glass. An herbalized wine, Dubonnet, is an ingredient in cocktails with a Gin or other spirit base. The Dubonnet Cocktail is made of Dubonnet (red or blonde), 1 1/2 ounces of Gin and a lemon twist. Red Robbin on the rocks requires equal parts of Vodka and Dubonnet poured over ice cubes, with a twist of lemon peel added.

In noting changes in taste, consider the novelty of new drinks evolving from Tequila, the spirit distilled in Mexico from the fermented juice of the mescal plant. The popularity of Tequila spread from California and the American Southwest to many other areas. Tequila is used in almost any drink recipe that calls for Gin or Vodka —for instance, a Bloody Maria or Screwdriver. It also constitutes the base ingredient in a number of cocktails particularly identified with the beverage from below the Rio Grande. A Margarita is one familiar example. This is made with 1 1/2 ounces of Tequila, 1/2 ounce of Triple Sec, 1 ounce fresh lime or lemon juice. The Tequila Toreador is more complicated. It is made with 1 1/2 ounces of Tequila, 1/2 ounce of Crème de Cacao and 1/2 ounce sweet cream, poured over cracked ice and shaken well. The contents are strained into a stemmed cocktail glass and topped with a small puff of whipped cream. The Matador calls for 1 ounce of Tequila, 2 ounces of pineapple juice and the juice of half a fresh lime. The contents are shaken with crushed ice and served in a Champagne glass or over the rocks in an Old-Fashioned glass.

New Cordial-type spirits have been introduced, such as Chocla Menthe and Koffie Menthe by John deKuyper & Son. These combine the luscious taste of mint with chocolate and coffee never before marketed in the liquor industry.

In the Rum group, the Mai-Tai has been added to the long-standing Daiquiri and Planter's Punch. The Mai-Tai is made with 1/2 ounce each fresh lime juice, Orgeat and Curaçao plus 2 ounces of Jamaica or Demerara Rum. The ingredients are stirred in a double-size Old-Fashioned glass half filled with finely cracked ice. This drink is decorated with tropical fruits and served with straws.

There has been an upsurge in the popularity of Sake. It is neither a spirit nor a wine, but a member of the beer family. It does not foam as does beer, and there is no carbonation. In Japan, Sake is taken slightly warmed (about 100° F). It is first poured into a china or pottery bottle with a narrow top, then the entire filled bottle is put into hot water, a *bain-marie*. Then it is poured into a shallow, stemmed saucer and sipped. In the United States, Sake is being used as an ingredient in a mixed drink with Gin, Vodka, Rye or other spirits. The Sakini, a version of the Martini, is traditionally 1 part Sake and 3 parts dry Gin or Vodka. What does it taste like? Not at all like beer; more like a dry Sauterne. A Sake Manhattan contains 1 part Sake and 2 parts Rye (or Bourbon), prepared in the regular way. It is low in calories and therefore as welcome as an aperitif of Vermouth or Dubonnet.

How much do people themselves change in a changing world? Many Americans in the past have preferred to live in Paris. In the 1920s, they sat in the cafés sipping aperitifs, criticizing postwar policy, just as their prototypes do today, 50 years later. In our present jet age, there are some 15,000 American expatriates—artists, writers, vagabond students, fugitives from mediocrity and the turmoil of the times—coming to Paris from Chicago, Houston, New York, Los Angeles, Minneapolis to seek a warmer, more meaningful life in France. In addition to this colony, there are some 30,000 more who live in Paris because of business or government assignments.

The Bohemian quarter on the Left Bank belonged to Sherwood

Anderson, Ezra Pound, Sinclair Lewis and Gertrude Stein. Today the spots most frequented are Deux Maggots, Café de Flore, Lipp or La Rotonde and Le Dome for inexpensive food and wine—Paris is now expensive. In 1921, Ernest Hemingway sailed to France as everyone did, but today you can breakfast in New York and after a seven-hour flight, dine in the evening on the Champs Elysees (today called Champs de Gaulle). Modern-day Paris boasts such writers as James Jones *(From Here to Eternity)* and Mary McCarthy *(The Group)*. Although much of a romantic aura still clings to the city, Paris between the two World Wars was not the same as it is today. The Paris constellation of artists of brush and pen in the 1920s and 1930s is gone.

There are signs of awareness of a new age throughout the world. It is encouraging to note the upward trend in amenities of precurtain and between-the-acts imbibing in New York, long a tradition among European theatergoers. Under the new licensing arrangements in New York as of 1967, the Vivian Beaumont Theater in Lincoln Center initiated a fully stocked bar that can provide over 200 drinks during the 10-minute intermission period.

To correct the image of the Ugly American, U.S. industry is developing a new breed of international executive. He is equally at home in London, Berlin or Rome. There has been a great need to acquaint American executives and their wives with the business and social customs abroad, for a lack of such social knowledge can impair the value of a company executive. The answer to this need is CETI. This is an international training center for executives initiated on February 13, 1967, in the Château de Mercues in southwest France. Transformed into a hotel, the ancient château offers its facilities as a training place for executives and their wives from many countries.

Endorsed by the French Government and by the United States State Department, the project is financed by private funds and supported by firms in America and Western Europe who contribute up to $17,000 each. American sponsors include Alcoa, Chrysler Corporation, Continental Grain, International Latex Corporation and Time, Inc. Classes are limited to 25 executives and their wives for each of three 10-week sessions a year. In luxurious hotel surroundings, they study the laws, business structures, sociological and cultural backgrounds of various nations. The courses include the foreign foods, wines and liquors.

CETI stands for Centre d'Exchanges Technologiques Internationaux. It charges $3,000 tuition (including accommodations) per couple. Lectures are given in English and French. Foreign representatives of corporations become better equipped to be unofficial ambassadors of their native countries and societies. CETI should prove of inestimable value not only to the corporations but to the countries represented, for it helps meet the needs of our changing world.

A new breed of men is emerging on the business scene: business-man, artist, scientist in one personality. He is responsible for com-plex business, technological and social changes, using computer applications to support his judgment and imagination in decision-making. He not only examines statistics but fathoms individual moti-vation and group dynamics. This type of man is socially responsible, sensitive to the interaction of business, government and society. He wants to know more about the cuisines and drinking customs of other countries as well as his own.

In juxtaposition to the influx of young people in our present world are those of forty-plus who are exploring what is truly a new time of life. We are in an era in which there is a lively opportunity for the new use of intelligence, taste, imagination and knowledge, a new develop-ment of psyche and charisma, a new eminence for men and women of years. Anne W. Simon calls it the vintage mind in her book *The New Years: A New Middle Age.* In a new way of growing older, people are provided with choices about home life, work life, marital life—choices unknown to their grandparents or parents. Young peo-ple, today's Renaissance men, will gravitate into this new milieu.

Of importance to the subject of home and professional hospitality, therefore, are the changes apparent in the educational and occupa-tional orientation of the population, factors that shape tastes and influence the patronage of restaurants and hotels and the respon-sibilities of a host or hostess in home entertainment.

An occupational profile of the American economy through 1975, prepared by the U.S. Bureau of Labor Statistics, reveals that the number of professional workers will increase 40 percent, technicians by 66 percent, and semiskilled workers by only 18 percent. On the basis of this projection, there should be 2,000,000 scientists by 1975, compared with 1,300,000 in 1964. There will be 332,000 college teachers, compared with 200,000 in 1964.

How do these figures translate into terms of alcoholic beverages? The change in occupations means considerable potential shifts in preference and demand. Merchandisers in the hospitality field will have to take into account greater discrimination and knowledgeabil-ity in taste through experience and reading; a more critical attitude toward service; and an interest in experiencing foods and drinks, the natural consequence of increased sophistication, earning power and education. The increase of leisure time provides opportunity for both at-home and away-from-home entertainment. The growing urban and suburban population with its social acceptance and usage of alcoholic beverages is reaching a high level in greater demand for the amenities offered by wine and spirits.

In the Age of Anxiety, it is sometimes wiser to turn to the soothing balm of liquor than to the expensive psychiatrist. It is more pleasant to gain a bit of euphoria or illusion through the wine glass than to discover some dark recess in one's psyche that causes discontent. Recently there has been more emphasis on the therapeutic powers of alcoholic beverages when wisely used, which has been given medical sanction. Dr. Morris E. Chafetz, in his book *Liquor: The Servant of Man,* says: "If liquor can overcome and suppress man's awareness of the little miseries and drudgeries in life, and thus set free and strengthen his enthusiasm for whatever dominant ideas he may cherish, and if it can lubricate the frictions and pains, and bring back once again the feeling of unity and freedom of flow, then humans would be fools to ignore this aid to civilization."

It happens that the Age of Anxiety coincides with the Age of Affluence. Many people previously used to abstain from wine and spirits because they could not afford to drink, not because of principle. But in prosperity, the abstainers diminish in numbers. It is estimated that by 1980, increased technology will enable 2 percent of the population to produce all of the goods and food the other 98 percent will be able to consume. In fact, the government will be paying millions of people *not* to work. The irony of this, and it is already apparent, is that professional and managerial people—those best attuned educationally and temperamentally, as well as economically, to know how to enjoy leisure—are the very ones who have the least opportunity to do so.

We have reached the point at which the key movers in our society are working 70 to 80 hours a week, taking home briefcases jammed with work. They find the days too crowded for a leisurely meal with wine and spirits, unless they attend business meetings in a restaurant, club or hotel where such hospitality is emphasized. But even then the concentration is on the deal, rather than on enjoying hospitality.

Oscar Wilde lamented that "youth is wasted on the young." Today he would see the busy elite in the business world with no decent leisure. The pursuit of wisdom, truth and beauty was the ideal of ancient civilizations such as the Egyptian, Greek, Roman and Etruscan. "Civilization," said Plato, "is the victory of persuasion over force." Much of this "persuasion" is exercised through hospitality in and out of the home.

In the face of spiraling changes in technology, space and religion, the humanities will somehow survive if individuals place sufficient importance on perpetuating the traditions of hospitality. The ancient custom of "breaking bread" and drinking "which makes the heart glad" may yet prove to be the salvation of health and sanity in a mad world.

The scouts sent out by Moses to the site of the Land of Canaan, carrying an enormous cluster of grapes: Numbers 8:23, "And they came unto the brook of Eschol, and cut down a branch from thence with one cluster of grapes, and they bare it between two on a staff."

And wine that makes glad the heart of man and bread which strengthens man's heart . . .

PSALM 104:15

Chapter **2**

Deep-Rooted In Antiquity

FEW social customs are as universal as drinking. People have enjoyed this pastime and written about it from time immemorial. The oldest Greek name for wine is *Woinos,* which in classical Greek became *Oinos.* In Etruscan and Latin it was *Vinum* and in Hebrew, *Vayin.*

An understanding of how wine and spirits have been present from earliest times, and their mystical connotation, gives a fascinating dimension to present consumption of wine and spirits.

Perhaps the earliest reference to an alcoholic beverage is contained in a Babylonian clay tablet of 2400 B.C. Cuneiform characters mention "two jars of must and twenty of beer" among the ceremonial vessels of a high priest. Some 4,000 years ago, Hammurabi, King of Babylon, wrote a book about the taverns and inns of his day. Concerned about the quality of wine and food they sold and the cleanliness of the premises, he laid down some rules and regulations for their control.

Beer was sacred to Isis, Goddess of Life, and wine to Osiris, Lord of Death. The carvings on an Egyptian tombstone dating to 1600 B.C.

depict the service of their beverages on the family table. Sehetep-ab, an overseer of the audience chamber of the Pharoah in Lower Egypt, is shown seated while his wife, Sedan-sat, stands over the festive board, laid with a roast goose, a roast duck and goblets of beer and wine.

Everything gastronomy could conceive of was represented in Egyptian feasts, with the exception of mutton because divine Ammon is portrayed with a ramlike head. Broiled and salted geese were accompanied by good brown stout and strong barleywine. Delicious roast beef dishes and plum puddings were borrowed by the Egyptian cooks from menus of the pleasure-loving Thebans. Before sitting down to a munificent repast, the guests were served strong Liqueurs as a spur to their appetites.

Egyptian rulers recognized wine as a necessity of life. Their soldiery, besides liberal pay allowance in land and exemption from tribute, daily received five pounds of bread, two pounds of meat and a quart of wine. With such rations, should they really have been bested by the Persians? For their part, however, the Persians had become even more interested in drink than in food. Their national boast was: "We Persians can drink deeper than any other men without seeming half so drunk."

From ancient times, wild grapevines extended from Turkestan deep in Asia along the Armenian southern slopes of the Caucasus range, the northern section of Asia Minor, and in Europe well into Thrace (parts of present-day Bulgaria, Turkey, and Greece). Grapes grew around the Caspian Sea, and from there the vines were brought to all continents.

Egypt produced wine around 2400 B.C., and in China before 2000 B.C. Wine culture is described many times in the Old and New Testaments of the Bible in the locale of Asia Minor. From that region it spread to the Mediterranean countries, which were sheltered and sunny—perfect for grape growing. Before 3000 B.C., a form of wine was being produced in Mesopotamia, the locale of the legendary Flood (about 2800 B.C.) as related in the eighth and ninth chapters of Genesis. It is related that when the turbulent waters subsided, Noah's ark came to rest on the summit of Mount Ararat, the highest peak of the great Caucasus range. God bade Noah and his sons Shem, Ham and Japheth to go forth, to be fruitful and to multiply, and to replenish the water-ravaged earth. Noah became a husbandman and "he planted a vineyard and drank of the wine." Wine became a popular beverage in the Bronze Age with the people of Syria and Palestine and among the Minoans and the Mycenaean Greeks.

When the children of Israel were led out of Egyptian bondage, they complained to Moses and his brother Aaron, who had brought them out of their captivity, that now they found themselves in "a dry and barren land where there were neither figs nor vines." Finally, after 40 years of wandering in the wilderness, they came into the Promised Land and, says the Bible, it was "the time of the first ripe grapes."

When Moses sent scouts out from Kadesh-barnea to spy the land of Canaan, they searched from the wilds of Zim to Rehob and came to the brook of Eshcol. Here they cut down a great branch bearing a single enormous cluster of grapes; the branch was so huge they had to attach it to a stout pole supported on the shoulders of two strong men. When the scouts returned after searching the land for 40 days, they reported to Moses: "We came into the land where you sent us and surely it flows with milk and honey and this is the fruit of it."

The Prophet Jeremiah foresaw great prosperity for his people in Canaan: "Therefore they shall come and sing in the height of Zion and shall flow together in the goodness of the Lord for wheat and for wine and for oil." Ecclesiastes said: "Go your way. Eat your bread with joy and drink your wine with a merry heart for God now accepts your works."

The Book of Kings tells of King Solomon's tables being spread with delicacies and elegant wines worth a king's ransom. The Book of Esther relates the great feast given by the Persian king Ahasuerus replete with exotic foods and wine. Nevertheless, the most costly dinner ever given in the ancient world is attributed to the glamorous Egyptian queen Cleopatra, who served her Roman lover Mark Anthony a dessert that featured a 74-carat melted pearl worth six million sesterces . . . and an array of the most precious wines.

The mythological Dionysus, the god of wine, was sired by Zeus, who fell in love with the mortal maiden Semele, one of the daughters of Cadmus and Hermione. Semele's desire to see her celestial lover cost her her life. Zeus came in all of his majesty with thunder and lightning, consuming Semele. But Vulcan, god of fire, cut the immature infant from his mother's body and he was put into the god's thigh for the balance of his term of gestation. Then the nymphs nursed Dionysus until he was passed along to the Muses and taught viniculture and the making of wine.

The Greeks felt wine was so joyously alive it had to ensconce a god in its being. A god was the soul of the grape and the juice was his blood, so in drinking the wine, one partook of the godhead, who thereupon entered into man's blood and his life. Dionysus, who was depicted with bull's horns, was also the god of dancing and drama; he brought the gift of wine to men to assuage their sorrows.

The frenzied madness with which Dionysus was worshipped gave us the word *ecstasy,* and the Greek word *enthousiasmos* gave us *enthusiasm.* When Phoenician merchants and traders brought the grapevine into Italy in the seventh century B.C., the Romans readily adopted the Greek god Dionysus, calling him Bacchus.

Not only did the Greeks deify the fruit of the vine, but their poet Homer immortalized wine in the *Iliad* and the *Odyssey,* which glow with wine in a Grecian atmosphere of vintages, libations and feastings. The exquisitely wrought shield of Achilles in the eighteenth book of the *Iliad* depicts a vineyard scene. When the shield is lost to Hector, Achilles is no longer able to fight. When the new shield is fashioned, it shows scenes of a vineyard and country dancers. Homer constantly mentions the endless meals and quaffing of unceasing cups of wine by Ulysses even in his old age.

Wine and the social customs it inspires is often depicted in the art of ancient peoples. A black-figured vase in the Louvre in Paris, dating from 550 to 540 B.C., shows vine trails, using an old tree trunk and wooden props for support, and grapes in clusters being gathered by men and boys. Vases and frescoes show ancient methods of making wine. Grapes were thrown into a large stone vat to be trodden by many feet in a rhythmical dance to the accompaniment of simple vintage melodies. Such customs still persist in present-day Greece, Spain, but much less in Italy than heretofore.

The ancient world had three main exportable commodities: corn, oil and wine. The grape and the vine were often placed on contemporary coins. As soon as organized cultivation and exportation of wine was developed, the connoisseur emerged to sample brands, vintage and proof. Such a critic was the Greek author Athenaeus, who wrote the famous book *The Sages at Dinner,* in which many wines are catalogued.

Xenophon, a historian and traveler who lived in the fifth century B.C., noted at Damascus the famous wine called Chalybon, reserved for the cellars of the kings of Persia, just as Imperial Tokay was kept exclusively for the House of the Hapsburgs of modern times. Xenophon tells of villages in Mesopotamia replete with grain and wine; of the Kurds on the borders of Media and Armenia keeping quantities of wine in great cemented cisterns; how Greeks and their mercenaries were billeted in a town above the River Tigris where they found "old wine with a fine bouquet"; and that when the marchers in 400 B.C. reached the Greek city of Trapezus on the coast of the Black Sea, they enjoyed "an abundance of wine."

The wine of the gods was said to be even more potent and splendid than the superb wine devised for mortal man. Red and thick like Port, the last book of the *Iliad* tells how it was poured and passed at a divine banquet. Called nectar, there is still a brand today in Greece known as Nektar. Roman wines, also very strong, some as thick as jelly, were diluted with water before being served. Herbs and spices were added as flavoring, as well as aloes, myrrh and even perfumes.

The Romans drank three times as much as the Greeks, and Roman poets paid due tribute to the wine god Bacchus. Pliny Secundus, who died in the volcanic holocaust in Pompeii in 79 B.C., devotes a whole chapter in his book *Natural History* to the famous drunks of Rome. Horace wrote an ode to a wine jar. Ansonius, born in southern France, glorified the vines of Bordeaux and Moselle in verse.

The Greeks as early as 600 B.C. brought vines to Massalia (Marseilles) on the Mediterranean coast and spread their colonies in Provence, Nicea (Nice) and Antipolis (Antibes). In Julius Caesar's time (100 to 44 B.C.), every country along the Mediterranean produced wine for table use. At times, wine served as a medium of exchange, with debts and taxes being paid partly in wine. Among the Romans, all law business was suspended during vintage time; this long vacation for Roman bar members still extends from August 22 to October 15.

The Romans borrowed Grecian methods of viticulture and vinification, including lining earthenware receptacles with resin or pitch because the pottery was porous. In addition to earthen jars, the Romans used glass bottles for their wine, and corks to seal them. Romans took great pride in the excellence of wine from various parts of the empire. For instance, Julius Caesar mentions in *Commentaries* the wine he particularly enjoyed in Piedmont, which he brought back with him to Rome: "From the little village of Murra [Morra] we brought the best wine to our city of Rome."

That elegant Roman social reporter Gaius Petronius—whose book *Satyricon of Petronius* recounts the fantastic banquet of the wealthy Trimalchio, renowned for its outrageous extravagance and poor taste—was in fact the official Arbiter of Taste to the mad emperor Nero. The *Satyricon,* perhaps the world's first novel, is a brilliant rambling narrative of dining, wining and other social customs in the era of paganism. From such books we learn that wine of the ancient Greeks was red, white, pale straw color, brown or amber, while that of the Romans was white and red (sanuieus) and niger, very dark red.

The Etruscans, who flourished in the sixth century B.C., have left paintings on their tombs that reveal they were a gay, life-accepting people. They wined, dined, laughed and danced to the music of seven-stringed lyres and flutes amid the gray olive trees. Etruria and Tuscany were their lands; music and merriment the center of their lives. Etruscan archaeology illustrates the high vitality of this strange race, who migrated to Italy from Anatolia (formerly a district in Asia Minor). They wore Ionic garments and imported many luxuries from their former homes in Asia Minor.

Expertly prepared food and exquisite wine were served at Etruscan banquets. In contemporary paintings, men and women are seated together on banquet couches at tables in gala attire, with precious jewels on their fingers. They are served viands in wrought dishes and wine in goblets by young female slaves, nude except for elaborate necklaces and girdles to enhance the enjoyment of the diners in an ethereal sense of beauty unveiled. Etruscan women, known for their remarkable beauty, enjoyed friendships with many men. The women were "terribly bibulous." The Etruscans were nevertheless powerful and feared by Romans, Latins and Italiote Greeks. A banquet scene painted about 475 B.C. in the tomb of the Leopards at Tarquinia shows a wine bearer leading a flutist and a lyre-player, wearing colorful scarves in an aura of joyousness. Even the Greeks and Romans, who were no slouches in the art of enjoying themselves, were scandalized by the privileged place of women in Etruscan society. The Greeks and Romans excluded women from their feasts to avoid distraction from gustatory concentration, but they included music, perfumes and incense. Of course, after dessert the gorgeous courtesans made their appearance.

Tuscany is the locale of the ancient Chianti Wine praised by Dante, Boccaccio, the Borgias. Long before the straw-covered fiaschi (bottle) came into general use, St. Francis of Assisi loved the Chianti Wine of Tuscany, from where grapevines were brought to Gaul to initiate the vineyards of what became the country of France.

Sicily is another land renowned in antiquity for its wine. Homer wrote of the "spontaneous wine which from weighty clusters flow." The vines for what became the famous Sicilian Marsala were brought in from Samos, Crete, Cyprus and many other Greek islands. The vineyards in Sicily are said to date back to the seventh century B.C., the era in which the cult of Dionysus was very strong.

At the end of the seventh century B.C., the frenzied cult of Dionysus and Bacchus reached its most violent form. It entered Athens by way of Phrygia and Thrace. The phenomenon struck quiet, intellectual and civilized Greece with a furor of mystical, barbaric worship, but it receded by the sixth century B.C. How did the Grecian rulers treat the horrifying outbursts of unbridled drinking, sensuality and debauchery? Understanding human nature, they refused to outlaw the revels. They accepted Dionysus and his worship, sublimating it to a religion.

What has become of Dionysus and his votaries? Paganism and its deities were not uprooted to make room for Christianity. On the contrary, paganism served as a foundation for the new scheme of Christian saints, retaining pagan customs within the pale of the church. For the simple people of the vineyards, the memory of the old gods and goddesses still lingers in tradition. In Greece on the island of Naxos, once devoted to the worship of Dionysus, the church now credits Saint Dionysus with the introduction of the grape. On the nearby isle of Paros, Saint George is worshipped as Methystes, the Inebriate, whose festival on November 15 is the signal for broaching the new wine with singing, unrestrained joyousness and bubbling laughter. Wine was the core of life for the deities of Mount Olympus, and the peoples of the once-pagan world continued its mission of joy into the Christian era.

Some of the Old Testament prophets, such as Hosea, bitterly denounced too much imbibing, saying "whoredom and wine and strong drink" take away the heart. The influence of the Greeks is felt in the New Testament, in which wine drinking is advocated but there is warning against its abuse. "Drink no water but use a little wine for your stomach's sake," suggested Timothy. The Gospel of St. John tells of the preparations for a marriage feast in Cana of Galilee attended by Mary and her son Jesus. The Master bade the servants fill the waterpots with water when it was evident that no wine had been provided for the festivities. These He transformed into an abundance of wine for the wedding party . . . His first miracle. The wine served at the Last Supper became the Holy Sacrament of Communion: "Take. Drink. This is my blood." And at the last ordeal, the crucifixion on Mount Calvary, Jesus refused the comfort of wine mingled with myrrh offered to Him by His enemies.

In both the Old and New Testaments of the Bible, the divine command appears: "Rejoice!" The wine instinct is the natural urge for joy; and wine, the symbol of captured sunshine, encompasses the whole of man's history. The fearful sailors of Christopher Columbus' crew murmured that their captain was taking them over a trackless ocean, bringing them away from the olive trees and the vineyards of Spain.

The church was the greatest single factor in the spread of vineyards and the development of wine throughout the Middle Ages. After the fall of the Roman Empire (476 A.D.), wine making became the province of the monasteries. They preserved its knowledge so that it could survive through the Dark Ages. Centuries ago, religious orders established some of today's most famous European vineyards, and even later the hand of the church was felt in some of the newer wine-producing areas of the world. In California, for example, viticulture was begun by the Franciscans in the years following 1769.

Wine was again in wide social use in the 14th and 15th centuries during the Renaissance. Then the sumptuous banquets of such enormously wealthy Italian families as the Medicis and the Barberinis were replete with precious wine served in golden goblets.

Down through the years of the Middle Ages, the monks and friars performed considerable service in preserving ancient recipes and inventing new ones in vinification. The convents devised many food delicacies, and some of the best French Liqueurs were made at La Cote by the Visitandine nuns. Church-owned vineyards brought renown to the ecclesiasts. In Germany, they produced such famous wines as Johannisberg, Steinberg, Hochheimer, Dom Dechanei, Rauenthal-Pfaffenberg, Rheingau, Forster Kirchenstück of the Jesuit-garten of the Rheinpfalz Stain and Leisten wine of Franconia, Liebfraumilch, Enclos Klöstergarten and Rhenish Hessia of the Kloster Neuberg of Austria.

From the Côte d'Or comes Romanée Chambertin; from the Rhone comes Clos de Vougeot; from the Gironde come the well-known Hermitage and Châteauneuf-du-Pape wine, Saint-Emilion and Sainte-Croix-du-Mont and the priceless growths for Haut-Médoc.

Of course, there is the classic example of ecclesiastical ingenuity in the invention of Champagne by the Monk Dom Perignon in Eper-nay, France. He was the cellar-master at the Abbey of Hautvillers from 1670 to 1715. The Carthusian friars of Dauphine gifted the world with their green and gold Chartreuse. The cenobites of La Grace Dieu produced Trappistine. The Trappists of L'Allier evolved in their quiet cloister the elixir de Sept-Fonds, and the praying father of the Rouen invented the exquisite balm of Bon-Secours.

The famous Benedictine Liqueur invented by monks was later made by the monks of Fecamp in Normandy. Curaçao was discovered by a French curé, and Maraschino by an Italian frater. Santa Cruz was invented by a Spanish sacerdote as the Rum of the Holy Cross.

In 1371, Pope Gregory XI made the abbot of Clos de Vougeot a full cardinal in gratitude for his exquisite gift of a basket of the monastery's best old wine. The celebrated vineyard of Clos de Voug-eot belonged to the Bernardin monks before it was confiscated as national property. It was no small item for the monks to terminate their association with the vineyard. Dom Gobelot was the father-cellarer, and when forced to retire to private life, he brought with him to his home at Dijon 1,200 bottles of a famous year of his monastic vineyard. Soon the fame of Dom Gobelot's wine reached Napoleon Bonaparte. When the little emperor returned from the battle of Marengo, after his conquest of Italy, he dispatched a messenger to Dom Gobelot at Dijon requesting Clos de Vougeot. But the father did not comply to the request, proudly replying: "If Napoleon wishes 40-year-old Vougeot, let him come and drink it here at my table, for it is not for sale."

Napoleon, who favored the fine wine produced in the French mon-asteries, showed a marked deference and respect for the aging Cardinal Jean Baptiste de Belloy at Dijon, who lived to be almost 100, having all the while a remarkable appetite for fine food and good wine. Indeed, the cardinal was a living symbol of *la bonne vie*. Across the pages of history, his corpulent image of glowing good health reaches us. His patriarchal countenance shone with anticipation when an important dish and a good accompanying wine were placed before him, and he would proceed through the ritual of the meal with increasing pleasure. In his whole deportment, he paid tribute not only to the bountiful gifts of nature but to those who had so carefully prepared and served for his enjoyment such choice viands and wine.

The vineyards of Burgundy, France, were also originally connected with the Burgundian monasteries. There were no better and more dedicated vignerons than the monks, who were partial to caring for the vines—enjoying their grapes and wine. Chambertin of Burgundy was another favorite wine of Napoleon Bonaparte. The *vinum dulce* was obtained after drying the grapes in the sun for three days and then crushing them by foot during the hottest hours of the fourth day. Napoleon was faithful to Burgundy as long as he could secure it, but when he was exiled to Saint Helena, he took to drinking Bordeaux because he discovered that Chambertin lost its best qualities in transit.

There was a specific reason the vine was closely linked to the church in the whole of ancient Christendom. Transportation was precarious, and a local viticulture was needed to provide the wine for the celebration of the Mass. Keeping the faith was dependent on the zones in which the vine could enjoy ideal exposure to bring forth its fruit. The Master promised that "I will drink with you the new wine in the Kingdom of my Father" (Matthew 26:29). All of the archbishops since Saint Peter and Saint Augustine have been very vigilant as to viticulture.

In the Bordeaux region, the priests became viticulturists from the moment they donned the cope and the mitre. Pey Berland was the archetype of these Princes of the Church, and he did not disdain to promote the trade of Bordeaux wine by using his high religious and political functions to be the first to sell his harvest to the English buyers. His successors, down to the present Archbishop of Bordeaux, declared themselves, without any restriction, the spiritual protectors of the vine.

La Journée Vinicole Export of March 1967 tells of a Pope who was a founder of vineyards. The viticulturist Bertrand de Got, Archbishop of Bordeaux, was enthroned in 1305. Before becoming Primate of Aquitaine, he had been Bishop of Cummings and counselor to Philip the Fair, where he fulfilled the role which later fell to Cardinals Mazarin and de Richelieu. Bertrand de Got had worked in the paternal vineyard for a long time before entering the Orders. The future Pope was then doubly a vinegrower: by birth and by archiepiscopal consecration. He was vinegrower by vocation as well. In the year 1300, he inherited from his uncle, Gailhard de Got, a fine domain in the parish of Pessac, where he lost no time in planting vines. He thus added another fine vineyard to the many others he already possessed in the Bordeaux region. Today this property is known under the name of the Château Pape Clement, in memory of Bertrand de Got who became Clement V.

In Italy from the 11th to the 14th centuries, there were two political factions. One supported the German emperor and the other supported the Pope. A person opposed to the Pope was known as a Ghibelline. At the time Clement V was to be crowned, Italy was in the throes of the Ghibelline difficulties. He therefore selected Avignon as his residence, and for the next 68 years, Clement's successors continued to reside there. In addition to his strenuous responsibilities to church and king, Pope Clement V remained a vinegrower. He created the vineyard of Châteauneuf about 10 miles from Avignon. Alphonse Daudet, in his charming story *La Mule du Pape,* perpetuates the legend of Pope Clement making his weekly visits to the Papal vineyards. Every Sunday, after vespers, the head of the Catholic Church went to pay his court to the vine. When he reached the hilltop, he seated himself in the sunshine, his mule and cardinals nearby. There, near the vines, they would uncork and enjoy a bottle of wine, the wine since called Châteauneuf-du-Pape. Popes John XXII and Urban V were also winegrowers.

From Gallic France, cuttings of grapevines reached ancient Britain with the Romans, who conquered and occupied the country for four centuries. Many picturesque localities in southern England once produced good wine grapes. Monastery gardens were famous for their fine grapes and for the wine that monks produced from them. The little village of Durweston near Blandford in Dorsetshire was once noted for its unusual grapes and wine, which was similar to that restricted Rhenish locality of Germany whose grapes produce the precious Liebfraumilch.

When William of Normandy defeated the English at the Battle of Hastings in 1066 in what became known as the Norman Conquest, he brought French customs into England, initiating the wine trade with France. Trade was considerable by the time English kings conquered parts of France and became proprietors of the French wine districts therein. Of all the French wine, Burgundy, which exhilarates the drinker without intoxicating, was the most difficult to transport to England. The bottles were covered with cottony paper and even bedded down in salt, to protect the delicate living wine from the rigors of shipboard travel.

The demand for French wine helped Britain rise to a maritime power, some say. King Edward III and his wealthy courtiers in the 14th century sent ships with protecting convoys to Bordeaux for the wine supplies for his cellars. In the 17th century, Champagne was introduced to England by the Marquis de Sillery, one of the most wealthy vineyard owners of the Champagne region. Since he was in great favor at the French royal court, he presented to the king the sparkling white wine of Champagne. In time, the Marquis became the first exporter to ship Champagne to England for the elite. Then there was St. Evremond, gourmet, courtier, soldier of adventure, who went to London and became a leading social light. He loved Champagne and lost no time in making it fashionable among his coterie. Its popularity spread, and ever since the English have been recognized as the most discriminating connoisseurs of Champagnes and the best customers of France's Champagne region.

The vineyards of Germany are also very ancient. Many in Moselle, Hessia and the Pfalz date to the dawn of the Christian era, a century or so after Caesar took Gaul. The Latin poet Ausonius, for whom the Château Ausone in France is named, published a poem about the Moselle and its wines in 200 A.D. From the great palace he built at Ingelheim on the Rhine River near Mainz, the Emperor Charlemagne could look at the slope across the river (now called Rheingau) where snow melted earlier than anywhere else. Charlemagne ordered the area planted with grapevines, and it is now the steep vineyard of Schloss Johannisberg. Many vineyards were created by monasteries, and the Cathedral of Trier still sells the wine produced by its monks.

Pliny wrote of the Romans developing strong, frost-proof vines on some Alpine uplands, and introducing these into the Bordeaux country, and along the valleys of the Rhine, Saône, Youne, Marne and Seine—in fact, as far as Rheims and the site of what became the city of Paris—as well as on the banks of the Moselle and Rhine beyond Treves as far as Coblenz. After the fall of the Roman Empire, the early Christian missionaries carried the vines much farther north to make sacramental wine for the church ritual. As early as the fourth century A.D., the vines were brought into lands bordering on the North Sea; at the beginning of the 12th century, into the lands of the Baltic states. St. Otto, the Bishop of Bamberg, planted the first vineyards for the church in Pomerania in north-central Prussia in 1127.

Cicero's works refer to the vineyards of Lusitania, the Roman name for Portugal. By the time of Roman Emperor Probus, 282 A.D., Portuguese wines were being shipped to Italy. Since Portugal became an independent nation and kingdom in 1143, wine production has been the major staple of the country, its viticulture dating back to the 10th century.

From the ancient Persian city of Shiraz came the vine of Sherry wine of Cádiz and Jerez in Spain. Persian by birth, the vine was cradled on the slopes of the hilly regions of the southern shores of the Caspian Sea, in Caucasus and in Cashmere (Kashmir), where wild vines still climb and cling to the highest trees. This is the land of 11th-century Omar Khayyám (the tentmaker). When the sultan became his patron of science, he was given a royal pension in Nishapour, his birthplace. He became Royal Astronomer and the author of works on algebra, but his renown rests on his 12th-century *Rubaiyat,* translated from the Persian in 1859 by Edward Fitzgerald, the English poet:

A book of verses underneath the bough
A jug of wine, a loaf of bread
And thou beside me, singing in the wilderness
Ah wilderness were paradise enough.

I'm not ambitious, I never was proud
I sigh but for sherbet and ease
. . . Do I wish for commend in dark history's page,
Do I long in fond record to shine?
Yes, let me have sway, till the last sigh of age
Over cohorts of old Shiraz wine.

An intimate dinner party in the wine cellar of Le Chateau Richelieu.

Claret is the liquor for boys. Port for men. But he who aspires to be a hero must drink Brandy.

SAMUEL JOHNSON (1709–1784)

Chapter 3   Brandy, Cognac And Cordials (Liqueurs)

IT would be impossible to comment in detail on all of the wine, spirits and liqueurs produced in the world that contribute to conviviality. Some, better known than others, have interesting histories. It can be safely said, for instance, that even in the most remote parts of the world, at least two French words are familiar—Paris and Cognac, which takes its name from the region that is the home of Cognac Brandy. This work of art, a masterpiece of nature, France offers with just pride to the world.

Brandy occupies a well-nigh sacred place for all who appreciate fine living. What makes Brandy so special that people hold it in almost mystical regard? This antique drink has been the favorite after-dinner libation of royalty and the high-born for centuries. Nothing is more gratifying than extended hospitality, and when a private host or restaurateur serves Cognac, he honors both himself and his guests. After a good dinner, Cognac creates an optimistic, relaxing atmosphere with its unique way of warming the spirit and lightening the burden of care. That is why, it is averred, the people of the

Brandy

Cognac district of France live for such a long time and are so remarkably alert and spry even in their very old age.

Although Peter the Great of Russia and his consort Catherine were not imperial in their taste, he would order Hungarian or French wine (preferably Burgundy) to finish their plebian repast of cabbage soup, gruel, roast pig with sour cream sauce, cold roast meat with pickled cucumbers or salad greens, salt meat, ham and Limburg cheese. During the meal he quaffed quass, a sort of inferior beer that would have disgusted an ancient Egyptian with his excellent brew. Yet, Peter held Brandy in the highest respect. Old records tell how he and Catherine once arrived at Stuthof in Germany where they claimed not only the hospitality of the table but lodging for the night. The owner of the country house at which they sought to be guests was a Herr Schoppenhauer.

He readily agreed to give up to them a small bedroom, which the czar himself said "would do." The room had no stove or fireplace, a brick floor without rugs and bare walls. It was bitter cold, and the question was how could the chamber be warmed? The willing host soon solved the problem. Several casks of Brandy were brought in and their contents emptied on the floor, the furniture first being removed, and the precious spirit set on fire. The czar screamed with delight as he saw the sea of blue flames and smelt the delicious Cognac odor. No sooner was the fire extinguished than the bed was replaced and Peter and Catherine straightway betook themselves to their repose in their flambéed nest. The monarchs not only slept profoundly through the night in this gloomy German bower, amid the delicate fumes of burnt Brandy, but they rose in the morning in cheerful spirits, thoroughly refreshed and delighted with their unique experience.

The ruler was particularly pleased because ingenuity had been displayed. Napoleon loved to be so served at his tables when he was in the field of combat. He was irregular in the hours of his repasts and ate rapidly and without ceremony. The absolute regal will he applied to most things was exercised also in matters pertaining to the appetite, so that as soon as a sensation of hunger was experienced, it had to be appeased. His table service was so arranged that in any place and at any hour he had but to give expression to his will and he was promptly served with roast fowls, cutlets, steaming coffee and his favorite wine and Brandies. In deference to Cognac and Champagne, he would partake of these delights when time was not too pressing.

Usually Brandy is sniffed for its aroma. The hands surround the glass to warm the Brandy and release fumes from the special balloon-shaped glass. Brandy is definitely an after-dinner drink—after a banquet, an important dinner at home or when dining out, usually when it is an important occasion. Being limited in quantity, good Brandies are always expensive. To drink Brandy when one has been chilled by cold weather is incorrect, for Bourbon, Scotch or Rye can be used for such a purpose. Cognac is traditionally a man's drink, although it is not improper for a lady to be served with a Brandy, particularly a fruit one, or even for her to request it. At the authors' restaurant, the ladies lean more to Cordials or Liqueurs. For a woman to handle a large Cognac glass would be tantamount to her smoking one of the gentleman's cigars.

At home, Brandy is kept either in a bar or cabinet. At a business place, where large quantities are on hand, the bottles are always tilted in the same manner as wine bottles, in a wine cellar, so that the corks remain moist at all times and will not become dry and crumble when uncorked. Among the better known uses for Brandy are an Alexander, Manhattan, Flip, Sour, Grasshopper, Old-Fashioned, French 75, Jack Rose Cocktail, Stinger, and other delectable drinks. Recipes for these drinks are included in the Cocktail section of this book. Under no circumstances will an initiate ask for a Brandy on the rocks; this is a crime, denigrating the bouquet of the Brandy. Brandy is a delightful ingredient in the preparation of desserts such as Crepes Suzette and Cherry Jubilee, in the beverage Café Diable and in dishes to be included in the recipe section.

Actually, Brandy is not used in a heated drink in the manner of a Hot Scotch Toddy or a Rum Toddy, the two most popular warm drinks. However, Brandy should be served slightly warmer than room temperature. If a glass has not been heated by being rinsed in hot water, a common procedure is to pour a drop of Brandy in the sniffer and ignite it. When the glass has thus been warmed, the Brandy is poured in.

What exactly is Brandy? It may be defined as a hard liquor distilled from grapes. To be exact, first a wine is made from the grapes, and then Brandy is distilled from the wine.

The word "Brandy" comes from the Dutch *brandewijn* and the German *Branntwein*, or burned wine, because it is distilled, cooked or burned wine. The French call it *eau-de-vie* and the Scandinavians *aquavit* from the Latin *aqua vitae*, water of life.

Brandy is made in many countries throughout the world, including the United States. There is no question, in our opinion, that France produces the finest Brandies in the world; for centuries, French kings considered it the royal drink. Some of the preferred Brandies are Remy Martin, Martell Cordon Bleus, Otard, Courvoissier, The Christian Brothers Brandy and Paul Masson Brandy, the latter two from California. The well-known Grappa, Italian Brandy, is produced by several companies.

A number of years ago, Distillerie Stock Company began to distribute to the United States its Brandies, Vermouths and Liqueurs. Lionello Stock was only 17 when he founded his company in Trieste in 1884. At that time, there were no major Brandy distilleries in Europe, but only local producers for local consumption. Signor Stock set up a widely operating organization that concentrated on quality.

Up to Signor Stock's time, producers in the 19th century sold their Brandy in casks. Stock pioneered in selling his products bottled and labeled with his name on each bottle, refusing to sell Brandy in casks for fear the liquor might be diluted along the line before reaching the consumer. Realizing the importance of experimentation and scientific application, Stock was the first in his field to work with Europe's famous universities. Following the pattern set by their founder, the Distillerie Stock Company still collaborates with universities at Trieste, Vienna, Zurich, Rome and Bologna in efforts to produce an even finer product.

The story of this innovator is fascinating. Lionello Stock was determined to control his own shipments, and therefore he contrived to acquire his own ships, trucks and finally railroad cars. While this would be a natural procedure for a steel tycoon in America, it was a bit unusual for an entrepreneur of the wineries of his time. From the Turin distillery of Stock (a familiar name in Italy), where Stock is known not only for Brandy, identifying the distillation of pure grape, but also for fruit-flavored Liqueurs and a sweet Marsala. The Liqueurs are made of 10-year-old Brandy. The company, with headquarters in Trieste, Italy, has issued a recipe for an Italian Manhattan: three parts Italian Brandy and one part Italian Vermouth. It has become popular all over Europe.

By 1918 this company, founded by a very young man with the determination to attain his dream, had factories and distilleries in Austria, Poland, Switzerland, Yugoslavia, Hungary, Egypt, Israel, Brazil and France. Lionello Stock died in 1948 after a lifetime devoted to the advancement of his company. Many high honors were bestowed upon him for his achievements. Perhaps the honor he prized the most was his designation as "purveyor to the Vatican."

American Brandy According to *Grossman's Guide to Wines, Spirits, and Beers,* production of Brandy since Repeal has reached some five million gallons annually. Most of it comes from California made from California grapes. Average production per year, in addition, reaches approximately 33 million gallons of "high proof" Brandy used commercially in processing fortified wines and as a base for Cordials. Storing and aging takes place in 50-gallon capacity white oak barrels. The oak imparts a characteristic wood flavor and a golden color. There are some 14 million tax gallons of mature American Brandy now warehoused. This is an excellent showing inasmuch as the Brandy industry in the United States had only been initiated in 1933. It takes time to mature spirits but each year will accrue larger stocks of older and older American Brandies for our market.

Unquestionably, Cognac is the best of all Brandies, serving in itself as France's goodwill ambassador-at-large to the world. As early as the 17th century, merchants from foreign countries acclaimed the uniqueness of Cognac. In the busy harbor of La Rochelle, vessels bearing in their holds shipments of this precious liquid sailed for all parts of the globe where good dining also meant the best in wine and spirits.

Cognac

In western France, Cognac lies midway between north and south on the Atlantic Ocean. There are approximately 150,000 acres planted with vines surrounding Cognac, the small ancient town in the Charente District north of Bordeaux. From these vines come grapes that yield a natural Brandy of unrivaled quality, and Cognac can only be produced from the wine of this district. The peculiarity of the soil and climate, plus the proximity of the sea, combines in this district to give Cognac its distinct taste and character.

Cognac is made just as it was centuries ago. The hard, white wine of the Cognac district is distilled twice (the farmer calls it "burning his wine"). The old-fashioned pot stills are used, and the resulting Brandy is left to age in large barrels made from the wood of the nearby forest of Limousin. Trees there are a particular type of hard oak. If aged in any other type of wood, the Brandy takes on a different flavor. Brandies remain in oaken barrels 3 to 60 years, in the heavily charged atmosphere of darkened warehouses as if in a primordial womb. As time goes by, the raw, colorless Brandy takes on a golden brown color from the tannin in the oakwood. The action of the wood and of the air give the Brandy its incomparable bouquet and flavor.

During this resting period, evaporation is substantial. In the old town of Cognac, many warehouses where Brandy barrels are stored are blackened as they might be after a fire and are covered with soot. The blackness is caused by the alcohol fumes. After half a century, the proof is down to 80, which is a good time to drink the Brandy. But that is very costly, so many Brandies are bottled after only a few years; burned sugar is added to give Cognac its caramel coloring and a little vanilla added for flavor. This is an insult to Cognac and should never be confused with fine Brandy. Once it is in the bottle, it no longer ages.

There are other Brandies produced outside France that are sometimes called Cognac, but anyone who has tasted genuine Cognac can never be deceived. The French Excise and the National Bureau of Cognac control production, aging and distribution, which guarantees the Brandy's authenticity. The territory was delimited by decree on May 1, 1909.

Cognac is divided into seven subdistricts: Grande Champagne,

Petite Champagne, Les Borderies, Les Fins Bois, Les Bons Bois, Les Bois Ordinaires and Les Bois Communs. The closer the vineyard is situated to the center of the Cognac district, the better the product. The Cognac shipping firms mix Brandies of various vintages and from different subdistricts so as to balance each other in the best possible blend. For the last four centuries, most of the land in these various districts has belonged to the same families of vintners. Long and successful tradition has ensured them a place of their own within the economy of France.

You can spend anywhere from $10 to even $50 a bottle for Cognac, depending on its age. Price is definitely an indicator of quality. Why is Cognac expensive? Because it takes 10 bottles of wine to distill one bottle of Cognac.

The various qualities of Cognacs are generally indicated by stars: one, two or three in ascending indications of quality. In the excellent book *Grossman's Guide to Wines, Spirits, and Beers,* Harold J. Grossman suggests that all wine people are superstitious, as they may well be since the whole cycle of vine culture and wine making is so dependent on the caprices of nature. One of their beliefs is that comet years produce fine wine, and the legend goes that in the comet year of 1811, when a superb Brandy was produced, one of the shippers decided to designate the Brandy of that year with a star. When an equally superior Brandy was produced in the following year, he designated it by two stars. He stopped when he had reached five stars. However, the firm of Hennessy claims they originated the star system. Standards represented by the stars vary with different producers. All three-star brands will not be equal, for one house might give three stars to a 6-year Brandy, another to a 10-year Brandy and still another to a 20-year Brandy.

Better qualities of Brandy are labeled with letters representing English words, not French ones: *E* means Especial, *F* means Fine, *V* means Very, *O* means Old, *S* means Superior, *P* means Pale, *X* means Extra and *C* means Cognac. *V.S.* on the neck label of a bottle of Cognac means simply Very Superior; *S.F.C.* means Superior Fine Cognac.

In all French wine districts, distilled wine is made from the marc, the residue of stems, with the pulp remaining in the vats after the wine is pressed. The best are Marc de Bourgogne and Marc de Champagne, but they are grapy, leathery, hard tasting, so that they have not become popular in America. The Italian variety, called Grappa, is even less delicate. Brandies of Cognac were made famous in France by Napoleon, who took along a barrel of Cognac Brandy into every major battle. Napoleon Brandy became the Brandy of Distinction, and ever since, the large Cognac firms call their best blends after the French emperor. Courvoisier Cognac, "The Brandy of Napoleon," is 80 proof, produced and bottled by Courvoisier Jarnon and solely imported by W. A. Taylor & Company from France. Of course, no real Napoleon Brandy is still in existence.

E. Remy Martin, established in 1724, produces a Fine Champagne Cognac (Qualité du Centaure) bottled in the typical bottle with a three-inch neck that is slightly hipped. This type of bottle is reserved for the expensive Brandies to differentiate them from less expensive qualities, which are sold in a normal, standard Bordeaux-type bottle. There are some V.S.O.P.'s that have a typical mandolin-shaped squat bottle, developed by Brandy producers and traditionally used.

Hennessy is a very famous Cognac Brandy that had its inception in 1763 when Richard Hennessy settled in Cognac, France. An Irishman in the Irish Brigade, he had come to fight as a mercenary for the King of France and to enjoy some adventures. He was so delighted with the local Brandy that he sent a few casks home to his friends in Ireland. They sent letters overwhelming him with praise and requests, so he began to export Cognac Brandy on a business basis. Richard's son James founded the firm of Jas. Hennessy & Co. and began shipping to all parts of the world. The House of Hennessy is now in its seventh generation of direct descendants of Richard.

Until 1860, Hennessy Cognac was shipped to the United States in casks. Thereafter it was imported already bottled. The symbol of Hennessy is the woeful-looking Saint Bernard dog, depicted with a little oaken cask tied about his neck. True Cognac of France is in the cask, ready to resuscitate any stranded traveler. Hennessy comes into its own when an élégante of the old school places a bouillon or dessert spoon in which there is a cube of sugar over a demitasse of hot black coffee, adds an ounce of Hennessy (or any other Cognac) and sets it blazing. When the blue flame begins to fade, the contents are poured into a coffee cup. Café Royale, the beverage prepared in this way, is the perfect ending to a fine dinner.

It is not simple to buy good Brandy, for even cheaper blends usually have three stars and are from three to six years old. The bottles marked V.O. and V.E., "very old" and "very extra," range from 7 to 12 years; the best, called V.S.O.P., "very superior old pale," are over 10 years old. The safest way to buy a good Cognac is to buy a bottle that is expensive and shows the name of a world-famous firm. Sometimes the words "Old Liqueur Brandy" denote good quality.

Cognac, which is truly the fiery spirit of wine, is best from a balloon- or tulip-shaped glass. Some Cognac glasses are outsized. When the palms of the hands warm it, the subtle and marvelous aroma satisfies the most discriminating gourmet. To take it this way after a fine repast is called *neat.* It also imparts its delicate and striking flavor to a cocktail, and enhances the dish in which it is added as an ingredient.

Armagnacs   Next to the Brandies from Cognac, the Brandies from Armagnac are the best known in France. The Armagnacs come from Gascony, the fabled land of the Three Musketeers. The finest are often known as "Reserve d'Artagnan," so d'Artagnan did for Armagnac what Napoleon did for Cognac. Vines of Armagnac country cover the greater part of the Gers Department and reach the border of the immense Forest of the Landes, which protects the region from the sea air coming from Hossegor and Biarritz.

Armagnacs are distilled in a slow, single process. The raw Brandy, 104 proof, is poured into barrels made from local oak, which gives more tannin to the aging Brandy than other oaks. Good Armagnac is strong and heady, with a distinctive flavor. This is derived from the soil of the Gascon country in which the grape vines grow. The best Armagnacs are just as expensive as fine Cognacs, and even more difficult to find. Generally they are sold in round, flat bottles with a long neck, or in flute-shaped bottles. Near the town of Auch the old Château de Marsan now belongs to the Marquis de Montesquieu, an authentic descendant of d'Artagnan. The young, elegant Marquis provides small decanters of Armagnac in each of his guestrooms at night, and it is considered a grave affront to the hospitality of the château if, in the morning, any Armagnac is still in the decanter. The legend that Armagnac is an aphrodisiac in disguise still persists; there may be a kernel of truth therein, for the famous Brandy certainly advanced d'Artagnan's amorous fortunes.

All Marquis de Caussade Armagnac bears the registered phrase "The Brandy of Lafayette." Marquis de Caussade Fine Grand Armagnac, V.S.O.P., is aged in wood for 10 years. A ⅘ths quart, 84 proof, is imported by Park, Benziger & Co. Inc., New York, N.Y.

On the slopes of the hills of Cognac and Armagnac grow extra-fine quality grapes from which the famous Armagnac Brandy is made. In 1908, the French Chamber of Deputies established the exclusive right of these two supervised grape-growing regions to label their Brandies with their district names. No other grape Brandy produced in France or elsewhere is permitted this privilege. Armagnac de Caussade is one of the oldest Armagnac Brandies, esteemed in France for over 500 years for its rare excellence and distinguished traditions. Each importation into the United States is numbered and accompanied by an Acquit Régional Jaune d'Or (Certificate of Origin) issued by the French government. Some wines, like rare books, are also numbered, such as Château Rothschild Lafite, Château Mouton Rothschild and Cheval Blanc.

Brandy covers the family of liquors distilled from the wine of grapes *Fruit*
or other fruits. When the name "Brandy" stands alone, it always *Brandies*
identifies a distillation of pure grapes and no other fruit.

Brandy is a soft, smooth, velvety liquor, distinguished for its great
bouquet and subtle fragrance of the original grapes or fruits. The
term Brandy covers the group of Cognac, Armagnac, Spanish, Greek,
Israeli, Italian, American, Kirsch, Kirschwasser (Cherry Brandy), Calvados (Apple Jack), Slivovitz (Plum Brandy) and other fruit Brandies.
All are potable spirits, aged in wood obtained by distilling wine or
a fermented mash of fruit.

Many countries produce fruit Brandies when they have an abundance of fruit. The prime example is the Calvados of Normandy,
which comes from the district that is one vast apple orchard. In
Normandy, where meals are enormous, Apple Brandy was discovered in the 11th century to be the pause between courses to restore
flagging appetites. The time-honored custom is called *le trou Nor-
mand,* the Norman hole. Calvados is not sipped, but washed down
with gusto.

Somewhere between the grape Brandies and the Liqueurs are the
water-colored, dry, unsweetened Brandies made from various fruits.
The French call these *alcool blanc.* Most are colorless because they
are aged in crockery instead of wooden barrels. Framboise is the
most famous of them, short for Eau-de-Vie de Framboise, and is not
to be confused with Crème de Framboise, that is a pure distillation
of raspberries. Small, often unknown producers in Alsace make the
best Framboise, which is pure, aromatic and strong. It takes 60
pounds of raspberries to make one bottle of good Framboise, but
some say the Alsatians, like the Irish, are fond of tall stories.

The Brandies aged in wood have a golden brown color such as the
Plum Brandies, called Slivovitz, of Central Europe (Hungary, Rumania, Yugoslavia). The Apricot Brandy of Hungary, called Barack
Palinka, and some Blackberry Brandies have their color enhanced by
adding darkly colored juice to the matured spirit. The colorless,
un-aged group of Brandies are water-white. These include the Brandies distilled from a fermented mash of cherries (Kirschwasser) aged
in earthenware containers or casks lined with paraffin to avoid taking
on any color from the oak casks. Mirabelle comes from the mirabelle
and quetsch varieties of plum. Pear Brandy is made from the Williams
pear in Switzerland and France. The maximum fruit aroma is
achieved by distilling off at 100 proof or less, then it is promptly
bottled so as not to lose any of the natural fruit fragrance.

The United States and France are the two sources for Apple
Brandy called Apple Jack in the United States and Calvados in France
from the town of Calvados in Normandy, center of apple and cider
production. Calvados is not usually sold until aged in wood for ten

years. Apple Jack, on the other hand, is aged only two to five years in wood. This Brandy's charm is its characteristic apple flavor distilled from fermented cider of the best apples in the crop.

Brief Summary of Cognacs and Brandies

While French Cognac is the oldest commercially produced spirit, today the largest volume of sales is accounted for by Brandies produced in the United States. Brandy has been defined as "a potable spirit distilled from wine or a fermented mash of fruit, usually aged in the wood." In practically all countries that grow fruit, Brandy is produced locally.

Cognac: Considered by experts as the most famous Brandy of them all. It is usually aged in casks made of limousin oak from the forest of Limoges. Cognac labels include the various symbols of the individual shippers: *V*—very; *S*—superior; *O*—old; *P*—pale; *X*—Extra; *E*—Especial; *F*—Fine.

Armagnac: After Cognac, this is the best known Brandy. It is produced in Southern France and often shipped as a vintage Brandy, i.e., the distillation of a particular year. Often it has a fuller body and is drier than Cognac.

Brandy (California): This State accounts for 66 percent of the Brandy consumption in the United States. Everything is done by one organization: growing grapes, making wine, distilling, aging, bottling, marketing. In contrast to this American method, European farmer-distillers sell their Brandies to the blender-shippers. Since Repeal, many fruit Brandies have been imported to the United States from abroad.

Apple Brandy: Wherever apples grow and cider is fermented, Apple Brandy or Apple Jack can be produced. The latter is the best known in the United States. Apple Jack Brandy is aged in charred oak barrels for four to seven years and is bottled at both 84 and 100 proofs. In the United States, it was one of the first distilled spirits in pot stills. Its history in this country goes back to the 1600s.

Calvados: Apple Brandy produced in Normandy, France.

Grappe: This is a very popular Brandy in Italy, a distillation from the grape pomace of the wine press. It is clear, without color. Some is distilled in California.

Slivovitz: This Brandy is distilled from a fermented mash of prunes. The stones are allowed to remain during fermentation. In France, Brandy distilled from this fruit is called Quetsch and Mirabelle, and is brown in color. Slivovitz is the national drink of the Balkans.

Kirsch or Kirschwasser: A Brandy distilled from a fermented mash of cherries. The stones are left in during fermentation. The most famous of the Kirsches is the Schwartzwalder Kirschwasser, the Cherry Brandy of the Black Forest. The French have their Alsatian Kirsch, the Swiss their Kirschwasser. This Brandy is colorless.

Barack Palinka: Brown in color, this Brandy is distilled from a fermented mash of apricots and is made only in Hungary.

Man has known the comfort of Liqueurs since earliest history. In the tombs of the Egyptian Pharaohs have been found formulas and replicas of stills. The Athenians wrote of the delight of Liqueurs. Actual commercial production, however, dates from the Middle Ages, the period in European history between classical antiquity and the Renaissance (usually regarded as extending from the downfall of Rome in 476 A.D. to about 1450). Liqueurs were the creation of physicians, alchemists and monks searching for an elixir of life.

Cordials and Liqueurs

At first, Liqueurs served as medicine and sometimes as love potions, aphrodisiacs and multipurpose panaceas. Indeed, many of the seeds, herbs, roots and fruits used in Liqueurs are found in today's pharmacy: caraway, cumin, coriander, angelica root, oil of orange, oil of lemon, peppermint and others. A number of Liqueurs are still made from ancient and closely guarded formulas.

The making of Liqueurs in Europe dates from the 13th century. At that time, Ramón Lull, a Spaniard from Majorca, and Arnaud de Villeneuve, a Frenchman, brought back to Europe the secrets of distillation they found during their travels either in North Africa or in the East—which area is not known precisely. Thereafter, for the next three or four centuries, manufacturers brought out bad-tasting aqua vitae or eau-de-vie until someone rediscovered the value of using spices and fruits in making distilled Liqueurs, just as the ancients had used flowers, rare spices and herbs to flavor their wine.

While Liqueurs began to receive some recognition between 1750 and 1800, they did not achieve a place of their own until the improved transportation of the modern world brought all countries closer together geographically and exotic herbs, spices and fruits became more readily available. Meanwhile, modern science introduced improved manufacturing methods.

Liqueurs, sweet alcoholic beverages, are labeled and advertised as Liqueurs if they are imported, for that is the term for them used abroad. If they are produced in the United States, they will properly be called Cordials. Much has been produced in the United States, and

90 percent of the sales since World War II have been of native production. While Liqueurs and Cordials are popularly served as an after-dinner drink, they can also be served over shaved ice, in highballs or cocktails, or be used to flavor fresh fruits, sauces, ice creams and soufflés.

Two major types of Cordials and Liqueurs are available: the common, general varieties; Apricot-, Peach-, Cherry-flavored Brandies, Rock and Rye, Crème de Cacao, Crème de Menthe, etc., and the world-famous, specific proprietary brands made for centuries such as Bénédictine D.O.M, B and B Liqueur D.O.M, Chartreuse, Drambuie, Grand Marnier, Cherry Heering, Cointreau.

How are Cordials and Liqueurs created? Renowned elixirs, they are sweetened by flavoring with fruits and plants, and produced by combining the flavors with a previously prepared spirit base—generally Brandy or neutral spirits—and adding sweetening. According to U.S. federal regulations, Cordials are produced by mixing or redistilling neutral spirits, Brandy, Gin, and so on with or over fruits, flowers or plants for flavoring, to which has been added sugar or dextrose, not less than 2 1/2 percent of the weight of the finished product. Some of the more popular Cordial types are: Anisette, which is licoricelike; Blackberry-, Apricot-, Cherry- and Peach-flavored Brandies, which have the flavor and aroma of ripe fresh fruit of the respective types; Crème de Cacao, which is made by the creamy blending of chocolate and vanilla; Sloe Gin, which has a tangy flavor like wild cherries. In the mint family there are Chocla Menthe and Koffie Menthe, which are produced by John deKuyper & Son.

A Liqueur is defined as an alcoholic beverage which is sweetened and flavored. By United States law it must contain a minimum of 2 1/2 percent of sugar, but generally it contains considerably more —from 10 percent to 35 percent. This is a simple definition of rather exotic drinks made since ancient times.

The word "Liqueur" derives from the Latin *liquefacere* which means to melt or dissolve. The word "Cordial" has the identical meaning to Liqueur and is so indistinguishable from the point of view of nomenclature that the two words are always mentioned together in Federal and state laws and regulations. In France they are called *digestif.* Over the years these beverages have also been known as elixirs, oils, balms, cremes, and so forth. Sometimes they were also called "ratafia," which originally was any Liqueur drunk at the ratification of a treaty or agreement. Later ratafia meant any fruit Liqueur, particularly those flavored with the pits as well as the fruit.

Fruit Liqueurs are produced by placing some fresh and some dried pieces of a particular fruit in Brandy, where it is allowed to steep for six to eight months. This process infuses the Brandy with the color, aroma and flavor of the added fruit. After the Brandy is drawn off and sweetened, it is matured in a wood, stone or crockery vat for about a year, at which time it is ready to serve.

Plant Liqueurs are produced by distillation. The peels, seeds or roots of the plant are softened in Brandy for 48 hours, and then the Brandy and flavors are placed in a pot still and distilled. The product of distillation is always colorless, so coloring and sweetening are added before the plant Liqueur is aged for a year and marketed.

In the 18th century, it was quite fashionable for Liqueurs to have romantic-sounding names such as Parfait Amour, which, as it so happens, managed to survive. This Perfect Love Liqueur is flavored with citron peel, lemon peel, cloves and other spices. It is colorless when completed, but artificially tinted violet to be more significant supposedly of purple passion. In the New York Japanese restaurant Nippon, of all places, we found a Perfect Love cocktail made of the violet Liqueur, dry Gin and passion fruit nectar.

A word about Crème de Menthe, the popular after-dinner drink. Made from peppermint, it is either white or green. There is no basic difference in taste, quality or potency, but there are reasons for the variation. The natural distillate of mint results in a colorless liquid. Green is added for eye appeal and because it is a cool color and as refreshing as mint is to the taste. Generally the green of Crème de Menthe does not come from mint but from a combination of saffron and indigo, the yellow and blue creating green.

White Crème de Menthe is more suitable when used as a mixing ingredient with other multicolored spirits; for example, in making the Stinger Cocktail, which is made with 1 ounce of white Crème de Menthe and 1 1/4 ounces Brandy. If green Menthe were added to the golden Brandy, the drink would be the same in taste but its color would probably resemble soiled river water.

Drambuie, classified as a Liqueur, is made from an ancient secret formula brought to Scotland by a French courtier of Prince Charles Edward in 1745, which explains its accolade as Prince Charles Edward's Liqueur. It is made with the finest old Highland Malt Scotch Whisky and heather honey, 80 proof.

Falernum has no connection with the famous old wine of Italy beloved by the ancient Romans, for it is made in the West Indies and in the United States. Falernum was concocted over 200 years ago in Barbados, British West Indies, by a sugarcane planter. It is a pleasant flavoring syrup to which 6 percent alcohol has been added. Its ingredients are simple syrup, lime, almond, ginger and other spices, and it is white.

Kümmel is principally flavored with caraway seed and cumin seed. From the latter is obtained the highly therapeutic cumin oil. Gilka Kümmel, made in Berlin, Germany, has been accepted as the standard of quality for almost a century. However, the old firm of Bols in

Holland claims that their Bolskümmel was the original Kümmel, distilled by Erven Lucas Bols in 1575. A visiting czar from Russia secured the recipe and saw to it that it was produced; eventually Russia became the principal producer and consumer of Kümmel, 86 proof.

Anise has been the favorite flavor since Greek and Roman times throughout the whole Mediterranean area from Syria to Spain, whereas the caraway seed and cumin are favored in North Central Europe for the manufacture of Kümmel. Americans lean toward the flavor of mint. Anise or Anisette, which has a licorice taste, is the basic flavor used in Greek Ouzo and Mastikha and in the Arrack of Syria and Lebanon. In Spain, anise is used in Ojen. Anis del Mono comes from near Barcelona, and a truly superior Anisette from Andalusia in southern Spain. In France, anise appears in Pastis de Marseilles, the best known being Ricard. Pernod, a derivative of Absinthe, does not contain the forbidden wormwood, but has all the flavor and eye appeal of yesteryear. When mixed with water it takes on a milky, opalescent hue. In Italy, the preferred Liqueur with anise flavoring is called Anesone. The best anise without a doubt comes from Spain and the South of France, where Marie Brizard from Bordeaux is made with green anise, a small gray seed of a plant quite common in Europe.

Curaçao, a small island in the Dutch West Indies, gives its name to Curaçao. Made from bitter Curaçao orange peel, 60 to 90 proof, it is one of the most successful Liqueurs in preparing soufflés, for flaming crepes and to accompany other elegant desserts. Triple Sec, a colorless orange-flavored Curaçao, is really not dry as its name would imply, and is certainly not triply dry; it is usually higher in alcohol than Curaçao.

Cointreau was originally a form of Triple Sec. Orange Curaçao sold in a distinctive square-shaped bottle under the name of Triple Sec. Cointreau is colorless and orange-flavored. The firm of Cointreau Ltd. now also manufactures Cordials in the United States at its plant in Pennington, New Jersey. Grand Marnier, which has Cognac as its base, is not unlike Curaçao. Likewise Cointreau, white Curaçao and Triple Sec are very similar to each other, with Cointreau being the sweetest of the three.

Cordial Médoc, which is produced in Bordeaux, France, is made of Crème de Cacao, Curaçao and some other flavors. Crème de Cacao itself is a heavy Liqueur made from cocoa beans, usually with the addition of vanilla and chocolate flavoring; it is excellent when served as a sauce over ice cream or custard. Crème de Moka (Mocca) is made from coarsely ground coffee and bitter almonds, left to steep 24 hours in high-proof alcohol, then distilled, colored, sweetened and reduced in proof. Crème de Cassis, which is made from black currants, is chiefly produced in Burgundy, France.

Bénédictine D.O.M Liqueur, still being produced at the same place where its secret formula was devised in 1510, still defies imitation. There is now a reconstruction of the original Bénédictine Abbey of Fécamp where botanist-monk Dom Bernardo Vincelli first offered his marvelous elixir to his brother monks for their edification, especially to cheer them when fatigued or sick. D.O.M, which appears on the bottle's label, stands for Deo Optimo Maximo—To God, most good, most great. No longer connected with any religious order, the company was founded by Monsieur Alexandre Le Grand in 1863. The secret formula is very closely guarded. Only three persons ever have complete knowledge of it at one time. Of course, there are hundreds of counterfeits. It can be classified as a plant Liqueur made of various herbs, plants and peels on a Cognac Brandy base.

Although the Bénédictine Abbey at Fécamp is somewhat off the beaten tourist track, it is attracting an increasing number of visitors. Fécamp nestling among the coastal fishing towns and natural beauty of Normandy, is 40 miles north of Le Havre and 125 miles from Paris. The Abbey offers much of interest: a fine palace, a museum of art treasures and the famed distillery where Bénédictine is made and has been made since it was first developed by Dom Bernardo Vincelli. And guests will not want for hospitality since luncheon or dinner is a happy experience at one of the charming provincial inns at Fécamp, bringing one even closer to historic Normandy. Julius Wile is sole importer of Bénédictine. A large table model of the ancient buildings is in view at Julius Wile headquarters, 320 Park Avenue, New York City.

Chartreuse, an aromatic plant Liqueur, is produced by the Chartreuse Fathers of the Carthusian Order, near Grenoble, France. The Order was founded in 1084 by Bruno, a famed instructor at the University of Reims. Withdrawing into the desert of Chartreuse with six companions, Bruno founded a monastery dedicated to prayer and solitude. The monks grew herbs and sold wood; in the 17th century, they began to make the Liqueurs that have become so famous. In 1605, Marshal d'Estrees, who was in the court of King Henry IV of Navarre, gave the Chartreuse monks a secret formula for making Liqueur. This mysterious elixir was concocted of aromatic herbs. The formula was so complicated that the old manuscript was ignored by the monks for years. However, in 1735, Brother Jerome Maubec studied the original recipe and succeeded in perfecting the formula. He developed the green Liqueur. The yellow Liqueur was discovered a century later in 1840 by Brother Bruno Jacquet. The green and yellow Liqueurs were produced in the monastery's pharmacy, and Brother Charles went by mule to sell them in Grenoble and Chambéry.

Chartreuse has been called Queen of Liqueurs for its mellow softness. Excellent base Brandies are used from selected wine; the secret formula uses 130 herbs. The Liqueurs develop in oaken vats with a capacity of over 2500 gallons. The herbs and Brandy are distilled together in the still, where the herbs surrender their properties and aroma to the Brandy. Among other ingredients, Chartreuse contains balm leaves, orange peel, dried hyssop tops, peppermint, angelica seed and root, cinnamon, mace, cloves, tonka beans, calamus aromatics and cardamon.

During the French Revolution, the monks were driven away from their Monastery of La Grande Chartreuse, but later they returned and faithfully rebuilt their quarters damaged by war. Shortly after 1900, the monks were again expelled and their distillery and trademark sold to a commercial firm, which came into possession of everything except the formula itself and the knowledge of its manufacture. During the years of their expulsion, the monks were at Tarragona in Spain, where they continued to make their famous Chartreuse until they were finally able to return to France in 1929.

During the enforced absence of the Carthusian monks from France, pre-expulsion Chartreuse (i.e., prior to the early 1900s) brought high prices in France and abroad. Likewise, the Liqueur the Brothers produced while in exile in Tarragona was considered to be of a high order. Today there is no other source for obtaining Chartreuse than from les Pères Chartreux at La Grande Chartreuse in Grenoble, France.

The Chartreuse distillery is now not too far from the monastery located in the little town of Voiron. The cellars of the Compagnie Française de La Grande Chartreuse are the largest Liqueur cellars in the world, containing a double row of gigantic vats. When you are next in France, perhaps you will have the opportunity to visit Voiron, located in the midst of breath-takingly beautiful scenery. Since 1961 visitors have been allowed there by the Chartreux Fathers (every day except Sunday from 8 to 12 and 2 until 6). Voiron lies directly on the main route between Paris and the French Riviera. Along the way are roadside inns where the food is simple but excellent; and the monks of Chartreuse welcome travelers.

Green and yellow Chartreuse are shipped to the United States, but a third Liqueur, called by the mystic name of Elixir, Végétal de La Grande Chartreuse, considered a pharmaceutical medicinal, 136 proof, is not available in the United States. The green Liqueur (110 proof) is very pleasing to the taste, containing a large number of herbs, and is excellent after meals. The yellow Liqueur (86 proof) is milder than the green and of a different taste. The sole distributor in the United States is Schieffelin & Co. of 30 Cooper Square, which by coincidence happens to be the oldest pharmaceutical house in this country. They have been importing since 1794.

Another old French house that produces a distinguished Liqueur with a Cognac base is Etablissements Marnier Lapostolle, founded in 1827 deep in the château country by J. B. Lapostolle. Eugene Lapostolle succeeded his father as director of the distillery in 1859. It was Eugene's son-in-law, Marnier Lapostolle, who formulated what is today known as Grand Marnier. It was created from distilled orange peel and the fine Champagne Cognac found only in the Charentes region surrounding their establishment. The strict formula has been followed ever since, and it is guaranteed by the French State Excise Department, which carefully guards the Wine industry. Grand Marnier is the perfect accompaniment to Crepes Suzette. In France, you will also find popular the Cherry Marnier, which has a rich, fresh, cherry flavor.

The legendary Liqueur of old Ireland is Irish Mist. The story of its origin goes back nearly 1,000 years . . . to the days when Ireland was ruled by warring clans. The drink of these ancient Irish warriors was "Heather Wine," a Cordial based on Whiskey and wild heather extract. The secret of making Heather Wine was carefully guarded. Then came the Danish and Norman invaders—and, in the 16th century, the armies of Queen Elizabeth I. Gaelic Ireland was lost—and so was the secret of making Heather Wine. Ireland's nobles, clerics and fighting men left their native land in a centuries-long exodus—known as "the flight of the Wild Geese"—to enter France, Germany, Austria and Spain. And the secret recipe for Heather Wine went somewhere, somehow with them.

"Twas a sad loss for Ireland," said Daniel E. Williams, a fine 19th-century Irish distiller. From his Tullamore Whiskey Distillery, he began a search for the precious recipe among all the countries of Europe. At the same time, he experimented with Whiskey, heather honey and herbs at home, hoping to duplicate the Heather Wine formula.

His sons carried on the search, and his grandsons after them. And then, one day in 1948, into his great-grandson's office at Tullamore came an Austrian refugee. He brought a recipe for a Liqueur based on heather honey and Whiskey that had been in the family for generations and that he knew was of Irish origin.

The 100-year-long search was ended! This was the recipe the Williams family had been looking for—and it excelled in quality, appearance, bouquet and taste anything their trial-and-error experiments had previously produced.

Liqueurs and Cordials retain their names in all languages. For instance, Kirschwasser, which is wild cherry, retains this name (although more commonly simply called Kirsch) no matter in what country it is consumed. There are several Cordials made in only

specific countries, such as Cherry Heering, which is Danish in origin.
Following is a list of some of the popular Cordials and their dominant flavors and colors:

Cordial	Flavor	Color
Amer Picon	Bitter	Tawny amber
Anesone	Anise-licorice (Italy)	Clear white
Anisette	Anise seed	Clear white
Bénédictine D.O.M	Herb Bénédictine	Tawny
B&B Liqueur D.O.M	Drier Bénédictine	Tawny
Blackberry	Blackberry	Black
Chartreuse	Aromatic of many herbs	Yellow and green
Cherry	Wild Cherry	Black
Cointreau	Orange	Orange and white
Cordial Médoc	Blend of Cognac and Curaçao	Tawny
Crème d'Ananas	Pineapple	Yellow
Crème de Banane	Banana	Yellow
Crème de Cacao	Cacao and vanilla	Dark and white
Crème de Cassis	Black currants	Black
Crème de Fraises	Strawberry	Pink
Crème de Framboise	Raspberry	Deep red
Crème de Menthe	Peppermint	White and green
Crème de Noyaux	Fruit stones, bitter almond	Light tawny
Crème de Roses	Rose petals and vanilla	Pink
Crème de Vanille	Vanilla beans (Mexico)	Tawny
Crème Yvette	Violets and vanilla (U.S.A.)	Violet
Curaçao	Orange	Orange
Danziger Goldwasser	Kümmel, spices with gold flakes	White
Drambuie	Heather, honey, spicy (Scotland)	Golden
Fiori Alpini	Alpine flowers (North Italy or Switzerland)	Yellow

Cordial	Flavor	Color
Forbidden Fruit	Grapefruit (U.S.A.)	Yellow
Galliano	Flavor of yellow sweet Chartreuse (Livorno, Italy)	Yellow
Gilka Kümmel	Caraway seed flavor (Germany)	White
Grand Marnier	Orange Curaçao (Cognac, France)	Tan
Izarra	Basque Liqueur with Armagnac Brandy (Pyrenees)	Yellow and green
Kahlúa	Coffee (Mexico)	Coffee
Kümmel	Caraway seed	White
Mandarine	Tangerine	Tangerine
Maraschino	Marasca cherries	White
O Cha	Green tea (Japan)	Olive green
Ouzo	Anise seed (Greece)	Clear
Peach	Peaches	Deep brown
Pernod	Star anise (France)	Yellow
Peppermint GET	Mint (France)	Green and white
Prunelle	Plum	Brown
Quetsch	Plum (Alsace)	White
Raspail	Herbs and spices	Brown
Rock and Rye	Rye, rock candy	Brown
Sloe Gin	Sloeberry, Hawthorn berries	Red
Southern Comfort	Peaches and bourbon (U.S.A.)	Reddish
Strega	Plant Liqueur (Italy)	Yellow
Swedish Punch	Rum base (originally called Arrack Punsch, Java Rum)	Light Brown
Tia Maria	Coffee (Jamaica)	Coffee
Triple Sec	Curaçao	White

Cordial	Flavor	Color
Van der Hum	Spicy plant Liqueur (South Africa)	
Vieille Curé	Plant Liqueur (France)	Green and yellow

Being both sweet and potent, Cordials or Liqueurs contain certain beneficial essential oils, so they are natural digestifs. For this reason, they are popular after-dinner drinks. In fact, this was once their primary and historic use. But at the present time, with more and more people seeking to enlarge their scope of favorites, they have become increasingly popular as cocktail ingredients.

While a Cognac should be served in a sniffer shaped with a large belly and a small lip, a Cordial is served in a glass better known to the trade as a London dock, a miniature Whiskey-Sour glass, tulip-shaped. A Cordial should be sipped when one is in a relaxed mood, while conversing pleasantly or smoking—it should never be hurried or gulped.

There are no specific Cordials for a specific occasion, but there are certainly specific ones for taste preferences. For example, a Soufflé Grand Marnier would be flambéed with Grand Marnier Liqueur (recipe included at the end of this book). There should be some coordination between the type of spirit consumed during the meal and the after-dinner drink. A Scotch drinker usually asks for Drambuie because it has a Scotch base or flavor. If the beverage during the meal was wine, then the after-dinner drink definitely should be Cognac, which is basically made from distilled wine.

Men often prefer a smoky, harsh type of drink such as Cognac or Armagnac, while women usually lean toward a sweet, fruity-flavored drink such as Grand Marnier, Cherry Heering or Mint, green or white. There used to be a pale pink Mint, but it is no longer on the market.

The most simple drink using Liqueurs as an ingredient calls for a float of Liqueur on top of a drink. For instance, the Rusty Nail requires a float of Drambuie on a Scotch on the rocks. An Angel Tip calls for a float of sweet cream on Kahlúa, the coffee-flavored Cordial from Mexico. It is in order to call for a float of any Liqueur from Pernod to Drambuie to top a Martini.

Probably the most popular cocktails using Liqueurs are a Sidecar, Aquavit Bloody Mary, Pisco Sour, Banana Daiquiri, Alexander, Grasshopper and Pink Squirrel. More exotic drinks using Liqueurs that are becoming better known are a Prince of Wales, Morning Mist, Sunbeam, White Lady and Pink Cloud. Recipes for these are included in the cocktail chapter.

Typical of bitter Liqueur is Campari Bitters, extensively used as an ingredient of the Negroni cocktail. You can also make several after-dinner drinks with Vodka and Liqueurs (see recipe section).

Curaçao is famous for its marriage to Crepes Suzette. Various Cordials are delicious with ice cream or sherbets. Occasionally a drop of Anisette in a cup of espresso gives it an exotic flavor. Kirsch—wild cherry—is appropriate on half a grapefruit, added to a fruit cup or fruit salad.

Stock's after-dinner Liqueurs are justly famous. They include Anisette, Apricot, Blackberry, Cherry, Peach, Crème de Menthe, Crème de Cacao, Crème de Mocca, Crème de Marsala and Maraschino Liqueur. Liqueurs are often a blend of extract, natural and artificial, with spirits. Stock's Liqueurs, made of 10-year-old Brandy with pure distilled fruits, are delightful in flavor.

Marie Brizard Liqueurs run from 50 to 100 proof and are exclusively imported by Schieffelin & Co., New York: Anisette, Apry (Apricot), Banane, Blackberry, Café Brizzard, Cherry, Crème de Cacao, Crème de Menthe, Crème de Cassis, Curaçao, Kirsch, Kümmel, Mandarine, Marasquin, Parfait Amour, Peach, Prunelle and Triple Sec.

Liqueurs, the gay toys of the palate, come from tropical lands and exotic places, from Venezuela, France, the Alps, Denmark, the Spice Islands and Andalusia. A medieval atmosphere surrounds their production, with its ancient vocabulary of essences, elixirs, tinctures, creams, infusions. The Arabians contributed the words alcohol, alchemy and alembic, and also the glass or metal apparatus used in distillation. To appeal to the fancy and to the eye, the special bottles to contain Liqueurs are fashioned of porcelain from Limoges, delftware and flacons of Venetian glass, so that many of these charming containers become collectibles.

In our home we have treasured for years an emptied bottle of Marie Brizard Anisette Liqueur. You would hardly suspect its original purpose. A lovely porcelain lady stands erect in a full, bright blue dress that falls gracefully over a hooped skirt with ermine panels from waist to toe over a white underskirt, her hands demurely hidden in a matching ermine muff; a brilliant blue hood over her blonde head ends in an abbreviated cape at the shoulders. The removable head discloses a small cork and the secret that this old-fashioned doll is a bottle once filled with delectable Liqueur.

Philistines may scoff that Liqueurs would taste the same if mundanely contained in cheap utilitarian bottles. This is not true, no more than an expensive, delicate perfume would smell the same if placed in a mustard bottle or Champagne taste as delicious if served in a mug or plastic cup. Likewise, beautifully planned and prepared dinners would not taste the same if served on a plastic cloth in colored, heavy pottery dishes. There is a harmony, a style, a propriety in the whole subject of food and drink that appeals as much to the imagination as to the taste. Of great importance in gastronomy is what, where, with whom, how and why. The intangibles are the real values that make partaking food, wine and spirits a worthwhile social experience. Restaurateurs call it atmosphere, and a great deal of money, time and effort is allocated to providing elegantly appointed restful surroundings for the public's dining and drinking enjoyment.

Aperitifs It is interesting to note that during the past ten years or so, more European ways of using wine and liquor have become familiar to Americans. An example of this is the word "aperitif," whose meaning was once only vaguely understood, connoting a way of life and beverages completely foreign to the taste habits of Americans. Only Americans who had lived or traveled abroad (and, until recently, they represented a very small segment) had a clear idea of the role of the aperitif.

Now this drink has established itself on the American scene and the visitor who asks for one either in a bar or in a home receives it as a matter of course—and this not always in large cities but in unexpected places. Time was when a guest would receive an uncomprehending look a number of years ago. Today, if a particular requested aperitif is out of stock, he will receive a polite apology and perhaps a suggestion of a substitute. In the same vein, Americans can freely order an aperitif without feeling they are affecting airs.

What, then, is an aperitif? The term denotes the use to which a drink is put, namely, as a before-meal appetizer, and does not signify a specific beverage. Correctly speaking, almost any drink that stimulates the appetite may be regarded as an aperitif—if it does not dull the ability of the palate to perceive flavor. An aperitif may be made of wine or spirits, it may be herbalized, aromatized, or otherwise flavored. It may be sweet or bitter. Vermouth or Sherry may serve as an aperitif, or the drinks whose names for so many decades have become synonymous with the term aperitif: Dubonnet, Campari, also Raphael, Lillet, Byrrh, Ricard, Pernod, and so on. The Vermouths are closely related to these. These exotic beverages are often called for even as a preluncheon drink and are in favor among many of the businessmen who hold memberships in the luxurious luncheon clubs. The light alcoholic content makes an aperitif more suitable for a business luncheon followed by an afternoon still packed with activity.

The aperitif wine probably more heavily advertised than any other is Dubonnet. Unlike its competitive aperitifs, manufactured abroad and shipped in bottles, Dubonnet has been manufactured for some years in the United States by a Schenley subsidiary under a franchise granted by the French owners of the brand name.

Dubonnet was formulated over a century ago by Joseph Dubonnet.

This wine wholesaler was not content with the aromatized wine then on the market. He decided to blend his own for some relatives, friends and himself, but he kept the formula secret and only passed it on to his son Marius shortly before his death. Marius began to manufacture Dubonnet at a small plant in Paris, and before the turn of the century, demand for it soared. He had designed an unusual label for it: a cat contentedly winding its lithe body around a bottle.

How does one drink Dubonnet? Slightly chilled, and served in a cocktail glass, certainly before meals. Early in this century, a restaurateur invented what became known eventually as the Dubonnet Cocktail: 1/2 Gin, 1/2 Dubonnet, stirred well with cracked ice, strained and served with lemon peel.

The French process called for steeping the aroma-adding herbs in the wine, producing a red Dubonnet. For some years now, Dubonnet blonde, dryer than the red and more subtly herbalized, has been produced and sold on the American market. Some say it is the number-one aperitif both in Paris and in the United States.

Campari, the largest-selling aperitif in Italy, has more recently come into favor here, distributed by Austin Nichols & Co., Inc. Spirit-based, it has a distinctive bitter-sweet flavor. Campari is prepared in the Campari plant in the outskirts of Milan and shipped here in a concentrated form. At the Austin Nichols plant, it is blended with spirits and bottled at the standard 48 proof at which Campari is marketed.

Two drinks, well-known in Italy and elsewhere, are coming into favor here: the Americano and the Negroni. The Americano is made of equal portions of Campari and dry or sweet Vermouth plus a twist of lemon over ice and served with Soda, if desired. The Negroni calls for Campari, Vermouth, Soda Water and Gin in equal parts.

Raphael is the largest selling aperitif wine in France. It is red and bittersweet, enjoyed on-the-rocks or in cocktails. It is imported by Julius Wile Sons & Co., Inc.

Lillet is gaining wider appreciation in the United States since the post-war years. It has been distributed for a number of years by Dreyfus, Ashby, Inc., a division of Schenley. Widely enjoyed in France and particularly popular in southwestern France, extending from Bordeaux southward to the Pyrenees, Lillet is billed by its label as an aperitif Vermouth. It is imported in both red and blonde form, being prepared and bottled at Podensac in the Gironde district about 25 miles outside of Bordeaux. Its distinctive characteristic is its orange flavor.

Ricard takes its name from its inventor, Paul Ricard. It is an aniseed-flavored aperitif diluted with water when served. This product was perfected in 1932, when Ricard was 23 years old, in a rudimentary laboratory in the midst of the worldwide Depression. The House of Ricard gave up the wine trade and specialized in making and selling its new product, establishing warehouses in Sète, Nice, Grenoble and Lyon. But the capitulation of France in 1940 to the Germans plunged his concern into a long run of misfortunes. The enemy needed alcohol for military purposes, and they prohibited manufacture of the aperitif. After many tribulations, it has not only survived but has continued to be particularly renowned.

What more than mirth would mortals have? The cheerful man is a king.

ISAAC BICKERSTAFF (1735–1812)

Chapter 4 Whiskeys, Other Spirits And Beer

MAN cannot possess either food or drink. He consumes them and they are gone, yet hunger and thirst remain his constant companions. Only the memory lingers of the taste, place, company, gratifyingly happy hours spent in dining and drinking—the complete experience that poignantly emphasizes the true meaning of life, increases strength and vitality and lifts the spirits. Perhaps that is why certain liquors are called spirits.

This chapter includes liquors (strong alcoholic beverages) usually 86 proof or more, which derive their principal flavor mostly from the process of manufacture and not from infusion of flavors and aromatics. For example, Whiskeys are flavored from being in charred oak casks, whereas Liqueurs (sweet alcoholic beverages) are infused with the flavor and aroma of spices, herbs, fruits and aromatic substances. While their alcoholic strength may be low, many Liqueurs are as strong as the strongest hard liquors. Some specialties such as Gin or Aquavit are on the borderline. Both are strong and flavored by botanicals, but they are not sweet, so their classification always has and always will be controversial.

There are three main types of American whiskeys: Ryes, Bourbons and Blends, all distilled from a fermented mash of assorted grains, usually consisting of rye, corn and malt. Those who drink Rye, Bourbon and Blends often cannot tell the difference between them. However, this unawareness is blissful and harmless since it does not diminish the enjoyment of the drink. Those who can tell the difference derive extra pleasure out of the subtle skills of the various distillers and blenders. Each distiller, vintner and rectifier performs in an individual way and often by secret formula. This accounts for the distinction between brands.

To be called a Bourbon, the mash must contain a minimum of 51 percent corn; a Rye. 51 percent rye. As a rule, all Bourbons contain Rye and most Ryes contain corn. There are also so-called "pure Rye Whiskeys," which are distilled from a mash containing rye grain only. Blended Whiskeys are straight whiskeys blended with neutral grain spirits.

Bourbon happens to be the only Whiskey that is truly native to the United States. Like the whalemen's scrimshaw carvings, it can be considered indigenous to America. By coincidence, the time of its birth coincides with that of the United States Government in 1789, the year George Washington took the oath as first President. At one time, Bourbon replaced currency, and it was praised by Daniel Boone, Andrew Jackson and William Henry Harrison. When Senator Daniel Webster honored Harrison at a great Log Cabin Ball, guests were served Old Crow Bourbon, which had been created by James Crow in Kentucky. Light and mild, it is 86 proof.

Bourbon is distinguished from all other Whiskeys by its distinctive flavor derived from American corn. After the Revolutionary War, hundreds of soldiers flocked to the Kentucky hills and began making Bourbon in Bourbon County, Kentucky. There the native corn, rye, wheat and malt were mixed with the iron-free water that had run over limestone rocks. Kentucky abounds in springs of water. They rush upward through layers of limestone, which filter out impurities and provide water generally conceded to be the best in the United States for the manufacture of Bourbon. There are also some important Whiskey distilling areas in the limestone-water regions of western Pennsylvania and southern Indiana.

Before the Civil War, Bourbon was sold only by the barrel, and there were no brand names when it was bottled. Then came professional distillers and bonded warehouses, which ended the backyard-farmer production begun by the early Scottish and Irish settlers in the United States. The immigrants brought with them their native skills and magical yeast for their household craft of Whiskey making. The conversion of surplus grain into Whiskey was a welcome economic expedient. In 1872, Isaac W. Bernhaim established a distillery in Louisville and made a fine Bourbon that was sold by his salesman,

I. W. Harper. Mr. Harper cleverly promoted the sale of his Whiskey by putting it in fancy decanters, and the company bearing his name still dispenses some fine Bourbons.

Nobody really knows who first used a charred keg for aging Whiskey. The first historical reference to such kegs dates from 1840. The Bourbon Institute relates three versions. In order to save money, a distiller planned to use kegs in which fish had been stored. To get rid of the odor, he scorched the inside of the barrels with a blazing pine knot. Later, he found the Whiskey had a pleasant flavor and a ruddy hue. Another story is that an early-day cooper carelessly burned some barrel staves he was heating before curving, and then decided to use them anyway. Months later, a customer told him the Whiskey from the charred barrel was very good. Another version is that the discovery was made in Jamaica when a Rum warehouse burned and it was found the Rum from the charred barrels was better than from the others.

Bourbon is aged in charred kegs made from *new* wood, preferably white oak either from the Ozarks or the hills of Tennessee. The cost of these kegs runs about $22 to $25 each, and they cannot be used again. Once used, they are sold to Scotch and Canadian Whisky people, who buy them at $1 or $2 each. The use of new casks adds a great deal to the price of the product. Another serious factor in the cost of Bourbon is taxes. The first excise tax was levied in 1791 for a badly depleted Federal treasury and enforced by the Secretary of the Treasury, Alexander Hamilton. The farmers in Pennsylvania took rather violent exception to the Federal levy of 11 cents a gallon, and this brought on the Whiskey Rebellion recounted in history books.

In ensuing years, taxes and regulations, both Federal and state, have proven a heavy burden to the industry. In 1897, came the Bottling-in-Bond Act; in 1913, the Webb-Kenyon Act; in 1919, the Eighteenth Amendment to the Constitution establishing Prohibition; the Repeal Amendment; and in 1935, the Federal Alcohol Administration Act. During the War of 1812, the tax was 9 cents a gallon. During the Civil War, it went from 60 cents a gallon to $2 to raise funds, but moonshining forced the tax down to 50 cents. During World War I the tax rose from $2.40 to $6.40 just before Prohibition. In 1934, it was back to $2. Today, after several years, the Internal Revenue Alcohol Director says it is still set at $10.50 a gallon. In its general usage, this excise tax is levied by the United States Government on distilled spirits, malt beverages and wines.

It is not true that most Bourbon drinkers live in rural areas. On the contrary, a survey conducted by W. R. Simmons Associates, Inc. (and published in *New Yorker* magazine) indicated that 79.3 percent of those who prefer Bourbon are metropolitan and suburban residents, while only 20.7 percent live in nonmetropolitan areas. The study, in fact, showed that 45.1 percent of users were college graduates. Bourbon has been around a long time. Old Forester Kentucky Bourbon celebrated its centennial in 1970, with an original leaded-glass Tiffany lamp as a customer coupon offer.

There are many brands for your choice. Old Grand Dad is a straight Bourbon, 86 proof, Old Grand Dad bottled-in-bond has 100 proof; Wild Turkey, 101 proof—straight good Bourbons. The high proof, such as 101 Wild Turkey, will burn the tongue. Old Taylor is a good brand, and likewise Jim Beam. Brand names help to establish a reputation for integrity and quality, but actually there is very little difference in taste between the brands. The only way you can differentiate would be on the basis of the proofs. As a matter of fact, Bourbon is often distilled and then distributed to name brands which bottle and label them, so essentially there is no basic difference.

As for identifying whether the brand you are drinking is of high quality, if you do not see the bottle from which it is served, you cannot actually decide whether it is excellent or less than excellent. It would depend a great deal on the intangibles such as the company, companionship, atmosphere and the personal mood of the drinker. There are, of course, many less expensive brands for large consumption, and price is the key to its value.

The Brand Names Foundation, now in its 27th year, has done a notable job of strengthening public confidence of consumers by joining stores with manufacturers and advertising media in stressing the importance of the brand competitive system of America. Many a brand name familiar to Europeans during our Colonial years still enjoys a faithful following. For instance, Crosse and Blackwell dates from 1706; Royal Worcester porcelains from 1751; Wedgwood china from 1759; and *The Encyclopaedia Britannica,* fount of so much knowledge, from 1768. The Foundation records over 300,000 trademarks and 20,000 brand names in use which stimulate sales, and it is interesting to note that the oldest brand name at the Foundation is Cherry Rocher, a French Liqueur. The oldest American native brand is alcoholic, too. It is Old Medford Brand Rum. This dates from 1776. James E. Pepper's distilled spirits and Caldwell's Rum came along as early as 1790.

Many of the whiskey manufacturers have built reputations for impeccable products. Seagram's reliable Seven Crown, American Blended Whiskey, 86 proof, 65 percent grain neutral spirits, is said to be America's largest-selling brand, outselling other brands for 22 straight years. For over 80 years, Four Roses Blended Whiskey has been a great American spirit, 86 proof, 65 percent neutral spirits, blended and bottled by the Four Roses Distillers Company, New York City.

Fleischmann's celebrated one century of progress (1870 to 1970) with such well-known and respected brands as Old Medley; Kentucky

Straight Bourbon Whiskey, 90 proof; Davies County; Kentucky Straight Bourbon Whiskey, 86 proof, matured in oak casks, labeled as "four years old" with a heritage from 1874. Fleischmann's also offers Preferred Blended Whiskey, 90 proof, 65 percent grain neutral spirits; Fleischmann's Bottled in Bond, Straight Kentucky Bourbon Whiskey, 100 proof, solely distributed by Fleischmann Distilling Corporation, New York City.

All of the fine brands available to the American taste cannot be included, so many worthy of mention do not appear here. Mr. W. L. Lyons Brown, former Chairman of the Brown-Forman Distillers Corp., Louisville, Kentucky, tells us that his century-old company gained its foothold on the American market because of Old Forester. Later they added brands such as Early Times. This company first introduced the year-round gift package in the mid-1930s, with Old Forester being marketed in a colonial-style bottle.

Before the Civil War, doctors for years had been prescribing Bourbon as a remedy for malaria, bronchitis, dyspepsia and other ailments. W. L. Lyons Brown's grandfather, George Garvin Brown, who was a young wholesale drug salesman, recognized the need for a Bourbon of quality and uniformity, since the Whiskey then available was many times unreliable in quality because it could be tampered with while in barrels. He packaged it in bottles instead of shipping it in barrels, with a tamper-proof closure on the bottle. This was the first American Whiskey ever sold exclusively in a distiller-sealed bottle: Old Forester Bourbon Whiskey.

In the good years of prosperity following World War II, the American public became more sophisticated in its drinking habits, and the industry responded with different types of Liquor. At this point, Brown-Forman acquired (in 1956) the Jack Daniel Distillery Co. of Lynchburg, Tennessee, maker of the famous Jack Daniel Black and Green labels. In 1956, they also acquired Jos. Garneau Co., a 114-year-old wine and spirits manufacturing firm in New York City. This added Usher's Green Stripe Scotch, Cruse French Wines, Veuve Clicquot Champagnes and Anheuser German Wines to the Brown-Forman line.

Scotch

There was scarcely a time when the Scots were not making their distinctive beverage, having exactly what they needed: barley, clean water and peat. They mixed the water with the barley, used the peat to dry out and flavor the malt, and then proceeded with the distillation to its potent conclusion. Almost every farmhouse had a distillery, or, if not, used a neighbor's. Through the 18th century and the first half of the 19th century, this Whisky was Everyman's drink. Soon the government discovered a taxable item, but nobody really felt it was a crime to outwit the Government inspector. In 1777, more than 400 illicit stills were found in Edinburgh alone. Eventually, however, the stills were controlled. A significant change came about when grain was substituted for barley and a new process made distillation cheaper and quicker. The makers blended the grain Whiskeys with the single malt Whiskeys in proportions that are today company formula secrets. The blends make up the great bulk of the Scotch imported into the United States but it is the unblended malt Whiskeys to which those initiated give their devotion. The malt Whiskeys varied not only from area to area but also within a given area, much as wines do in France. There was a time in history when the distillers religiously used only local barley, peat and water. Now the barley comes from as far as Australia and India without altering the quality of the product.

All Scotch Whisky must be imported. This is an expensive process: not only is transportation involved, but taxes in the form of import duties and the United States excise tax of $10.50 per 100-proof gallon paid by the importer. This tax rate and the way the law is worded has led to one of the great marketing innovations of the post-World War II era—bulk import. Most Scotch bottled in Scotland is bottled at 86.6 proof. The importer therefore gets 14 percent less Whisky than he is really paying tax on. Bulk Scotch Whisky brought into this country and reduced and bottled here is usually shipped at 110 to 115 proof, and in this way the importer pays tax on the actual proof of the Whisky he brings in.

Many brands of Scotch Whisky bottled in the United States have achieved substantial sales and wide recognition, such as Inver House, King George IV, Bullock and Lade, Clan MacGregor and Peter Dawson. The taste for light-bodied Whiskies is achieved by distilling at a higher proof and by blending American Whiskey which is naturally full-bodied, with 75 to 80 percent neutral spirits.

A recent development is the shipment of Scotch and other spirits in huge stainless steel tanks with a capacity of 5,000 American wine gallons by a certain shipping firm. In order to comply with United States Government regulations, these tanks actually are only filled with 4,800 gallons. Most bulk Scotch is bottled at 80 proof. When the tanks reach the bottling plant, custom officials break the seal and determine the tax due. Few bottling plants have the facilities at the present time to store and reduce the proof of these huge quantities of spirits.

What is the advantage to Scotch being bottled in the United States? Most of these bulk-imported Scotches sell from $1 to $1.50 less than their bottled-abroad brothers. This has led, of course, to an increase in consumption as many more people are now able to afford Scotch, which was once considered a wealthy man's prerogative. Once a city seller, Scotch is now reaching all over the country.

Other countries enjoy Scotch, although the United States is the greatest consumer. France, which has contributed so much to the treasury of mankind in wines, is now becoming an increasingly responsive market for the alcoholic beverage produce of other countries. France is the third largest market in the world for Scotch Whisky, after the United States and the United Kingdom.

Tradition always plays a very important part in the blending of Whiskies and in maintaining the prestige of an old and trusted name. There are many fine Scotches. The House of Haig, established in 1627, is the oldest distiller in Scotland. Distilled by the pot-still method, the Whisky of this old firm ages for at least three years in uncharred oak barrels or used Sherry casks. Ballantine's is blended and bottled by George Ballantine & Son in Dumbarton, Scotland, 86 proof, imported by "21" Brands, Inc., New York City.

Superb flavor and eight years of careful aging makes a fine Sandeman Scotch, solely imported from the House of Sandeman in London by W. A. Taylor & Co., New York City. The largest selling brand of Scotch Whiskies in the United States is J. V. B. Rare imported by Paddington Co., closely followed by Cutty Sark imported by Buckingham Co., #3 Dewars White Label and #4 Johnny Walker Red Label imported by Schenley and Somerset respectively.

John Begg, distilled in Balmoral and shipped by John Begg in Glasgow, established in 1845, is a reliable Scotch; the Antiquary, 86.8 proof, Edinburgh, sole importers Carillon, New York City; the familiar White Horse, 86 proof, from Glasgow; Ambassador, 86 proof, eight years old, imported by Jos. Garneau; Heather Dew, imported by Sovereign Importers, Ltd.; Thistle Scotch, Buchanan's and Pinch, House of Haig, short indented bottle. Then there is the squat bottle of Grand Old Parr, 12 years old, named for Thomas Parr, whose white-bearded visage appears on the back label with the legend he lived to be 152 years of age. MacDonald Greenlees, Ltd., Leith, Scotland, distills for the sole United States distribution of Peartree Imports, New York City. We conclude our collection with King's Ransom, 94 proof, William Whiteley & Co., Leigh, Scotland.

Among the fine Scotches in the Richelieu Wine Cellar are Teacher's Highland Cream, William Teacher & Sons, Glasgow, Scotland, imported by Schieffelin & Co., New York; Butler, Royal Blended Scotch Whisky, London, established in 1667 during the reign of Charles II, 86 proof; House of Lords, 86 proof, William Whiteley & Co., Leith, Scotland; Seagram's 100 Pipers, Aberdeen, Scotland; Bell's Royal Vat, 12 years old, Arthur Bell & Sons, Perth, Scotland, established 1825; Catto's Gold Medal, a blended Scotch, Aberdeen, Scotland, imported by Victor Fischel & Co., New York City. Along the River Spey are the three distilleries of Knockando, Strathmill and Glen Spey in the heart of the Highlands, which distill malt Whiskies, giving Catto's its essential character and style.

By law, Scotch Whisky needs only three years to mature, but citing the distillers, five years should be the minimum. Twelve years is even better, but the average consumer would balk at the price.

Most of the better-known Scotches have a regular Scotch, an eight-year-old with the same name (same Scotch) and a twelve-year-old, and the price increases as the age increases. It is good to remember that once out of the charred oak casks, the aging process stops because Whiskies, unlike wine, do not age in bottles. So a 100-year-old bottle of Whisky or Whiskey with the label reading "six years old," is only a curio. Qualitatively, the spirit is only six years old.

When you are in Scotland or England, you have to remember that British 70 proof is equal to American 80 proof. The American visitor in England who enjoys a few extras because he thinks he is drinking something lighter may feel the full effects of his folly on the morrow.

The high proof of a product is the reason for many hangovers or after-effects, although the mixture with which the drink is made also has much to do with it. In other words, if you were having a Scotch and water, it would give you one effect. If you were having the drink with Club Soda, instead of water, it would give a quicker reaction because of the Carbonated Water.

The British take a rather dim view of the almost universal American practice of chilling their Scotch by adding ice cubes to the glass, or muddying the flavor of the beverage by adding Angostura Bitters, fruit juices, Soda Water or other foreign bodies. Only a few Americans drink in the way Scotch authorities consider correct—i.e., neat.

Connoisseurs never mix Scotch with Ginger Ale because the latter tends to kill the smoky flavor for which Scotch is prized. This flavor is most pungent when imbibed at room temperature with either Club Soda or water, and the experts say this holds true as well for American Whiskeys. The smart drinker combines his Scotch with water.

Brief Summary of Whiskeys The Irish called their favorite drink by its Gaelic name, "Usigabeatha," after the Latin "aqua vitae," water of life. This was Anglicized to Whisky or Whiskey.

WHISKY: To clarify confusing spellings, *Whisky,* is the name identifying the distilled spirits of Scotland and Canada. Some Canadian brands are Calvert Extra Blended Whisky and Canadian Lord Calvert, also Windsor Canadian. Some American distillers use this spelling to label their products, and the United States Treasury Department uses Whisky in its regulations. *Whiskey,* however, is the Irish spelling, and most American products conform to the Irish preference.

STRAIGHT WHISKEY: By Federal regulation, this is a Whiskey such as Bourbon, Rye, corn or wheat, an alcoholic distillate from a fermented mash of a grain distilled at not more than 160 proof and withdrawn from the cistern room of the distillery at not more than 110 and not less than 80 proof. It is aged for not less than 24 calendar months in new, charred oak barrels. Aging brings out the character (as in the aging of tobacco or cheese) and is nature's way of awarding an excellence for the virtue of patience. Character has been defined as "that combination of a Whiskey's sensory qualities which distinguishes it from another Whiskey." There are so many brands because each distiller has his own favorite formula, a time for mashing, temperature, and the particular proof at which to distill his Whiskey. A master distiller gives his skill, and in the end talented tasters render their judgment before the product reaches the consumer.

BOURBON: First distilled in Bourbon County, Kentucky, 51 percent of the grain used is mash corn. This makes America's most popular straight Whiskey (spelled with an *e*). It is wonderful for blending and a truly American product. It is distilled from mash of corn, rye and barley malt, with corn as the determining factor. (To qualify as Bourbon, at least 51 percent and less than 80 percent of the grain must be corn.) Bourbon is distilled out below 160 proof, then aged for two years.

BLENDED WHISKEY: In many states, this drink is first man on the totem pole. Blending is the judicious combination of carefully selected straight Whiskeys with grain neutral spirits. From the straights, the new Whiskey derives its aroma, flavor, character and body. The grain neutral spirits give the result a lightness and velvetiness, which does not eliminate character. It is possible to secure by the science of blending a uniform product that always is identical to the desideratum.

CANADIAN WHISKY: Canadian law permits greater freedom than American law. In Canada, a distiller may use any grains he feels suit his needs. He uses barley malt, corn and rye, and is not limited to proof nor to methods of blending. The government bows to the knowledge of the distiller, and his skill is recognized in world markets. New casks are not needed, and used cooperage is acceptable. Proofs of imports vary from 80 to 90.4. A light-bodied, pleasant Whisky, it contains no distilled spirits less than two years old. Canadian distillers may blend their Whiskies either before aging or during the aging period, and most Canadian Whiskies exported to the United States are blends. United States regulations do not permit labeling Canadian Whiskies as "straights."

BRITISH WHISKY: Intercontinental Wine & Spirits, Ltd., Lake Success, New York, imports a British Whisky called Britannia (recipe included on p. 156 in recipe section).

IRISH WHISKEY: Spelled with an *e,* this is a full-bodied, straight Irish Whiskey or a blended Irish Whiskey (which is much lighter). Straight and malt Whiskeys are distilled off the pot stills at about 140 proof from fermented mash of barley malt and some small grain. The smoky taste of the barley malt is eliminated by drying out in coal-fired kilns. Usually, Sherry casks are used for Irish Whiskeys. When imported, they are at least four years of age. John Jamieson & Son exports a blended Irish Whiskey, 86 proof, from Dublin. Made solely from barley malt, wheat and oats, and matured at least seven years in oak casks, it is pot-stilled to produce a light, delicate Whiskey with a tantalizing flavor. It is considered ideal for Irish coffee and certain cocktails such as a Bloody John and Irish Sour (recipes included in recipe section). The same firm in Dublin exports a 12-year-old J. J. & S. Liqueur.

RYE WHISKEY: Early Americans, including George Washington, distilled a good Rye Whiskey that was popular in the eastern part of the country. This has a darker color and a heavier body than Bourbon. Taste patterns were disturbed by Prohibition, so the taste for a full-bodied malty Rye Whiskey has since declined. Rye is defined by Licensed Beverage Industries, Inc., of New York City as "Whiskey distilled at not more than 160 proof from a fermented mash of grain containing at least 51 percent rye grain." When a person asks for Rye, he gets either a blended Whiskey or Canadian Whisky. He expects it to have a deeper color and to be heavy.

SCOTCH WHISKY: The popularity of Scotch in world markets began 100 years ago. Barley was used exclusively in the traditional products of years ago, with the Highlands providing the most abundant of grains. In producing the malt Whiskies, barley lends a distinctive character not to be imitated elsewhere. To suit palates in locations other than those of the cold, northern hills of Scotland, a blend was achieved with other grains. Shortages always prevail because of the four-year waiting period required. Since Whisky in a blend is not used until fully developed, it sometimes takes as many as 8 years and even 12 years. The malt Whiskies that come from the Highlands, Lowlands, Cambeltown and Islay have a smoky aroma due to the drying of the sprouted barley malt over open peat fires.

Official Trade Terms

TAX GALLON: The unit of distilled spirits subject to the Federal excise tax is the United States gallon (231 cubic inches at 60 degrees Fahrenheit) of 100 proof alcoholic strength, on which the Federal tax is $10.50. On the other hand, a wine gallon is a physical measure of actual liquid volume; the standard United States gallon contains 231 cubic inches as compared to the British wine or imperial gallon, which contains approximately 20 percent more by volume than the United States wine gallon. The British Imperial Gallon contains 277.4 cubic inches, as does the Canadian Imperial Gallon.

BOTTLED IN BOND: The United States Bureau of Internal Revenue affixes a strip stamp tax-paid over the closure of every bottle of distilled spirits. Green stamps are used for bottled-in-bond spirits and reddish-pink stamps for all other distilled spirits. The Federal Government does not guarantee quality, but does guarantee compliance with the regulations: Straight Whiskey distilled in one plant in one season must be aged in new charred oak barrels for at least four years, and must be bottled at 100 proof.

U.S. GOVERNMENT BONDED WAREHOUSE: A warehouse established under the laws and regulations of the Internal Revenue Service in which distilled spirits are stored in bond, before payment of tax. Although the proprietor of a bonded warehouse is a private individual or firm, the operations as well as the warehouse itself are kept under the direct supervision of officers of the Internal Revenue Service, who carry the keys to the warehouse and keep a governmental record of all entries and withdrawals of spirits. The warehouse owner may enter the premises only in the presence of a Government officer, and no spirits may be withdrawn except with governmental permission.

Gin

Gin is the soul and main body of the Martini, America's leading cocktail. Immediately after Prohibition, it consisted of two parts Gin and one of Vermouth, plus about 25 percent water from diluted ice. Since then the proportions have fluctuated so that now the proportions are up to six to one and more. What the proper preparation should be is a matter of opinion, and manufacturers of Vermouth and Gin have divergent views, each in favor of their own product. The more Gin used, the dryer your drink will be and the more potent. Because it is rather inexpensive, Gin is more popular than other liquors, comparable in quality, strength and universal taste appeal.

New equipment is constantly being designed and new procedures being tested for the manufacture of Gins that are not aged and are colorless spirits containing about 80 proof. The Spanish called Gin *ginebra,* the Dutch *genever,* the French *genièvre* (juniper).

The main flavoring agent is the juniper berry, and Gin has been made in a pot still ever since it was discovered in the 16th century by a doctor-scientist, Francis de la Boe, at the University of Leyden in Holland. It was first made in the Netherlands, notably at Schiedam, and called Holland Gin.

Actually, Vodka and Gin production begins more or less in the same way with a high proof of grain neutral spirits. In what follows, however, the production of Vodka and Gin differ radically. In making Vodka, any perceptible character, taste or aroma is taken out of the spirits; in making Gin, taste, aroma and character are added by the use of botanicals.

The Federal regulations that define Gin say that "distilled Gin is a distillate obtained by original distillation from mash, or by the redistillation of distilled spirits, over or with juniper berries and other aromatics customarily used in the production of Gin, and deriving its main characteristic flavor from juniper berries and reduced at times of bottling to not less than 80 proof; and includes mixtures of such products."

The redistilling takes place in the presence of juniper berries and other botanicals and herbs such as aniseed, coriander, caraway seeds, almonds, cassia bark, fennel, orrisroot, licorice, bitter orange peel and lemon peel. Some Gins acquire a golden hue from being stored in wood as had been done in recent years, and sometimes Gins are flavored with orange or mint. Gin is ready for bottling immediately after distillation, since there are no aging requirements. Sometimes a simple syrup is added, as in the case of Old Tom, which is a dry, slightly sweetened Gin.

When members of the Charles Dickens Fellowship made an interesting pilgrimage to the novelist's haunts in London, they discovered the author used to buy Gin and other beverages from the wine and spirits merchants, Seager, Evans and Co., a company that began its long history as distillers of Gin. Seager, Evans, now 75 percent owned by Schenley, asked the members of the Fellowship to their West End offices to see many Dickens mementoes including a fine bas relief head of the author, some of his checks for purchase of Seager, Evans products, and the like. Just recently, when English novelist Lawrence Durrell was traveling in the United States to promote his latest book titled *Nunquam,* he announced a discovery. "What I thought was a slight earthquake going through the whole place that made me thirsty all the time was actually your Gin. It's 90 proof. Ours in London is only 60."

Some claim the higher the proof of the distilled spirits, the better the botanicals' flavor comes through in the Gin. In any event, the formulas and processes involved in the making of Gin are jealously-guarded secrets.

Most imported Gins are bottled at a higher proof than their American counterparts. We prefer English Gin. In their promotion, the purity of the product is always emphasized. Gin is usually pushed with an English connotation, whereas Vodka bears a Russian one. Companies that have both a Vodka and a Gin often employ two promotion approaches but some, like Hiram Walker, market and promote them as companion items. Gordon's, Gilbey's and Fleischmann split the two items completely and have a separate promotion for the individual brands. Calvert has emphasized the fact that theirs is an American Gin made for the American Martini drinker. They may call attention to the fact that in addition to botanicals from all over the world, they also use hand-cut lime peel, and they distill over and over again to create a particularly dry product.

The makers of Beefeater Gin are very proud of the continuing family control for this product by James Burrough, Ltd., of London. The bottles are still numbered, and a record is kept of each one. It is 94 proof, and its importer, Kobrand Corporation, directs its promotion almost entirely to the consumer. Coates Plymouth Dry Gin, 94.4 proof, is bottled by Coates of Plymouth, England, established in 1793; they remind you that it is made in the building housing the former refectory room of the Black Friar Dominicans, where the provisions were stored for the Pilgrims before they embarked on the *Mayflower.*

Booth's House of Lords, the one significant bulk Gin on the United States market today, makes much of the fact that their product is unchanged in quality for 227 years. There are six rampant lions on their label. The fact that the English quality of Gin is always emphasized harks back to medieval times when the water in London was renowned for its purity. This purity was due in part to the geological formation of rock existing around London, which has a high degree of limestone that would tend to purify the water by its filtering through it. It is from this fact that London Dry Gin gets its name. However, now that most Gins employ some kind of purification in the water used to reduce their grain neutral spirits, this is not so important.

Sir Robert Burnett's White Satin English Gin is distributed by Four Roses Distillers Company. Other Gins include Bombay Gin, still distilled from a 1761 recipe, 86 proof, by Bombay Spirits Company in London; sole distributors are Carillon Importers, Ltd., who bring in Bombay Vermouth. Recipes are included in the recipe section for Bombay Martini, Gimlet and Bombay Tonic. Old Gentry, London Dry Gin, 94.8 proof, is imported by Dolphin Imports, Inc., New York City; J & B, Justerini & Brooks, comes from England; Squire's Gin is solely imported by Victor Fischel and Co., Inc.; Old Lady's Dry Gin, 96 proof, comes from Marie Brizard, established in 1755 in Bordeaux, France, solely distributed by Schieffelin and Co. Two more English Gins in our Wine Cellar are Tanqueray and Boodles British Gin. Cork Dry Gin from Cork, Ireland, is imported by Austin Nichols. Among the good American Gins are Calvert Gin, 90 proof, and Seagram's Extra Dry Gin.

Gin used to be sold in cloudy bottles, but this practice is now disappearing. The idea was to give the buyer a frosty cool visual impression of an iced drink. We no longer receive Gin stock in frosted bottles at Richelieu. The same holds true for stemware, which is no longer available frosted.

Vodka   Vodka's progress from the "little water" of Russia, from its original inception in the 11th century in Persia, has been nothing short of phenomenal. Vodka is a neutral spirit, distilled usually from grains and filtered through activated carbon to remove any taste of the spirits. In this country, the good Vodkas are distilled from a grain mash, including portions of malt, rye, wheat, and so on. Contrary to general belief, most of the Vodka consumed is produced in the United States. This colorless liquor can be made from any starch material such as grains, potatoes or sugar beets. It is distilled at a high proof (190 or higher) and filtered, so virtually none of the flavors in the mash come through. This results in a spirit that is called neutral and, even after the proof has been reduced for palatability, ardent.

The Government definition of Vodka is: "Neutral spirits distilled from any material at or above 190 degrees proof, reduced to not more than 110 degree proof and not less than 80 degree proof, and after such reduction in proof, so treated by one of the accepted methods as to be without distinctive character, aroma or taste."

To deserve its classification, Vodka must be devoid of flavor or aroma, be colorless and not aged. Therefore, it lends itself well to combining with any other liquid. It becomes a Screwdriver with orange juice, a Bloody Mary with tomato juice, a Vodka Martini with dry Vermouth (recipes included in recipe section) and can be taken with cider, coffee or tea. A Vodka Stinger means Vodka is substituted for Brandy in combination with Menthe.

New fashions in Vodka drinks continue to make their impact. The Black Russian is made with 1 1/2 ounces Vodka and 3/4 ounce Coffee Liqueur poured over ice cubes in an Old-Fashioned glass. The White Russian adds cream. The same ingredients in the same proportions, plus the addition of a dash of lemon juice and a twist of peel, makes an interesting variation called Black Magic.

The Moscow Mule originally called for 1 jigger Vodka, the juice of half a lime plus the rind, ice cubes and service in a copper cup. This has been outdistanced by the Smirnoff Mule, for which Skitch Henderson wrote a hit tune. It calls for 1 jigger Vodka, the juice of 1/4 lime and 7-Up to desired strength.

Vodka got its start in California after World War II. The idea spread throughout the nation, permanently changing the drinking pattern of many Americans. The difference between a domestic brand of Vodka and an imported one is very slight, if any. In large part, the success story of Vodka is due to Heublein, Inc., who for years have shown their belief in this product by expending intelligent effort in the promotion of their Smirnoff brand. California still out-ranks other areas as a market for Vodka; it is strong in the West and Northeast, a leading favorite among Americans particularly in the more affluent or trend-setting urban communities. There are now more than 50 brands of Vodka on the market, with the list growing. Kamchatcka enjoys great popularity both in package stores and in bars in Los Angeles.

For all practical purposes, Vodka in this country is bottled at 80 proof, the most popular (although most companies also have a 100-proof product). The charcoal method of purification was invented by the Russians where Vodka production has been a government monopoly since the 11th century. In 1780, the Russian czar commis-sioned a Prussian chemist, Theodore Lowitz, to find a method to make the national drink of the Russians more healthful.

One American Vodka producer has patented his process of pro-ducing Vodka: Gordon's, 80 proof, produced and bottled by the Distillers Company, Ltd., Linden, New Jersey, and Plainfield, Illinois, for Gordon's Dry Gin Company, Ltd., patent No. 2,879,165. Meth-ods of production of imported Vodka are not well-known, although the two brands imported from England are made much as are the American product. Most of the imported Eastern European Vodkas are flavored, mostly with buffalo grass known as Zubrowka, and there is one imported French Vodka made from potatoes.

By Slavic custom, Vodka is served in small glasses. It is gulped, not sipped, as an accompaniment to appetizers or snacks. The use of Vodka as a base for mixed drinks is largely an American innovation that has happily given rise to a Vodka industry here using grain only and rectifying with charcoal. Originally taken straight or neat in Russia, there now seems to be an undercurrent to revive this practice in the United States. Victor Fischel makes much of the fact that Wolfschmidt is the one Vodka that you dare to drink straight.

There tends to be a Russian emphasis on Vodka—many Russian-sounding brand names are used—but there are exceptions, most notably Gordon's, Gilbey's, Wolfschmidt and the two English im-ports, Masquers and Cavendish. Some names hark back to the Rus-sian nobility—Czarina of Bartons, Romanoff of Julius Wile Co. Others relate to the Russian people—Park Avenue Import's Bolshoi, a French import. Smirnoff is the largest-selling Vodka in the United States.

Tequila

Tequila, distilled from the mescal or agave plant, is perhaps one of the oldest spirits known. It is Mexico's national drink. The Indians of Mexico used to eat the cooked mescal hearts, but it was not until the coming of the Spaniards that the product was distilled. The mescal plant has grown wild in the deserts of Mexico for over 1,000 years, and was first commercially cultivated in the Mexican state of Jalisco, near Guadalajara, more than a century ago. The plant matures in 8 to 14 years; when harvested, the leaves are sheared off, exposing the heart, which resembles a pineapple. This heart is only partly used. The juice is extracted, fermented and then distilled. Tequila Sauza, 86 proof, is imported by Munson G. Shaw Co., New York.

It is almost impossible for a non-Mexican to take Tequila neat because it is a very strong beverage. The way it is drunk in Mexico is a ritual in itself. The drinker takes half a lime or lemon, tilts his head back and squeezes some of the juice on his tongue, then he puts a little salt on his thumbnail and combines this with the juice on his tongue. All is done very deftly. Then he gulps the Tequila as a Russian takes his Vodka. Margarita (recipe included) is a very popular cocktail which utilizes the salt idea on the rim of the cocktail glass.

Rum Rum belongs to our own hemisphere rather than to Europe. Christopher Columbus, on his second voyage to this part of the world in 1493, planted sugarcane cuttings in St. Croix, Virgin Islands. Columbus had become familiar with cane and its sugar while he lived on the Portuguese island of Madeira. Prior to this, he had brought a cargo of Madeira sugar back to Genoa. From the root shoots of cane, called ratoons, planted in the soil of what became Haiti, emerged the great Caribbean sugar industry. As early as the middle of the 16th century, it included the making of Rum. In the 17th century, New York and New England set up Rum distilleries, using West Indian molasses. The residue of sugar manufacturing was used for sugarcane molasses, and the leftover portions after the molasses were made were distilled to create alcohol. Then the product was aged in wood for the production of Rum.

Using Rum as currency, a valuable factor in trade, New Englanders initiated the Triangle Trade, exchanging Rum for natives in Africa and trading these natives for molasses in the West Indies, where slave labor was needed. The molasses were brought to New England, where they were distilled into more Rum, and the cycle was repeated.

Although George Washington was partial to Madeira, he also favored Rum drinks, and ordered Rum regularly from the West Indies (the use of Rum in America predates Whiskey). New Englanders, for their part, quickly found that Rum made their bitter winters more bearable, and they experimented with the creation of such drinks as Toddy, Stonewall and Flip. Rum was also popularly used as an ingredient for medicinal preparations. Here is one from New England: "Into ye heavy cream, put a good measure of strong syder and some sugar. Whip until it peaks, stirring in as much Rum as ye cream will hold. Put powdered nutmeg on top." This pleasant, puddinglike sweet was recommended for "sweating in ye bed to relieve aches and paynes." As early as 1733, King George of England attempted to impose a Rum tax on his American colonies. Forty years later, the War of Independence was helped along by the imposition—among other burdens—of the British Molasses Act, which forbade the colonies to buy molasses from any place in the Caribbean area except the British West Indies.

Rum was a staple on British ships ever since Admiral Edward Vernon in 1745 found it cured his crew of the dread disease scurvy, because of its Vitamin C content. By accident, he had replaced the daily beer ration with Rum. Buccaneers took their Rum with water, lemons or limes, calling it Grog. The first places established to supply pirate crews on islands such as St. Thomas were called Grog Shops. Virgin Islanders retain their own version of the original Rum, water and lime mixture, which is similar to today's Daiquiri. In the tropical islands, fruit flavors are added and sometimes Cointreau. Rum is a favorite for such warm-weather drinks as Planters Punch and the tall, cool Rum punches (recipes included in recipe section).

Modern Rums are divided into (1) traditional Rums and (2) lighter-bodied and less pungent Rums. Jamaica is the base for traditional Rums, where the large and wealthy estates are famous for growing special varieties of cane selected for flavor by Jamaican distilleries to produce dark Rum rich in aroma. This increases when aged in wood. The full-bodied, traditional Rums from the British West Indies come from old-fashioned pot stills at a much lower proof. The more pungent Rums marketed in the States come from Jamaica, Trinidad, Barbados, British Guiana, Martinique, Madagascar and Reunion Island, where they are known as Rum, Rhum, Ran, Cana, etc. Demerara Rums, as dark as mahogany, are produced in British Guiana. Other full-bodied Rums under British labels are those of Barbados and Trinidad. France brings Rum from Martinique and imports molasses for distillation in France.

Jamaican Rum brought to England benefits from the peculiarities of the English climate, being stored and blended and named for the location where this process takes place, and thus becoming the finest London Dock Rums.

Usually the dry, light-bodied Rums, distilled out in column stills at fairly high proof, come from Puerto Rico and Cuba. Batavia Arak, from the Island of Java in the Indonesian Republic, is a very pungent Rum, yet it is light-bodied. The lighter-bodied Rums are, indeed, a Cuban innovation dating from the last quarter of the 19th century. The Cubans carried the distilling process to the point where much of the pungency—deriving from the fermented molasses—is eliminated, the product being more neutral than the traditional Rums.

There are many proofs and types of Rum and variations in color and taste. The lighter they are in color, the lower the proof. Proof runs from 86 up. A very high proof is Lemon Hart, imported by Julius Wile, which is 151 proof. The higher the proof, of course, the more intoxicating it is.

White Label and Gold Label are the two Cuban types standardized for the import trade. Since 1933, both of these types have been imitated by the Rum industry of Puerto Rico and the Virgin Islands.

White Label generally identifies a light-bodied Rum that is pale in color and has a delicate aroma and flavor. This Rum is suitable for cocktails and makes drinks in which the Rum flavor should not be predominant. Gold Label identifies the darker Rums that have a stronger flavor and aroma and are most appropriate in drinks in which the Rum flavor predominates. This Rum combines well as a flavoring for cakes, pastries (Baba Rum) and candies.

Beer and Ale

Beer and ale have quenched the thirst of man from ancient times. Early man accidently discovered that a refreshing drink could be produced by the fermentation of cooked cereals. (Spontaneous fermentation of sun-warmed cereals was made possible by airborne yeasts.) Thus brewing followed fast upon all-important agriculture in the dawn of history.

Some of the earliest historical records excavated in the valleys of the Euphrates and the Nile, the cradles of two ancient civilizations, concern beer. Deciphered are transactions of the sale of grain, surveying measurements of fields in which millet and barley were grown, and tools for the malting and brewing trades. Also included are recipes and formulas for making beer. There were coarse beers available to the laborers and peasants; they contained spent grain husks that had to be chewed. Drawings and bas reliefs show priests, warriors and kings drinking special brews through long clay pipes from jugs containing beer filtered through screens woven from willow branches.

The Goddess Isis, who represented the female principle of life, is said to have introduced brewing into Egypt. In 1935, American archaeologists unearthed in Mesopotamia a tablet of baked pottery at least 6,000 years old. Two men with sticks are shown stirring the contents of a brewing vat. The Babylonians and peoples of ancient India produced a kind of beer, and Kiu, a beerlike drink, was known to the Chinese as far back as the 23rd century B.C.

The Greeks called beer *Zythos* and the Romans *Cerevisia,* but wine overshadowed beer in ancient Greece and Rome. In the German town of Alzey, once an outpost of the Roman Empire, a jug was found containing beer mash evidently set aside for beer fermentation. The find is dated as 300 B.C.

In Wales, a tax in the form of ale contributed to officials was levied in 694. The Anglo-Saxon epic *Beowulf,* dating from 1000 A.D., makes frequent references to beerlike beverages, including mead and fermented honey-water. By the 14th century, brewery workers were organized into powerful guilds.

When the Dutch settled New Amsterdam in 1624, the breakfast beverage was beer, and beer was served at every meal thereafter—as well as a refresher between meals. During the American Revolution, when the English occupied New York for eight years, the officers (who were traveled and cultivated Englishmen) introduced table wine for dining, importing expensive wine from England and elsewhere to be served at table. But the drink of every commoner was beer, which was used as a substitute for water—not always obtainable.

A deficit of beer caused the Pilgrims to settle in Massachusetts. Governor William Bradford wrote in his journal, which became his *History of the Plymouth Plantation,* that it was necessary for the *Mayflower* to seek harbor because "we could not now take time for further search or consideration, our victuals being much spent, especially our beer. . . . " However, the first commercial breweries in the Colonies are said to have been built by the Dutch West Indian Company in lower Manhattan in 1623. Robert Sedgwick built one in 1637 in the Massachusetts Bay Company. Large farms and plantations were always equipped with bakeries and breweries.

What does brewing mean? Brewing and baking are twin arts. Both use cereals and depend on enzymes and yeast for fermentation, in which alcohol, carbon dioxide, and aromatic flavoring contribute to the brew.

The verb *to brew* derives from the German verb *brauen,* referring broadly to boiling, steaming or extraction of carefully blended ingredients. Today the term means the process of preparing beer from malted cereals. A sweet liquid (wort) results after mashing and it is then separated from the spent grains, boiled with hops, cooled, fermented with yeast and finally aged and carbonated.

Malting is simply the controlled germination of any grain, stopped at the desired stage by means of dry heat. One of the main objects of malting is the development of dormant enzymes, proteinlike substances, from barley and other grains. In connection with brewing, unless specified by the term wheat malt or rice malt, malting generally refers to the production of malted barley, and at present the production of malt has become a separate industry.

Malting barley is usually the fully ripened, spring-sown, six-rowed barley such as Oderbrucker, Wisconsin Barbless and Velvet, grown in the Mississippi Valley. Atlas and Bay Brewing are produced on the Pacific Coast. In Europe, two-rowed varieties are grown known as

Chevalier and Hannchen. Since 1955, good malting barleys have been grown westward from the Great Plains to the Dakotas, Montana and Nebraska, and also in Colorado and Kansas. Barley malt is the one indispensable brewing material often referred to as "the soul of the beer."

The mild, pleasing, bitter taste and delicate aroma of quality beers are the result of the intelligent use of fine hops. Hops are the dried female flowers of a vinelike plant, harvested in early autumn. American hop culture is chiefly concentrated in Oregon, Washington and California, comparing to the famous Bohemian, Austrian and Bavarian hop industries. Hops reach back far into ancient times. Their mention in literature antedates the Christian era. There were breweries in all of the medieval monasteries, and the earliest recorded hop gardens are said to be those of Pepin the Short, who at the Monastery of St. Denis in 760 A.D., used hops for making beer, and the herb flavorings of mint, tansy, sage, wormwood, dandelion and other plants.

American brewing followed the pattern of English and German brewers. When the Germans came to the United States in great numbers in 1848, they preferred the milder, lighter beers to the stronger ale, and so the bottom-fermented lager beer was introduced from Bavaria by forerunners who came in 1837. By 1870, mechanical refrigeration served to meet the lower cellar temperatures necessary in bottom fermentation. This was a welcome innovation. It meant that it was no longer necessary to excavate cellars four stories down in the earth.

There are many fine German beers imported in bottle for American use. Löwenbräu, brewed and bottled in Munich, the birthplace of brewing, dates from the 14th century. In 1383, the first keg of Löwenbräu, or Lion's Brew, was tapped in Munich. By 1516, Bavaria's breweries had so flourished that Duke Wilhelm IV decreed the Reinheitsgebot regulating the purity of beer. Thus through the centuries, Munich has become synonymous with fine beer. True to the ancient tradition, Löwenbräu is made with the classic malt, hops and yeast, brewed with matchless Alpine water and naturally carbonated by at least three months of aging. The importance of water, comprising 97 percent of the beer, cannot be overemphasized. Löwenbräu is imported by Hans Holterbosch, Inc., New York City.

Beer and ale, alcoholic, fermented malt beverages, are prepared from grains and flavored with hops, the predominate grain being malted barley, with specially prepared corn and rice also being used. At one time, beer and ale were indeed very different products than what has been evolved in our own time. In 15th-century England, for instance, ale was strong in alcohol, and no hops or other flavoring were used. However, beer was flavored with hops or other herbs and had a somewhat lower alcohol content than ale. Today the two terms have very little difference in meaning. The tendency is to designate as ale those brews prepared with top-fermenting yeast, and to designate as beer those prepared with a bottom-fermenting yeast.

Lager beer is a type which, after the main fermentation is finished, is subjected to a longer storage period in tanks in a cold storehouse or *lager,* the German term, for the purpose of clarification and flavor maturation.

Bock beer, a special, heavy kind of beer, usually darker and richer in flavor than regular beer, is prepared in early spring. Legend says it originated in Einbeck in Germany, and later this word became merged with *ein Bock,* a goat, the symbol widely used in promoting this beer.

Near beer (used in Prohibition times) contains less than 0.5 percent alcohol by volume. First a normal beer is brewed, and then by a distillation process, the alcoholic content is reduced. Porter beer from Ireland and England, a type of dark, top-fermented ale, is usually somewhat sweeter and less hoppy than regular ale. It is said to have received its name because it was once so popular with the porters of the London open-air markets.

What causes the foaming of a freshly dispensed glass of beer? The foamy collar begins with the release of myriads of tiny bubbles of carbon dioxide gas as the beer enters the drinking tumbler. The bubbles move upward in the liquid and tend to collect surface "skins" of colloidal materials present in the beer. The colloids give strength to the walls of the separate bubbles and cause the formation of the foam, which persists for a time. The gas bubbles of Carbonated Waters and Sparkling Wines do not generally form foams because they do not contain colloids capable of merging into a foam formation and foam stabilization.

In the United States, pale beers are mostly in demand because of their moderate satiating power and reduced bitterness; there is also some emphasis on a beer with a dry or a sweet taste. Hop content has been reduced in order to achieve an overall blandness, and there is a greater use of corn and rice as raw materials, along with malted barley in the mashing process.

The trend of preference continues toward packaged beer to be enjoyed at home and elsewhere. This is sold pasteurized in sealed bottles and cans. Packaged beer has reached over 78 percent of all beer sales. Is beer good for you? Yes, if you enjoy it, because beer is a delicate food product similar to the value of milk. It has been stabilized against spoilage by the process of pasteurizing. The filled bottles or cans are subjected to submersion in huge pasteurizers, warming them up to 140° F. in 20 minutes. After 18 minutes they are reduced to about 80° F. for 20 minutes.

Classification of Beers
(Service: Not too cold—48° to 50° F.)

LAGER OR BOTTOM-FERMENTED BEER:

Pilsener, Dortmunder: Most American draught and bottle beers are of this type; pale, medium hoppy, 3 to 3.8 percent alcohol.

Vienna: Amber colored and less bitter beers.

Munich: This type includes Bock, Salvador, Wuerzbuerger; dark brown, full-bodied, slightly sweet, not very hoppy, 2.5 to 5 percent alcohol.

Near Beer: Cereal beverage or near beer Pilsener type of less than 0.4 percent alcohol.

Malt Tonics: Low in alcohol, fortified with iron and vitamins.

Steam Beer: California tart, effervescent beer.

TOP-FERMENTED BEER:

Ale: Pale in color, hoppy taste, tart, of 4 to 5 percent alcohol.

Porter: A dark brown, full-bodied beer, less hoppy and slightly sweeter than ale, 5 percent alcohol.

Stout: Very dark, strong, hoppy, bitter and sweet beer with a malty taste, 5 to 6.5 percent alcohol.

Weiss: Made from wheat malt; pale, tart and has a rich foam.

American: This refers to the common beers that are inexpensive, dark amber, locally brewed.

No country is as proud of its pubs and taverns as England, where Guinness Stout is to be found in every pub. The favorite drink of the British pub is, quite naturally, beer. This beverage has kept pace from ancient times. In England, beer is taxed heavily enough, but not so steeply as spirits. Beer lasts longer as a drink than wine and spirits, and fits in with casual bar games such as darts, shove half-penny and dominoes in the "poor man's clubs." Little wine is drunk in pubs, although some Port and Sherry are, with light wines occasionally in demand. The standing of some Scotches and Gins, such as Black and White Scotch, Dewar's, Teacher's and Grant's, have no peers.

The trend in London is the invasion of the pub in drug stores, which go modern to satisfy the public, providing for a pub lounge area, as in the Chelsea Drugstore. Brewers have their own pubs, acting as bulk purchasers from themselves, getting maximum discounts and reselling to the tenants who own their pubs. The oldest licensed pub in England is Ye Old Fighting Cocks, in St. Albans; it dates back to 795 A.D.

The great beer halls of Germany are, of course, beyond imitation with their vastness and lofty rafters. In beer gardens, beer on draft is king. In Salzburg, Austria, birthplace of Mozart and the music festivals, beer halls can seat 1,500 people. Bottled beer is served, but the demand is beer on draft from the barrel. There is probably little taste difference; it is a matter of the atmosphere and prevalence of *gemütlichkeit.* It is true, however, that in the matter of Champagne, the larger the bottle the better the taste; a split of Champagne is hardly worthy of its name. The kegs of beer for parties come in sizes of 1/4 and 1/2, which are aluminum, with the 1/8 being wood. The 1/8 contains two gallons, the 1/4 four gallons and the 1/2 eight gallons.

Beer is consumed all over the world. For instance, it has become the most popular drink in the bars of Manila, Philippines, where San Miquel is the only beer available.

Beer consumption by Americans is on the rise, and many restaurants, hotels and bars encourage the ordering of beer by women by serving malt beverages in goblets, Pilsener and fine glasses with fluted bases. In addition, many places wisely serve imported malt liquors in Champagne-type glasses. At home, hosts and hostesses have adapted the idea and are now serving malt liquors in more appealing and appropriate glasses that enhance their enjoyment. Beer should be served not too cold, say from 48° F. to 50° F. If taken in moderation, beer is a liquid food, nonintoxicating, containing 170 calories per 12 ounces.

Sake

Sake is neither a spirit nor a wine but a member of the beer family. Americans are becoming more and more intrigued with the traditional Japanese beverage that has been in use in Japan since the 8th century. Sake tastes something like a wine and looks like a clear wine; it does not foam as beer does, and there is no carbonation. The Japanese Sake Brewers' Central Association suggests the word *Sake* stems from the word *Sakamizu,* which means "water of prosperity," rather than from the town of Osaka, long famous for the Sake brewed there (and now renowned for the Expo '70 World's Fair).

Growing interest in Sake may be due partly to the surge of popularity food, art and other aspects of Japanese life and culture have experienced in America. How is Sake made? In its manufacture, steamed rice, called kofi, is treated with a culture of special yeast, Aspergillus oryzae, which converts the starch into sugar. The kofi is added to a thin paste of freshly boiled starch in a vat. The resulting mix is called moto. Fermentation begins and continues slowly for four or five weeks. Then fresh rice and koji are added to the moto. There is second fermentation, lasting from 8 to 10 days. At this point the liquor, now Sake, is drawn off, filtered, heated and put into casks for a brief maturing. The action of the yeast performs the combined functions of saccharification, converting the starch of the grain into sugar, and fermentation. Thus it does the work of the diastase of malt and the yeast in an American brewery.

In Japan, Sake is taken slightly warmed, to about 100° F., poured into a china or pottery bottle with a narrow top. The entire filled bottle is put into hot water in a container, like a *bain marie.* Then the Sake is poured into a shallow stemmed saucer, and sipped. In the United States, the trend is to enjoy Sake by using it as an additive to mixed drinks containing Gin, Vodka, Rye or other spirits. For instance, the Sakini is a version of the Martini. Use 1 part Sake and 3 parts dry Gin or Vodka. A Sake Manhattan contains 1 part Sake and 2 parts Rye (or Bourbon). We include recipes for Sake Collins, Sake Sour, Sake Cobbler, Sake Buck, Sake and Bitters, and Sake on the Rocks.

Many people trying Sake straight for the first time say it is similar to a dry Sauterne in flavor. Alcoholic content? Rather low, about 17 percent, and for this reason some bars will offer it as a change from such aperitifs as Vermouth, Dubonnet, Byrrh or Saint Raphael, using the aforementioned mixtures. It has a quick, but not lasting, intoxicating effect.

From left to right: Cocktail glass, Old-Fashioned glass, Whiskey Sour, Delmonico, Highball, Tom Collins, small Brandy Sniffer, large Brandy Sniffer, Pousse-café, Cordial, Port (Sherry or Madeira) glass, on Richelieu's bar.

Edward Moran Studio

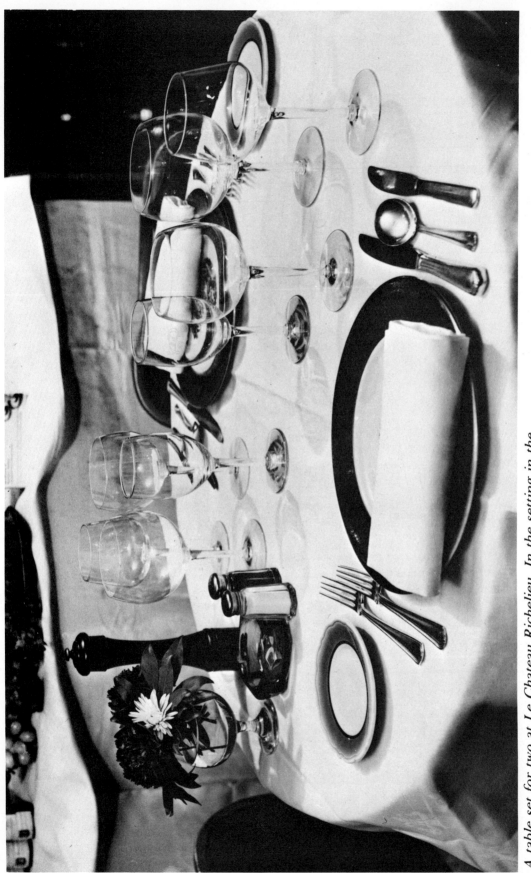

A table set for two at Le Chateau Richelieu. In the setting in the foreground the glasses are, left to right, white wine, Bordeaux (red), Burgundy (red), Champagne glass (Minners Company glasses).
Edward Moran Studio

Festive display for celebration of publication of Much Depends on Dinner, *with cheeses of all nations banked by Charles Heidsieck wine, Almadén Rosé, green and yellow Chartreuse liqueurs, Stock's dry and sweet Vermouth, Paul Masson Cabernet Sauvignon.*

Edward Ozern

Bar of Le Chateau Richelieu, the only all-copper bar in New York City. Body of bar combines sheet and ribbed copper strips; red metal glows behind the bar and sheathes the lower wall in front, while top is of gleaming sheet copper. Mural is half of collage by Helen Watkins, depicting Le Chateau Richelieu of Le Cardinal de Richelieu in Poitou, France.

James Vincent

Mint Juleps and Bourbon decanters in a Kentucky hunt breakfast arrangement by interior designer Valerian Rybar in a table setting exhibit at Tiffany's.

Courtesy Tiffany & Company

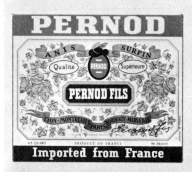

Products and imports of Julius Wile Sons & Co., Inc.

Mr. Robotti warms brandy for flambéeing a dessert.

Dr. David W. Burg

Peter Robotti in the wine cellar of Le Chateau Richelieu.

Standard Flash

*The Richelieu bar
with its montages on
the front wall.*

It is not good that man should be alone.
                                GENESIS 2, v. 18

Take your ease. Eat, drink and be merry.
                                ST. LUKE 12, v. 19

Chapter 5   Cocktails And Other
                     Mixed Drinks

NOBODY really knows where the word *cocktail* originated, but it is
considered an American invention. The earliest reference to it has
been found in *The Balance,* an American periodical, of May 13, 1806,
which would bring the age of the cocktail to well over a century and
a half. That publication said: "Cocktail is a stimulating liquor, com-
posed of spirits of any kind, sugar, water and bitters. It is vulgarly
called "bittered sling" and is supposed to be excellent as an election-
eering potion." *Cocktail* probably originated from "to concoct."

We have drawn upon our own resources of bar experience over the
period of many years at Le Chateau Richelieu from its inception in
1933 (locations at 13 West 51st Street, 37 West 51st Street, and
finally in its present home since Christmas 1957 at 48 East 52nd
Street, New York City).

The cocktails and other mixed drinks listed in this chapter were
compiled in this manner: The drinks in the *Savoy Cocktail Book,*
authored by the late Harry Craddock, Bartender of the Savoy Hotel
in London, first published in 1930, were checked against the *Standard Bartender's Guide* by Patrick Gavin Duffy, first published in 1940

71

(and in Permabook in 1955), including those cocktails that had survived into 1955.

We checked with many guides and finally with the *Cocktail and Wine Digest* by Oscar Haimo, President of the Bar Managers' Association, in its 28th edition, published in 1969. This method of research gives us a span of four decades of prevalent cocktail and mixed drink recipes.

Beyond some of the classic drinks that have survived into the 1970s, we include new drinks that have recently come into prominence—tastes *do* change with the times. Here also are some odd and unfamiliar drinks out of the past, for they should be part of a collection as comprehensive as this one. By the same token, it would be impossible for us in a single chapter to include all known drinks on record, nor would it serve any purpose because many are no longer current.

As with culinary success, skill in mixing drinks comes with knowledge and practice. The ideal cocktail, like the ideal dish, is a blend with no conflict in flavors. In the Prohibition era, strange cocktails were born because bartenders in speakeasies had to conceal the inferior quality of their liquors.

Recipes for the cocktails are presented according to the base or main ingredients.

The host (or hostess) must be the judge of how extensive he wishes his collection to be of spirits, wines, cordials and flavorings. It is better to possess a few good bottles than many lesser in quality, for a drink is no better than its ingredients.

SOME RULES TO FOLLOW: When in doubt, measure with a jigger. Mixing drinks is a culinary art that can be achieved by following directions. When mixing drinks containing fruit juices, egg, cream, milk and/or sweetening, pour the spirits last and use only fresh fruit juices, never canned. Do not use chemical preparations when the recipe calls for white of egg for foaming cocktails, and do not use squeezed juice that has been in the refrigerator more than 24 hours. Use powdered sugar, not confectioners' sugar. Ice is nearly always an absolute essential for any cocktail. Be sure it is clean, and do not use the same ice twice. Ice may be called for as cracked (for cocktails, Cobblers, Collins, Coolers, Crustas, Cups, Daisies, Eggnogs, Flips, Sangarees, Slings, Sours, Zooms); as shaved ice (for Frappés); as cubes (for Fizzes, Highballs, Puffs, Rickeys, Shrubs, Juleps). If commercial cracked or shaved ice is not available, put ice cubes in a napkin and fold napkin over. Dash against a hard surface or hammer to obtain cracked ice. If you do not have a shaver or a blender, pound the cracked ice until it resembles shaved ice.

If a recipe says stir, then stir, and do not shake. Stirring makes a clear drink; shaking produces a cloudy one. Remember that the ingredients mix better in a shaker somewhat larger than necessary to hold them. Do not just rock the shaker. Shake it as hard as you can. You are trying to vitalize the drink, not lullaby it to sleep. If possible, ice the glasses by placing in shaved ice upside down before using them. And have your guests drink the cocktails as soon as possible.

BAR ESSENTIALS: Champagne cooler, mixing glass and stirring spoon, cocktail shaker, corkscrew, funnel, two-way jigger (1 1/2 ozs.), wire-rimmed and handled strainer, lime squeezer and lemon squeezer, swizzle stick, spoon stirrer with long handle, ice scoop, muddler, fruit cutting board and stainless steel fruit knife, ice pick, snow ice shaver, straws, drink stirrers, toothpicks, cocktail napkins and ice trays.

ESSENTIAL STOCK TO HAVE ON HAND: Scotch, Rye, Bourbon, Gin, Rum, Vodka, Southern Comfort, Tequila, Cognac or Brandy, Crème de Menthe, dry Vermouth, sweet Vermouth, dry Sherry, Champagne, Port Wine, white Wine, Grenadine, Aromatic Bitters.

INGREDIENTS: Lemons, limes, fresh lemon juice, lemon peel, oranges, fresh pineapple, tomato juice, maraschino red cherries, pitted green olives, pearl onions, powdered sugar, eggs, nutmeg, cream and milk, Worcestershire sauce, salt and pepper.

GLASSWARE: Wash glasses with a detergent. Remember that a tablespoon of vinegar added to the rinse water will make the glasses sparkle. Cobblers take water goblets; cocktails, cocktail glasses; Collins and Coolers, Collins glasses; Crustas, cocktail or wine glasses; Cups, a glass pitcher; Daisies, highball glasses. Eggnogs take Collins glasses; Fixes and Fizzes, highball glasses; Flips, Delmonico or wine glasses; highballs, highball glasses; Juleps, tankards or Collins glasses; Old-Fashioneds, Old-Fashioned glasses. For Punches you need bowls, cups, Collins glasses or tankards; Puffs, Collins glasses; Rickeys, highball glasses; Sangarees, highball glasses; Shrubs, tumblers (made in pitcher and bottled); Slings, Collins glasses; Smashes, Old-Fashioned glasses; Sours, Delmonico glasses. Swizzles use a pitcher and highball glasses; Toddies, Old-Fashioned glasses; Tom & Jerries, a coffee cup or Tom & Jerry mug; Zooms, a wine glass.

MEASUREMENTS: A pony or cordial glass contains 3/4 to 1 ounce; Whiskey or liquor, 1 to 2 1/2 ounces; Sherry or Port, 2 to 2 1/2 ounces; cocktail, 2 to 3 1/2 ounces; wine glass or punch cup, 4 to 5 ounces; Old-Fashioned glass, 4 to 10 ounces; Delmonico, 5 to 7 ounces; highball, 8 to 10 ounces; goblet, tumbler, mug or cup, 8 to 12 ounces; Tom Collins, 10 to 14 ounces; Zombie glass, 14 to 16 ounces.

TRAY CUBE ICE: This is the standard form for all drinks calling for ice cubes. Stirrers go into any iced drink whether in an average cocktail or a tall glass, but a straw goes into a tall, mixed cocktail such as a Collins, Planter's Punch, Fizz, and so on calling for ice cubes. The tiny, strawlike, usually plastic striped stirrers, found wherever bar appliances are sold, are not used in sophisticated bars or restaurants.

There is really no cardinal rule in making mixed drinks. You should use the ingredients the recipe calls for, varying the quantity of ingredients to suit individual taste. In our opinion, there are certain rules that should not be violated in practice, such as drinking Scotch with Tonic Water. This is an insult to the Scotch. In Ireland, they will not drink Guinness and Tonic Water, but in England, the combination of Guinness and Tonic Water is recognized as the poor man's Black Velvet (Champagne and Guinness). As far as the Irish are concerned, they think that to mix Guinness with anything at all is an insult to the old Shamrock.

Remember that proof means the measurement of alcoholic strength. Each degree of proof equals ½ of 1 percent of alcohol. Thus 100 proof is equal to 50 percent alcohol. Quick effects are obtainable with strong drinks. A Manhattan is a potent drink, and so is a Martini (regular), not on the rocks. Southern Comfort, a Cordial, is 100 proof, and when included in a Cocktail such as a Manhattan, it is very potent. Green Chartreuse taken straight as an after-dinner drink, 110 proof, is very potent. In general, take note of the base of the drinks and check proofs for potency.

High-powered drinks comprise high proofs. A Black Russian is half Vodka and half Kahlúa, each being 90 proof. A Rusty Nail (also known as a Scotch Kiss) comprises equal parts of 90-proof Drambuie and Scotch (and Drambuie is a Scotch-base liqueur). Other strong drinks would be a Sandmartin Cocktail and a Scarlet O'Hara, made with Southern Comfort, 110 proof.

For people who do not care for the taste of liquor, you can offer them a Jack Rose (recipe included), which contains Apple Jack, Grenadine and a little lemon juice. Compari, Italian Bitters, and Soda served in a highball glass with lemon twist is a good choice, as is Blackberry Brandy Sour, which is Blackberry Brandy with fresh lemon juice.

How do you know if you are getting what you ask for or anticipate? In a high-class bar, a guest has no need to worry about anything in regard to mixed drinks, but in a lesser bar, you may order a Bloody Mary and be served one with tomato juice and spice seasoning without the Vodka. To protect your purchase, you may order the tomato juice spiced and the shot of Vodka on the side. This precaution also applies to a Screwdriver because Vodka is tasteless. Tonic Water has such a strong taste that you should order your Vodka shot on the side, if you have any doubts about the bar's reliability.

In dining out and you are not satisfied with the drink you have ordered, tell your waiter to bring it back to the bar and bring to your table the specified bottle. Have him pour it in front of you. This should be done as a matter of course and not with any antagonism; it is acceptable social behavior even in a very good bar or in the dining rooms of such restaurants as Le Chateau Richelieu.

Now, a word of wisdom about bartenders. Most of these experts respond to respect. Their profession is a complicated one; a bartender must possess exacting knowledge, and he also carries the social burden of being a Father Confessor. It is always better to stay in the good graces of the bartender in a valued place because you build up a relationship at the bar, and it is important to you to keep it. Anytime you have a grouse on about your job or problems at home, you pass them on to the bartender, who is your captive audience. After confiding in him, you feel better and consequently your life is better because of your bartender. The ethics of the profession forbid disclosure, and whatever is said is held in strict confidence and goes no further. Good bars give correct measurements and never use thickened glasses or glasses with false bottoms to decrease the amount of the contents you have paid for. There is a great deal of pride on the part of the bartender in working for a top place. He understands that drinking is a very personal matter, and he respects the varying wishes of his clientele.

Toasts of the Nations

As a matter of proper etiquette, formal toasts are with wine, not cocktails or liqueurs. However, the brief toast familiar to many nations is in order with cocktails and liqueurs, and these are given here. As to toast with wine, anyone may propose an informal toast. A person does not drink a toast to himself, but waits until it has been drunk by others before sipping his wine.

At the time of the War of Independence and its sequel, the War of 1812, great naval and military dinners were given in the City of New York. Officers in full regalia enjoyed banquets with fine wines. The formal toast required the toaster to rise to his feet. He would then drink to another's health, to his patriotism, to his valor and deeds, to his wife or sweetheart, the charms of women, the President of the country . . . until all were pretty well in their cups.

An informal toast is acknowledged with a smile, nod of the head and a thank you. Nondrinkers should join in the toast by substituting water or another beverage for wine.

American	Your health!	Irish	Slainte!
Arabian	Fi Schettak!	Israel	Lochaim!
Australian	Bottom's Up!	Italian	Salute!
Brazilian	Viva!	Japanese	Banzai!
British	Cheerio!	Jugoslavian	No Zravlje!
Chinese	Kong Chien!	New Zealand	Kia ora!
Czechoslo-vakian	Nazdar!	Polish	Na Zdrowie!
Dutch	Gezondheidt!	Portuguese	A vassa Saude!
French	À votre sante!	Roumanian	Noroc!
German	Prosit!	Russian	Vasha Zdarovia!
Greek	Is Yan!	Scandinavian	Skoll!
Hawaiian	Meli Kalikama!	Scotch	Hoot mon!
Hungarian	Egeszsegere!	Spanish	Salud!
Iranian	Salamati Shemoh!	Turkish	Serifinize!

How Many Drinks per Bottle? In planning a party, remember that the number of drinks required will depend on how many each guest will take. In designing parties for up to 1,000 persons, professional caterers figure on an average of three drinks each; some people take only one drink, or none, while others take up to five.

American Whiskey ⅘ bottle	25 drinks (1 oz. each)
Imported Scotch ⅘ bottle	25 drinks (1 oz. each)
Imported French Brandy ⅘ bottle	25 drinks (1 oz. each)
American Cordial	25 drinks (1 oz. each)
Wines, good American brands	8 drinks (3 ozs. each)
Champagne	6-8 drinks to a bottle and more (depending on size of bottle)

Selected Cocktails Read ingredients and instructions for each recipe completely. Be certain you have on hand everything required, including the correct glass.

Where two liquors or a wine and a liquor are called for in a bar recipe, we include the recipe under the dominant ingredient. If two liquors are of an equal quantity, we refer (Cf.) to its other ingredient under the base involved without repeating the recipe.

Where a recipe calls for simple syrup, syrup or sugar syrup, this is easily prepared by dissolving 1 cup sugar in 1 cup water and bringing to a boil, skimming or clarifying and storing in a bottle. Syrup of Citron is produced by adding sugar to taste to fresh lemon juice. It is a cardinal rule that all cocktails calling for lime, lemon, grapefruit, orange or other juices have to be shaken with ice cubes (with the exception of the Screwdriver). Drinks with cream or milk are also shaken with ice cubes. Other drinks are stirred.

Index for Cocktails

East India Cocktail
Elk Cocktail
Empire Cocktail
Frank Sullivan Cocktail
Froupe Cocktail
Gazette Cocktail
Gilroy Cocktail
Gloom-Chaser Cocktail
Grasshopper
Harry's Pick-Me-Up Cocktail
Honeymoon Cocktail
"Hoopla!" Cocktail
Hop Toad Cocktail
Horse's Neck
Ich Bien Cocktail
Jack Rose Cocktail
The Judgette Cocktail
Loud Speaker
Manhattan
Morning Glory Cocktail
Moulin Rouge Cocktail
Nicolaski Cocktail
Nightcap Cocktail
(Brandy) Old-Fashioned
Olympic Cocktail
Paradise Cocktail
Pick-Me-Up I.B.F. Cocktail
Saratoga (No. 1)
Shriner Cocktail
Side Car Cocktail
(Brandy) Stinger
Stomach-Reviver Cocktail
Tempter Cocktail
Three Miller Cocktail
Thunder and Lightning Cocktail
Thunderclap Cocktail
Tinton Cocktail
Tulip Cocktail
Valencia Cocktail (No. 1)
Victor Cocktail
Washington Cocktail
Waterbury Cocktail
Young Man Cocktail

Champagne Base
(Begin on p. 103)

Alfonso Cocktail
Black Velvet
Champagne Cocktail

French "75" Cocktail

Cordial (or Liqueur) Base
(Begin on p. 103)

Angel's Kiss Cocktail
Angel's Tip Cocktail
Aquavit Bloody Mary (Danish Bloody Mary)
Banana Daiquiri (No. 2)
Black Baby
Byrrh Cassis
Café Kirsch Cocktail
Cointreau on the Rocks
Diana Cocktail
Dream Cocktail
Golden Cadillac
Grasshopper
"Hoopla!" Cocktail
Lily Cocktail
Maui
Montmartre
Morning Mist
Palm Beach
Parisian Cocktail
Pernod Suissesse
Pink Cloud
Pink Squirl
Prince of Wales
Rainbow Cocktail
Rusty Nail
St. Germaine
Sandmartin
Scarlett O'Hara Cocktail
Spring Feeling Cocktail
Stars and Stripes Cocktail
Strega Witches' Brew
Sunrise Cocktail
Third Rail Cocktail (No. 1)
Tipperary Cocktail (No. 2)
Union Jack
Vermouth and Cassis Cocktail
White Lady
Wild Redhead

Galliano Liquore Base
(Begin on p. 108)

Apollo 8
Apollo Moon Maiden
Aruba Trade Wind

Auburn
Banana Italiano
Barracuda
Beano
Bossa Nova Special
Bronx Discotheque
Bumble Bee Sting
Café Galliano
Carabini
Caribbean
Cavalier
Chevoney
Dumb Denny
Fantasia
Florida
Flying Tiger
Frangi Pangi
Freddy's Special
G. & C.
Galaxy
Galliano Gimlet
Galliano L'Amore
Galliano Margarita
Galliano Mist
Galliano Screwdriver
Galliatini
Golden Cadillac
Golden Dragon
Golden Dream
Golden Glow
Golden Lilli
Goldfinger
Homestead
Irish Dream
Island in the Sun
Italian Orange Blossom
Las Vegas
Moon Dust
Morning Mist
Naples Delight
Old Charles
Orange Cadillac
Palm Beach
Pink Elephant
La Primavera
Raffaello
St. Vincent
Smutney
Snoopy

Snowflake
Southern Dream
Southern Gal
Suissesse Milanese
Terrazza
Three Faces
Tropicale
Tropicana Belle
Tyrol
Unie-K
Upstater
Viking
Volare
Warlock

Gin Base
(Begin on p. 119)
Admiral Cocktail
Alexander Cocktail (No. 2)
Alexander's Sister Cocktail
Alfonso Special Cocktail
Allies Cocktail
Army Cocktail
Australian Cocktail
Aviation Cocktail
Bijou Cocktail
Bloody Danish
Blue Moon
Bombay Marrino
Bombay Tonic
Bronx Cocktail
Bronx (Silver) Cocktail
Bull-Dog Cocktail
B.V.D. Cocktail
Chorus Lady Cocktail
Claridge Cocktail
Clover Club Cocktail
Clover Leaf Cocktail
Club Cocktail
Cointreau Screwdriver
Colonial Cocktail
Cooperstown Cocktail
Damn-the-Weather Cocktail
Darb Cocktail
Desert Healer Cocktail
Dolly O'Dare Cocktail
Douglas Cocktail
Du Barry Cocktail
Dubonnet Cocktail

Dunhill Cocktail
Eagle Cabin Cocktail
Eclipse Cocktail
Eddie Brown Cocktail
Elk Cocktail
Eton Blazer Cocktail
Everglade Cocktail
Fairbanks Cocktail (No. 1)
Fairy Belle Cocktail
Fallen Angel Cocktail
Favorite Cocktail
Fernet Branca Cocktail
Fifty-Fifty Cocktail
Fine and Dandy Cocktail
Flamingo Cocktail
Florida
Franken-Jack Cocktail
Froth-Blower Cocktail
Gene Tunney Cocktail
Gibson Cocktail
Gilroy Cocktail
Gimblet Cocktail
Gimlet Cocktail (No. 1)
Gimlet Cocktail (No. 2)
Gin Buck
Gin Cocktail
Gin Wink
Golden Ermine Cocktail
Golden Gate Cocktail
Grapevine Cocktail
Grand Royal Clover Club
  Cocktail
Great Secret Cocktail
Green Dragon Cocktail
Guard's Cocktail
Gypsy Cocktail
Hakam Cocktail
H & H Cocktail
Hanky Panky Cocktail
Harrovian Cocktail
Hawaiian Cocktail
Hoffman House Cocktail
Holland House Cocktail
Homestead Cocktail
Honolulu Cocktail (No. 1)
H.P.W. Cocktail
Hula Hula Cocktail
Hurricane Cocktail
Ideal Cocktail

Imperial Cocktail
Income Tax Cocktail
International Cocktail
Jack Dempsey Cocktail
Journalist Cocktail
The Judge Jr. Cocktail
The Judgette Cocktail
Knickerbocker Cocktail
Kraatz Special (No. 1)
Leap Frog Cocktail
Leap Year Cocktail
Leave-It-to-Me Cocktail (No. 1)
Lily Cocktail
Little Devil Cocktail
London Buck Cocktail
Long Glen Cocktail
Lord Suffolk Cocktail
Loud Speaker
Luigi Cocktail
Magnolia Blossom Cocktail
Maiden's Blush Cocktail (No. 1)
Maiden's Prayer Cocktail
Marguerite Cocktail
Marny Cocktail
Martinez Cocktail
Martini (Dry)
Martini (Medium)
Martini (Special)
Martini (Sweet)
Melon Cocktail
Millionaire Cocktail (No. 2)
Minnehaha Cocktail
Mississippi Mule Cocktail
Monkey Gland Cocktail
Monte Carlo Imperial Cocktail
Montpelier Cocktail
Montmartre
Moonlight Cocktail
Moonshine Cocktail
Napoleon Cocktail
Negroni
Nightingale Cocktail
One Exciting Night Cocktail
Opal Cocktail
Opera Cocktail
Orange Blossom Cocktail
Orange Martini Cocktail
Pall Mall Cocktail

Paradise Cocktail
Parisian Cocktail
Perfect Love Cocktail
Perfect Martini Cocktail
Pink Baby Cocktail
Pink Gin Cocktail
Pink Lady Cocktail
Pink Rose Cocktail
Pinky Cocktail
Plaza Cocktail
Polo Cocktail (No. 1)
Polo Cocktail (No. 2)
Raspberry Cocktail
Red Lion Cocktail
Richmond Cocktail
Rose Cocktail (French Style
    No. 2)
Royal Clover Club Cocktail
Royal Cocktail (No. 1)
Ruby Cocktail
St. Vincent
Salome Cocktail
Salty Dog Cocktail
Silver Bullet Cocktail
Silver Cocktail
Society Cocktail
Southern Gin Cocktail
Spencer Cocktail
Spring Feeling Cocktail
Susan-Shirley Cocktail
Sweet Patotie Cocktail
Thunderclap Cocktail
Velocity Cocktail
Vie Rose Cocktail
Webster Cocktail
Wedding Belle Cocktail
Wembley Cocktail (No. 1)
West Indian Cocktail
Western Rose Cocktail
White Cargo Cocktail
White Baby Cocktail
White Lady Cocktail
White Plush Cocktail
White Rose Cocktail
White Wings Cocktail
Windsor Cocktail
Yale Cocktail
Yellow Daisy Cocktail
Zanzibar Cocktail

Rum Base
(Begin on p. 142)

Apple Pie Cocktail
Bacardi Cocktail
Banana Daiquiri (No. 1)
Banana Daiquiri (No. 2)
B.V.D. Cocktail
Bolero
Daiquiri Cocktail
Dunlop Cocktail
Fair and Warmer Cocktail
Fluffy Ruffles Cocktail
Gradeal (Special) Cocktail
Jack Dempsey Cocktail
Jacqueline Cocktail
The Judge Jr. Cocktail
Little Devil Cocktail
Little Princess Cocktail
Mary Pickford Cocktail
Millionaire Cocktail (No. 1)
Nevada Cocktail
Palmetto Cocktail
Parisian Blonde Cocktail
Planter's Cocktail (No. 1)
Poker Cocktail
President Cocktail
El Presidente Cocktail
Robson Cocktail
Santiago Cocktail
September Morn Cocktail
Sevilla Cocktail (No. 2)
Shanghai Cocktail
Spanish Town Cocktail
Stanley Cocktail
Sunshine Cocktail (No. 2)
West Indies Yellowbird
White Mink
White Mule
Windmill
Yellow Bird

Southern Comfort Base
(Begin on p. 147)

Atomic Cocktail
Black Widow
Cuba Libre Supreme
Flying Grasshopper Cocktail
French "90"

Frozen Southern Comfort
Omar's Delight Cocktail
Oscar Haimo Cocktail
Pacific Cocktail
Puffs
Puzzler Cocktail
Rhett Butler Cocktail
Royal Southern Comfort
   Cocktail
Southern Comfort Daiquiri
   Cocktail
Southern Comfort Manhattan
   Cocktail
Southern Comfort 'n Bourbon
Southern Comfort
   Old-Fashioned
Southern Comfort on the
   Rocks
Southern Dream
Southern Gal

Tequila Base
(Begin on p. 150)

Acapulco
Bloody Maria
Daiquiri Tequila
Manhattan Tequila
Margarita
Martini Tequila
New Life
Sauza and Tonic
Sauza Highball

Vodka Base
(Begin on p. 151)

Auburn
Ballet Rousse
Black Russian
Bloody Bullshot
Bloody Mary
Blushin' Russian
Boyar
Brave Bull
Chevoney
Flying Grasshopper
Flying Tiger
Galliatini
Golden Lilli
Goldfinger

Ivan the Terrible
Katinka
Las Vegas
Lower Depths
Moscow Mule
Ochl
Palm Beach
Pushkin
Russian Cocktail
Sea Gull
Tovarich
Troyka
Vodka Martini
Vodka Richelieu
Volga Boatman
White Nights
White Russian
White Spider

Whiskey Base
(Begin on p. 155)

Barbary Coast
Bloody John
Bobby Burns Cocktail
Boiler Maker
Britannia
Brooklyn Cocktail
Byrrh Cocktail
Commodore Cocktail
Cowboy Cocktail
Creole Cocktail
Crow Cocktail
Dandy Cocktail
De Rigueur Cocktail
Dixie Whiskey Cocktail
Duppy Cocktail
Elk's Own Cocktail
Everybody's Irish Cocktail
Everything-But Cocktail
Fox River Cocktail
"Hoots Mon" Cocktail
Hot Deck Cocktail
Hurricane Cocktail
Ink Street Cocktail
John Wood Cocktail
Jupiter Cocktail
King Cole Cocktail
Los Angeles Cocktail
Mamie Taylor

Manhattan Cocktail
Manhattan Cocktail (Dry)
Manhattan Cocktail (Sweet)
Mickie Walker Cocktail
Morning Glory Cocktail
Mountain Cocktail
New York Cocktail
Oh Henry! Cocktail
Old-Fashioned Cocktail
"Old Pal" Cocktail
Opening Cocktail
Paddy Cocktail
Palmer Cocktail
Rattlesnake Cocktail

Rob Roy Cocktail
Shamrock Cocktail
Silent Third
Soul Kiss (No. 2)
Stone Fence
Strawberry Cocktail
Thistle Cocktail
Thunderclap Cocktail
Up-to-Date Cocktail
Ward Eight Cocktail
Wembley Cocktail (No. 2)
Whiskey Special Cocktail
Whisper Cocktail
Zazarak

Aperitif and Wine Bases

Amer Picon Cocktail	*1/2 Italian Vermouth*	*1/2 Amer Picon*

Shake well with ice cubes and strain into cocktail glass.

Americano

1 oz. Campari
2 ozs. dry or sweet Vermouth

Soda Water
Twist of lemon peel

Put Campari and Vermouth in Collins glass and fill with Soda Water. Serve with twist of lemon peel.

Black Martini

2/3 dry Vermouth
1/3 Blackberry Brandy

Twist of lemon peel

Stir Vermouth and Brandy into glass or serve on the rocks. Add twist of lemon peel.

Bronx Cocktail

Juice of 1/4 orange
1/4 French Vermouth

1/4 Italian Vermouth
1/2 dry Gin

Shake well with ice cubes and strain into cocktail glass.

Bronx (Silver) Cocktail

Juice of 1/4 orange
White of 1 egg
1/4 French Vermouth

1/4 Italian Vermouth
1/2 dry Gin

Shake well with ice cubes and strain into large wine glass.

Cherry Mixture Cocktail

1 dash Angostura Bitters
1 dash Maraschino Liqueur
1/2 French Vermouth

1/2 Italian Vermouth
1 cherry

Shake well with ice cubes and strain into cocktail glass. Serve with cherry.

Chorus Lady Cocktail

Juice of 1/4 orange
1/3 dry Gin
1/3 Italian Vermouth

1/3 French Vermouth
Slice of orange
Cherry

Shake well with ice cubes and strain into cocktail glass. Add slice of orange and a cherry.

Claridge Cocktail

1/3 dry Gin	*1/6 Apricot Brandy*
1/3 French Vermouth	*1/6 Cointreau*

Shake well with ice cubes and strain into cocktail glass.

Cooperstown Cocktail

1/3 French Vermouth	*1/3 dry Gin*
1/3 Italian Vermouth	

Shake well with ice cubes and strain into cocktail glass. If available, add sprig of mint.

Crystal Bronx Cocktail
(This is a good one for teen-agers.)

Juice of 1/4 orange	*1/4 Italian Vermouth*
1/4 French Vermouth	*Soda Water*

Pour all ingredients except Soda Water into cocktail glass. Add one ice cube. Fill glass with Soda Water.

Cupid Cocktail

3 ozs. Sherry	*1 teaspoon powdered sugar*
1 fresh egg	*A little cayenne pepper*

Shake well with ice cubes and strain into cocktail glass.

Dandy Cocktail

1/2 Rye or Canadian Club Whisky	*1 dash Angostura Bitters*
1/2 Dubonnet	*3 dashes Cointreau*

Shake well with ice cubes and strain into cocktail glass. Serve with twists of lemon and orange peels.

Darb Cocktail

1/3 French Vermouth	*1/3 Apricot Brandy*
1/3 dry Gin	*4 dashes lemon juice*

Shake well with ice cubes and strain into cocktail glass.

Davis Cocktail

1/4 Jamaica Rum	*2 dashes Grenadine*
1/2 French Vermouth	*Juice of 1/2 lemon or 1 lime*

Shake well with ice cubes and strain into cocktail glass.

Devil's Cocktail

1/2 Port Wine
1/2 French Vermouth

2 dashes lemon juice

Shake well with ice cubes and strain into cocktail glass.

Diabola Cocktail

2 dashes Orgeat syrup
(purchased in a
Gourmet Shop)

2/3 Dubonnet Blonde
1/3 Gin

Shake well with ice cubes and strain into cocktail glass.

Diabolo Cocktail
(For 6 people)

6 ozs. (4 jiggers) Brandy
6 ozs. French Vermouth

1 teaspoon Angostura
Bitters
2 teaspoons Orange Bitters

Pour Brandy and Vermouth into shaker. Add Bitters and shake with ice cubes. Strain. Serve with lemon rind and an olive or cherry.

Diplomat Cocktail

1 dash Maraschino Liqueur
2/3 French Vermouth
1/3 Italian Vermouth

Cherry
Lemon Peel

Shake well with ice cubes and strain into cocktail glass. Add cherry. Squeeze lemon peel on top.

Dolly O'Dare Cocktail

2 teaspoons Apricot Brandy
1/2 French Vermouth

1/2 dry Gin

Shake well with ice cubes and strain into cocktail glass. Squeeze orange peel on top.

Dubonnet Cocktail

1/2 Dubonnet

1/2 dry Gin

Stir well and strain into cocktail glass. (Juice of 1/2 orange may also be added.)

Duke of Marlborough Cocktail	1/2 Sherry 1/2 Italian Vermouth	3 dashes Orange Bitters

Stir well and twist orange peel on top.

Dunhill Cocktail	1/2 oz. Gin 1/2 oz. Sherry Wine 1/2 oz. French Vermouth	1 dash Pernod 2 dashes Curaçao

Stir with ice cubes. Strain into prechilled cocktail glass.

East Indian Cocktail	1/2 French Vermouth (sweet)	1/2 Sherry 1 dash Orange Bitters

Shake well with ice cubes and strain into cocktail glass.

Elk's Own Cocktail	White of 1 egg 1/2 Canadian Club Whisky 1/2 Port Wine	Juice of 1/2 lemon 1 teaspoon powdered sugar

Shake well with ice cubes. Strain into wine glass and add very thin slice of pineapple.

Five-Fifteen Cocktail	1/3 French Vermouth 1/3 Curaçao	1/3 heavy cream

Shake with ice cubes and strain into cocktail glass.

Fluffy Ruffles Cocktail	1/2 Italian Vermouth	1/2 Rum

Shake well with ice cubes and strain into cocktail glass. Add twist of lime or lemon peel.

Froupe Cocktail	1/2 Brandy 1/2 Italian Vermouth	1 teaspoon Bénédictine

Stir well and strain into cocktail glass.

Galliano Gimlet
(Cf. Galliano Liquore Base)

| **Gazette Cocktail** | ¹/2 Italian Vermouth | 1 teaspoon simple syrup |
| | ¹/2 Brandy | 1 teaspoon lemon juice |

Shake well with ice cubes and strain into cocktail glass.

———————————————————————

| **Gibson Cocktail (Dry)** | ¹/3 French Vermouth | ²/3 Gin |

Shake well with ice cubes and strain into cocktail glass. Twist lemon peel over drink. Serve with pickled onion.

———————————————————————

| **Golden Ermine Cocktail** | ¹/8 Italian Vermouth | ¹/2 dry Gin |
| | ³/8 French Vermouth | |

Shake well with ice cubes and strain into cocktail glass.

———————————————————————

| **Green Room Cocktail** | ¹/3 Brandy | 2 dashes Curaçao |
| | ²/3 French Vermouth | |

Shake well with ice cubes and strain into cocktail glass.

———————————————————————

| **Gypsy Cocktail** | ¹/2 Italian Vermouth | ¹/2 Plymouth Gin |

Shake well with ice cubes and strain into cocktail glass.

———————————————————————

| **Hakam Cocktail** | ³/4 oz. dry Gin | 1 dash Orange Bitters |
| | ³/4 oz. Italian Vermouth | 2 dashes Cointreau |

Shake with ice cubes and strain into a prechilled cocktail glass.

———————————————————————

| **Hanky Panky Cocktail** | ¹/2 dry Gin | 2 dashes Fernet Branca |
| | ¹/2 Italian Vermouth | |

Shake well with ice cubes and strain into cocktail glass. Squeeze orange peel on top.

Homestead Cocktail
(Cf. Gin Base)

H.P.W. Cocktail

1/2 Italian Vermouth	1/2 Tom Gin

Shake well with ice cubes and strain into cocktail glass.

Imperial Cocktail

1 dash Maraschino Liqueur	1/2 French Vermouth
1 dash Angostura Bitters	1/2 dry Gin

Stir well and serve with olive.

Inca Cocktail

1 dash Orgeat syrup	1/4 Sherry
1 dash Orange Bitters	1/4 French Vermouth
1/4 Gin	1/4 Italian Vermouth

Shake well with ice cubes and strain into cocktail glass.

Income Tax Cocktail

1 dash Angostura Bitters	1/4 Italian Vermouth
Juice of 1/4 orange	1/2 dry Gin
1/4 French Vermouth	

Shake well with ice cubes and strain into cocktail glass.

John Wood Cocktail

2 parts Irish Whiskey	1 part Kümmel
4 parts Italian Vermouth	1 dash Angostura Bitters
2 parts lemon juice	

Shake well with ice cubes and strain into cocktail glass.

The Judgette Cocktail

1/3 Peach Brandy	1/3 French Vermouth
1/3 Gin	1 dash lime juice

Shake well with ice cubes and strain into cocktail glass.

Kir Cocktail

2/3 dry white Wine	1/3 Crème de Cassis

Serve cold or on the rocks.

Little Princess Cocktail	*1/2 Italian Vermouth*	*1/2 Rum*

Shake well with ice cubes and strain into cocktail glass.

Lone Tree Cocktail	*2 dashes Orange Bitters*	*1/3 French Vermouth*
	1/3 Italian Vermouth	*1/3 dry Gin*

Shake well with ice cubes and strain into cocktail glass.

Luigi Cocktail	*1 teaspoon Grenadine*	*1/2 dry Gin*
	1 dash Cointreau	*1/2 French Vermouth*
	Juice of 1/2 tangerine	

Shake well with ice cubes and strain into cocktail glass.

Manhattan Cocktail	*2 dashes Curaçao or Maraschino Liqueur*	*3 dashes Angostura Bitters*
	1 pony Rye Whiskey	*4 ozs. Vermouth*

Shake well with 2 ice cubes and strain into Claret glass. Put 1/4 slice of lemon in the glass and serve. (If preferred very sweet, add 2 dashes of simple syrup.)

Manhattan Cocktail (Dry)	*1/4 French Vermouth*	*1/4 Rye or Canadian Club Whisky*
	1/4 Italian Vermouth	

Stir well and strain into cocktail glass.

Manhattan Cocktail (Sweet)	*1/2 Rye or Canadian Club Whisky*	*1/2 Italian Vermouth*

Stir well and strain into cocktail glass.

Martinez Cocktail (For 6 people)	*6 ozs. (4 jiggers) Gin*	*1 teaspoon Curaçao or Maraschino Liqueur*
	6 ozs. French Vermouth	
	1 1/2 teaspoons Orange Bitters	

Put ingredients in shaker with ice cubes. Shake well, strain and serve with a cherry and lemon rind.

Minnehaha Cocktail	*1/2 oz. dry Gin* *1/2 oz. Italian Vermouth* *1/2 oz. French Vermouth*	*1 dash fresh orange juice* *2 dashes Pernod*

Shake all ingredients except Pernod with ice cubes and strain into prechilled double cocktail glass. Top with Pernod.

Moonlight Cocktail (For 6 people)	*1 1/2 glasses (8 oz. size) grapefruit juice* *2 jiggers Gin*	*1/2 jigger Kirsch* *2 jiggers white wine*

Put ice cubes in shaker. Add ingredients and shake thoroughly. Serve in cocktail glasses, adding thinly shaved lemon peel. This is a very dry Martini.

Moonshine Cocktail (For 6 people)	*6 ozs. Gin* *2 wine glasses French Vermouth*	*1 jigger (1 1/2 ozs.) Maraschino Liqueur* *Pernod*

Before shaking with ice cubes, add a drop of Pernod. Serve in cocktail glasses.

Mountain Cocktail	*White of 1 egg* *1/6 lemon juice* *1/6 French Vermouth*	*1/6 Italian Vermouth* *1/2 Canadian Club Whisky*

Shake well with ice cubes and strain into medium-size glass.

Orange Martini Cocktail
(Cf. Gin Base)

Pall Mall Cocktail
(Cf. Gin Base)

Sanctuary Cocktail This cocktail derived its name because the Savoy of London has an inner American Cocktail Bar where only men were allowed. The privilege of Sanctuary was abolished by "The Escape from Prison Act" in 1697, outlawing sanctuary to escapees from such jails as The Clink, Deadman's Place, Fullwood's Rents, The Mint, Mitre Court, Baldwin's Gardens and Stepney.

1/4 Cointreau   *1/2 Dubonnet*
1/4 Amer Picon

Shake well with ice cubes and strain into cocktail glass.

Sangria
(For 4 people)

1 bottle (1 pint, 7 ozs.) red   *1/2 orange, sliced*
Spanish Wine   *2 ozs. Cointreau*
2 tablespoons powdered   *2 ozs. Spanish Brandy*
sugar   *12 ozs. Club Soda*
1 lemon, sliced   *24 ice cubes*

In large pitcher, combine wine, sugar, sliced lemon and orange. Stir in remaining ingredients. Let stand 15 to 20 minutes. Serve in tall glasses.

Sherry Twist Cocktail (No. 1)
(For 6 people)

1 jigger (1 1/2 ozs.) Brandy   *2/3 jigger Cointreau*
1 jigger French Vermouth   *1/3 jigger fresh lemon juice*
1 jigger Sherry

Shake well with ice cubes. Strain into cocktail glasses and add to each a small piece of cinnamon stick.

Soul Kiss Cocktail (No. 1)

1/6 orange juice   *1/3 French Vermouth*
1/6 Dubonnet   *1/3 Italian Vermouth*

Shake well with ice cubes and strain into cocktail glass.

Soul Kiss Cocktail (No. 2)

1/6 orange juice   *1/3 French Vermouth*
1/6 Dubonnet   *1/3 Canadian Club Whisky*

Shake well with ice cubes and strain into cocktail glass. Add orange slice.

Tango Cocktail

2 dashes Curaçao   *1/4 Italian Vermouth*
Juice of 1/4 orange   *1/2 dry Gin*
1/4 French Vermouth

Shake well with ice cubes and strain into cocktail glass.

Tempter Cocktail
(Cf. Brandy Base)

Third Rail Cocktail (No. 1)
(Cf. Cordial Base)

| Three Stripes Cocktail | 2/3 dry Gin | 1 dash fresh orange juice |
| | 1/3 French Vermouth | |

Shake well with ice cubes and strain into cocktail glass.

Thunderclap Cocktail
(Cf. Brandy Base)

| Trinity Cocktail | 1/3 French Vermouth | 1/3 dry Gin |
| | 1/3 Italian Vermouth | |

Shake well with ice cubes and strain into cocktail glass.

Twin Six Cocktail	1/4 Italian Vermouth	Juice of 1/2 orange
	3/4 dry Gin	White of 1 egg
	1 dash Grenadine	

Shake well with ice cubes and strain into cocktail glass.

| Van Dusen Cocktail | 2/3 dry Gin | 2 dashes Grand Marnier |
| | 1/3 French Vermouth | |

Shake well with ice cubes and strain into cocktail glass.

Velocity Cocktail
(Cf. Gin Base)

Vermouth and Cassis Cocktail
(Cf. Cordial Base)

Yellow Daisy Cocktail
(Cf. Gin Base)

Zanzibar Cocktail	6 ozs. (4 jiggers) Gin	Juice of 1 1/2 lemons
(For 6 people)	6 ozs. French Vermouth	1 spoonful Orange Bitters
	1 or 2 dessert spoons sugar syrup	(optional)

Shake well with ice cubes and serve in cocktail glasses garnished with lemon rind.

Brandy Base

After-Supper Cocktail	1/2 Apricot Brandy 1/2 Curaçao	4 dashes lemon juice

Shake well with ice cubes and strain into cocktail glass.

Alexander Cocktail (No. 1)	1 oz. Crème de Cacao (light or dark)	1 oz. Brandy 1 oz. heavy cream

Shake well with ice cubes and strain into large cocktail glass.

Apple Jack Cocktail	1 dash Angostura Bitters 1/2 Italian Vermouth	1/2 Calvados or Apple Jack Brandy

Shake well with ice cubes and strain into cocktail glass.

Apricot Brandy Cocktail	1/4 lemon juice 1/4 orange juice	1/2 Apricot Brandy 1 dash dry Gin

Shake well with ice cubes and strain into cocktail glass.

Between the Sheets Cocktail	1/3 Brandy 1/3 Cointreau	1/3 Rum 1 dash lemon juice

Shake well with ice cubes and strain into cocktail glass.

Brandy Sour Cocktail	1 jigger (1 1/2 ozs.) Brandy Juice of 1/2 lemon	1/2 teaspoon powdered sugar

Shake with ice cubes and strain into cocktail glass. Decorate with fruit.

Brandy Vermouth Cocktail	3/4 Brandy 1/4 Italian Vermouth	1 dash Angostura Bitters

Stir well and strain into cocktail glass.

Calvados Cocktail *(For 6 people)*	4 ozs. Calvados (Apple Jack Brandy) Juice of 2 oranges	2 ozs. Cointreau 2 ozs. Orange Bitters

Add plenty of ice and shake carefully.

Carol Cartaino Cocktail

2/3 Brandy *1/3 Italian Vermouth*

Stir well and strain into cocktail glass. Add walnut or pearl onion.

Cherry Blossom Cocktail
(For 6 people)

3 dashes dry Curaçao *2 1/2 jiggers Cherry Brandy*
Juice of 1 lemon *2 jiggers Brandy*
3 dashes Grenadine

Shake with ice cubes. Strain and serve in cocktail glasses.

Cold Deck Cocktail

1/4 white Crème de Menthe *1/2 Brandy*
1/4 Italian Vermouth

Shake well with ice cubes and strain into cocktail glass.

Corpse Reviver (No. 1)

1/4 Italian Vermouth *1/2 Brandy*
1/4 Apple Jack Brandy or Calvados

Shake well with ice cubes and strain into cocktail glass.

Cuban Cocktail (No. 2)

Juice of 1/2 lime or 1/4 lemon *1/3 Apricot Brandy*
2/3 Brandy

Shake well with ice cubes and strain into cocktail glass.

Davis Brandy Cocktail

1 dash Angostura Bitters *1/3 French Vermouth*
4 dashes Grenadine *2/3 Brandy*

Shake well with ice cubes and strain into cocktail glass.

Deauville Cocktail

1/4 Brandy *1/4 Cointreau*
1/4 Calvados *1/4 lemon juice*

Shake well with ice cubes and strain into cocktail glass.

Depth Bomb Cocktail	$^1/_2$ Brandy $^1/_2$ Calvados or Apple Jack Brandy	1 dash lemon juice 4 dashes Grenadine

Shake well with ice cubes and strain into cocktail glass.

Depth Charge Brandy Cocktail *(For 6 people)*	2 $^1/_2$ jiggers Brandy 2 $^1/_2$ jiggers Calvados	4 dashes Grenadine 1 jigger fresh lemon juice

Shake together and serve in cocktail glasses.

Diabolo Cocktail
(Cf. Aperitif and Wine Base)

East India Cocktail	1 dash pineapple juice 1 dash Orange Curaçao	1 dash Angostura Bitters 1 jigger (1 $^1/_2$ ozs.) Brandy

Stir with ice cubes and strain into cocktail glass.

Elk Cocktail	$^1/_2$ Prunelle Brandy 2 dashes French Vermouth	$^1/_2$ dry Gin

Shake well with ice cubes and strain into cocktail glass.

Empire Cocktail	$^1/_4$ Apricot Brandy $^1/_2$ Gin	$^1/_4$ Calvados or Apple Jack Brandy

Shake well with ice cubes and strain into cocktail glass.

Frank Sullivan Cocktail	$^1/_4$ lemon juice $^1/_4$ jigger Kina Lillet	$^1/_4$ jigger Cointreau $^1/_4$ jigger Brandy

Shake well with ice cubes and strain into cocktail glass.

French "75" Cocktail
(Cf. Champagne Base)

Gilroy Cocktail	$^1/_6$ fresh lemon juice $^1/_6$ French Vermouth $^1/_3$ Cherry Brandy	$^1/_3$ dry Gin 1 dash Orange Bitters

Shake well with ice cubes and strain into cocktail glass.

Gloom-Chaser Cocktail	1/4 lemon juice 1/4 Grenadine	1/4 Grand Marnier 1/4 Curaçao

Shake well with ice cubes and strain into cocktail glass.

Grasshopper	3/4 oz. white Crème de Cacao 3/4 oz. green Crème de Menthe	3/4 oz. Brandy 1 1/2 ozs. sweet cream

Shake well with ice cubes and strain into cocktail glass.

Harry's Pick-Me-Up Cocktail	1 teaspoon Grenadine 1 jigger Brandy	Juice of 1 lemon Champagne

Combine Grenadine, Brandy and lemon juice and shake well with ice cubes. Strain into medium-size Wine glass. Top with Champagne.

Honeymoon Cocktail	Juice of 1/2 lemon or orange 3 dashes Curaçao	1/2 Bénédictine 1/2 Apple Brandy

Shake well with ice cubes and strain into cocktail glass.

"Hoop La!" Cocktail	1/4 lemon juice 1/4 Kina Lillet	1/4 Cointreau 1/4 Brandy

Shake well with ice cubes and strain into cocktail glass.

Hop Toad Cocktail	1/4 lemon juice	3/4 Apricot Brandy

Shake well with ice cubes and strain into cocktail glass.

Horse's Neck (English version. The American version is a plain Ginger Ale with lemon rind.)	Lemon peel cut in spiral 2 ozs. Brandy	1 dash Angostura Bitters Ginger Ale

Drop peel into highball glass with end hanging over edge of glass. Fill glass with cracked ice. Add Brandy and Bitters and top with Ginger Ale.

Ich Bien Cocktail	Yolk of 1 egg 4 ozs. milk	1/4 Orange Curaçao 3/4 Brandy

Shake well with ice cubes and strain into medium-size glass. Top with nutmeg.

Jack Rose Cocktail	1 1/2 ozs. Apple Jack (Apple Brandy)	Juice of 1/2 lime 1 dash Grenadine

Shake with ice cubes and strain into cocktail glass.

The Judgette Cocktail
(Cf. Aperitif and Wine Base)

Loud Speaker	1 dash fresh lemon juice 1 dash Cointreau	1/2 dry Gin 1/2 Brandy

Shake well with ice cubes and strain into cocktail glass.

Manhattan	1 jigger (1 1/2 ozs.) Brandy or Rye	1/2 oz. sweet Vermouth

Stir well with ice cubes. Strain into cocktail glass and add cherry, or serve on the rocks in Old-Fashioned glass.

Morning Glory Cocktail	3 dashes simple syrup 2 dashes Curaçao 2 dashes Bitters 1 dash Pernod	1 jigger Brandy 1 jigger Whiskey Club Soda Twist of lemon peel

Shake all ingredients except Club Soda and lemon peel with ice cubes. Pour with ice cubes into highball glass and top with Club Soda. Add twist of lemon peel.

Moulin Rouge Cocktail	3 dashes Grenadine 1/2 Apricot Brandy	1/4 Orange Gin 1/4 fresh lemon juice

Shake well with ice cubes and strain into cocktail glass.

Nicolaski Cocktail	2/3 Brandy 1 slice lemon	1/2 teaspoon powdered sugar

Place Brandy in cocktail glass. Spread sugar over lemon and place in glass. Drink through the prepared lemon with a straw.

Nightcap Cocktail	Yolk of 1 egg 1/3 Anisette	1/3 Curaçao 1/3 Brandy

Shake well with ice cubes and strain into cocktail glass.

(Brandy) Old-Fashioned	1 lump sugar 1 squirt Seltzer Water 2 dashes Aromatic Bitters	1 jigger (1 1/2 ozs.) Brandy Orange and lemon slices Cherry

Muddle lump sugar with Seltzer Water and Aromatic Bitters in Old-Fashioned glass. Add Brandy and 2 ice cubes. Squeeze twist of lemon peel over drink and then drop into glass. Decorate with orange and lemon slices and a cherry.

Olympic Cocktail	1/3 orange juice 1/3 Curaçao	1/3 Brandy

Shake well with ice cubes and strain into cocktail glass.

Paradise Cocktail	1 dash lemon juice 1/4 orange juice	1/2 Gin 1/4 Apricot Brandy

Shake well with ice cubes and strain into cocktail glass.

Pick-Me-Up I.B.F. Cocktail	3 dashes Fernet Branca 3 dashes Curaçao	1 jigger (1 1/2 ozs.) Brandy Champagne

Place 1 ice cube in a Wine glass. Add Fernet Branca, Curaçao and Brandy. Top with Champagne. Stir. Squeeze lemon peel over drink and serve.

Saratoga (No. 1)	2 dashes Maraschino Liqueur 2 dashes Angostura Bitters	Club Soda 1/4 slice pineapple

Shake Liqueur and Bitters well with ice cubes. Strain into cocktail glass. Top with Club Soda. Add pineapple.

Shriner Cocktail	1/2 jigger Sloe Gin 1/2 jigger Brandy	2 dashes sugar syrup 2 dashes Peychaud's Bitters

Stir well with ice cubes and strain into glass. Serve with peel, lemon, orange or lime.

Side Car Cocktail	1 oz. Cointreau 1 oz. Cognac or French 　　Brandy	1 oz. lemon juice

Shake well with ice cubes and strain into cocktail glass.

Brandy Stinger	1/4 white Crème de Menthe	3/4 Brandy

Shake well with ice cubes and strain into cocktail glass.

Stomach-Reviver Cocktail	1 teaspoon Angostura 　　Bitters 1 teaspoon Fernet Branca	2/3 Brandy 1/3 Kümmel

Shake well with ice cubes and strain into cocktail glass.

Tempter Cocktail	1/2 Port Wine	1/2 Apricot Brandy

Shake well with ice cubes and strain into cocktail glass.

Three Miller Cocktail	1 teaspoon Grenadine 1 dash lemon juice	2/3 Brandy 1/3 Bacardi Rum

Shake well with ice cubes and strain into cocktail glass.

Thunder and Lightning Cocktail	Yolk of 1 egg 1 teaspoon powdered sugar	1 jigger (1 1/2 ozs.) Brandy Cayenne pepper

Shake well with ice cubes and strain into cocktail glass. Top with cayenne pepper.

Thunderclap Cocktail (For 6 people)	2 jiggers (1 1/2 ozs. each) 　　Brandy 2 jiggers Scotch Whisky	2 jiggers Gin 3 dashes Orange Bitters

Thoroughly shake Brandy, Gin and Whisky with ice cubes. Add Bitters. Serve in 8-oz. highball glasses, then run for your life!

Tinton Cocktail   *1/3 Port Wine*   *2/3 Apple Jack or Calvados*

Shake well with ice cubes and strain into cocktail glass.

Tulip Cocktail   *1/6 lemon juice*   *1/3 Calvados or Apple*
1/6 Apricot Brandy   *Brandy*
1/3 Italian Vermouth

Shake well with ice cubes and strain into cocktail glass.

Valencia Cocktail   *2/3 Apricot Brandy*   *4 dashes Orange Bitters*
(No. 1)   *1/3 orange juice*

Shake well with ice cubes and strain into cocktail glass.

Victor Cocktail   *1/4 Brandy*   *1/4 dry Gin*
1/2 Italian Vermouth

Shake well with ice cubes and strain into cocktail glass.

Washington   *2 dashes Angostura Bitters*   *2/3 French Vermouth*
Cocktail   *2 dashes sugar syrup*   *1/3 Brandy*

Shake well with ice cubes and strain into cocktail glass.

Waterbury   *2 dashes Grenadine*   *1 jigger (1 1/2 ozs.) Brandy*
Cocktail   *1/2 teaspoon powdered*   *Juice of 1/4 lemon or 1/2*
sugar   *lime*
White of 1 egg

Shake well with ice cubes and strain into cocktail glass.

Young Man   *1 dash Angostura Bitters*   *1/4 Italian Vermouth*
Cocktail   *2 dashes Curaçao*   *3/4 Brandy*

Shake well with ice cubes and strain into cocktail glass. Add olive or cherry.

Champagne Base

Alfonso Cocktail

1 lump sugar	*1 dash Dubonnet*
2 dashes Secrestat Bitter	*1 split Champagne*

Put sugar in medium-size wine glass. Add Bitter and an ice cube. Pour on Dubonnet. Top with Champagne and add squeezed lemon peel. Stir slightly.

Black Velvet

1/2 Guinness Stout	*1/2 Champagne*

Pour very carefully into a tall tumbler.

Champagne Cocktail

1 lump sugar	*Lemon peel*
1 dash Angostura Bitters	*1 slice orange*
Champagne	

Put sugar into a wine glass. Saturate with Bitters. Add 1 ice cube and top with Champagne. Squeeze lemon peel on drink and serve with orange slice.

French "75" Cocktail

1 jigger (1 1/2 ozs.) Brandy	*Juice of 1 lemon*
Champagne	*1 lump sugar*

Shake Brandy, lemon juice and sugar with ice cubes. Strain into highball glass. Top with Champagne and stir slightly.

Cordial (or Liqueur) Base

Angel's Kiss Cocktail

1/4 Crème de Cacao	*1/4 Crème de Violette*
1/4 Prunelle Brandy	*1/4 light cream*

Use liqueur glass. Pour carefully so that ingredients do not mix.

Angel's Tip Cocktail *3/4 jigger Crème de Cacao*   *1/4 fresh cream*

Put Crème de Cacao into liqueur glass and float cream on top.

Aquavit Bloody Mary
(Danish Bloody Mary) *1/4 Aquavit*   *Dash Worcestershire sauce*
3/4 tomato juice

Blend Aquavit with tomato juice and season with Worcestershire sauce.

Black Baby
(Courtesy Le Chateau Richelieu Bar) *1/2 Kahlúa*   *1/4 syrup of citron*
1/4 Cointreau

Shake well with ice cubes and strain into cocktail glass.

Byrrh Cassis *1 jigger (1 1/2 ozs.) Byrrh*   *Soda Water*
1/2 jigger Crème de Cassis

Pour Byrrh and Crème de Cassis into medium-size glass. Fill up with Soda Water.

Café Kirsch Cocktail *White of 1 egg*   *1/2 tablespoon sugar*
1 jigger (1 1/2 ozs.) Kirsch   *1 jigger cold coffee*

Shake well with ice cubes and strain into cocktail glass.

Cointreau on the Rocks Pour 2 jiggers (1 1/2 ozs. each) Cointreau over ice cubes in an Old-Fashioned glass. As Cointreau chills, drink turns pearly and opalescent in color.

Diana Cocktail *3/4 Crème de Menthe*   *1/4 Brandy*

Fill cocktail glass with shaved ice. Add Crème de Menthe and top with Brandy.

Dream Cocktail *1/3 Curaçao*   *1 dash Pernod*
2/3 Brandy

Shake well with ice cubes and strain into cocktail glass.

| Golden Cadillac | 1 oz. Galliano | 1 oz. light cream |
| | 1/2 oz. Triple Sec | 1/2 oz. orange juice |

Shake well with ice cubes and serve in stemmed glass.

"Hoop La!" Cocktail
(Cf. Brandy Base)

| Lily Cocktail | 1 dash lemon juice | 1/3 Kina Lillet |
| | 1/3 dry Gin | 1/3 Crème de Noyaux |

Shake well with ice cubes and strain into cocktail glass.

| Maui | 2 ozs. unsweetened pineapple juice | 2 ozs. Cointreau |

Shake well with ice cubes. Strain into cocktail glass or serve on the rocks.

| Montmartre | 1/2 oz. Cointreau | 1 1/4 ozs. Gin or Vodka |
| | 1/2 oz. sweet Vermouth | |

Stir well with cracked ice and strain into cocktail glass. Garnish with cherry.

| Morning Mist | 2 parts Irish Mist | 1 part Bénédictine |
| | 1 part dry Sherry | 1 part orange juice |

Shake vigorously with ice cubes and serve in cocktail glass.

| Palm Beach | 2 jiggers (1 1/2 ozs. each) Cointreau | Grapefruit juice |

Pour Cointreau over ice cubes in 10-oz. highball glass. Top with grapefruit juice and stir.

| Parisian Cocktail | 1/3 French Vermouth | 1/3 Gin |
| | 1/3 Crème de Cassis | |

Shake well with ice cubes and strain into cocktail glass.

Pernod Suissesse (Licorice in flavor, anise)	White of 1 egg 2 ozs. Pernod	1 teaspoon powdered sugar 1/2 oz. heavy cream

Shake with ice cubes and strain into tall glass.

─────────────

Pink Cloud	1/4 light cream 1/4 white Crème de Cacao	1/2 Cherry Heering

Combine ingredients. Shake vigorously with ice cubes and strain into cocktail glass. (Omit cream if drink is to stand more than 15 minutes before consumption, for there is a possibility of curdling.)

─────────────

Pink Squirl	1/3 Crème de Noyaux Red 1/3 white Crème de Cacao	1/3 heavy cream

Shake with ice cubes. Strain into cocktail glass.

─────────────

Prince of Wales (very expensive)	1 part Cointreau 2 parts lemon juice	5 parts Cognac Champagne

Combine all ingredients except Champagne in a cocktail shaker. Shake with ice cubes and strain into a highball glass containing two ice cubes. Top with Champagne.

─────────────

Rainbow Cocktail	1/7 Crème de Cacao 1/7 Crème de Violette 1/7 yellow Chartreuse 1/7 Maraschino Liqueur	1/7 Bénédictine 1/7 green Chartreuse 1/7 Brandy

Use liqueur glass and carefully pour each ingredient as given so that they do not mix.

─────────────

Rusty Nail The strength of this drink depends on the person's taste. The Drambuie is floated on top of the Scotch.

	3/4 Scotch	1/4 Drambuie

Pour Scotch on the rocks and add Drambuie.

─────────────

St. Germaine	Juice of 1/2 lemon Juice of 1/4 grapefruit White of 1 egg	1 jigger (1 1/2 ozs.) green Chartreuse

Shake well with ice cubes and strain into cocktail glass.

San Martin $^1/_2$ *dry Gin*   *1 teaspoon green*
     $^1/_2$ *Italian Vermouth*   *Chartreuse*

Shake well with ice cubes and strain into cocktail glass.

Scarlett O'Hara *1 jigger (1 $^1/_2$ ozs.) Ocean*   *1 jigger Southern Comfort*
Cocktail   *Spray cranberry juice*   *Juice of $^1/_4$ fresh lime*
      cocktail

Shake well with ice cubes and strain into cocktail glass.

Spring Feeling $^1/_4$ *lemon juice* $^1/_2$ *Plymouth Gin*
Cocktail $^1/_4$ *green Chartreuse*

Shake well with ice cubes and strain into cocktail glass.

Stars and Stripes $^1/_3$ *Crème de Cassis* $^1/_3$ *green Chartreuse*
Cocktail $^1/_3$ *Maraschino Liqueur*

Use liqueur glass. Pour each ingredient carefully and in order as listed so that they do not mix.

Strega Witches' $^3/_4$ *oz. Strega*   *1 oz. orange juice*
Brew $^1/_2$ *oz. Gin* $^1/_4$ *oz. lemon juice*

Combine ingredients in shaker. Shake well and pour over rocks into Champagne glass. Add twist of lemon.

Sunrise Cocktail $^1/_4$ *Grenadine* $^1/_4$ *yellow Chartreuse*
     $^1/_4$ *Crème de Violette* $^1/_4$ *Cointreau*

Carefully pour ingredients into liqueur glass in order as listed so that they do not mix.

Third Rail *1 dash white mint*   *2 ozs. French Vermouth*
Cocktail (No. 1)   *1 dash Curaçao*
(Cf. Aperitif and Wine
Bases)   Shake well with ice cubes and strain into cocktail glass.

Tipperary Cocktail (No. 2)
1/6 orange juice
1/6 Grenadine
1/3 French Vermouth
1/3 dry Gin

Shake well with ice cubes and strain into cocktail glass. Add 2 sprigs green mint, if available.

Union Jack
1/3 Grenadine
1/3 Maraschino Liqueur
1/3 green Chartreuse

Carefully pour ingredients into liqueur glass in order as listed. so that they do not mix.

Vermouth and Cassis Cocktail
1 jigger (1 1/2 ozs.) French Vermouth
1 jigger Crème de Cassis
Soda Water

Pour Vermouth and Crème de Cassis into medium-size glass. Fill with Soda Water.

White Lady
1/4 Triple Sec
1/4 lemon juice
1/2 Sloe Gin

Shake with ice cubes and strain into cocktail glass.

Wild Redhead
1 jigger Denmark's Cherry Heering
3/4 oz. fresh lemon or lime juice

Shake well with cracked ice. Serve in Whiskey Sour glass. Garnish if desired.

Back-O-Town
(Companion recipe of Wild Redhead from bars in Bermuda.)
2/3 Cherry Heering
1/3 Pernod or Ricard

Serve on the rocks.

Galliano Liquore Base
Distilled in Lovorno, Solaro, Italy, close to Florence, this cordial comes in a fifth, imported exclusively by McKesson Liquor Co., New York. The flavor is a combination of lemon peel and Anisette. This golden-colored liqueur, 80 proof, is marketed in a distinctively tall, tapered bottle. As an after-dinner liqueur, it can be served neat in a pony glass.

Apollo 8
(Al Domanski, Traverse
City, Michigan)

¹/2 oz. Liquore Galliano	¹/4 oz. Tequila
¹/4 oz. Curaçao (blue)	Sweet cream

Stir together and float cream on top.

Apollo Moon Maiden
(George A. Stephens,
Westmont, New Jersey)

1 oz. Liquore Galliano	1 tablespoon vanilla ice cream
1 oz. Brandy	
1 ¹/2 ozs. heavy cream	Lime slice

Shake well with ice cubes and serve in cocktail glass. Garnish with lime slice.

Aruba Trade Wind
(Vincent Mardenborough,
Aruba Sheraton Hotel,
Aruba, W.I.)

³/4 oz. Liquore Galliano	¹/2 oz. sweet cream
¹/2 oz. Grand Marnier	Cherry
1 dash Apricot Brandy	

Shake well with ice cubes. Strain into cocktail glass and garnish with cherry.

Auburn
(Kurt Behringer,
California Bartenders'
Guild, Westminster,
California)

¹/2 oz. Liquore Galliano	¹/2 oz. Crème de Cassis
1 oz. Vodka	¹/2 oz. fresh orange juice

Add crushed ice, shake well with ice cubes and strain into cocktail glass.

Banana Italiano
(Garceau,
Fontana-on-Geneva Lake,
Wisconsin)

1 oz. Liquore Galliano	1 oz. sweet cream
¹/2 oz. Banana Liqueur	

Shake with ice cubes. Strain into Champagne glass.

Barracuda
(Expensive; St. Vincent
Italy Competition:
Benito Cuppari, Genoa,
Italy)

¹/2 oz. Liquore Galliano	1 dash sugar syrup
1 oz. gold Rum	Champagne
1 oz. pineapple juice	1 fresh pineapple shell
1 dash lime juice	

Shake together all ingredients except Champagne with ice cubes. Pour into pineapple shell made by slicing lid off top and digging out pineapple flesh. Fill with champagne. Garnish with lime and cherry.

Beano
(G.W. Kenny, Columbus, Ohio)

1/3 Liquore Galliano
1/3 Tia Maria
1/3 Cognac

3 or 4 whole roasted coffee beans (optional)

Shake with ice cubes. Serve very cold in cocktail glass.

Bossa Nova Special
(Nassau Beach Hotel Competition, Nassau, Bahamas: Cecil E. Roberts, Head Barman, winner)

1 oz. Liquore Galliano
1 oz. light Rum
1 dash Apricot Brandy

2 ozs. pineapple juice
White of 1 egg
1 dash fresh lemon juice

Shake well with ice cubes and pour contents, including ice cubes, into tall glass. Decorate with orange slice and cherry.

Bronx Discotheque

1/2 jigger Liquore Galliano
1/2 jigger dry Gin
1 dash dry Vermouth

1 dash sweet Vermouth
Juice of 1/2 orange

Shake well with ice cubes and strain into cocktail glass.

Bumble Bee Stinger*
(A very potent drink invented by Andy L. Nonella, Bay Harbor, Florida)

3/4 oz. Liquore Galliano
1 oz. Brandy

1/2 oz. Pernod

Combine ingredients with small quantity shaved ice in blender. Blend for short time. Strain and serve in cocktail glass.

Café Galliano
(A strong after-dinner drink to be served at the table. Created by Arthur W. Young, Edgartown, Massachusetts)

1 oz. Liquore Galliano
1 oz. cold, very dark black coffee

1 oz. Brandy
Heavy cream

Shake violently with ice cubes. Pour into cocktail glass and float a little heavy cream on top.

Carabini
(Reginold Mind, Princess Hotel, Bermuda)

1 oz. Liquore Galliano
1 oz. lime juice

1 oz. orange juice
3/4 oz. Crème de Noyaux

Shake well with ice cubes and strain into cocktail glass.

* Use a blender in recipes marked with * after the title.

Caribbean
(Miss Patricia Deuley, Miami, Florida)

1/4 Liquore Galliano
1/4 lime juice
1/4 orange juice

1/4 light rum
Club Soda

Shake all ingredients except Club Soda well with ice cubes. Pour into Tom Collins glass, top with Club Soda, and garnish with fruit.

Cavalier*
(Chuck Schafer, Colorado Springs, Colorado)

1 oz. Liquore Galliano
1/2 oz. Tequila

1 oz. orange juice
1/2 oz. heavy cream

Place in blender at low speed, briefly. Serve on the rocks in an Old-Fashioned glass.

Chevoney*
(Norbert F. Karch, Bailey's Harbor, Wisconsin)

1 oz. Liquore Galliano
1/2 oz. Grand Marnier
1/2 oz. Vodka

1 small scoop vanilla ice cream

Put in blender (without ice) for short time. Serve in prechilled cocktail glass.

Dumb Denny
(Dennis Mellor, Pittsburgh, Pennsylvania)

1 oz. Liquore Galliano
1/2 oz. lemon juice
1/2 jigger Gin

1 dash Grenadine
1 oz. heavy cream
1 dash Triple Sec

Shake well with ice cubes and strain into Champagne glass.

Fantasia
(Winner in Early Times National Mixed Drink Competition)

1/2 oz. Liquore Galliano
1 1/2 ozs. (1 jigger) Early Times Bourbon

1/2 oz. Triple Sec
1 oz. lime juice

Shake with ice cubes and serve in cocktail glass or on the rocks.

Florida
(Gigi Cesaro, Il Pirata, Burgh Heath, Surrey, England)

3/4 oz. Liquore Galliano
1 1/2 ozs. (1 jigger) grapefruit juice

1 oz. Gin
1 dash Campari Bitters

Shake well with ice cubes and strain into cocktail glass. Garnish with orange slice.

Flying Tiger
(Joseph Saba, Whiteland, Indiana)

1/3 Liquore Galliano   1/3 white Crème de Menthe
1/3 Vodka (80 proof)

Serve on the rocks in cocktail glass.

Frangi Pangi*
(Leslie Supersaad, Port Royal Grog Shoppe, Kingston, Jamaica)

3/4 oz. Liquore Galliano   1 dash sugar syrup
1 oz. light Rum   2 ozs. grape juice
Juice of 1/2 lime

Mix in blender. Dress with fruit and serve in tulip-shaped glass with shaved ice.

Freddy's Special*
(Harry Heins, Jacksonville, Florida)

1/3 Liquore Galliano   1/3 Gin
1/3 Cognac   1 dash heavy cream

Place in blender for short time with cracked ice. Serve in 7-oz. cocktail glass.

G. & C.
(Joe D'Agostino, Winter Park, Florida)

7/8 oz. Liquore Galliano   1/8 oz. Cognac

Put Galliano in 1-oz. pony glass and float Cognac on top.

Galaxy
(J. Garceau, Fontana-on-Geneva Lake, Wisconsin)

1 1/2 ozs. (1 jigger) Liquore   3 ozs. orange juice
   Galliano   White of 1 egg
1/2 oz. Triple Sec

Shake with ice cubes. Pour ice and all into 12-oz. Collins glass. Garnish with orange slice.

Galliano Gimlet
(Reta Gow Celatano, Penfield, New York)

1 1/2 ozs. (1 jigger) Liquore   Juice of 1/2 lime
   Galliano   1 dash of bitters
1 oz. dry Vermouth   Soda Water

Stir all ingredients except Soda Water with ice. Strain. Top with Soda Water and serve in 7-oz. highball glass.

Galliano L'Amore
(James Christian, Lombard, Illinois)

1/3 white Crème de Menthe   1/3 Liquore Galliano
1/3 dark Crème de Cacao

Gently float ingredients in given order in Pousse-café glass.

Galliano Margarita
(Bob Reggiani, Los Angeles, California)

1 oz. Liquore Galliano
1 oz. Tequila

1/2 oz. fresh lime juice
Salt

Shake all ingredients except salt with ice cubes and pour into saucer Champagne glass that has been rimmed with salt.

Galliano Mist

1 oz. Liquore Galliano

1/4 section fresh lime

Fill Old-Fashioned glass with cracked ice. Pour in Galliano over ice cubes and squeeze lime into glass. Add lime shell. Stir and serve.

Galliano Screwdriver
(C. Charles Fiore, Boston, Massachusetts)

1 oz. Liquore Galliano
3 ozs. orange juice

1/2 teaspoon fresh lemon juice

Pour over ice cubes and stir. Serve in 8-oz. highball glass.

Galliatini
(Michael Kahier, Sheffield, Massachusetts)

1/3 Liquore Galliano
2/3 Vodka

Twist of lemon peel

Instead of using dry Vermouth as in a Martini, you use Galliano. Stir with ice cubes and strain into cocktail glass. Garnish with lemon twist.

Golden Cadillac
(As served at Le Chateau Richelieu)

1 oz. Liquore Galliano
1 dash Triple Sec or Cointreau

2 dashes Vodka
1 oz. heavy cream

Shake vigorously with ice cubes and strain into Champagne glass.

Golden Dragon

1 1/2 ozs. (1 jigger) Liquore Galliano
1 egg yolk

1 dash cream
3/4 oz. white Crème de Cacao

Mix or shake with ice cubes and serve in cocktail glass.

Golden Dream
(Very similar to Golden Cadillac. United Kingdom Bartenders' Guild winner, Leroy Sharon, Marineland, California)

1 oz. Liquore Galliano
1/2 oz. Cointreau

1/2 oz. orange juice
1/2 oz. heavy cream

Shake with ice cubes and strain into cocktail glass.

Golden Glow
(H. T. Kranz, Williamston, Michigan)

1 oz. Liquore Galliano
1 oz. Drambuie

1 oz. Gin

Shake well with ice cubes. Serve in Martini glass.

Golden Lilli
(Jimmy Jones, Los Angeles, California)

1/2 oz. Liquore Galliano
1 1/2 ozs. Canadian Whisky

1/2 oz. Banana Liqueur

Shake with ice cubes and serve in cocktail glass.

Goldfinger
(Jimmy Sastro, Bar Algabeno, Can Picafort, Majorca, Spain)

1 oz. Liquore Galliano
1 1/4 ozs. Vodka

1 oz. pineapple juice

Shake well with ice cubes and serve in cocktail glass or on the rocks.

Homestead
(John F. Willett, Jr., Exeter, New Hampshire)

1 oz. Liquore Galliano
3/4 oz. orange juice

1/2 oz. Grenadine
1/2 oz. heavy cream

Shake with ice cubes and serve over crushed ice in Champagne glass.

Irish Dream
(John Finnegan, Palm Springs, California)

1/2 oz. white Crème de Cacao
1/2 oz. green Crème de Menthe

1/2 oz. Liquore Galliano
1/2 oz. heavy cream

Shake with ice cubes and strain into Champagne glass.

Island in the Sun
(Lawrence Adderley, Jack Tar Hotel, West End, Grand Bahama)

1 oz. Liquore Galliano
1/2 oz. dark Rum
1/2 Apricot Brandy

2 ozs. pineapple juice
1/2 lemon juice
1/2 oz. simple syrup

Shake well with ice cubes. Serve in tall glass with ice cubes. Decorate with fruit.

Italian Orange Blossom
(Mrs. Sophia Dodge, Daly City, California)

1 jigger (1 1/2 ozs.) Liquore Galliano

Juice of 1 orange
1 dash Tequila

Shake well with ice cubes and strain into cocktail glass.

Las Vegas
(Pasquale Esposito, Londres Hotel, Naples, Italy)

1/6 Liquore Galliano
5/6 Vodka

1 dash fresh lemon juice

Shake with ice cubes and strain into cocktail glass.

Moon Dust
(Angelo Zola, Principe & Savoia Hotel, Milan, Italy)

3 parts Liquore Galliano
4 parts Palo Viejo Rum or Añejo
2 parts lemon juice

1 part Blue Curaçao
3 dashes Grenadine
3 dashes Orgeat

Shake with ice cubes in mixing glass and serve in cocktail glass or on the rocks. Garnish with green Maraschino cherry.

Morning Mist
(Mrs. Susan Canale Parenteau, Bellingham, Massachusetts)

1 jigger (1 1/2 ozs.) Liquore Galliano

Juice of 1/2 orange

Pour over crushed ice in Old-Fashioned glass and serve with a straw.

Naples Delight
(John Johnson, Winter Park, Florida)

1 oz. Liquore Galliano
1 oz. Crème de Cacao (dark)

1 oz. heavy cream

Shake with ice cubes and strain into 6-oz. cocktail glass.

Old Charles
(Lucien Riffis, Barbados Hilton Hotel, Barbados, West Indies)

2 ozs. Liquore Galliano
1 oz. Barbados Rum
2 ozs. grapefruit juice

1 dash Grenadine
1/2 oz. Rose's lime

Shake with ice cubes and pour contents, including ice cubes, into Old-Fashioned glass. Decorate with lime slice, passing two short straws through the lime.

Orange Cadillac*
(Joe Beaudry,
Jacksonville, Florida)

1 oz. Liquore Galliano
*3/4 oz. white Crème de
Cacao*

1/4 oz. orange juice
1 oz. heavy cream

Place in blender for short time with cracked ice. Serve in old-time 5-oz. cocktail glass.

Palm Beach

1 oz. Liquore Galliano
1 oz. Vodka

White of 1 egg

Shake with ice cubes. Pour into highball glass. Top with Sparkling Water and garnish with wedge of lime.

Pink Elephant
(Australasian United
Kingdom Bartenders'
Guild: Peter Zorbas, Potts
Point, Australia Winner)

1/5 Liquore Galliano
1/5 Vodka
1/5 Crème de Noyaux
1/5 orange juice

1/5 sweet cream
1 dash Orange Bitters
1 dash Grenadine

Mix first 5 ingredients. Add Orange Bitters and Grenadine. Shake with ice cubes and strain into cocktail glass. Dust with cinnamon.

La Primavera
(Marshall Stoneham,
Princess Hotel, Bermuda)

3/4 oz. Liquore Galliano
1 oz. orange juice

1 oz. Gin

Shake with ice cubes and strain into cocktail glass.

Raffaello
(Angelo Zola, Principe &
Savoia Hotel, Milan,
Italy)

1/3 Liquore Galliano
1/3 Inca Pisco
1/3 white sweet Vermouth

1 dash Angostura Bitters
*1 dash Grand Marnier or
Triple Sec*

Shake with ice cubes and serve in Old-Fashioned glass.

St. Vincent
(Associazione Italiana
Barmen e Sostenitori,
Italy)

1 oz. Liquore Galliano
1 oz. light cream

1 oz. Gin
1 dash Grenadine

Shake with ice cubes and serve in cocktail glass.

Smutney

1 oz. Liquore Galliano
1 oz. orange juice

*1 oz. white Crème de
Menthe*

Shake with ice cubes and pour into cocktail glass.

Snoopy
(Piero Reggioli, Ritz Hotel, Florence, Italy)

1 oz. Liquore Galliano
1 1/2 ozs. J. W. Dant Bourbon Whiskey
1 oz. Campari Bitters
1/2 oz. Grand Marnier
Drops of lemon juice

Shake with ice cubes and strain into cocktail glass. Garnish with lemon peel.

Snowflake
(Don Humm, Chilcotin Inn, Williams Lake, British Columbia)

3/4 oz. Liquore Galliano
1/4 oz. Cointreau
1/4 oz. yellow Chartreuse
1 1/4 ozs. heavy cream

Shake with ice cubes and serve in Champagne glass. Garnish with cherry.

Southern Dream
(Ben C. Evans, Dania, Florida)

1 oz. Liquore Galliano
1/2 oz. Southern Comfort
1/2 oz. fresh orange juice
1 oz. heavy cream (or small scoop vanilla ice cream)

Shake well with ice cubes. Strain. Serve in Champagne glass.

Southern Gal

3/4 oz. Liquore Galliano
3/4 oz. Southern Comfort
3/4 oz. Cointreau

Shake with ice cubes and serve in cocktail glass.

Suissesse Milanese

1 1/2 ozs. (1 jigger) Liquore Galliano
1/2 oz. Anisette
Egg white

Shake with ice cubes and pour into cocktail glass.

Terrazza
(Edwardo Giaccone, Salo, Italy)

1 1/2 ozs. (1 jigger) Liquore Galliano
1 1/2 ozs. Vodka
2 ozs. pineapple juice
1/2 oz. light cream

Shake with ice cubes and strain into large cocktail glass. Garnish with cherry.

Three Faces
(Horacio Santana Ascenedo, La Fonda del Callejon, San Juan, Puerto Rico)

1 oz. Liquore Galliano
1 oz. light Rum
1/2 oz. Campari Bitters

1 dash Soda Water
Twist of orange peel

Serve on the rocks. Garnish with orange peel.

Tropicale
(Teodoro Rivera, Caribe Hilton Hotel, San Juan, Puerto Rico)

1 oz. Liquore Galliano
1 oz. Ronrico white Rum
1/2 oz. Cointreau

1/2 oz. grapefruit juice
1 dash Angostura Bitters

Shake and serve in Old-Fashioned glass over ice cubes.

Tropicana Belle*
(This drink is similar to a Frozen Daiquiri. It was created by Robert Taylor, Las Vegas, Nevada.)

1/2 oz. Liquore Galliano
1/2 oz. Geneva (Holland) Gin

1/2 oz. Calvados
1 dash Maraschino cherry juice

Put ingredients into blender, adding 1 cup shaved ice. Blend for a few moments. Spoon frozen mixture into small Brandy snifter. Decorate with cherries and serve with a straw.

Tyrol
(Michael Bauer, Baltimore, Maryland)

1 oz. Liquore Galliano
1/2 oz. Brandy

1/2 oz. green Chartreuse
1/2 oz. heavy cream

Shake well with ice cubes and serve in cocktail glass. Dust with grated nutmeg.

Unie–k
(Dominie Bovienzo, Pittsburgh, Pennsylvania)

1 1/2 ozs. Liquore Galliano
1 oz. Vodka

1 dash Grenadine
Juice of 1 lime

Shake with ice cubes and pour into Champagne glass. Serve with half-moon of lime rind perched on rim of glass.

Upstater

1 1/2 ozs. Liquore Galliano
1 oz. Vodka

1 dash Peach Brandy

Shake well with ice cubes and strain into cocktail glass.

Viking

1 oz. Liquore Galliano

1/4 oz. Akvavit (ice cold)

Pour Galliano into tapered Cordial glass. Float Akvavit on top, by pouring it over a spoon in a reverse position.

Volare
(Dr. F. Feldman, Elizabeth, New Jersey)

1 oz. Liquore Galliano   *Juice of 1/2 lemon*
1 oz. Apple juice

Shake with ice cubes and strain into cocktail glass

Warlock

1/2 oz. Vodka   *1 jigger (1 1/2 ozs.) Liquore*
Juice of 1/2 orange   *Galliano*

Shake with ice cubes and strain into cocktail glass.

Gin Base

There were 13.93 million cases of Gin sold in the United States in 1969. Of this total, 1.43 million cases were imported, mostly from England. Twenty-five English Gins are sold here, but the two leading brands are Beefeater (Kobrand's import) and Tanqueray (James M. McCunn's import in the green bottle). Schenley's Plymouth Gin, 170 years old, is now being promoted in New York City and San Francisco, the two big pockets of English Gin drinkers. Of the variety of good native Gins, a steady seller at our bar is Gordon's Distilled London Dry Gin. Originating in 1769, it is distilled and bottled in the United States. Another notable Gin is Lloyds, a native produce of Julius Wile Sons & Co.

Admiral Cocktail

Juice of 1/2 lime   *2 ozs. Gin*
1/2 oz. Cherry Cordial

Shake with ice cubes and strain into cocktail glass.

Alexander Cocktail (No. 2)

1/2 dry Gin   *1/4 heavy cream*
1/4 Crème de Cacao

Shake well with ice cubes and strain into cocktail glass.

Alexander's Sister Cocktail

1/3 Gin   *1/3 Crème de Menthe*
1/3 sweet heavy cream

Shake well with ice cubes and strain into cocktail glass.

Alfonso Special Cocktail	1 dash Angostura Bitters 4 dashes Italian Vermouth 1/4 dry Gin	1/4 French Vermouth 1/2 Grand Marnier

Shake well with ice cubes and strain into cocktail glass.

Allies Cocktail	3/4 oz. dry Vermouth 2 dashes Kümmel	2 ozs. Gin

Shake with ice cubes and strain into cocktail glass.

Army Cocktail	3/4 sweet Vermouth 2 ozs. Gin	2 dashes Orange Bitters Twist of orange peel

Shake well with ice cubes. Strain into cocktail glass and top with orange peel.

Australian Cocktail	3/4 oz. Apricot Brandy 3/4 oz. Gin	2 dashes lime juice 2 dashes orange juice

Shake with ice cubes and strain into cocktail glass.

Aviation Cocktail	Juice of 1/2 lime 3 dashes Maraschino Liqueur	3 dashes Triple Sec 2 ozs. Gin

Shake with ice cubes and strain into cocktail glass.

Bijou Cocktail	1/2 oz. Chartreuse 4 dashes sweet Vermouth	2 ozs. Gin

Stir with ice cubes and strain. Decorate with cherry and lemon peel.

Bloody Danish The only difference between this and a Bloody Mary is that this calls for Akvavit instead of Vodka. Aquavit, the national Danish drink, was first distilled in 1846. Danes drink it neat and very cold, sometimes first taking a cracker with cheese. It is good right out of the refrigerator (where it should be kept) as an aperitif or after-dinner drink straight, never diluted. Akvavit is imported by Munson Shaw from Aalborg in North Jutland.

	1 dash lemon juice	1 dash or more Lea and
	2 ozs. Akvavit	Perrins Sauce
	3 ozs. tomato juice	Salt and pepper to taste

Shake well with ice cubes. Strain into 8-oz. glass or serve on the rocks.

Blue Moon *1/2 oz. Crème Yvette* *White of 1 egg*
2 ozs. Gin

Shake with ice cubes and strain into cocktail glass.

Bombay Marrino *1/5 dry Vermouth* *4/5 Bombay Gin*

Fill cocktail shaker to top with ice cubes or chopped ice. Stir ingredients rapidly. Pour into chilled cocktail glass. Twist freshly cut lemon peel over top and serve immediately.

Bombay Tonic *1/4 squeezed fresh lime* *Quinine Water*
1 1/2 ozs. Bombay Gin

Fill an 8-oz. highball glass with ice cubes. Add lime and Bombay Gin. Fill to top with Quinine Water.

Bronx Cocktail
(Cf. Aperitif and Wine Bases)

Bronx (Silver) Cocktail
(Cf. Aperitif and Wine Bases)

Bull-Dog Cocktail *Juice of 1 orange* *Ginger Ale*
1 jigger (1 1/2 ozs.) Gin

Put 2 or 3 ice cubes into a large tumbler. Add juice and gin. Top with Ginger Ale.

B.V.D. Cocktail *1/3 Bacardi Rum* *1/3 French Vermouth*
1/3 dry Gin

Shake well with ice cubes and strain into cocktail glass.

Chorus Lady Cocktail
(Cf. Aperitif and Wine Bases)

Claridge Cocktail
(Cf. Aperitif and Wine Bases)

Clover Club Cocktail

This drink is similar to a Pink Lady, but a Pink Lady also calls for Apple Jack.

Juice of 1/2 lemon or 1 lime	*White of 1 egg*
1/3 Grenadine	*2/3 Gin*

Shake well with ice cubes and strain into cocktail glass.

Clover Leaf Cocktail

This drink is the same as Clover Club but with a sprig of fresh mint on top.

Club Cocktail

2/3 dry Gin	*1 dash yellow Chartreuse*
1/3 Italian Vermouth	

Shake well with ice cubes and strain into cocktail glass.

Cointreau Screwdriver

1 oz. Cointreau	*Orange juice*
2 ozs. Gin (or Vodka)	

Pour Cointreau and Gin over 2 ice cubes in a 10-oz. highball glass. Top with orange juice and stir well.

Colonial Cocktail

2/3 dry Gin	*3 dashes Maraschino*
1/3 grapefruit juice	*Liqueur*

Shake well with ice cubes and strain into cocktail glass.

Cooperstown Cocktail
(Cf. Aperitif and Wine Bases)

Damn the Weather Cocktail

3 dashes Curaçao	*1/4 Italian Vermouth*
1/4 orange juice	*1/2 dry Gin*

Shake well with ice cubes and strain into cocktail glass.

Darb Cocktail
(Cf. Aperitif and Wine
Bases)

**Desert Healer
Cocktail**

Juice of 1 orange   ¹/2 jigger Cherry Brandy
1 jigger (1 ¹/2 ozs.) dry Gin   Ginger Beer

Shake all ingredients except Ginger Beer with ice cubes and
strain into long tumbler. Top with Ginger Beer.

**Dolly O'Dare
Cocktail**
(Cf. Aperitif and Wine
Bases)

Douglas Cocktail   ¹/3 French Vermouth   2/3 Gin

Shake Vermouth and Gin well with ice cubes and strain into
cocktail glass. Squeeze orange and lemon peels on top.

**Du Barry
Cocktail**

1 dash Angostura Bitters   2/3 Gordon's Dry Gin
2 dashes Pernod   Orange slice
¹/3 French Vermouth

Shake well with ice cubes and strain into cocktail glass. Add
orange slice.

**Dubonnet
Cocktail**
(Cf. Aperitif and Wine
Bases)

Dunhill Cocktail
(Cf. Aperitif and Wine
Bases)

**Eagle Cabin
Cocktail**

¹/4 Crème Yvette   White of 1 egg
³/4 dry Gin   1 teaspoon powdered sugar
Juice of ¹/4 lemon

Shake well with ice cubes and strain into cocktail glass.

Eclipse Cocktail   Grenadine   ¹/3 dry Gin
Olive   2/3 Sloe Gin

Put enough Grenadine in a cocktail glass to cover the olive.
Mix spirits together and pour gently onto the Grenadine so
that it does not mix. Squeeze orange peel on top.

Eddie Brown Cocktail	2 dashes Apricot Brandy	1/3 jigger Kina Lillet
	2/3 jigger dry Gin	

Shake well with ice cubes and strain into cocktail glass. Squeeze lemon peel on top.

Elk Cocktail
(Cf. Brandy Base)

Eton Blazer Cocktail	Juice of 1/2 lemon	1/4 Kirsch
	1/2 tablespoon powdered sugar	3/4 Gordon's dry Gin
		Club Soda

Shake all ingredients except Club Soda with ice cubes. Strain into long tumbler and top with Club Soda.

Everglade Cocktail	Juice of 1/2 lime	1 jigger (1 1/2 ozs.) Gin
	Juice of 1/2 orange	2 dashes Apple Jack
	4 dashes Curaçao	White of 1 egg

Shake well with ice cubes and strain into cocktail glass.

Fairbanks Cocktail (No. 1)	1 dash lemon juice	1/3 Apricot Brandy
	1 dash Grenadine	1/3 French Vermouth
	1/3 dry Gin	

Shake well with ice cubes and strain into cocktail glass.

Fairy Belle Cocktail	White of 1 egg	1/4 Apricot Brandy
	2 dashes Grenadine	3/4 dry Gin

Shake well with ice cubes and strain into Port Wine glass.

Fallen Angel Cocktail	1 dash Angostura Bitters	Juice of 1 lemon or 1/2 lime
	2 dashes Crème de Menthe	1 jigger dry Gin

Shake well with ice cubes and strain into cocktail glass.

Favorite Cocktail	1 dash lemon juice	1/3 French Vermouth
	1/3 Apricot Brandy	1/3 dry Gin

Shake well and strain into cocktail glass.

| *Fernet Branca Cocktail* | *1/4 Fernet Branca* *1/4 Italian Vermouth* | *1/2 dry Gin* |

Shake well with ice cubes and strain into cocktail glass.

| *Fifty-Fifty Cocktail* | *1/2 dry Gin* | *1/2 French Vermouth* |

Shake well with ice cubes and strain into cocktail glass.

| *Fine and Dandy Cocktail* | *1/4 lemon juice* *1/4 Cointreau* | *1/2 Gin* *1 dash Angostura Bitters* |

Shake well with ice cubes and strain into cocktail glass.

| *Flamingo Cocktail* | *Juice of 1/2 lemon* *3 dashes Grenadine* | *1/2 oz. Apricot Brandy* *2 ozs. Gin* |

Shake well with ice cubes and strain into cocktail glass.

Florida
(Cf. Galliano Liquore Base)

Franken-Jack Cocktail
(Cf. Aperitif and Wine Bases)

| *Froth-Blower Cocktail* | *White of 1 egg* *1 teaspoon Grenadine* | *1 jigger Gin* |

Shake well with ice cubes and strain into Port Wine glass.

| *Gene Tunney Cocktail* | *1 dash orange juice* *1 dash lemon juice* | *1/3 French Vermouth* *2/3 Gin* |

Shake well with ice cubes and strain into cocktail glass.

Gibson Cocktail
(Cf. Aperitif and Wine Bases)

Gilroy Cocktail
(Cf. Brandy Base)

| *Gimblet Cocktail* | *1/4 lime juice* | *Club Soda* |
| | *3/4 dry Gin* | |

Shake lime juice and Gin well with ice cubes. Strain into cocktail glass and top with Club Soda.

| *Gimlet (No. 1)* | *1/4 oz. Cointreau* | *Juice of 1/2 lime* |
| | *2 ozs. Gin (or Vodka)* | |

Shake well with ice cubes and strain into cocktail glass, or serve on the rocks.

| *Gimlet (No. 2)* | *1/4 Rose's lime juice* | *3/4 Bombay Gin* |

Fill shaker with ice cubes. Add lime juice and Gin. Shake well, strain and pour into chilled silver goblet or chilled cocktail glass, or serve on the rocks. Twist fresh-cut lime peel over the top.

| *Gin Buck* | *1 jigger (1 1/2 ozs.) Gin* | *1/4 lemon* |
| | *Ginger Ale* | |

Put ice cubes in a highball glass. Pour in Gin and top with Ginger Ale. Squeeze in lemon.

| *Gin Cocktail* | *4 dashes Orange Bitters* | *1 jigger (1 1/2 ozs.) dry Gin* |

Shake well with ice cubes and strain into cocktail glass.

| *Gin Wink* | *1 jigger (1 1/2 ozs.) Gin* | *Canada Dry "Wink"* |

Put Gin in highball glass with ice cubes. Top with Canada Dry "Wink" beverage.

Golden Ermine
Cocktail
(Cf. Aperitif and Wine
Bases)

Golden Gate Juice of 1/2 orange   1 jigger (1 1/2 ozs.) Gin
Cocktail Shake with ice cubes and strain into cocktail glass.

Grape Vine 1/4 grape juice   1/2 Gin
Cocktail 1/4 fresh lemon juice   1 dash Grenadine
  Shake well with ice cubes and strain into cocktail glass.

Grand Royal Juice of 1/2 lemon   1 egg
Clover Club 3 dashes Grenadine   1 jigger (1 1/2 ozs.) dry Gin
Cocktail Shake well with ice cubes and strain into cocktail glass.

Great Secret 1/3 Blonde Kina Lillet   1 dash Angostura Bitters
Cocktail 2/3 dry Gin
  Shake well with ice cubes and strain into cocktail glass.
  Squeeze orange peel on top.

Green Dragon 1/8 lemon juice   1/2 dry Gin
Cocktail 1/8 Kümmel   4 dashes Peach Bitters
  1/4 green mint (Marie
    Brizard or get 60 proof)
  Shake well with ice cubes and strain into cocktail glass.

Guard's Cocktail 2/3 dry Gin   2 dashes Curaçao
  1/3 Italian Vermouth
  Shake well with ice cubes and strain into cocktail glass.

Gypsy Cocktail
(Cf. Aperitif and Wine
Bases)

Hakam Cocktail
(Cf. Aperitif and Wine
Bases)

H & H Cocktail

2/3 dry Gin
1/3 Kina Lillet

2 dashes Curaçao

Shake well with ice cubes and strain into cocktail glass. Squeeze orange peel on top.

Hanky Panky Cocktail
(Cf. Aperitif and Wine
Bases)

Harrovian Cocktail

1 dash Angostura Bitters
1 dash orange juice

1 dash lemon juice
1 jigger (1 1/2 ozs.) dry Gin

Shake well with ice cubes and strain into cocktail glass.

Hawaiian Cocktail

1 part Curaçao (or any other of the orange Liqueurs)

4 parts Gin
2 parts orange juice

Shake well with ice cubes and strain into cocktail glass.

Hoffman House Cocktail

2 dashes Orange Bitters
2/3 Plymouth Gin

1/3 French Vermouth

Shake well with ice cubes and strain into cocktail glass. Squeeze lemon peel on top.

Holland House Cocktail

Juice of 1/4 lemon
1 dash pineapple juice
1/3 French Vermouth

2/3 dry Gin
4 dashes Maraschino Liqueur

Shake well with ice cubes and strain into cocktail glass.

Homestead Cocktail

Long before the name *cocktail* was current, this delightful drink was enjoyed in the old homesteads of the Southern states.

1 dash orange juice
2/3 dry Gin

1/3 Italian Vermouth

Shake well with ice cubes and strain into cocktail glass.

Honolulu Cocktail (No. 1)	*1 dash Angostura Bitters* *1 dash orange juice* *1 dash pineapple juice*	*1 dash lemon juice* *1 jigger (1 1/2 ozs.) dry Gin* *Little powdered sugar*

Shake well with ice cubes and strain into cocktail glass.

H.P.W. Cocktail
(Cf. Aperitif and Wine Bases)

Hula Hula Cocktail	*2/3 dry Gin* *1/3 orange juice*	*1 dash Curaçao*

Shake well with ice cubes and strain into cocktail glass.

Hurricane Cocktail (Cf. Whiskey Base)	*1/3 Whiskey* *1/3 Gin*	*1/3 Crème de Menthe* *Juice of 2 lemons*

Shake well with ice cubes and strain into cocktail glass.

Ideal Cocktail	*3 dashes Maraschino*
	   Liqueur
	1/3 Italian Vermouth
		2/3 dry Gin
		1 tablespoon grapefruit
		   juice

Shake well with ice cubes and strain into cocktail glass. Serve almond or walnut in glass.

Imperial Cocktail
(Cf. Aperitif and Wine Bases)

Income Tax Cocktail
(Cf. Aperitif and Wine Bases)

International Cocktail	*3/4 oz. dry Vermouth* *2 dashes Pernod*	*2 ozs. Gin*

Stir with ice cubes and strain into cocktail glass.

| Jack Dempsey Cocktail | 1 oz. Gin
1/2 oz. Bacardi Rum
1/2 teaspoon lemon juice | 1/2 teaspoon powdered
   sugar |

Shake with ice cubes. Strain into chilled cocktail glass.

| Journalist Cocktail | 2 dashes lemon juice
2 dashes Curaçao
1 dash Angostura Bitters | 1/6 French Vermouth
1/6 Italian Vermouth
2/3 Gordon's Dry Gin |

Shake well with ice cubes and strain into cocktail glass.

| The Judge Jr. Cocktail | 1/3 Gin
1/3 Rum
1/3 lemon juice | Powdered sugar
1 dash Grenadine |

Shake well with ice cubes and strain into cocktail glass.

The Judgette
Cocktail
(Cf. Aperitif and Wine Bases)

| Knickerbocker Cocktail | 1 dash Italian Vermouth
2/3 dry Gin | 1/3 French Vermouth |

Shake well with ice cubes and strain into cocktail glass. Squeeze lemon peel on top.

| Kraatz Special (No. 1) | 1 1/2 jiggers Gin
Schweppes Tonic Water | Rose's lime juice |

Pour Gin over ice cubes in a Collins glass. Top with equal amounts of Tonic Water and lime juice. Stir well and serve.

| Leap Frog Cocktail | 1 jigger (1 1/2 ozs.) Gin
1 split (7 ozs.) Ginger Ale | Juice of 1/2 lemon |

Serve in a long tumbler with one ice cube.

| Leap Year Cocktail | This delightful cocktail was created by Harry Craddock for the Leap Year celebrations on February 29, 1928 at the Savoy |

Hotel, London. It was credited with more proposals than any other cocktail that had theretofore been mixed.

1 dash lemon juice	*1/6 Grand Marnier*
2/3 Gin	*1/6 Italian Vermouth*

Shake well with ice cubes and serve in cocktail glass. Squeeze lemon peel on top.

Leave-It-to-Me Cocktail (No. 1)

1 dash lemon juice	*1/2 Plymouth Gin*
1/4 Apricot Brandy	*1 dash Grenadine*
1/4 French Vermouth	

Shake well with ice cubes and strain into cocktail glass.

Lily Cocktail
(Cf. Cordial Base)

Little Devil Cocktail

1/6 lemon juice	*1/3 Rum*
1/6 Cointreau	*1/3 dry Gin*

Shake well with ice cubes and strain into cocktail glass.

London Buck Cocktail

1/3 dry Gin	*2 dashes simple syrup*
2 dashes Pernod	

Shake with one ice cube and strain into cocktail glass.

Long Glen Cocktail

1 oz. Cointreau	*Bitter Lemon*
1 oz. Gin or Vodka	

Pour over ice cubes in Highball glass and add Bitter Lemon.

Lord Suffolk Cocktail

1/8 Italian Vermouth	*5/8 dry Gin*
1/8 Cointreau	*1/8 Maraschino Liqueur*

Shake well with ice cubes and strain into cocktail glass.

Loud Speaker
(Cf. Brandy Base)

Luigi Cocktail
(Cf. Aperitif and Wine Bases)

Magnolia Blossom Cocktail	*1/4 fresh lemon juice* *1/4 heavy cream*	*1/2 Gin* *1 dash Grenadine*

Shake well with ice cubes and strain into cocktail glass.

Maiden's Blush Cocktail (No. 1)	*1 dash lemon juice* *4 dashes Orange Curaçao*	*4 dashes Grenadine* *1 jigger (1 1/2 ozs.) dry Gin*

Shake well with ice cubes and strain into cocktail glass.

Maiden's Prayer Cocktail	*3/4 oz. dry Gin* *3/4 oz. Cointreau*	*1 dash fresh orange juice* *1 dash fresh lemon juice*

Shake with ice cubes and pour into cocktail glass.

Marguerite Cocktail	*1/3 French Vermouth* *2/3 dry Gin*	*1 dash Orange Bitters* *Twist of orange peel*

Shake well with ice cubes and strain into cocktail glass. Twist orange peel on top.

Marny Cocktail	*1/3 Grand Marnier*	*2/3 dry Gin*

Shake well with ice cubes and strain into cocktail glass.

Martinez Cocktail
(Cf. Aperitif and Wine
Bases)

Martini (Dry)	*1/3 Italian Vermouth*	*2/3 dry Gin*

Stir and strain into cocktail glass.

Martini (Medium)	*1/4 French Vermouth* *1/4 Italian Vermouth*	*1/2 dry Gin*

Shake well with ice cubes and strain into cocktail glass.

Martini (Special) *(For 6 people)*	*4 jiggers (1 1/2 ozs. each)* Gin *1 1/2 jiggers Italian* *Vermouth*	*1/3 jigger orange-flower* *water* *1 dash Pernod* *2 dashes Angostura Bitters*

Pour ingredients into shaker with ice cubes. Stir. Strain into cocktail glasses.

Martini (Sweet)	*1/3 French Vermouth*	*2/3 Gin*

Stir well and strain into cocktail glass.

Melon Cocktail	*1/8 lemon juice* *3/8 Maraschino Liqueur*	*1/2 Gin*

Shake well with ice cubes and strain into cocktail glass.

Millionaire *Cocktail (No. 2)*	*1 dash Anisette* *White of 1 egg*	*1/3 Pernod* *2/3 dry Gin*

Shake well with ice cubes and strain into cocktail glass.

Minnehaha *Cocktail* *(Cf. Aperitif and Wine* *Bases)*		
Mississippi Mule *Cocktail*	*2/3 dry Gin* *1/6 lemon juice*	*1/6 Crème de Cassis*

Shake well with ice cubes and strain into cocktail glass.

Monkey Gland *Cocktail*	*3 dashes Pernod* *3 dashes Grenadine*	*1/3 orange juice* *2/3 dry Gin*

Shake well with ice cubes and strain into cocktail glass.

Monte Carlo *Imperial Cocktail*	*1/2 dry Gin* *1/4 lemon juice*	*1/4 white Crème de Menthe* *Champagne*

With ice cubes, shake well all ingredients except Champagne. Strain into cocktail glass and top with Champagne.

Montpelier Cocktail	*1/3 French Vermouth*	*2/3 dry Gin*

Shake well with ice cubes and strain into cocktail glass. Top with onion.

───────────────────────────

Montmartre
(Cf. Cordial Base)

Moonlight Cocktail
(Cf. Aperitif and Wine Bases)

Moonshine Cocktail
(Cf. Aperitif and Wine Bases)

Napoleon Cocktail	*1 dash Fernet Branca*	*1 dash Dubonnet*
	1 dash Curaçao	*1 jigger (1 1/2 ozs.) dry Gin*

Shake well with ice cubes and strain into cocktail glass. Squeeze lemon peel on top.

───────────────────────────

Negroni	*1/3 Campari*	*1/3 Gin or Vodka*
	1/3 sweet Vermouth	

Stir and pour into cocktail glass on the rocks.

───────────────────────────

Nightingale Cocktail	*1 oz. Coffee Southern*	*2 ozs. Gin*

Shake with ice cubes and strain into cocktail glass. Top with grated nutmeg.

───────────────────────────

One Exciting Night Cocktail	*1 dash orange juice*	*1/3 Italian Vermouth*
	1/3 French Vermouth	*1/3 Plymouth Gin*

Frost edge of Port Wine glass with sugar. Shake ingredients well with ice cubes and strain into glass. Squeeze lemon peel on top.

───────────────────────────

Opal Cocktail *(For 6 people)*	*3 jiggers (1 1/2 ozs. each) Gin*	*Powdered sugar to taste*
	2 jiggers orange juice	*Orange-flower water (buy in gourmet shop)*
	1 jigger Cointreau	

Shake with ice cubes and serve in cocktail glasses.

Opera Cocktail

1/6 Maraschino Liqueur   *1/6 Dubonnet*
2/3 dry Gin

Shake well with ice cubes and strain into cocktail glass. Squeeze orange peel on top.

Orange Blossom Cocktail

3/4 oz. orange juice   *1/4 teaspoon powdered*
2 ozs. Gin   *sugar*

Shake with ice cubes and strain into cocktail glass.

Orange Martini Cocktail
(For 6 people)

2 1/2 jiggers Gin   *Rind of 1 orange*
2 jiggers French Vermouth *Orange Bitters*
1 jigger Italian Vermouth

Combine Gin and Vermouths. Steep in this mixture the grated rind of 1 orange, white pith removed. Allow to soak for 1 to 2 hours. Then add ice cubes and shake well. Rinse out 6 cocktail glasses with Orange Bitters. Strain Gin and Vermouth mixture into these glasses and serve.

Pall Mall Cocktail

1 dash Orange Bitters   *1/3 Italian Vermouth*
2 dashes white Crème de   *1/3 French Vermouth*
*   Menthe*   *1/3 Plymouth Gin*

Shake well with ice cubes and strain into cocktail glass.

Paradise Cocktail

3/4 oz. orange juice   *2 ozs. Gin*
4 dashes Apricot Brandy

Shake with ice cubes and strain into cocktail glass.

Parisian Cocktail

1 oz. dry Vermouth   *3 dashes Crème de Cassis*
1 1/2 ozs. Gin

Shake with ice cubes and strain into cocktail glass.

Perfect Love Cocktail	1 dash Perfect Love Liqueur	1 jigger passion fruit nectar
	1 jigger (1 1/2 ozs.) dry Gin	

Stir with ice cubes and strain into cocktail glass.

Perfect Martini Cocktail	3/4 oz. dry Vermouth	3/4 oz. sweet Vermouth
	1 1/4 ozs. Gin	

Stir with ice and strain into cocktail glass. Add twist of orange peel.

Pink Baby Cocktail	1/2 Gin	1/4 syrup of citron
	1/4 Grenadine	White of 1 egg

Shake well with ice cubes and strain into cocktail glass.

Pink Gin Cocktail	1 dash Angostura Bitters	1 jigger (1 1/2 ozs.) Gin

Stir well and strain into cocktail glass.

Pink Lady Cocktail	White of 1 egg	1 jigger (1 1/2 ozs.) dry Gin
	3 dashes Grenadine	

Shake well with ice cubes and strain into cocktail glass.

Pink Rose Cocktail	White of 1 egg	1 dash heavy cream
	2 dashes Grenadine	1 jigger (1 1/2 ozs.) dry Gin
	1 dash fresh lemon juice	

Shake well with ice cubes and strain into cocktail glass.

Pinky Cocktail	1/2 dry Gin	White of 1 egg
	1/2 Grenadine	

Shake well with ice cubes and strain into cocktail glass.

Plaza Cocktail	1/3 Italian Vermouth	1/3 dry Gin
	1/3 French Vermouth	Pineapple slice

Shake Vermouths and Gin well with ice cubes. Strain into cocktail glass. Add slice of pineapple.

Polo Cocktail *(No. 1)*	*Juice of 1/4 lemon or 1/2* *lime* *1/3 Italian Vermouth*	*1/3 French Vermouth* *1/3 dry Gin*

Shake well with ice cubes and strain into cocktail glass.

Polo Cocktail *(No. 2)*	*1/6 orange juice* *1/6 grapefruit juice* *2/3 Plymouth Gin*	*Powdered sugar to taste* *(optional)*

Shake well with ice cubes and strain into cocktail glass.

Raspberry
Cocktail
(For 6 people)

Delightfully refreshing on a hot summer's day.

1 cup plus 6 additional *fresh raspberries* *2 jiggers (1 1/2 ozs. each)* *Gin*	*1 jigger Kirsch* *8 ozs. white wine (such as* *Moselle, Graves or* *Chablis)*

Slightly bruise 1 cup raspberries and add Gin. Soak for 2 hours, then strain. Add Kirsch and wine. Add cracked ice and shake well. Place a raspberry in 6 cocktail glasses and serve.

Red Lion *Cocktail*	*Juice of 1/2 lime* *3 dashes Grenadine*	*3 dashes Grand Marnier* *2 ozs. Gin*

Shake with ice cubes and strain into cocktail glass.

Richmond *Cocktail*	*1/3 Kina Lillet* *2/3 Plymouth Gin*	*Lemon peel*

Shake well with ice cubes and strain into cocktail glass. Squeeze lemon peel on top.

Rose Cocktail *(French Style No. 2)*	*1/4 Cherry Brandy* *1/4 Kirsch*	*1/2 dry Gin*

Stir well and strain into cocktail glass.

Royal Clover
Club Cocktail

This is similar to a Pink Lady.

	Juice of 1/2 lemon	Yolk of 1 egg
	2 dashes Grenadine	1 jigger (1 1/2 ozs.) Gin

Shake well with ice cubes and strain into cocktail glass.

Royal Cocktail (No. 1)

Juice of 1/2 lemon — 1 egg
1/2 tablespoon powdered sugar — 1 jigger dry Gin

Shake well with ice cubes and strain into cocktail glass.

Ruby Cocktail

4 dashes Grenadine — 1/2 oz. Apple Jack
2 ozs. Gin

Shake with ice cubes and strain into cocktail glass.

St. Vincent
(Cf. Galliano Liquore Base)

Salome Cocktail

1/3 French Vermouth — 1/3 Dubonnet
1/3 dry Gin

Shake well with ice cubes and strain into cocktail glass.

Salty Dog Cocktail

2 ozs. Gin or Vodka — Salt
Grapefruit juice

Put ice cubes in highball glass. Add Gin or Vodka and fill glass with grapefruit juice. Add salt to taste.

Silver Bullet Cocktail

1/2 Gin — 1/4 Kümmel
1/4 lemon juice

Shake well with ice cubes and strain into cocktail glass.

Silver Cocktail

2 dashes Maraschino Liqueur — 1/4 French Vermouth
2 dashes Orange Bitters — 1/2 dry Gin

Shake well with ice cubes and strain into cocktail glass.

| Society Cocktail | 3/4 oz. dry Vermouth
4 dashes Grenadine | 2 ozs. Gin |

Shake with ice cubes and strain into cocktail glass.

| Southern Gin
Cocktail | 2 dashes Curaçao
2 dashes Orange Bitters | 1 jigger dry Gin |

Shake well with ice cubes and strain into cocktail glass.

| Spencer Cocktail | 1 dash Angostura Bitters
1 dash orange juice | 1/3 Apricot Brandy
2/3 dry Gin |

Shake well with ice cubes and strain into cocktail glass. Add cherry, and squeeze orange peel on top.

Spring Feeling Cocktail
(Cf. Cordial Base)

| Susan-Shirley
Cocktail | 1 dash Angostura Bitters
1/3 Italian Vermouth | 2/3 dry Gin |

Stir well. Strain into cocktail glass with 1 ice cube. Squeeze lemon peel on top.

| Sweet Patotie
Cocktail | 1/4 orange juice
1/4 Cointreau | 1/2 dry Gin |

Shake well with ice cubes and strain into cocktail glass.

Thunderclap Cocktail
(Cf. Brandy Base)

| Velocity Cocktail | 1/3 dry Gin
2/3 Italian Vermouth | 1 slice of orange or a cherry |

Shake Gin and Vermouth well with ice cubes and strain into cocktail glass. Garnish with fruit.

| Vie Rose
Cocktail | 1/6 lemon juice
1/6 Grenadine | 1/3 dry Gin
1/3 Kirsch |

Shake well with ice cubes and strain into cocktail glass.

Webster Cocktail $^1/_8$ *lime juice* $^1/_4$ *French Vermouth*
$^1/_8$ *Apricot Brandy* $^1/_2$ *Plymouth Gin*

Shake well with ice cubes and strain into cocktail glass.

Wedding Belle $^1/_6$ *orange juice* $^1/_3$ *dry Gin*
Cocktail $^1/_6$ *Cherry Brandy* $^1/_3$ *Dubonnet*

Shake well with ice cubes and strain into cocktail glass.

Wembley   *1 dash Apricot Brandy* $^1/_3$ *French Vermouth*
Cocktail (No. 1)   *2 dashes Calvados or Apple* $^2/_3$ *dry Gin*
Jack

Shake well with ice cubes and strain into cocktail glass.

West Indian   *1 teaspoon sugar*   *1 jigger Burrough's*
Cocktail   *4 dashes Angostura Bitters*   *Beefeater Gin*
1 teaspoon fresh lemon
juice

Put sugar in medium-size tumbler, add other ingredients plus
1 ice cube. Stir and serve in same glass.

Western Rose   *1 dash lemon juice* $^1/_4$ *Apricot Brandy*
Cocktail $^1/_4$ *French Vermouth* $^1/_2$ *dry Gin*

Shake well with ice cubes and strain into cocktail glass.

White Baby $^1/_2$ *Gin* $^1/_4$ *syrup of citron*
Cocktail $^1/_4$ *Cointreau*

Shake well with ice cubes and strain into cocktail glass.

White Cargo   *1 scoop vanilla ice cream*   *1 jigger (1 $^1/_2$ ozs.) Gin*
Cocktail*

No ice is necessary. Put ingredients in blender. When
thoroughly mixed, serve in champagne glass.

White Lady Cocktail	*1/2 dry Gin* *1/4 Cointreau*	*1/4 lemon juice*

Shake well with ice cubes and strain into cocktail glass.

White Plush Cocktail	*1 jigger (1 1/2 ozs.)* *Maraschino Liqueur*	*1 jigger (1 1/2 ozs.) dry Gin* *1/2 pint of milk*

Shake well with ice cubes and strain into tall tumbler.

White Rose Cocktail	*1/4 Maraschino Liqueur* *3/4 dry Gin* *Juice of 1/4 orange*	*Juice of 1/4 lemon or 1/2 lime* *White of 1 egg*

Shake well with ice cubes and serve in cocktail glass.

White Wings Cocktail	*1/3 white Crème de Menthe*	*2/3 dry Gin*

Shake well with ice cubes and strain into cocktail glass.

Windsor Cocktail	*3/4 oz. green Crème de Menthe*	*2 ozs. Gin*

Stir and decorate with twist of lemon peel.

Yale Cocktail	*2 dashes Orange Bitters* *1 dash Angostura Bitters*	*1 jigger (1 1/2 ozs.) dry Gin* *Little syphon water*

Stir well Bitters and Gin and strain into cocktail glass. Add Club Soda and squeeze lemon peel on top.

Yellow Daisy Cocktail
(For 6 people)

This cocktail was invented by Richard William Clark, who died in 1884. He was a one-time Custer Scout, Pony Express rider, inspiration for the Deadwood Dick novels of E. L. Wheeler, and a friend of Buffalo Bill, Wild Bill Hickok, Poker Alice Tubbs, Calamity Jane. While his cocktail lives after him, Clark rests on Sunrise Mountain overlooking Deadwood Gulch, South Dakota.

2 jiggers (1 1/2 ozs. each) Gin *2 jiggers French Vermouth*	*1 jigger Grand Marnier* *3 dashes Pernod*

Shake well with ice cubes and strain into cocktail glass.

Zanzibar Cocktail
(Cf. Aperitif and Wine Bases)

Rum Base Popular rums include Rum Rico, Bacardi, Bacardi Añejo (expensive), Boca Chica, Puerto Rican, Rum Lemon Hart, dark Demerara, Three Daggers, dark Jamaica Rum, Don Qu, Puerto Rican, Rhum Megrita (dark) from the West Indies.

Apple Pie Cocktail

1/2 Rum
1/2 Italian Vermouth
4 dashes Apricot Brandy

2 dashes Grenadine
4 dashes lemon juice

Shake well with ice cubes and strain into cocktail glass.

Bacardi Cocktail

To make a Daiquiri, just eliminate the Grenadine.

Juice of 1/2 lime
2 ozs. Bacardi Rum

4 dashes Grenadine (or 1/2 teaspoon sugar)

Shake well with ice cubes and strain into cocktail glass.

Banana Daiquiri (No. 1)

1/3 ripe banana, chopped
1 level teaspoon sugar
1/2 oz. lime juice

1 1/2 ozs. white or silver Puerto Rican Rum

Put chopped banana in blender, add other ingredients and crushed ice. Blend for 10 to 20 seconds. Pour into Champagne glass.

Banana Daiquiri (No. 2)

1 part lime juice
1 part Banana Liqueur

3 parts dry Rum
Sugar to taste

Shake vigorously with ice cubes and strain into cocktail glass.

B.V.D. Cocktail

This cocktail is like a Rum Dry Martini.

Bolero

Juice of 1/2 lime
4 dashes fresh orange juice

1 oz. Brandy
1 oz. Rum

Shake with ice cubes and strain into cocktail glass.

Daiquiri Cocktail   To create a Frozen Daiquiri, put the ingredients into a blender with shaved or cracked ice.

1 jigger (1 1/2 ozs.) Rum   Juice of 1/4 lemon or 1/2
    (either Meyers, which is   lime
    dark, or Bacardi, which   1 teaspoon powdered sugar
    is golden amber)

Shake well with ice cubes and strain into cocktail glass.

Dunlop Cocktail   *1 dash Angostura Bitters   2/3 Rum*
    1/3 Sherry Wine

Shake well with ice cubes and strain into cocktail glass.

Fair and Warmer   *1/3 Italian Vermouth   2 dashes Curaçao*
Cocktail   *2/3 Rum*

Shake well with ice cubes and strain into cocktail glass.

Fluffy Ruffles
Cocktail
(Cf. Aperitif and Wine
Bases)

Fox Trot   *Juice of 1/2 lemon or 1 lime   1 jigger (1 1/2 ozs.) Rum*
Cocktail   *2 dashes orange Curaçao*

Shake well with ice cubes and strain into cocktail glass.

Gradeal (Special)   *1/4 dry Gin   1/2 Bacardi Rum*
Cocktail   *1/4 Apricot Brandy*

Shake well with ice cubes and strain into cocktail glass.

Jack Dempsey
Cocktail
(Cf. Gin Base)

| *Jacqueline Cocktail* | 1 oz. Cointreau
2 ozs. Rum | 1 oz. lime juice
Pinch sugar (optional) |

Shake well with ice cubes and strain into cocktail glass.

The Judge Jr.
Cocktail
(Cf. Gin Base)

Little Devil
Cocktail
(Cf. Gin Base)

Little Princess
Cocktail
(Cf. Aperitif and Wine Bases)

| *Mary Pickford Cocktail* | 1/2 Rum
1/2 pineapple juice
1 teaspoon Grenadine | 2 dashes Maraschino
    Liqueur |

Shake well with ice cubes and strain into cocktail glass.

| *Millionaire Cocktail (No. 1)* | Juice of 1 lime
1 dash Grenadine
1/3 Sloe Gin | 1/3 Apricot Brandy
1/3 Jamaica Rum |

Shake well and strain into cocktail glass.

| *Nevada Cocktail* | 1 1/2 jiggers light Rum
Juice of 1/2 grapefruit
Juice of 1 lime | 1 dash Angostura Bitters
1 teaspoon powdered sugar |

Shake well with ice cubes and strain into cocktail glass.

| *Palmetto Cocktail* | 2 dashes Orange Bitters
1/2 Italian Vermouth | 1/2 St. Croix Rum |

Shake well with ice cubes and strain into cocktail glass.

| *Parisian Blonde Cocktail* | 1/3 heavy cream
1/3 Curaçao | 1/3 Jamaica Rum |

Shake well with ice cubes and strain into cocktail glass.

Planter's Cocktail *(No. 1)*	*1/2 Rum* *1/2 fresh orange juice*	*1 dash fresh lemon juice*

Shake well with ice cubes and strain into cocktail glass.

───────────────────────────────────────

Poker Cocktail	*1/2 Italian Vermouth*	*1/2 Bacardi Rum*

Shake well and strain into cocktail glass.

───────────────────────────────────────

President Cocktail

This cocktail is similar to a Daiquiri. Orange juice is used instead of lemon juice to make it more golden in color.

2 dashes Grenadine   *1 jigger (1 1/2 ozs.) Rum*
Juice of 1/4 orange

Shake well with ice cubes and strain into cocktail glass.

───────────────────────────────────────

El Presidente Cocktail

3/4 oz. sweet Vermouth   *1 dash Curaçao*
2 ozs. Rum

Stir with ice cubes and strain. Add twist of orange peel.

───────────────────────────────────────

Robson Cocktail

1/8 lemon juice   *1/4 Grenadine*
1/8 orange juice   *1/2 Jamaica Rum*

Shake well with ice cubes and strain into cocktail glass.

───────────────────────────────────────

Santiago Cocktail

2 dashes Grenadine   *1 jigger Bacardi Rum*
2 dashes lemon juice

Shake well with ice cubes and strain into cocktail glass.

───────────────────────────────────────

September Morn Cocktail

Juice of 1/2 lemon or 1 lime   *1 jigger (1 1/2 ozs.) Bacardi*
1 dash Grenadine   *Rum*
White of 1 egg

Shake well with ice cubes and strain into cocktail glass.

───────────────────────────────────────

Sevilla Cocktail (No. 2)

1/2 teaspoon powdered   *1/2 Port Wine*
    sugar   *1/2 Bacardi Rum*
1 egg

Shake well with ice cubes and strain into cocktail glass.

Shanghai Cocktail

2 dashes Grenadine
3/8 lemon juice
$^1/_8$ Anisette
$^1/_2$ Jamaica Rum

Shake well with ice cubes and strain into cocktail glass.

Spanish Town Cocktail
(For 6 people)

5 jiggers Rum
1 teaspoon Curaçao

Pour ingredients into shaker and add large quantity of ice. Shake thoroughly. Serve in cocktail glasses with a little grated nutmeg.

Sunshine Cocktail (No. 2)

Juice of $^1/_4$ lemon
2 dashes Crème de Cassis
$^1/_2$ French Vermouth
$^1/_2$ Bacardi Rum

Shake well and strain into cocktail glass.

West Indies Yellowbird
(Tony Richardson, King's Inn, Freeport, Grand Bahamas)

1 oz. Liquore Galliano
1 $^1/_2$ ozs. light Rum
$^1/_4$ oz. Crème de Banane
2 ozs. pineapple juice
2 ozs. fresh orange juice
Fruit

Shake well with ice cubes. Pour into a tall glass with the ice cubes and decorate with fruit.

White Mink*
(Ted Barbera, New Smyrna, Florida)

1 oz. Liquore Galliano
3/4 oz. white Crème de Cacao
$^1/_2$ oz. Brandy
1 $^1/_2$ ozs. heavy cream
1 small scoop vanilla ice cream

Place in blender for short time until ice cream floats. Serve in 5 oz. cocktail glass.

White Mule
(Al Japur, Jacksonville, Florida)

1 oz. Liquore Galliano
3/4 oz. Anisette
3/4 oz. Vodka

Shake with ice cubes and strain into cocktail glass.

Windmill
(L. F. Nota, The Hague, Holland)

1/4 oz. Liquore Galliano
3/4 oz. Vodka

1/4 oz. white Crème de Cacao

Shake with ice cubes and strain into cocktail glass.

Yellow Bird

1/3 jigger Liquore Galliano
1 jigger White Rum

2 dashes Triple Sec
Juice of 1 lime

Shake with ice cubes and strain into stemmed glass. Garnish with slice of lime.

Southern Comfort Base

Used like an ordinary Whiskey, Southern Comfort, which is sweet Bourbon, 100 proof, tastes very different than any other basic liquor. It is an old-time American favorite. In the olden days of New Orleans, a talented gentleman, dissatisfied by the taste of even the finest Whiskeys of his day, combined rare and delicious ingredients to create this unusually smooth, special kind of basic liquor. Its formula is still a family secret.

Atomic Cocktail

Juice of 1/2 lime
2 ozs. Southern Comfort

3/4 oz. Akvavit
4 dashes Brandy

Shake with ice cubes and strain into cocktail glass.

Black Widow

2 ozs. Rum
1 oz. Southern Comfort

Juice of 1/2 lime
Sugar to taste

Shake with ice cubes and strain into cocktail glass.

Cuba Libre Supreme

1 jigger (1 1/2 ozs.) Southern Comfort

Juice and rind of 1/2 lime
Coca-Cola

Squeeze lime over ice cubes in tall glass. Add rind and Southern Comfort. Top with Coca-Cola, stir and serve.

Flying Grasshopper Cocktail

3/4 oz. white Crème de Menthe

3/4 oz. Southern Comfort
3/4 oz. Vodka

Shake well with ice cubes and strain into cocktail glass.

French "90"   Juice of 1/2 lemon   1/2 teaspoon sugar
2 ozs. Southern Comfort (or   (optional)
    Brandy)   Champagne, chilled

Shake all ingredients except Champagne well with ice cubes. Strain into tall glass containing shaved ice. Top with Champagne.

Frozen Southern   Juice of 1/2 lime   1 dash Maraschino Liqueur
Comfort   1/2 teaspoon sugar   2 scoops shaved ice
2 ozs. Southern Comfort

Serve unstrained in Champagne glass with short straws.

Omar's Delight   Juice of 1/2 lime   1 jigger (1 1/2 ozs.)
Cocktail   4 dashes lemon juice   Southern Comfort
3 dashes Curaçao

Shake well with ice cubes. Strain and serve in Champagne glass.

Oscar Haimo   Mr. Haimo is President of the International Bar Managers'
Cocktail   Association.

1 jigger (1 1/2 ozs.)   2 dashes Canada Dry Club
    Southern Comfort   Soda
3 dashes Campari Bitters

Put Southern Comfort and Bitters in Old-Fashioned glass with ice cubes. Top with Club Soda. Add lemon peel and stir.

Pacific Cocktail   3/4 oz. heavy cream   2 ozs. Southern Comfort

Shake with ice cubes and strain into cocktail glass.

Puffs   1/2 pint milk   Club Soda
2 ozs. Southern Comfort

Shake with ice cubes and strain into tall glass containing one cube of ice. Top with Club Soda. Serve with straws.

| *Puzzler Cocktail* | *1 jigger (1 1/2 ozs.)* | *Pineapple-grapefruit juice* |
| | *Southern Comfort* | |

Pack a tall glass with cracked ice. Add Southern Comfort. Top with juice and serve.

Rhett Butler Cocktail	*1 jigger (1 1/2 ozs.)*	*1/2 teaspoon sugar*
	Southern Comfort	*Juice of 1/2 lime*
	1 teaspoon Curaçao	*Juice of 1/2 lemon*

Shake with ice cubes. Strain into cocktail glass.

| *Royal Southern Comfort Cocktail* | *3/4 oz. heavy cream* | *2 ozs. Southern Comfort* |
| | *3/4 oz. Crème de Moyaux* | |

Shake well with ice cubes and strain in Champagne glass.

| *Southern Comfort Daiquiri Cocktail* | *Juice of 1/2 lime* | *1 jigger (1 1/2 ozs.)* |
| | *1 teaspoon sugar* | *Southern Comfort* |

Shake well with ice cubes. Strain into cocktail glass.

| *Southern Comfort Manhattan Cocktail* | *1/2 oz. French dry Vermouth* | *1 dash Aromatic Bitters (optional)* |
| | *1 jigger (1 1/2 ozs.) Southern Comfort* | |

Stir with ice cubes until thoroughly chilled. Strain into cocktail glass and top with cherry.

| *Southern Comfort 'n Bourbon* *(Very potent!)* | *1/2 jigger (3/4 oz.) Southern Comfort* | *1/2 jigger (3/4 oz.) Bourbon* |

Pour over cracked ice in short glass. Serve with twist of lemon peel.

| *Southern Comfort Old-Fashioned* | *1 dash Angostura Bitters* | *1/2 oz. Sparkling Water* |
| | *1/2 teaspoon sugar (optional)* | *1 jigger (1 1/2 ozs.) Southern Comfort* |

Stir Bitters, sugar and Sparkling Water in glass. Add ice cubes and Southern Comfort. Garnish with fruit, if desired.

Southern Comfort on the Rocks	Pour 1 jigger (1 1/2 ozs.) Southern Comfort over ice cubes in a short glass. Add twist of lemon peel, if desired.

Southern Dream
(Cf. Galliano Liquore Base)

Southern Gal
(Cf. Galliano Liquore Base)

Tequila Base

Acapulco

1/2 oz. Cointreau
2 ozs. Tequila
Juice of 1/2 lime

6 dashes unsweetened pineapple juice

Shake with ice cubes and strain into cocktail glass.

Bloody Maria

1 1/2 ozs. Tequila Sauza
3 ozs. tomato juice
1/2 oz. fresh lemon juice

1 dash Worcestershire sauce
Salt and pepper to taste

Shake with ice cubes and strain into 8-oz. Delmonico glass, or serve on the rocks in a tall glass.

Daiquiri Tequila

1 jigger (1 1/2 ozs.) Tequila Sauza

Juice of 1/2 lime
1 teaspoon powdered sugar

Shake well with ice cubes and strain into cocktail glass.

Manhattan Tequila

1 1/2 ozs. Tequila
1/2 oz. sweet Vermouth

1 dash Angostura Bitters (optional)

Stir with ice cubes. Strain into cocktail glass and serve with a cherry.

Margarita

1 1/2 ozs. Tequila

1 oz. lime juice

Shake with ice cubes. Rub rim of glass with lime, then dip into salt. Sip over salted edge.

| *Martini Tequila* | *3 parts Tequila*
1 part dry Vermouth | *Olive, pearl onion or twist*
of lemon peel |

Stir with ice cubes until chilled. Strain and serve with green olive, pearl onion or lemon twist.

| *New Life* | *1 lump sugar*
5 drops Angostura Bitters | *1 1/2 ozs. Tequila Sauza*
Twist of lemon peel |

Muddle sugar and Bitters in Old-Fashioned glass. Fill glass with ice cubes. Add Tequila Sauza and twist of lemon peel. Stir well and serve.

| *Sauza and Tonic* | *2 ozs. Tequila Sauza* | *1/2 lime or lemon* |

Squeeze lime over ice cubes in 8-oz. glass. Add Tequila Sauza and top with water or Soda. Stir.

Sauza Highball Pour 1 1/2 ozs. Tequila Sauza into highball glass filled with ice. Top with water or soda. Stir.

Vodka Base When enjoying caviar, it is customary to serve Vodka in a jigger (1 1/2 to 2 ozs.) and to place the jigger in a nest of crushed ice in an Old-Fashioned glass. Then it is drunk neat. The imported Vodkas used at the Richelieu Bar are Stolichnaya, 80 proof, distilled and bottled in Moscow, imported by Kraus Bros. of Philadelphia; Russkaya, 80 proof, imported by Munson Shaw; Borzoi, an English Vodka, 91 proof, imported by Kobrand Corporation; and Masquers English Vodka, 91 proof, imported from England by Mohr International.

Auburn
(Cf. Galliano Liquore
Base)

| *Ballet Rousse* | *2 ozs. Vodka*
1 dash fresh lemon juice | *1 dash Crème de Cassis* |

Shake with ice cubes and strain into cocktail glass.

Black Russian	*1 jigger (1 1/2 ozs.) Vodka*	*3/4 oz. Kahlúa*

Serve in Old-Fashioned glass over ice cubes.

Bloody Bullshot	*1 jigger (1 1/2 ozs.) Vodka*	*Beef bouillon (cold)*
	Tomato juice	

Combine ingredients and serve in highball glass on the rocks.

Bloody Mary	*1 jigger (1 1/2 ozs.) Vodka*	*1 dash Worcestershire sauce*
	2 jiggers tomato juice	*Salt and pepper to taste*
	1/3 jigger lemon juice	

Shake well with ice cubes and strain into Delmonico glass, or serve on the rocks in a highball glass.

Blushin' Russian

This is made with Russian Vodka imported by Munson Shaw. Russkaya is produced from grain in Russia, and is marketed at 80 proof. Chambraise is made with the tiny wild strawberries of France, known as Fraises des Bois, in Chambery, a small town in the French Alps district known as La Haute Savoie. It is made by the firm of Chambery-Comoz, famous since 1854. The color of this cocktail is a cheerful red.

1/2 Russkaya Vodka	*Tonic Water*
1/2 Chambraise	

Mix Vodka and Chambraise over ice cubes in highball glass. Top with Tonic Water.

Boyar	*2/3 Vodka*	*1/3 Cherry Liqueur*

Stir over ice cubes and strain into cocktail glass.

Brave Bull	*2 parts Vodka*	*1 part Tequila*

Serve over ice with a lemon twist in an Old-Fashioned glass.

Chevoney
(Cf. Galliano Liquore
Base)

Flying Grasshopper
(Cf. Southern Comfort Base)

Flying Tiger
(Cf. Galliano Liquore Base)

Galliatini
(Cf. Galliano Liquore Base)

Golden Lilli
(Cf. Galliano Liquore Base)

Goldfinger
(Cf. Galliano Liquore Base)

Ivan the Terrible   2 ozs. Gordon's Vodka   1 oz. green Chartreuse

Stir and serve on the rocks in an Old-Fashioned glass.

Katinka   2 ozs. Masquers English   1 dash fresh lemon juice
              Vodka   1 oz. Apricot Liqueur·

Shake with ice cubes and strain into cocktail glass.

Las Vegas
(Cf. Galliano Liquore Base)

Lower Depths   2/3 Vodka   Black coffee
                   1/3 Irish Whiskey

Pour Vodka and Whiskey over shaved ice in an Old-Fashioned glass. Top with hot black coffee.

Moscow Mule   1/2 lime   Schweppes Ginger Beer
                  2 ozs. Vodka

Squeeze juice from lime into mug. Add remaining piece of lime and Vodka. Top with Schweppes Ginger Beer. Stir.

Ochi   1/2 Vodka   1/4 sweet Vermouth
           1/4 dry Vermouth   Black Olive

Stir and strain into cocktail glass. Serve with a black olive.

Palm Beach
(Cf. Galliano Liquore Base)

Pushkin   *2/3 Vodka*   *1/3 Crème de Cacao*

Stir and strain into cocktail glass, or serve on the rocks.

─────────────────────────────────

Russian Cocktail   *1/3 Crème de Cacao*   *1/3 Vodka*
                         1/3 dry Gin

Shake well with ice cubes and strain into cocktail glass.

─────────────────────────────────

Sea Gull   *2 ozs. Vodka*   *1 oz. Apricot Brandy*
                 1 dash dry Vermouth

Shake with ice cubes and strain into cocktail glass.

─────────────────────────────────

Tovarich   *1 jigger (1 1/2 ozs.)*   *2/3 jigger Kümmel*
                 Russkaya Vodka   *Juice of 1/2 lime*

Shake with ice cubes and strain into cocktail glass.

─────────────────────────────────

Troyka   *2/3 Vodka*   *Juice of 1/2 lime*
               1/3 Jamaica Rum

Shake with ice cubes and strain into cocktail glass.

─────────────────────────────────

Vodka Martini   To make a Vodka Gibson, serve with cocktail onions instead of olive or lemon twist.

1/3 dry Vermouth   *2/3 Vodka*

Stir and strain into cocktail glass, or serve on the rocks. Garnish with olive or lemon twist.

─────────────────────────────────

Vodka Richelieu   *1 jigger (1 1/2 ozs.) Vodka*   *Juice of 1/2 lemon or lime*
                        1 jigger Cherry Heering

Shake with ice cubes and strain into cocktail glass.

Volga Boatman	*1 jigger (1 1/2 ozs.) Vodka* *1 jigger Cherry Brandy*	*1 jigger fresh orange juice*

Shake well with ice cubes and strain into cocktail glass.

Warlock
(Cf. Galliano Liquore
Base)

White Nights	*2 ozs. Vodka*	*1 dash Pernod*

Shake with ice cubes and strain into cocktail glass.

White Russian	*3/4 oz. white Crème de Cacao*	*1 jigger (1 1/2 ozs.) Vodka*

Stir together and serve on the rocks.

White Spider	*1 oz. white Crème de Menthe*	*2 ozs. Vodka*

Stir together and serve on the rocks.

Whiskey Base Scotch and Rye drinks come under this Whiskey classification. Whiskey is a very old spirit known to the ancient Chinese, the Arabs and the Moors, but it is likely the Celts invented Whiskey. It contains barley malt as part of the mash, plus other carefully blended grains. Only time in wood can soften the taste. The mash is grain and water brought to a boil, cooked awhile, then allowed to ferment for a few days, producing a beer that is then distilled. Some Whiskey is aged in old Sherry casks from Spain, or in other casks called "plains" that have never contained Whiskey. Still other casks are rebuilt from Rum barrels or American barrels that once held Bourbon. Thus each Whiskey develops an individual subtlety. These are blended in various proportions to make the famous brands. The aging is the most important part of the process, done in cool climates in storehouses that are damp. Each brand has its own character and its own following.

Barbary Coast	*1 dash heavy cream* *1 dash Crème de Cacao* *1/2 oz. Gin*	*1/2 oz. Scotch* *1/2 oz. Rum*

Shake with shaved ice and strain into Champagne glass.

Bloody John	1 jigger (1 1/2 ozs.) tomato juice	1 dash fresh lemon juice
	1 jigger John Jamieson Irish Whiskey	1 dash Worcestershire sauce

Shake well with ice cubes and strain into Delmonico glass, or serve on the rocks in a highball glass.

Bobby Burns Cocktail	1/2 Italian Vermouth	3 dashes Bénédictine
	1/2 Scotch Whisky	

Shake well with ice cubes and strain into cocktail glass. Add lemon twist if desired.

Boiler Maker	1 jigger (1 1/2 ozs.) Scotch	Beer

Mix Scotch in a glass of Beer.

Britannia	1 jigger (1 1/2 ozs.) Britannia Whisky	1/2 Calvet Orange

Pour over crushed ice in cocktail glass and add twist of lemon.

Brooklyn Cocktail	1 dash Amer Picon	2/3 Canadian Club Whisky
	1 dash Maraschino Liqueur	1/3 French Vermouth

Shake well and strain into cocktail glass.

Byrrh Cocktail	1/3 French Vermouth	1/3 Byrrh
	1/3 Canadian Club Whisky	

Shake well with ice cubes and strain into cocktail glass.

Commodore Cocktail	1 dash Grenadine	1 jigger Canadian Club Whisky
	2 dashes Orange Bitters	
	Juice of 1/2 lime or 1/4 lemon	

Shake well with ice cubes and strain into cocktail glass.

Cowboy Cocktail	*2/3 Whiskey*	*1/3 heavy cream*

Shake well with ice cubes and strain into cocktail glass.

Creole Cocktail	*1/2 Rye or Canadian Club Whisky*	*2 dashes Bénédictine*
	1/2 Italian Vermouth	*2 dashes Amer Picon*

Stir well and strain into cocktail glass. Twist lemon peel on top.

Crow Cocktail	*1/3 Whiskey*	*1 dash Grenadine*
	2/3 fresh lemon juice	

Shake well with ice cubes and strain into cocktail glass.

Dandy Cocktail
(Cf. Aperitif and Wine Bases)

De Rigueur Cocktail	*1/2 Whiskey*	*1/4 honey*
	1/4 grapefruit juice	

Shake well with ice cubes and strain into cocktail glass.

Dixie Whiskey Cocktail *(For 6 people)*	*2 lumps sugar*	*6 jiggers Whiskey*
	1 teaspoon Angostura Bitters	*1 teaspoon Curaçao*
	1 teaspoon fresh lemon juice	*2 teaspoons Crème de Menthe*

Add ice cubes and shake carefully. Serve in cocktail glasses.

Duppy Cocktail *(For 6 people)*	*6 jiggers (1 1/2 ozs. each) Whiskey*	*5 drops Orange Bitters*
	Few cloves	*3 jiggers Curaçao*

Put ingredients in shaker with ice cubes. Shake well and serve in cocktail glasses.

Elk's Own Cocktail
(Cf. Aperitif and Wine Bases)

Everybody's Irish Cocktail

This is a real St. Patrick's Day favorite.

3 dashes green Crème de Menthe
6 dashes green Chartreuse

1 jigger (1 1/2 ozs.) Irish Whiskey

Shake well with ice cubes and strain into cocktail glass. Garnish with green olive.

Everything-But Cocktail

1/4 Whiskey
1/4 Gin
1/4 fresh lemon juice
1/4 fresh orange juice

1 egg
1 dash Apricot Brandy
Powdered sugar

Shake well with ice cubes and strain into cocktail glass.

Fox River Cocktail

4 dashes Peach Bitters
1/4 Crème de Cacao

3/4 Canadian Club Whisky

Stir and pour into wine glass. Squeeze lemon peel on top.

"Hoots Mon" Cocktail

1/4 Kina Lillet
1/4 Italian Vermouth

1/4 Scotch Whisky

Stir well and strain into cocktail glass.

Hot Deck Cocktail

1 dash Jamaica Ginger
1/4 Italian Vermouth

3/4 Canadian Club Whisky

Shake well with ice cubes and strain into cocktail glass.

Hurricane Cocktail
(Cf. Gin Base)

Ink Street Cocktail

1/3 Canadian Club Whisky
1/3 fresh orange juice

1/3 fresh lemon juice

Shake well with ice cubes and strain into cocktail glass.

John Wood Cocktail
(Cf. Aperitif and Wine Bases)

Jupiter Cocktail

1 oz. Coffee Southern Liqueur	1 oz. Scotch
3/4 oz. dry Vermouth	3 dashes orange Curaçao

Stir with ice cubes and strain. Decorate with cherry.

King Cole Cocktail

1 jigger (1 1/2 ozs.) Rye or Canadian Club Whisky	1 dash Fernet Branca
	2 dashes sugar syrup

Add 1 lump ice and stir well; decorate with slices of orange and pineapple, if desired.

Los Angeles Burg-Farnham Cocktail
(For 4 people)

Juice of 1 lemon	4 teaspoons powdered sugar
4 jiggers (1 1/2 ozs. each) Whiskey	1 dash Italian Vermouth
1 egg	

Shake well with ice cubes and strain into cocktail glasses.

Mamie Taylor

2 ozs. Scotch Whisky	Canada Dry Ginger Ale
1 lemon slice	

Place 2 ice cubes in a tall glass. Add Scotch and lemon. Fill with Ginger Ale. Serve with stirrer.

Manhattan Cocktail
(Cf. Aperitif and Wine Bases)

Manhattan Cocktail (Dry)
(Cf. Aperitif and Wine Bases)

Manhattan Cocktail (Sweet)
(Cf. Aperitif and Wine Bases)

Mickie Walker Cocktail	1 dash Grenadine 1 dash fresh lemon juice	1/4 Italian Vermouth 3/4 Scotch Whisky

Shake well with ice cubes and strain into cocktail glass.

Morning Glory Cocktail
(Cf. Brandy Base)

Mountain Cocktail
(Cf. Aperitif and Wine Base)

New York Cocktail	1 jigger (1 1/2 ozs.) Rye Whiskey 1 dash Grenadine	1/2 teaspoon powdered sugar Juice of 1/2 lime

Shake well with ice cubes and strain into cocktail glass. Top with twist of orange peel.

Oh Henry! Cocktail	1/3 Bénédictine 1/3 Whiskey	Ginger Ale

Stir well and serve in 8-oz. Delmonico glass. Top with Ginger Ale.

Old-Fashioned Cocktail	1/2 lump sugar 1 dash Aromatic Bitters 2 dashes Club Soda	1 jigger (1 1/2 ozs.) Spirits (Scotch, Rye or Bourbon, as desired)

Muddle sugar saturated with Aromatic Bitters. Add Club Soda in Old-Fashioned glass with ice cubes. Top with spirit desired. (Sometimes water is used instead of Club Soda.)

"Old Pal" Cocktail	1/3 Canadian Club Whisky Bourbon or Scotch	1/3 French Vermouth 1/3 Campari

Shake well with ice cubes and strain into cocktail glass.

Opening Cocktail	1/4 Grenadine 1/4 Italian Vermouth	1/2 Canadian Club Whisky

Shake well with ice cubes and strain into cocktail glass.

Paddy Cocktail | *1/2 Paddy Irish Whiskey* | *1 dash Angostura Bitters*
1/2 Italian Vermouth

Shake well with ice cubes and strain into cocktail glass.

Palmer Cocktail | *1 jigger (1 1/2 ozs.)* | *1 dash Angostura Bitters*
Canadian Club Whisky | *1 dash fresh lemon juice*

Shake well with ice cubes and strain into cocktail glass.

Rattlesnake Cocktail
(For 6 people)

4 jiggers (6 ozs.) Rye Whiskey | *White of 2 eggs*
Few dashes Pernod

Shake very thoroughly with ice cubes and strain through a fine sieve. Serve in cocktail glasses.

Rob Roy Cocktail

3/4 oz. sweet or dry Vermouth | *2 ozs. Scotch*
1 dash Angostura Bitters

Stir with ice cubes and strain. Garnish with cherry or lemon peel.

Shamrock Cocktail

3 dashes green Crème de Menthe | *1/2 French Vermouth*
3 dashes green Chartreuse | *1/2 Irish Whiskey*

Shake well with ice cubes and strain into cocktail glass.

Silent Third

1 oz. Cointreau | *1 oz. fresh lemon juice*
2 ozs. Scotch Whisky

Shake well with ice cubes and strain into cocktail glass.

Soul Kiss (No. 2)

1/6 fresh orange juice | *1/3 French Vermouth*
1/6 Dubonnet (Blend or Red) | *1/3 Canadian Club Whisky*

Shake well with ice cubes and strain into cocktail glass. Top with orange slice.

Stone Fence	*1 jigger (1 1/2 ozs.) Scotch Whisky*	*2 dashes Angostura Bitters Soda Water*

Use tall tumbler and one ice cube. Add Whisky and Bitters, then fill with Soda Water.

Strawberry Cocktail
(For 6 people)

This is a good drink for beginning drinkers. Pass 1 pound of fresh strawberries through a hair-sieve and pour the juice into a shaker together with juice of 1 orange and a dash of Whiskey. Add a few ice cubes. Shake carefully and serve in cocktail glasses.

Thistle Cocktail	*2 dashes Angostura Bitters* *1/2 Italian Vermouth*	*1/2 Scotch Whisky*

Stir and strain into cocktail glass.

Thunderclap Cocktail
(Cf. Brandy Base)

Up-to-Date Cocktail	*2 dashes Grand Marnier* *2 dashes Angostura Bitters*	*1/2 Sherry* *1/2 Canadian Club Whisky*

Shake well with ice cubes and strain into cocktail glass.

Ward Eight Cocktail	*2 dashes Grenadine* *1/4 fresh orange juice*	*1/4 fresh lemon juice* *1/4 Rye Whiskey*

Shake well with ice cubes and strain into cocktail glass.

Wembley Cocktail (No. 2)	*1/3 Scotch Whisky* *1/3 French Vermouth*	*1/3 pineapple juice*

Shake well with ice cubes and strain into cocktail glass.

Whiskey Special Cocktail *(For 6 people)*	*3 jiggers (1 1/2 ozs. each) Whiskey*	*2 jiggers French Vermouth* *1 jigger orange juice*

Shake with ice cubes. Strain into cocktail glasses and serve, adding a little grated nutmeg.

Whisper Cocktail
(For 6 people)

3 jiggers (1 1/2 ozs. each)
Whiskey

3 jiggers French Vermouth
3 jiggers Italian Vermouth

Pour into a shaker half full of cracked ice. Shake well and strain into cocktail glasses.

Zazarak

This is similar to an Old-Fashioned except for the use of Pernod.

1 dash Pernod
1 dash Bitters

1 lump sugar
1 jigger (1 1/2 ozs.) Rye

Put Pernod in Old-Fashioned glass. Swirl it around inside of glass, then add Bitters and sugar. Serve Rye on the side in the jigger. Guest or waiter pours this into the drink when it is served.

Index for Other Mixed Drinks

Grog
(Begins on p. 177)

Highballs
(Begin on p. 178)

Addington Highball
Amer Picon Highball
American Glory Highball
Apple Jack Highball
Barbary Coast Highball
Black Velvet
Bon Soir Highball
Brandy Highball (No. 1)
Brandy Highball (No. 2)
Bulldog Highball
Cassis-Kirsch Highball
Durkee Highball
Harry's Highball
Harvard Highball

Juleps
(Begin on p. 180)

Champagne Julep
Mint Julep
Southern Mint Julep

Puffs
(Begin on p. 181)

Southern Comfort Puff

Punches
(Begin on p. 181)

Bombay Punch
Celebration Punch
Champagne Punch
Claret Punch
Daiquiri Punch (No. 1)
Daiquiri Punch (No. 2)
Gin Rickey Punch
Milk Punch
Sensation Punch

Rickeys
(Begin on p. 183)

Apple Jack Rickey
Royal Rickey

Rum Rickey
Whiskey Rickey

Sangarees
(Begin on p. 184)

Brandy Sangaree
Claret Sangaree
Hot Sangaree
Port Sangaree
Sauterne Sangaree

Scaffas
(Begin on p. 185)

Brandy Scaffa
Gin Scaffa
Rum Scaffa
Whiskey Scaffa

Slings
(Begin on p. 185)

Apple Jack Sling
Fancy Sling
Gin Sling
Hot Rum Sling
Raffles Hotel Sling
Singapore Sling
Straits Sling

Smashes
(Begin on p. 187)

Sours
(Begin on p. 187)

Swizzles
(Begin on p. 187)

Toddies
(Begin on p. 187)

Rum Toddy
Apple Jack, Brandy, Gin,
    Tequila, Vodka or Whiskey
    Toddy
Southern Comfort Toddy

Cobblers   Like the Julep, the Cobbler is a cooling, generous drink of American origin, a favorite in warmer climates. It is usual to decorate a Cobbler before serving.

———————————————————————————

Southern Comfort Cobbler

2 ozs. Southern Comfort   *4 dashes Curaçao*

Fill goblet halfway with cracked ice. Add Southern Comfort and Curaçao. Stir. Decorate with slice of lemon and a sprig of mint, if available.

———————————————————————————

Collins

Gin Collins   *1 oz. Cointreau*   *Carbonated Water*
            2 ozs. Gin   *Slice of lemon or orange*
            Juice of 1/2 lemon   *Cherry*

Shake Cointreau, Gin and lemon juice well with ice cubes. Strain into a 12-oz. Collins glass and add several more ice cubes. Fill with Carbonated Water and stir gently. Garnish with lemon or orange slice and a cherry.

———————————————————————————

John Collins   Same as a Tom Collins but use Holland Gin instead of Gin. In England as well as in America, Scotch Whisky is used instead of Holland Gin.

———————————————————————————

Rum Collins   Same as a John Collins or Tom Collins except it uses Rum as a base, with a choice of the Rums.

———————————————————————————

Tom Collins
(As served at Le Chateau Richelieu)

Juice of 1/2 lemon   *1 jigger (1 1/2 ozs.) dry Gin*
1/2 teaspoon powdered   *Soda Water*
*   sugar*

Shake lemon juice, sugar and Gin well with ice cubes. Strain into tall tumbler. Add ice cubes and top with Soda Water. Decorate with orange slice and cherry. Serve with a straw. (You may use a variety of liquors instead of the Gin: Apple Jack, Aquavit, Brandy, Sloe Gin, Tequila, Vodka or Whiskey. Each Collins bears the name of the liquor used.)

Coolers

Apricot Cooler

Juice *1/2* lemon or 1 lime	2 dashes Grenadine
1 jigger (1 *1/2* ozs.) Apricot Brandy	Club Soda

Shake juice, Brandy and Grenadine well with ice cubes. Strain into tall tumbler and fill with Club Soda.

Bourbon Cooler

Same as Remsen Cooler except Bourbon is used instead of Gin.

Calypso or Rum Cooler

Same as Remsen Cooler except Rum is used instead of Gin.

Champagne Cooler
(Expensive)

1 oz. Cointreau	Champagne
1 oz. French Brandy	

Pour Cointreau and Brandy into a 12-oz. Collins glass half-filled with cracked ice. Fill with Champagne. Stir gently. Decorate with sprig of mint, if available.

Country Club Cooler

2 jiggers (1 *1/2* ozs. each) dry Vermouth	1 dash Grenadine
	Club Soda

Place ice cubes in tall glass. Add Vermouth and Grenadine. Fill with Club Soda.

Harvard Cooler

Juice of *1/2* lemon or 1 lime	*1/2* tablespoon sugar
1 jigger (1 *1/2* ozs.) Apple Jack or Calvados	Club Soda

Shake all ingredients except Club Soda well with ice cubes. Strain into tall tumbler and fill with Club Soda.

Highland Cooler

1 teaspoon powdered sugar	2 dashes Angostura Bitters
Juice of *1/2* lemon	Ginger Ale

Shake sugar, juice and Bitters with ice cubes and strain into tall glass. Top with Ginger Ale.

Honolulu Cooler	Juice of 1/2 lime	Pineapple juice
	1 jigger Southern Comfort	

Pack 12-oz. glass with cracked ice. Add lime juice, then Southern Comfort. Fill glass with pineapple juice. Serve with a straw.

Lemon Cooler	1 jigger (1 1/2 ozs.)	Bitter Lemon
	Southern Comfort	

Pour Southern Comfort over ice cubes in a highball glass. Fill with Bitter Lemon. Serve with straw.

Lone Tree Cooler	Juice of 1/4 lemon	1/3 French Vermouth
	Juice of 1 orange	2/3 dry Gin
	1 dash Grenadine	Club Soda

Shake all ingredients except Club Soda well with ice cubes. Strain into tumbler and fill with Club Soda.

Long Tom Cooler	Juice of 1/2 lemon	1/2 tablespoon sugar
	1 jigger (1 1/2 ozs.) dry Gin	Club Soda

Shake lemon juice, sugar and Gin with ice cubes. Strain into tall tumbler and add the ice cubes. Fill with Club Soda.

Mint Cooler	1 jigger (1 1/2 ozs.) Scotch	Club Soda
	3 dashes Crème de Menthe	

Put Scotch and Crème de Menthe in tumbler with ice cubes. Fill with Club Soda.

Moonlight Cooler	1/2 tablespoon powdered sugar	1 jigger (1 1/2 ozs.) Calvados or Apple Jack
	Juice of 1 lemon	Club Soda

Shake all ingredients except Club Soda well with ice cubes. Strain into long tumbler. Fill with Club Soda. Decorate with slices of fruit in season.

Remsen Cooler	1 teaspoon sugar or 4 dashes Grenadine	2 ozs. Gin Club Soda

Put sugar (or Grenadine) and Gin into 12-oz. glass with ice cubes. Top with Club Soda. Decorate with spiral of lemon rind.

Shady Grove Cooler	1/2 tablespoon sugar 1 jigger (1 1/2 ozs.) dry Gin	Juice of 1/2 lemon Schweppes Ginger Beer

Put sugar, Gin and lemon juice into tall tumbler. Top with Ginger Beer.

Whiskey Cooler Same as a Remsen Cooler except Whiskey is used instead of Gin.

Wine Cooler Same as a Remsen Cooler except 3 ozs. of wine desired is used instead of Gin. Fill with Club Soda.

Cups Wine cups are refreshing mealtime companions, especially suitable for Thanksgiving and Christmas festivities. These miniature punches, made with fruits, liqueurs and wines, add a touch of gaiety to home dining.

Burgundy Cup
(For 4 people)
	1 jigger (1 1/2 ozs.)
	    Benedictine
	2 jiggers Brandy
	1 oz. white Curaçao
	1 pint Burgundy
		4 tablespoons powdered
		    sugar
		Orange slices
		Pineapple slices
		Cherries

Mix ingredients in large pitcher with ice cubes. Add fruit and stir well. Top with fresh mint, if available. Serve in wine glasses.

Champagne Cup
(No. 1)
(For 4 people)
	1 orange, sliced
	1/2 lemon, sliced
	3 slices pineapple
	1 jigger (1 1/2 ozs.)
	    Chartreuse
		1 jigger Maraschino Liqueur
		    or Cherry Liqueur
		1 jigger Brandy
		1 Bottle Champagne

Half fill large glass pitcher with cracked ice. Add fruit, Liqueurs and Brandy. Let chill thoroughly. Add chilled Champagne at last moment before serving in Champagne glasses.

Champagne Cup (No. 2)
(For 4 people)

2 ozs. Brandy
2 tablespoons powdered sugar
1 oz. orange Curaçao
1/2 oz. Maraschino Liqueur or Cherry Liqueur
1/2 oz. Grand Marnier
1 quart Champagne

Thoroughly mix sugar with Liqueurs in a large glass pitcher. Half fill with cracked ice. Garnish with slices of pineapple and orange, cherries or berries in season and a strip of cucumber peel. Top with chilled Champagne and add fresh mint, if available. Serve in Champagne glasses.

Cider Cup
(For 4 people)

1 jigger (1 1/2 ozs.) Maraschino Liqueur
1 jigger Curaçao
1 jigger Brandy
1 quart cider
1 split Club Soda

Stir ingredients gently in a small glass pitcher. Garnish with slices of fruit in season.

Claret Cup
(For 4 people)

1 jigger (1 1/2 ozs.) Maraschino Liqueur
2 jiggers Curaçao
2 tablespoons powdered sugar
1 quart Claret Burgundy

Stir gently in large glass pitcher with 4 cubes of ice. Decorate with slices of orange and pineapple, and a very small slice of cucumber peel. Top with 3 or 4 sprigs of fresh mint, if available.

Orange Cup
(For 12 people)

Juice of 6 oranges
16 ozs. Rum
2 pints light white Wine
2 ozs. Cointreau

Strain orange juice into punch bowl. Place large block of ice in bowl and add rest of ingredients. Stir well.

Peach Cup
(For 6 people)

1 or 2 ripe peaches
2 bottles light Still Moselle Wine
2 or 3 tablespoons powdered sugar
1 bottle Sparkling Moselle

Carefully peel peaches. Cut into small pieces, losing as little juice as possible. Place into a punch bowl or soup tureen. Pour 1 bottle of Wine over the fruit and add powdered sugar. Stir gently and cover carefully, allowing to stand for 20 to 30 minutes. Then add another bottle of Still Moselle, previously chilled. Before serving, add a bottle of Sparkling Moselle. Taste and add more sugar, if required. Serve in medium-size glasses, omitting fruit from glasses. (This Cup should be carefully iced, but on no acccount should ice be put into the Cup.)

Rhine Wine Cup
(For 4 people)

1 jigger (1 1/2 ozs.) Curaçao
2 jiggers Maraschino Liqueur

1/2 tablespoon sugar
1 quart Rhine Wine

Put 4 ice cubes in large glass pitcher. Add liquids. Garnish with slices of orange and pineapple and one very small cucumber peel. Add 3 or 4 sprigs of mint, if available, and serve in punch glasses.

Sauterne Cup

Same as a Rhine Wine Cup but substitute Sauterne for the Rhine Wine.

Daisies

Brandy Daisy

This is a long, refreshing, fruit-accented drink served in a stein or highball glass.

Juice of 1/2 lemon
4 dashes raspberry or Grenadine syrup

2 ozs. Brandy
Club Soda

Shake lemon juice, syrup and Brandy with ice cubes. Strain into 12-oz. glass. Top with Club Soda and decorate with fruit.

Southern Comfort, Gin, Rum, Vodka, or Whiskey Daisy

Same as the Brandy Daisy, but the desired liquor is used. Top with Club Soda.

Eggnogs The Eggnog, essentially an American beverage, is enjoyed throughout the world. During Christmastime in the South it is a long-time tradition. In Scotland, the Eggnog is known as "Auld Man's Milk."

Baltimore Eggnog
(One serving)

1 egg
1/4 teaspoon sugar
1/4 jigger Brandy

1/4 jigger Jamaica Rum
1/2 jigger Madeira
1 cup milk

Shake well with ice cubes and strain into a tall tumbler. Grate nutmeg on top.

Brandy Eggnog
(One serving)

1 egg
1 1/2 teaspoons powdered sugar

1 cup milk
2 ozs. Brandy
Grated nutmeg

Shake well with ice cubes and strain. Serve in tall glass. Grate nutmeg on top.

Bourbon, Gin, Rum, Vodka or Whiskey Eggnog

Same as Brandy Eggnog but use the liquor desired.

Breakfast Eggnog
(One serving)

1 egg
1/4 Curaçao

3/4 Brandy
1/2 cup milk

Shake well with ice cubes and strain into tall tumbler. Grate nutmeg on top.

Christmas Eggnog

This recipe produces a gallon, suitable for approximately 36 servings.

12 whites of eggs, well-beaten
12 yolks of eggs, well-beaten
1 cup powdered sugar
1 pint milk
4 ponies Crème de Cacao

1 quart vanilla ice cream
3/4 bottle (4/5 quart) Southern Comfort
3/4 bottle (4/5 quart) Jamaica Rum
1/2 bottle (4/5 quart) Brandy

Stir well with ice cubes in punch bowl. Ladle into punch cups or Delmonico glasses. Top with grated nutmeg.

*General
Harrison's
Eggnog*
(One serving)

This is a fine drink, still very popular along the Mississippi River. It was the favored beverage of William Henry Harrison, ninth President of the United States.

1 cup milk, chilled   *1 dash Apple Brandy*
1 teaspoon sugar   *1/4 teaspoon cinnamon*
1 jigger (1 1/2 ozs.) Cognac   *1/4 teaspoon grated nutmeg*
   or Rum

In a shaker, combine milk, sugar, Cognac or Rum, Apple Brandy and shake. Pour into 12-oz. glass and sprinkle with cinnamon and nutmeg.

---

*Southern
Comfort Eggnog*
(For 10 people)

8 ozs. (1 cup) Southern   *1 quart dairy eggnog mix*
   Comfort

Chill the mix and Southern Comfort. Blend by beating in a punch bowl. Dust with grated nutmeg. Serve in mugs, punch cups or Delmonico glasses.

Fizzes

The Fizz is characterized by one ice cube, liquor, lemon, and sugar, plus seltzer, Club Soda or Champagne.

Brandy Fizz

Juice of 1 lemon   *1 teaspoon powdered sugar*
1 jigger (1 1/2 ozs.) Brandy   *Club Soda*

Shake lemon juice, Brandy and sugar with one ice cube. Pour with cube into highball glass and top with Club Soda.

---

*Bourbon, Gin,
Rum, Sloe Gin,
Tequila, Vodka
or Whiskey Fizz*

Same as a Brandy Fizz except use the liquor desired. Top with Club Soda.

Bucks Fizz

2 ozs. Fresh orange juice   *Champagne*

Put fresh orange juice and an ice cube into highball glass. Top with champagne.

Cream Fizz Juice of 1/2 lemon   1 jigger (1 1/2 ozs.) dry Gin
              1/2 tablespoon powdered   1 dash fresh cream
                 sugar   Club Soda

Shake all ingredients except Club Soda well with ice cubes. Strain into highball glass and top with Club Soda.

Diamond Fizz Juice of 1 lemon   Champagne
                1 teaspoon powdered sugar

Put lemon juice and sugar into highball glass with an ice cube. Top with chilled Champagne.

Dubonnet Fizz Juice of 1/2 orange   1 jigger (1 1/2 ozs.)
                 Juice of 1/2 lemon   Dubonnet rouge
                 1 dash Cherry Brandy   Club Soda

Shake juices, Brandy and Dubonnet with one ice cube. Strain into medium-size glass and top with Club Soda

---

Golden Fizz Same manner as a Brandy Fizz except use Gin and the yolk of egg. Shake well to dissolve yolk. Top with Club Soda and serve in a highball glass.

Grand Royal Fizz Juice of 1/2 lemon   1 jigger (1 1/2 ozs.) Gin
                    1/2 tablespoon powdered   Juice of 1/4 orange
                       sugar   1 dash sweet cream
                    2 dashes Maraschino   Club Soda
                       Liqueur

Shake all ingredients except Club Soda well with one ice cube. Strain into medium-size glass and top with Club Soda.

Hoffman Fizz Juice of 1/2 lemon   Club Soda
                1 jigger (1 1/2 ozs.) Gin   1 dash Grenadine
                1/2 tablespoon powdered
                   sugar

Shake lemon juice, Gin and sugar well with ice cubes. Strain into medium-size glass and top with Club Soda. Add a dash of Grenadine.

Morning Glory Fizz	*1 jigger (1 1/2 ozs.) Scotch* *1 teaspoon powdered sugar*	*White of 1 egg* *Club Soda*

Shake Scotch, sugar and egg well with ice cubes. Strain into highball glass with a cube of ice. Top with Club Soda.

───

New Orleans Gin Fizz	*Juice of 1/2 lemon or 1/2 lime* *1/2 tablespoon powdered sugar* *White of 1 egg*	*1 jigger (1 1/2 ozs.) dry Gin* *3 dashes Fleur d'Orange* *1 dash heavy cream* *Club Soda*

Shake all ingredients except Club Soda well with ice cubes. Strain into tall tumbler. Top with Club Soda.

───

Orange Fizz	*Juice of 1/2 orange* *1 jigger (1 1/2 ozs.) dry Gin*	*Juice of 1/4 lemon or 1/2 lime* *Club Soda*

Shake juices and Gin well with ice cubes and strain into medium-size glass. Top with Club Soda.

───

Ostend Fizz	*1 dash Crème de Cassis* *1/2 jigger Kirsch*	*Club Soda*

Shake Crème de Cassis and Kirsch well with ice cubes. Strain into medium-size glass. Top with Club Soda.

───

Ramos Gin Gizz	*Juice of 1/2 lemon* *White of 1 egg* *1 oz. heavy cream* *1 teaspoon powdered sugar*	*2 ozs. Gin* *Club Soda* *3 dashes Fleur d'Orange*

Shake lemon juice, egg white, cream and sugar with ice cubes. Strain into highball glass with one ice cube and top with Club Soda. Add Fleur d'Orange.

───

Ruby Fizz	*Juice of 1/2 lemon* *1/2 tablespoon powdered sugar* *White of 1 egg*	*1 jigger (1 1/2 ozs.) Sloe Gin* *Club Soda* *Fruit*

Shake lemon juice, sugar, egg white and Sloe Gin well with ice cubes. Strain into medium-size glass. Top with Club Soda and decorate with fruit.

Silver Fizz *Juice of 1/2 lemon*   *White of 1 egg*
1 teaspoon powdered sugar   *Club Soda*
1 jigger (1 1/2 ozs.) Gin

Shake all ingredients except Club Soda with ice cubes. Strain into highball glass with a cube of ice. Add Club Soda.

Southern *Juice of 1/2 lemon*   *1/2 teaspoon powdered*
Comfort Fizz *1 jigger (1 1/2 ozs.)*   *sugar*
     Southern Comfort   *Club Soda*

Shake lemon juice, Southern Comfort and sugar well with ice cubes. Strain into highball glass and add 2 ice cubes. Top with Club Soda.

Southside Fizz *Juice of 1/2 lemon*   *1 teaspoon sugar*
1 jigger (1 1/2 ozs.) Gin   *Club Soda*

Shake lemon juice, Gin and sugar with ice cubes. Strain into highball glass with an ice cube. Add Club Soda.

Texas Fizz *Juice of 1/4 orange*   *1 jigger (1 1/2 ozs.) dry Gin*
Juice of 1/4 lemon   *Club Soda*
1 teaspoon powdered sugar

Shake juices, sugar and Gin well with ice cubes. Strain into medium-size glass. Top with Club Soda.

Flips A Flip takes Liquor, sugar, egg and nutmeg. No ice is used in shaking.

Brandy Flip *1 1/2 teaspoon powdered*   *2 oz. Brandy*
     sugar   *1 egg*

Shake well (without ice) and strain into Delmonico glass. Top with grated nutmeg.

Bourbon, Gin, Rum, Vodka, or Whiskey Flip Same as a Brandy Flip except use Liquor desired.

Port or Sherry Flip Same as a Brandy Flip except use Port or Bristol Cream Sherry.

Southern Comfort Flip

1 jigger (1 1/2 ozs.) Southern Comfort	White of 1 egg

Shake well (without ice) and strain into cocktail glass. Top with grated nutmeg.

Frappés The word frappé comes from the French *frapper,* to chill. A Liquor or Liqueur is poured over shaved ice.

Cointreau Frappé Fill a cocktail or Old-Fashioned glass with finely crushed or shaved ice. Pour in Cointreau. Serve with a straw.

B and B, Bénédictine, Grand Marnier, Cordial of Choice, Green or White Mint, Strega Galliano Frappé Same as Cointreau Frappé. Remember, it is not proper in making a Frappé to mix two spirits; use only one.

Grog This drink is similar to a Toddy and is a good remedy for a chill or a cold.

2 ozs. Bourbon, Brandy, Jamaica Rum, Southern Comfort or Wine	Juice of 1/2 lemon Cinnamon stick Lemon slice
1 lump sugar 2 cloves	4 cloves

Fill tumbler or mug with all ingredients except cinnamon stick and lemon slice. Top with boiling hot water. Add small piece of cinnamon stick and slice of lemon stuck with four cloves. Stir well.

Highballs   A Highball is characterized by Liquor, Ginger Ale or seltzer and one ice cube.

Addington Highball

1 jigger (1 1/2 ozs.) French Vermouth	*1 jigger Italian Vermouth Club Soda*

Stir Vermouths in highball glass with ice cube. Top with Club Soda. Twist orange peel over drink and serve.

Amer Picon Highball

2 ozs. Amer Picon	*Club Soda*
1 oz. Grenadine	

Stir together Amer Picon and Grenadine and strain into highball glass. Add one cube of ice. Top with Club Soda.

American Glory Highball

2 ozs. Champagne	*Club Soda*
2 ozs. fresh orange juice	

Stir Champagne and orange juice with one ice cube in highball glass. Top with Club Soda.

Apple Jack Highball

1 jigger (1 1/2 ozs.) Apple Jack	*1/2 teaspoon powdered sugar*
1 dash Brandy	*Seltzer Water*
1 dash fresh lemon juice	

Shake all ingredients except Seltzer with ice cubes. Strain into highball glass over one ice cube. Top with Seltzer Water.

Barbary Coast Highball

1 oz. Bourbon	*1 oz. heavy cream*
1 oz. Crème de Cacao	*Club Soda*
1 oz. Gin	

Shake all ingredients except Club Soda with ice cubes. Strain into highball glass over one ice cube. Top with Club Soda.

Black Velvet

1/2 Guinness Stout	*1/2 Champagne*

Prechill Stout and Champagne thoroughly. Pour simultaneously over one ice cube in tall highball glass. Do not stir.

Bon Soir Highball	1 oz. Bénédictine 1 oz. Crème Yvette	Ginger Ale

Stir Bénédictine and Crème Yvette in a muddling or mixing glass, then pour contents into highball glass. Top with Ginger Ale.

Brandy Highball (No. 1)	2 ozs. Brandy 1/2 teaspoon fresh lemon juice 3 dashes Orange Bitters	1/2 teaspoon powdered sugar Seltzer Water

Shake all ingredients except Seltzer Water with ice cubes. Strain into highball glass. Add an ice cube and top with Seltzer Water.

Brandy Highball (No. 2)	2 ozs. Brandy 1/2 teaspoon fresh lemon juice 3 dashes Pernod	1/2 teaspoon powdered sugar Seltzer Water

Shake all ingredients except Seltzer Water well with ice cubes. Strain into highball glass. Add an ice cube and top with Seltzer Water.

Bulldog Highball	3 ozs. Gin 1/2 jigger fresh orange juice	Ginger Ale

Shake Gin and orange juice with ice cubes. Strain into highball glass. Add an ice cube and top with Ginger Ale.

Cassis-Kirsch Highball	2 ozs. Crème de Cassis 1 oz. Kirschwasser	Club Soda

Stir Crème de Cassis and Kirschwasser well with ice. Drain into highball glass. Add an ice cube and top with Club Soda.

Durkee Highball

2 ozs. Rum
1 dash Curaçao
2 dashes sugar syrup

1 dash fresh lemon juice
Seltzer Water

Shake all ingredients except Seltzer Water with ice cubes. Strain into highball glass. Add an ice cube and top with Seltzer Water.

Harry's Highball

2 ozs. Brandy
2 dashes fresh lemon juice

1 dash Grenadine
Champagne

Shake Brandy, lemon juice and Grenadine with ice cubes. Strain into highball glass. Add an ice cube and top with chilled Champagne.

Harvard Highball

1 oz. Brandy
1 oz. Italian Vermouth
1 dash sugar syrup

2 dashes Angostura Bitters
Seltzer Water

Shake all ingredients except Seltzer Water with ice cubes. Strain into highball glass. Add an ice cube and top with Seltzer Water.

Juleps

This delightful drink emerged from the Southern States and was subsequently adopted by some foreign countries as a nostalgic bit of Americana. Always serve with straws.

Champagne Julep

1 lump sugar
2 sprigs mint

Champagne

Muddle mint with sugar in a tall glass. Fill with Champagne. Decorate with slices of fruit in season. Put mint leaf on rim and serve with straw.

Mint Julep

1/2 teaspoon sugar
4 sprigs mint
2 ozs. Bourbon

Jamaica Rum or Brandy
Mint sprigs

Muddle sugar and mint in Bourbon. Fill a silver mug or tall glass with shaved ice. Stir until outside of mug or glass is frosted. Top with Jamaica Rum or Brandy and decorate with mint sprigs. Serve with straws.

| *Southern Mint Julep* | 4 sprigs fresh mint
1/2 tablespoon powdered
   sugar | 1 jigger (1 1/2 ozs.)
   Bourbon, Rye or
   Canadian Club Whisky |

In a tall tumbler, muddle 1 mint leaf with sugar. Add spirits over cracked ice. Stir gently until glass is frosted. Top with 3 sprigs of mint and serve with straws.

Puffs

| *Southern Comfort Puff* | 2 ozs. Southern Comfort (or
   Rye, Scotch or Bourbon
   if desired) | 1/2 pint milk
Club Soda |

Shake ingredients except Club Soda with ice cubes. Strain into tall glass with one ice cube and top with Club Soda. Serve with straws.

Punches Punch is the answer to entertaining large groups because there is only one beverage to serve and only one kind of glass required. Everything can be mixed in advance to avoid last-minute preparations. If a punch bowl is not available, large pitchers can be substituted.

| *Bombay Punch*
(For 35 to 40 people) | 1 quart French Brandy
1 quart Sherry Wine
4 ozs. Maraschino Liqueur | 8 ozs. Cointreau
4 quarts Champagne
2 quarts Club Soda |

Place a block of ice in punch bowl. Add ingredients, sliced fruits and halved seeded grapes. Serve in Champagne glasses.

| *Celebration Punch*
(For 25 people) | 1 jigger (1 1/2 ozs.) light
   corn syrup
1 jigger brandy
1 bottle (4/5 quart) dry or
   sweet Sauterne Wine
1 bottle (28 ozs.)
   Carbonated Water | 1 bottle (4/5 quart)
   Champagne
1 pint whole strawberries,
   washed, or defrosted
   frozen strawberries |

Place ice block in punch bowl. Combine corn syrup and Brandy in punch bowl until well-blended. Stir in Sauterne. Just before serving, add Carbonated Water and Champagne. Add fresh, washed strawberries (not hulled) or defrosted frozen strawberries. Serve in 4-oz. glasses.

Champagne Punch
(For 28 people)

2 cans frozen lemonade
  concentrate, thawed
2 bottles (4/5 quart each)
  chilled Champagne

2 1-pint, 12-oz. bottles
  Carbonated Water
2 pints orange sherbert

Pour lemonade concentrate, Champagne and Carbonated Water over ice block in a large punch bowl. Stir gently. Drop spoonfuls of sherbert over top of punch and serve immediately in 5-oz. glasses.

Claret Punch
(For 20 people)

Juice of 12 lemons
Powdered sugar
8 ozs. Cointreau
1 pint French Brandy

3 quarts Claret or Red
  Bordeaux Wine
1 quart Club Soda
Sliced fruit

Strain lemon juice into punch bowl. Add enough powdered sugar to sweeten and stir well. Place large block of ice in bowl and add rest of ingredients. Mix well and decorate with fruits in season, sliced.

Daiquiri Punch (No. 1)
(For 25 people)

1 jigger (1 1/2 ozs.) light
  corn syrup
4 jiggers light Rum
2 cans (6 ozs. each) frozen
  Daiquiri mix, thawed

2 bottles (28 ozs. each)
  Carbonated Water,
  chilled
Lime slices

Mix corn syrup and Rum in punch bowl, stirring to blend well. Place ice block in bowl and add Daiquiri mix. Just before serving, add Carbonated Water. Decorate with lime slices.

Daiquiri Punch (No. 2)
(For about 12 people)

2 cans (6 ozs. each) frozen
  Daiquiri mix (or 1 bottle
  non-alcoholic Daiquiri
  mix)

20 ozs. light Rum
4 ozs. Cointreau
1 bottle Club Soda (28 ozs.)

Ahead of time, combine Daiquiri mix, Rum and Cointreau and refrigerate, stirring occasionally. Pour over block of ice in punch bowl (or over ice cubes in large pitcher). Stir in Club Soda.

Gin Rickey Punch
(For about 20 people)

1 jigger (1 1/2 ozs.)
  Grenadine
4 jiggers Gin
2 dashes Aromatic Bitters
1 can (6 ozs.) frozen pink
  lemonade concentrate,
  thawed

1 bottle (4/5 quart) Rosé
  Wine, chilled
1 bottle (28 ozs.) Ginger
  Ale
1 lemon, sliced

Combine Grenadine, Gin and Bitters in punch bowl. Add block of ice. Stir in lemonade. Just before serving, add Rosé Wine and Ginger Ale. Decorate with thin slices of lemon. Serve in 4-oz. glasses.

Milk Punch
(For 1 person)

1/2 pint milk
2 ozs. liqueur desired

1 1/2 teaspoons sugar
Nutmeg

Shake with ice cubes and strain into a tall glass. Top with grated nutmeg.

Sensation Punch
(For 8 people)

5 ozs. Cointreau
5 ozs. French Brandy
2 bottles (4/5 quart each)
  Champagne

Juice of 1 lemon
Fresh strawberries or
  raspberries

Place block of ice in punch bowl. Add ingredients. Garnish with fresh strawberries (washed but unhulled) or raspberries.

Rickeys

The Rickey is halfway between a Collins and a Sour. The essential procedure is to squeeze half a lime into a Rickey or small highball glass. Drop in shell and add Gin or any preferred Liquor along with some cracked ice. Top with Club Soda, Ginger Ale or Seltzer Water.

Apple Jack Rickey

1 jigger (1 1/2 ozs.) Apple
  Jack
1 dash Brandy

1 dash Grenadine
1 dash fresh lemon juice
Club Soda

Shake all ingredients except Club Soda with ice cubes. Top with Club Soda and serve in highball glass.

Royal Rickey

1/2 lime
1 dash Grenadine
2 ozs. Gin

1 oz. Italian Vermouth
Ginger Ale

Crush lime in highball glass with Grenadine. Shake Gin and Vermouth well with ice cubes and strain into the glass. Top with Ginger Ale.

Rum Rickey

1 jigger (1 1/2 ozs.) Rum
2 ozs. Bénédictine
1 dash Grenadine

1 dash fresh lemon juice
Club Soda

Shake all ingredients except Club Soda with ice cubes. Strain into highball glass and top with Club Soda.

Whiskey Rickey

1 jigger (1 1/2 ozs.)
*   Bourbon*
1/2 teaspoon Maraschino
*   Liqueur*

1 dash Brandy
1 dash fresh lemon juice
Seltzer Water

Shake all ingredients except Seltzer with ice cubes. Strain into highball glass and top with Seltzer Water.

Sangarees

These are an old-style drink characterized by the use of wine, either Sherry or Port, some form of sugar and a garnish of grated nutmeg.

Brandy Sangaree

3 ozs. Brandy (or Rum, Gin
*   or Whiskey if desired)*
1 dash sugar syrup

1 dash fresh lemon juice
Seltzer Water
Grated nutmeg

Shake Brandy, sugar syrup and lemon juice well with ice cubes. Strain into highball glass and add an ice cube. Top with Seltzer Water and dust with grated nutmeg.

Claret Sangaree

2 dashes sugar syrup

Claret Wine

In a 10-oz. highball glass, pour sugar syrup over several cubes of ice. Fill glass with Claret Wine and stir gently. Dust with grated nutmeg.

Hot Sangaree

1 cube sugar
Cinnamon stick
Twist of lemon peel
Whole cloves

1 jigger (1 1/2 ozs.) Whiskey
(or Scotch, Rum or
Bourbon if desired)

Dissolve sugar in boiling water in a Collins (8 ozs.) glass. Add 1 piece of cinnamon stick, lemon peel, several whole cloves and Whiskey. Serve a pitcher of hot water separate.

Port Sangaree

4 ozs. Port Wine
1 teaspoon powdered sugar

Seltzer Water

Stir Wine and sugar well with ice cubes in highball glass. Top with Seltzer Water and dust with grated nutmeg.

Sauterne Sangaree

4 ozs. Sauterne Wine

2 dashes sugar syrup

Mix in small highball glass. Fill with shaved ice. Stir and dust with grated nutmeg and serve with straws.

Scaffas These old-time drinks are served without ice.

Brandy Scaffa

1 oz. Brandy
1 oz. Maraschino Liqueur

1 dash Angostura Bitters

Stir and serve in a cocktail glass

Gin Scaffa

1 oz. Bénédictine
1 oz. Gin

1 dash Angostura Bitters

Stir and serve in a cocktail glass.

Rum Scaffa Same as a Gin Scaffa, but substitute Rum for Gin.

Whiskey Scaffa Same as a Gin Scaffa, but substitute Whiskey for Gin.

Slings A Sling is characterized by Liquor, fruit juice, Cordials and two ice cubes.

Apple Jack Sling	*2 jiggers (3 ozs.) Apple Jack (or Brandy, Rum or Whiskey if desired)* *Juice of 1/2 lemon*	*1/2 teaspoon sugar* *1 dash Angostura Bitters* *Seltzer Water*

Shake all ingredients except Seltzer Water well with ice cubes. Strain into Collins glass and add two ice cubes. Top with Seltzer Water. Add a dash of grated nutmeg.

Fancy Sling	*1 oz. Brandy* *1 oz. Bénédictine* *1/2 teaspoon fresh lemon juice*	*1 oz. Pernod* *1/2 teaspoon Maraschino Liqueur* *Seltzer Water*

Shake all ingredients except Seltzer Water with ice cubes. Strain into 10-oz. Collins glass with two ice cubes. Top with chilled Seltzer Water and dust with grated nutmeg.

Gin Sling	*1 teaspoon sugar* *1 jigger (1 1/2 ozs.) dry Gin*	*Club Soda*

Dissolve sugar in 8-oz. Collins glass with dash of water. Add two ice cubes and Gin. Stir and fill with Club Soda. (For a hot drink, mix in stem glass. Add boiling water and dust with grated nutmeg.)

Hot Rum Sling	*2 lumps sugar* *1 dash Angostura Bitters*	*Juice of 1/2 lemon* *2 ozs. Jamaica Rum*

Dissolve sugar with a little boiling water in a cup. Add Bitters, lemon juice, Rum and boiling water. Stir.

Raffles Hotel Sling	*1 oz. dry Gin* *1 oz. Bénédictine* *1 oz. Cherry Brandy*	*Club Soda* *1 lime*

Shake Gin, Brandy and Bénédictine with ice cubes. Strain into 10-oz. Collins glass containing 2 ice cubes. Top with Club Soda and garnish with a spiral peeling of a green lime.

Singapore Sling	*Juice of 1/4 lemon* *1/2 Cherry Brandy*	*1/4 dry Gin* *Club Soda*

Shake lemon juice, Brandy and Gin well. Strain into Collins glass and top with Club Soda. Add one ice cube.

Straits Sling
(For 6 people)

1 jigger (1 1/2 ozs.)	*Juice of 2 lemons*
Benedictine	*2 dashes Angostura Bitters*
4 jiggers Gin	*1 dash Orange Bitters*
1 jigger Cherry Brandy	*Club Soda*

Shake all ingredients except Club Soda with ice cubes. Top with Club Soda and serve in large Collins glasses.

Smashes
The Smash is really a Julep on a small scale. Use a medium-size glass. Dissolve in it 1 lump of sugar and add 4 leaves of green mint. Muddle mint and sugar very lightly. Place ice cube in glass. Then add 1 jigger of either Bacardi Rum, Brandy, Gin, Irish Whiskey or Scotch Whisky. Decorate with a slice of orange and squeeze lemon peel on top.

Sours
A sour is usually prepared from the following recipe:

1 jigger (1 1/2 ozs.)	*Juice of 1/2 lemon*
Bourbon, Brandy,	*1/2 tablespoon sugar*
Calvados, Gin, Rum,	*Club Soda*
Vodka, Whiskey, etc.	

Shake all ingredients except Club Soda well with ice cubes. Strain into medium-size glass and top with Club Soda. Add 1 slice of orange and a cherry. (An Irish Sour is made with John Jamieson Irish Whiskey.)

Swizzles
Here is a classic recipe for a Swizzle:

Juice of 1 lime	*1 jigger (1 1/2 ozs.) Gin*
1 dash Angostura Bitters	*1 teaspoon sugar*

Stir with swizzle stick until ingredients foam.

Toddies
A Toddy is characterized by Liquor, slice of lemon, sugar, cloves, and hot or cold water.

Rum Toddy

1 teaspoon sugar
1 slice lemon studded with
3 cloves

Small pieces cinnamon stick
1 jigger (1 1/2 ozs.) Jamaica
Rum

Place ingredients in Old-Fashioned glass and add boiling hot water for a Hot Toddy and cold water for a Cold Toddy. Stir.

Apple Jack, Brandy, Gin, Tequila, Vodka, Whiskey Toddy

Same as Rum Toddy except use Liquor desired.

Southern Comfort Toddy

1 teaspoon sugar
1 slice lemon studded with
3 whole cloves

1 piece cinnamon stick
1 jigger (1 1/2 ozs.)
Southern Comfort

Pour ingredients into Old-Fashioned glass. Add boiling hot water or, if you prefer, cold water.

I sometimes wonder what the vintner buys one half so precious as the stuff he sells.

OMAR KHAYYAM (1025–1123)

Chapter 6   Wine Around The World

IN Chapter 2, *Deep-Rooted in Antiquity,* we traced some of the story of the vine from Noah's ancient vineyard planted on top of Mount Ararat after the Deluge up to present times, imparting enough of its history, legend and tradition to indicate that the whole cycle of grapes-into-wine since time immemorial—dependent as it is on the elements and capriciousness of nature—gives the grape its mystic aura.

Many countries in the world produce wine to a greater or lesser degree. France is first and foremost. Italy is second, and also second in wine consumption. Germany follows, then Spain and Portugal. In South America there are Chile and Argentina. Among other wine-producing countries are Austria, Switzerland, tiny Liechtenstein, the Soviet Union, Greece, Israel, England, Canada, South Africa, and so on. We shall now cover in some detail countries not discussed later in separate chapters (France, Italy, and the wine-producing areas of the United States).

We are traversing this ground not only because it is interesting in itself, historically, geographically and for future traveling know-how, but also because we believe that an American wants to learn as much as he can about the wines that are imported into this country. The many good books available on the subject have different viewpoints: what the distinctive characteristics are of various national wines, how their prices range, what things to watch out for and to appreciate.

Wine makes a long journey to reach your table, from its origins of earth and sunshine, through the careful and devoted hands of the vigneron, the wholesaler, the shipper and distributor. Of all these, only the retailer—be he hoteler, restaurateur or shopkeeper—is in direct contact with the consumer, so it is up to him to advise and educate his clients, if they seek information. Indeed, his whole reputation and success depend on his doing so. The client feels obligated to remain with the supplier who gives him satisfactory service and caters to his requirements. Wine is not just a product for consumption but a part of modern civilization inherited from the past. By imparting honest knowledge to the person who seeks it, the supplier often finds he has not only made a convert but a friend.

German Wines This wine is becoming increasingly noticeable in world markets. Back in 1957, the *New York Herald Tribune* of July 23 announced that Germany would soon "challenge the leadership of France and Italy as the major wine suppliers of the United States market." In 1956, Germany's exports ranked fourth in volume, 7,000 gallons behind Spain. During the following years, steady importations reached the United States from Germany, which, paradoxically, is not a truly wine-drinking country.

Wine in Germany is regarded as a festive beverage for special occasions rather than a daily necessity as in France, Italy and other Latin countries. Beer is the favorite beverage of the Germans. West Germany, a leader in white wine, exports more white wine to the United States than even France. All German wines of any consequence are white, and those that are exported are excellent. According to the *Deutsche Weinzeitung,* citing figures from the West German Bureau of Statistics, a comparison of 1966 production (a good year) with the average figure for the previous five years, showed an 11 percent increase.

A valuable report was published on German wine by Frank Schoonmaker, who has made 21 extended trips through the German wine country in the past 24 years, testing 17,000 different kinds of German wine. He has kept a written record of over half. In his book *Wines of Germany* (published in 1956), he tells how the people of the vineyards belong to that timeless fraternity that has always united people of goodwill in all countries and in all centuries.

What makes German wine unique? They are the lightest in alcohol of the fine wines of the world, always refreshing, and easy to drink. Lord Byron loved the wine of the Rhineland and recommended drinking it with Spritzer, Soda Water. The few truly elite German great wines of this country are simply astonishing—from Hessia or Pfalz, from Moselle or Rhein.

In the great years, says Schoonmaker fervently, German wine is almost in the nature of "bottled poetry." Moselle and Rhine wines are pale, in the nature of cold country wine. To produce good wine, 100 sunny days are needed between May and October. This quota is reached almost every year. While not a wine-producing country in the same sense as Italy, France and Spain, Germany produces less wines than Chile, for example, yet attains a higher average of excellence than the wine of any other country in the world. Rhineland is wineland. The Rhine Valley and the valleys surrounding the tributaries of the Rhone River all have their wines. The Moselle waters meet those of the Rhine at Coblenz. A little farther south is the Nahe River area which produces admirable wines, not known outside of Germany, however.

In the Moselle and Saar regions, vines were first introduced by the Romans during their early occupation of Germany. The Rhine Gau was cultivated on the small stretch of land along the warm, sunny slopes of the Taunus mountains. The Riesling grape, which was early planted on the Eltville, Erbach, Hattenheim, Ruedesheim and Asomannshausen mountains, matures late. All of the wines that grow on the left bank of the Rhine between Worms and Bingen fall within the class of Rhenish Hesse or Rhinehessen. Mainz, which lies in the middle of the district, is also the chief center of the whole Rhine Wine trade. The wines Rhenish-Hessian, Niersteiner, Oppenheimer, Nackenheimer, Scharlachberger are for the export trade, plus Liebfraumilch (whose name is derived from the Convent of our Dear Lady, Liebfrauenstift at Worms, which owns the vineyards).

It is a rare treat to traverse the 314 easily navigated miles of the Moselle River with its picturesque villages, castles and vineyards. Bypassed by the bulk of tourists, here is a hidden world that still belongs to the barge masters, lock keepers and vintners. Originating in the Vosges Mountains of France, the Moselle River forms a border between Luxembourg and West Germany. Then it passes in a twisting course through the renowned wine district before joining the Rhine at Coblenz. After the Romans occupied the valley, the Moselle vineyards flourished on the steep hillsides of the river. The Roman poet Rusonius paid fervent tribute to the river and its vine-clad slopes in his poem *Moselle.*

It is really a sight to remember. The slate hills are covered with row upon row of vines, with their thick green leaves. Planted terraces look down from the steep cliff. The river in antiquity was the prime means of transportation, although a difficult passageway with its dangerous rapids and shoals. Margaret Durrance's article for the November 15, 1970, issue of *The New York Times* is illustrated with a picture of a second-century wineship carved in stone, depicting vintners crowded into a Roman oar-ship. Their kegs of wine are piled high behind them. Not until 1964 was the canalization of the Moselle completed, making the river safe for heavy barge traffic by the installation of 13 hidden locks. The giant *S. S. Europa* books passage for a thousand travelers on the Moselle during its one trip a month, but many yachts and smaller steamers are available.

As one might guess, Riesling is king in Germany. The wines of Moselle, Saar and Ruwer owe the floweriness of their bouquet to this grape. The Riesling grows grapes of yellow-green in tight little bunches. The vines were transplanted to California with much success, where the wines are known as White Riesling or Johannisberg Riesling, of great quality from the region around San Francisco Bay. The Riesling grape likewise went to Chile to produce the best of white wine in South America, called Johannisberg. Riesling is also grown in the vineyards of Soave, the source perhaps of the best Italian white wine, and it flourishes in Alsace overlooking the Rhine. Riesling is best, of course, in its native soil in Germany where success is largely a matter of climate and soil, creating Scharzhofberger, Marcobrunner, Forster Kirchenstück.

Pfalz or Palatinate is the largest wine-growing district of Germany, with some 35,000 acres of vines that annually produce 15 million gallons. This vast area is controlled by 42 vineyard owners grouped into an association of quality wine producers. There are some 50 separate holdings, the estate of Dr. Basserman-Jordan being the most famous. Of the major vineyards of Moselle-Saar-Ruwer, comprising 20,000 acres, less than one-third produce wine of superior quality in the yield of 10 million gallons.

Rheingau has 5,500 acres, with 4,200 acres in full production; two-thirds of its wine can be called good. Hessia has 31,000 acres under cultivation, with only 4,000 acres being within the eight townships. These acres produce top-quality wine, with a total yield of 13 million gallons annually. Other wine districts that are good producers are Nahe, with 4,500 acres yielding two million gallons; one-fourth of its wine is above average. While Franconia has some 7,000 acres, less than 10 percent produces superior wines. Baden-Württemberg has 33,000 acres yielding about 14,000 gallons; less than 2 percent produce superior wines.

When we toured the vineyards of Germany, we found the cellars to be of better physical quality than those of many other countries. With the national characteristic of thoroughness, the cellars are operated as cooperatives. The government has good viticulture schools for training in this prominent industry. The plants have good presses, filters, special fermenting tanks and insecticides for the vines.

Past masters in filtration processes, there is the great Seitz plant in Bad Kreuznach on the Nahe River, completely rebuilt since World War II. German scientists have introduced revolutionary methods that make possible early bottling and consequently early marketing of white wines, with a remarkable gain in quality. They have found a way of removing by filter the yeast cells that might produce a later fermentation. Ever since World War II, there has been a trend toward the presentation of younger wines with an age of 18 months or two years, rather than five to ten years. This is also the trend in wine making in France and in America. Since less time is involved in handling, such younger wine is less expensive to the purchaser. Bottles and corks are sterilized *without* pasteurization; since pasteurization involves heating the wine, it is highly detrimental to quality. Naturally, many winegrowers resisted any change in method from the tradition of centuries. However, they have had to concede that wines can be made with care, intelligence and love with the aid of modern science's achievements in the industry during the past six decades, as applied to wineries.

Germany uses two basic bottles that are easily recognizable. There is the slender, long-necked Flasche, traditional for the Moselle and Rhine Wine. The other bottle is the gaily designed Bocksheutel, a round-bellied flacon used for the wine of Franconia and occasionally for certain wine of Baden. Both of these traditional shapes have been imitated by Italy and also used by Chile and California. Color plays a part. The standard bottles are green for Moselle, brown for Rheingau and Hessia, green again for Pfalz and Alsace. You may notice that German vintners invariably use corks from Spain and Portugal, which are generally shorter than those used in France. Most of the corks are branded with the name and sometimes even with the coat of arms of the producer.

Points to remember about German wine:

1. Better wine carries the name of a specific town, plus the name of the vineyard.

2. Better wine is natural wine without the addition of sugar.

3. Better wine is estate-bottled and clearly marked.

4. Higher grades carry special, legally defined marks as to their quality and class.

Liebfraumilch is a white wine made from grapes grown in Rhineland vineyards. A favorite in the summer, it is deliciously refreshing when served cold. The Rhinelander calls the drink a Spritzer when Club Soda and a twist of lemon peel is added to the glass. Originally Liebfraumilch was the name for the wine produced from a vineyard around the church in Worms, the main city of the Rheinhessen, but now any wine of the province can properly be so called. The general run of wine from the province is made from Sylvaner grapes. This grape produces a soft and flowery wine. The best, coming from the townships of Oppenheim and Nierstein, bear the names of the town and of the vineyards. Some of the vineyards are planted in Riesling, the great Teutonic grape. The higher-priced Liebfraumilch can be truly superb. Usually a blend of lesser wine, it is the perfect accompaniment to a repast of fish, cold meats or cold chicken. The American market offers almost 100 different authentic Liebfraumilchs. You should buy them by the case when you strike the one you like.

Blue Nun, a white wine, is so famous it is known around the world. It can be bought in the cafés of Hong Kong as the best wine of all to accompany Oriental food, harmonizing with dishes from curry to sukiyaki.

Spätlese wine of the 1967 vintage is now on the market; Croever Nacktarsch Spätlese, and Graacher Himmelreich Spätlese. From vintage of 1964, Zeller Schwarze Katz Spätlese, Rudesheimer Rosengarten Spätlese and Bernkasteler Spätlese.

Crock bottle or stoneware wine of the 1966 vintage (24 ounces) are available: Moselblümchen Natur, Liebfraumilch Natur, Niersteiner Domtal and Zeller Schwarze Katz Natur.

In the Richelieu Wine Cellar bins we have some fine Moselles: Bernkasteler Doktor (Spätlese, late-picking), Bernkasteler Doktor (Auslese, selected picking), Piesporter Goldtröpfchen (Spätlese) and Bernkasteler Schlossberg (Spätlese). The Rhine wine includes: Johannisberger Riesling, Liebfraumilch, Steinberger Riesling, Steinberger Riesling (Spätlese), Schloss Johannisberger and Rheingau Spätlese. The Alsatian: Gewürztraminer (Trimbach and F. Brucker), Riesling and Château de Mittelwihr (Sylvaner).

Austrian Wines Delightfully fragrant, Austrian wine is increasing in exportation to the United States: the white wines, Anninger Perle, Gumpoldskirchner, Kremser, Loibner. The famous Klösterneuberger white wine comes from the vineyard of the old monastery by that name on the Danube. Grinzing, Sievering and Nussdorf are made from grapes grown in vineyards within the city limits of Vienna. In Vöslau, Lower Austria, and in Oggan, Burgenland, are produced Austria's best red wines, known as Vöslan, Oggan and Burgenland. Austria, which suffered vivisection in its many wars, especially after World War I, was left with few of its famous vineyards intact. Here good red and white table wine of local repute are produced, with the chief areas in Styria and Lower Austria.

Switzerland

The Rhine and Rhone Rivers, which rise in Switzerland, divide this mountainous country's wine regions. The wine of the Rhine section in Switzerland, contrary to the familiar white Rhine Wine, is red instead; and wine of the Rhone in Switzerland is white instead of red, except for Cortaillod. Twenty of the 22 cantons of Switzerland produce wine, but not enough for the country's needs. Switzerland therefore imports wine from Hungary, Italy, France and sometimes from distant Chile. Switzerland, in fact, is the largest importer of wine in the world, annually having twice the amount taken in by Great Britain and over six times the imports of the United States. About 90 percent of this large importation comprises red table wine, which is inexpensive to ship in from Italy and Spain (a small portion comes from France).

The best Swiss wine is white pale wine of Lavaux, Vallais and Neuchâtel. The vineyards of Neuchâtel are along the northern shore of Lake Neuchâtel in the northwest part of Switzerland near France. A red table wine is produced in Ticino (Tessin) around the Locarno and Lugano lakes, where Italian is the spoken language. A better red wine, Dôle de Sion from Vallais, is made from the Pinot Noir grape grown in the high rocky upper valley of the Rhone. Most Swiss wine is made from the Chasselas grapes for white wine or Fendant grapes for red wine, bottled when less than a year old, light and refreshing.

La Journée Vinicole Export of Paris, France, which reports on world wine production, concluded that 1966 was a year of strong contrasts and 1965 was very humid, which influenced the normal course of nature in the vineyards. Swiss vineyards were affected. Plants failed to grow as they should, and an average (but early) spring blossoming plus a rain-filled summer made the outlook for the vineyards appear bleak indeed. To further darken the picture, diseases jeopardized the vintage. However, an exceptionally fine autumn dramatically saved the harvest and blissfully provided viticulture and commerce with a good year and the consumer with very fine wine, except that shortages usually make prices go up and dampen the ardor of consumption. The years 1965 and 1966 are important to wine purchasers looking for mature wine in 1971 and later.

Liechtenstein

The smallest viticulture country in the world is the principality of Liechtenstein, pressed between Switzerland and Austria with its western frontier part of the Rhine. This little mountainous country—15 miles in length and 6 ½ miles wide, with 22,000 inhabitants—has not had a soldier in a century. Yet there are twelve gendarmes who at 1

A.M. enact curfew and hasten the closing of the local inns. The capital is the village of Vaduz, population 4,000.

The earliest records tell about vine growing in Liechtenstein in the ninth century. The Romans introduced the cultivation of vines here as in other parts of the European continent. At the present time, Prince Franz Joseph II is the most prominent vineyard owner. Second in importance is the engineer, Mr. Peter Rhanberger, who owns the historic Red House and its surrounding vineyards, once the property of monks. Here, as in the whole of this tiny country, only one vine plant is grown—the gray pinot of Burgundian origin. It subsists on the chalky soil called Dolomit. The quality of the wine produced is not notable, yet the price is very high. The Light Rosé, palatable enough and pleasant, is consumed by visitors to the principality. The white wine disappeared in 1940 in the wake of the war. The high price of the wine sold in the cafés and inns is due to the scarcity of vine plants and the small wine production of the few vineyard-growing parishes: Vaduz, Schaan, Triesen and Balzera. The inhabitants usually drink beer.

The Soviet Union Under the czars, Russia had many vineyards. These were expanded by the U.S.S.R. in the 1930s, but the German invasion of 1941 retarded these attempts. Efforts were later renewed, and vine growing is now in full expansion in Russia. Although no official statistics are available, it is known that newly planted areas yield more and more.

Crimea and Caucasus constitute the principal Russian wine regions with some wine being produced in Georgia, around the Black Sea at Baku, Batum, Transcaucasia, Turkestan, Bokhara and Samarkand. Shortly after Repeal, light red and white Crimean and Caucasian table wines from the Pinot and Riesling grape began coming into the United States; also Caucasian Champagne, not a bit dry, was imported, but we have not seen it anywhere for several years.

Production in the Soviet Union is expected to continue to progress. About 50 percent of Russian wine is table wine, chiefly consumed in the districts where it is produced. During World War II, Rumania which had Bessarabia since 1919 lost it again to the Russians, and thus the valuable regions of its white wines: Riesling, Leanyka and Furmint, the grape varieties grown in Bessarabia.

Yugoslavia and Hungary These countries have sufficient wine production. There is a small, high region in the northeast among the Carpathians that produces the superlatively sweet wine called Tokay. This wine comes from Furmint grapes left on the vine until they are almost dried. It takes years to develop the best, and it is said that this particular wine is almost immortal as it can live and improve in the bottle for centuries. The Slavic country of Bulgaria produces some wines, mostly for its own consumption. Czechoslovakia and Albania grow grapes for their local wines.

A great vineyard country, Spain has its heaviest production areas   *Spain*
along the Mediterranean coast, in the southern interior and in the Canary Islands. It is chiefly famous for its Sherry from the region around Jerez de la Frontera near Cadiz and for the dessert wine shipped from Malaga.

Spanish soil, 80 percent chalk with magnesia and clay, known as *albariza,* forms the first soil group for the production of Sherry wine. The second grade of soil is *barro,* or clay, and the third is *arenas,* sandy soil. The vineyards are well hidden from view of the dusty high roads and smoky railways of the hilly country. The Albariza district is five miles north and northwest of Jerez in the Carrascal and Macharnudo districts. The finest Sherries are produced here, where the House of Sandeman of London, England, maintain their holdings (known as El Corregidor and Cerro Viejo).

Vines in the Albariza district are planted in rows five feet apart to form squares, with some 2,000 vines per acre. The high yield of over 7,500 pounds of grapes per acre produce 500 gallons of Sherry. The yield from the other two sections, Barros and Arenas, is even larger, but the quality is not as fine as that of Albariza. The vines are supported in an unusual manner. Cultivated on a low trunk only 16 inches in height, the four branches are held up by forked props to keep the fruit off the ground. Only two of the four branches are allowed to produce fruit in alternate years. The grapes are so delicious that cultivators have to erect towerlike elevated structures in the vineyards (manned by armed guards during harvest time) to discourage theft of the clusters. The towers are called *Bien-te-veo,* meaning, "I can see you all right."

True Sherry—ranging from the very light and the very driest through a diversity of styles to wines that are dark, rich and sweet—comes only from that particular area in Spain with the requisite geological conditions. If a Jerez vine, for instance, was transplanted to another part of the world, it would not grow Sherry as in Jerez.

Tradition in Sherry production is very strong. Between Seville and Cadiz in southern Spain, around the little city of Jerez de la Frontera, are situated the original Sherry vineyards, barely changed in the past 100 years.

Sherry begins as a white wine. Fermentation is checked by the addition of grape Brandy before the natural grape sugar has been exhausted. A thin coating of mold yeast (called *flor del vino)* is allowed to form on the surface of the drier types of Sherry grapes. This causes mild secondary fermentation, or flowering, in the cask, which imparts the distinctive "rancio" flavor of Sherry.

The casks are purposely left open to the air and only seven-eighths filled in order for the flower of the wine to develop. Twice a year, in spring and in autumn, the flower accumulation falls to the bottom of the casks after periods of activity. It forms a crust there known as "mother of the wine" that markedly influences both the style and character of the Sherry. Great care is taken not to break this beneficial deposit similar to the "mother" used in making vinegar.

When Sherry does not undergo flowering, its flavor and color are achieved by aging the wine for extended periods in heated cellars or in casks exposed to the sun. Furthermore, solera systems are used in Jerez and elsewhere to maintain uniformity in Sherry from year to year by blending the newer wine with the older. The wine is taken for bottling from casks of older wine, on top of which rests tier upon tier of progressively younger wine. When a cask in the lowest tier, the oldest, has been partly emptied, it is replenished from the cask of the tier of younger wine immediately above it.

Vintage time in Spain is toward the end of September. Bands of vintagers, many from distant villages, trek to the vineyards. Equipped with small hooked knives, they cut off the bunches of grapes and place them in small baskets. The bunches are then emptied into larger baskets to bear a hundredweight of fruit. These are carried on the back to the nearby press-houses, the men moving slowly in single file. Carts with oxen or horses are used to transport the grapes if distance is involved. The grapes are deposited in lagars, stone tanks. They hold sufficient fruit for the production of 10 to 20 pipes of wine, a "pipe" being the old measurement of 115 gallons.

Barefoot men and women of all ages enter the tanks and tread the grapes to extract the juice. There is music, singing, high-spirited laughter and banter. Authorities claim that this antiquated procedure of pressing by the feet is superior to any other method. Inasmuch as the pips of the fruit are not crushed, the richness and color of the must—freshly pressed juice of grapes—are retained. This method avoids excessive astringency. After being tread, the must is removed from the tanks to vats to ferment.

Dry Sherry has no more than 2 1/2 percent natural grape sugar, medium dry Sherry no more than 4 percent. Sweet, Cream or Golden Sherry has no more than 7 percent natural grape sugar. Sherry is, indeed, a worldly sprite experiencing many marriages. Under the skilled hands of a blender matchmaker, perfect unions of various kinds of wine are attained by "marrying." Fashion conscious, too, Sherry changes its "robe" or color with the passage of time. You may purchase a very pale Sherry, only to find it has deepened in color by the time it is consumed.

While Sherry is the most renowned, there is other fine wine imported from Spain. Juan Hernandez of Valencia sends Burgundy,

Chablis, Sauterne and Rosé as well as Claret in wicker wrapping; his importer is San Martina Wines, Inc., Yonkers, New York. Ruby and tawny Port are also good Spanish wines.

This country sends its famous Port Wine around the globe, most *Portugal* especially to British concerns. This generous, full-bodied wine comes from the demarcated region of the Douro, matured and shipped from the harbor of Oporto, in the north of Portugal. The Douro region, demarcated by law since 1756, stretches along the valleys of the Douro River and of some of its tributaries in the north, from the Spanish frontier down to some 50 miles above Oporto. Only the grapes produced in the small district under very peculiar climatic and geological conditions possess the noble characteristics that are the basis of the unmatchable lusciousness of Port Wine. Port Wine is either white (made from white grapes) or red (from red grapes).

White Port presents these hues: pale white, straw-colored and golden. Red Port embraces several grades: full, red, ruby, tawny and light tawny. Both Red and White Port can be dry, medium-dry or sweet.

There are many types of Port. All of them, however, have something in common, and all are produced in a unique district—the Douro Valley. Therefore, Port is not a type of wine but a geographical designation of origin, representing only 3 percent of the wine production of Portugal.

A very efficient official Portuguese organization supervises the production of Port from vine to shipment and guarantees its genuineness by means of a Certificate of Origin. This is only granted after approval of the wine by a chamber of duly qualified tasters of the Port Wine Institute.

From the harbor of Oporto you may visit the Pais do Vinho, that lovely Port Wine country surrounding the River Douro, a region of wide valleys and deep river gorges. Outdoor cafés are in the European tradition, a very pleasant one at the Palacio da Crystal. The high double iron bridge over the deep river channel here was fashioned by Alexandre G. Eiffel of Paris.

A famous wine of Portugal is Lancers, the delicious Rosé in its familiar brown crock, imported by Vintage Wines Co. You will find others such as Rosicler's Portuguese Rosé, estate-bottled, in colored glass crocks and earthenware crocks. Red and white Borlido, estate-bottled, comes in a wicker bottle.

The precious Madeiras are justly famous, especially Rainwater, Sercial and Malmsey and Rare Rainwater in its wicker bottle, 1875 Solera. We were able to buy for our Wine cellar several cases of 1872 Rare Rainwater (medium-dry Madeira Wine) Bottle No. A. 93, being consumed at this writing (February 15, 1971) from the collection of

Sr. Henriques Estate, produced and bottled by Justino Henriques, Est. 1870, imported by Monsieur Henri Wines, New York. Using these precious bottles as Yuletide gifts brought forth adulation and expressions of appreciation from the recipients. Among the letters we received was one from Arnold Gingrich, publisher of *Esquire,* who expressed a fine tribute to the "precious Old Rainwater" bottled down a century ago, which, he said, he would broach on a very special occasion worthy of such a treasure.

By the end of the 15th century, Madeira was exporting wines to Europe. Shakespeare mentions Madeira in several of his plays, notably in *Henry* IV. The sailing vessels of the American Colonies and English ships made stops at Madeira for water and provisions, loading up with a few pipes of Madeira Wine. Baltimore was once the Madeira capital of the United States. Some shipowners gave the wines the name of the ship that imported them. "Rainwater" is the trade-marked brand today owned by Welch Brothers, the Madeira shippers. It was the fashionable wine for a long time.

Generally, Madeira Wine is sweet, although the Sercial is the least so. There is a bone-dry Gloria Mundi of Leacock & Co., which the late Andre L. Simon, the famous food and wine authority in London, once described as "a Madeira Wine so soft and refined that it has no body, no sugar, no color left, and yet it has bouquet and power, the sort of wine that Rabelais, had he known it, would have called 'a soul with a nose.' " One basic characteristic all Madeiras have in common is a subtle acid undertone or tang that is found in all wine produced from grapes grown in soils of volcanic origin. Madeira, a perfect aperitif, can be used in cooking in place of Sherry in most recipes, and finds a place in soups, sauces or desserts.

Chile Wine is served daily in all classes of homes in Chile. It appears on every restaurant menu as a table necessity as important as a knife, spoon or fork. Chile is said to produce the best wine of South America. Some is so fine, Americans and Europeans look for it in stores in the United States. The problem is that the Chilean wine commonly offered in the United States is a misrepresentation of the good wine Chile produces and drinks in great quantities. The red is pleasant, but the white wine is really superb—dry, crisp, fresh and full-bodied at the same time. Travelers in Chile, regardless of political upheavals and unrest short of an actual shooting war or revolution, will find good food and wine incredibly inexpensive. In fact, the price of wine in Chile is fixed, printed on the labels. A fine white wine in a half-bottle, marked to sell in a retail store in Santiago for 30 cents, is served chilled in a restaurant for 40 cents. But they do not ship these wines to the United States, unfortunately.

Since the Spaniards colonized this narrow country in the 16th century, grapes have been harvested from the plantings of the missionaries, who needed wine for church sacraments. European cuttings were the original source and, in recent years, California. The vines have grown strong in a sunny climate, blessed in escaping the usual diseases that plague vineyards.

Chilean wine has no vintage years because the weather is unvarying and the production almost unvaried. The Andes rise on one side of the length of this ribbon of a country, and on its other side is the Pacific Ocean with its cold Humboldt Current. The combination of breezes from the sea striking against the mountain wall produces an ideal climate for growing grapes, peaches, pears and melons. The finest wine is produced from the vineyard region near Santiago called Llano del Maipo. Lontué also produces wine of good repute. The wine regions begin at 30 degrees latitude around Coquimbo and continue south to Temuco, at 40 degrees. The wine area divides into three regions: Huasco and Elqui in the north; Aconcagua and Maipo in the central sections; and Itata and Cauquenes in the south. Summer comes in January, February and March, and winter in June. The eucalyptus and red pepper trees are reminiscent of those in California and the doleful poplars of northern Italy.

As in Europe, the harvesting of the grapes is an important social ceremony. In the tradition of my own home in Piedmont, the well-dressed entrepreneurs visit their vineyards, mingle with the workers, pick and eat grapes during the height of the harvest season. Communal singing and feasting are the high points anticipated all summer. This is festival time. In many sections, the carts bearing the grapes have the spokes of their wheels festooned with vines and clusters of grapes. Boys and girls in costumes of their region dance and sing in the streets. Much good food is prepared and enjoyed, and of course accompanied by much good wine.

In Chile, the special day of high festival, marking the conclusion of the grape harvest, is celebrated by singing, drinking Chica, sharing a barbecue and dancing the Cueca, the national dance. The countryman wears his native costume of tight black trousers, short jacket with 10 buttons on each sleeve, boots spurred with silver. The women wear colorful skirts and peasant blouses.

Chile consumes most of its wine, *Tinto* and *Blanco* (Red and White) being the large sellers. There is other wine, too. Riesling and Rhin (Rhine) wine is light, delicate and somewhat dry. The Sauternes and Haut-Sauternes are sweet, luscious, fragrant and full-bodied, the only wine produced outside of the Sauternais district of Bordeaux made in the identical manner. This means, of course, made of the same grape varieties: Sauvignon, Semillon and Muscadelle, the latter grapes remaining on the vines until *"pourriture-noble"* develops, meaning that its rich sweetness is a natural consequence.

Chilean Burgundy, obtained primarily from the Pinot Noir, is a great red wine—soft, well-rounded, full-flavored. They have a Cabernet lighter in body than the Burgundy, and a good Vin Rosé. Chile ships some of its Sparkling Burgundy to the United States. Most of the wine bears the name of the old House of Undurraga, whose first vineyards yielded their harvest in 1888, and are still owned and operated by this family. Vina Undurraga is packaged in a green bottle, almost round in shape, with the name pressed into the glass. This is one of the best Chile has to offer.

Argentina The most important wine-producing country in the Western Hemisphere, Argentina ranks after France, Italy, Spain and Algeria. In Argentina, the Province of Mendoza on the Chilean border was, only a century ago, a great desert, but Italian immigrants transformed it into a veritable Garden of Eden. The missionaries had begun the cultivation of some vines, and the enterprising Italians, long familiar with viticulture, continued and improved it. The Province of Mendoza gives Argentina 90 percent of its table wines. There are six very large Argentine producers in Mendoza who own some of the largest wineries and wine cellars in the world. Light beverage wines produced here account for 95 percent of production for home consumption.

The Province of San Juan, north of Mendoza, has a hotter climate and an arid soil in need of constant irrigation. Vineyards there yield grapes suitable for the production of dessert wine and Vermouth as well as table grapes and raisins. Argentina's best white wine and sparkling wine come from the territory of Río Negro, along the Río Negro, where little irrigation is needed. Like so many other wine regions of the world, the vineyards of Argentina—Mendoza and San Juan in particular—suffer from attacks of mildew, and that terrible plague of vines, phylloxera.

Supervision of the wine industry in Argentina is under the Bureau of Internal Revenue. It controls, among other things, vintage identification on labels. In many classifications, the wine is drunk young and travels well to nearby nationals, but not long distances. As in other Latin countries, red and white table wine is a necessary part of a meal. Rich and poor alike drink wine, and there is also wine on the tables of the servants.

Vermouth is very popular as an aperitif, with consumption running to 3 ½ million cases a year. Little wonder that in South America the hour before dinner is called *The Vermouth.*

Brazil This country produces wine from vinifera grapes on the Atlantic side of the continent, far from the Andean divide. The Brazilians, who consume all of their wine locally, favor sweet wine, especially Port and Muscatel. The wine is not of exportable quality, and Brazil imports most of the wine it consumes. Occasionally, Brazil exports some good Champagne.

Peru

On the Pacific slope Peru has a wine belt and, somewhat north, a fair amount of medium-quality wine is produced. The regions are Ica, Locumba, Lima and the Sicamba River valley. The grapes are the European variety and the wine is consumed locally. However, they have a distinguished Brandy, the Pisco Muscat, distilled from wine made in the Ica region, which is always shipped from the Port of Pisco.

Union of South Africa

This vast country is a wine producer of sorts. Viticulture was pioneered in 1653 upon the arrival of the first Dutch governor, Jan Van Riebeek. It was considerably advanced after 1688 by the Huguenots, who were familiar with the wine of their native France. Until the 19th century, the most famous wine of South Africa was the dessert wine from the Muscatel grapes in Constantia near Capetown. Later, European grape varieties were planted in several regions for white and red table wine. North Africa is also a producer, with Morocco, Algeria and Tunisia contributing heavy wine.

Greece

Thick, sweet wine is produced in Greece, and demand exists for its table wine, which include Marco and Tegea, the latter a pink wine from the mythical land of Arcadia. Greece has twice the wine production of Germany; the country exports her fortified sweet wine mostly in barrels to Switzerland, Malta and northern Europe. The Muscat of Samos and the wine made from the Mavrodaphne grape are of fairly good quality. Most Greek table wine, however, is flavored with resin. This gives the wine a slightly turpentine taste, for which an individual must acquire a taste. Cambas Greek wines exported to the United States include Roditys Rosé, Retsina, Kokinelli, Mantinia, Hymettus, Pendeli, Mavrodaphne. Empire Liquor Corporation, New York City, has a good list.

Turkey

Dry and sweet wine is produced in Turkey on the island of Tenedos near the entrance to the Dardanelles. It has a large vine-growing area, but wine production is relatively limited since a large portion of the grapes are used as table grapes and many others are designated for raisins. White wine is produced in Smyrna. There are wines from the Black Sea area and around Lake Van, formerly part of Armenia.

Israel

This young nation quickly developed its agriculture and grape-growing industry. By 1956, vineyards stretched across many acres; production doubled within a decade, and continues to increase. In

Biblical times in a land known for corn, oil and wine, the vine was cultivated in Palestine. The different wines named in the Bible are: Ahsis, perfumed wine (Song of Songs 8, v. 2); Khemer, Khamar; Khometz, small wine, poor or vinegar; Mesech, wine and water; Mimsach, translated as wine in Proverbs 23, v. 30, and liqueur in Isaiah 65, v. 11; Schechar, used 23 times, particularly in the sense of an intoxicating beverage; Soveh, not clear what type, Isaiah 1, v. 22; Tirosh, new or sweet wine, appears 38 times; Yayin, most commonly used name of wine, appears 140 times from Genesis 9, v. 21, the wine of Noah's vineyard, to Proverbs 21, v. 17.

The dispersion of the Hebrews and the conquest of the country by various nations caused the art of viniculture to almost disappear. Small amounts of wine were produced for religious purposes, but the Holy Land had no wine production for over 1,500 years. About 80 years ago, the wine renaissance was begun, chiefly by the efforts of Baron Edmond de Rothschild, one of the owners of France's Château Mouton Rothschild and Mouton d'Armailacq, the estates that initiated the flourishing vineyards there today. With the Baron's assistance, vines were planted and a winery constructed southeast of Tel Aviv at Rishon-le-Zion.

Centers of viticulture in Israel are: Zichron-Jacob, Nes-Ziona, Gedera and Rishon-le-Zion. Wine is named according to its center of origin: Adom Atic, a dry, red, Burgundy type; Hock, a dry, white, Rhine Wine type; Château Richon Vin Blanc d'Israel, a medium-dry, golden, Sauterne type; Château Richon Vin Rouge d'Israel, a moderately sweet, red wine; Rosé of Carmel, a semidry Rosé like an Anjou; Almog, a sweet, red, Malaga type; Partom, a sweet, full-bodied, red Port type; Sharir, a semidry, golden, Sherry type; and Topaz, a rich, sweet, golden, Tokay type.

Israel Wines, Ltd., New York City, has distributors in various states for its Jerusalem wines and liquors. Wines include: Sweet Grape (Malaga), Eretz Israel Concord, Light Golden Sweet (Tokay), Red Natural Sweet, White Medium, Dry White (Hock), Dry Red, Grand Vin Rosé (bottles and in half gallons and gallons), Golden Cream (Muscatel), Sweet Ruby (Port), Golden Medium (Sherry) and Vishnik-Cherry Wine. Imported here to the States by the same firm is Slivovitz (Plum Brandy), 100 proof; Brandy, 90 proof; Wishniak (Cherry Liqueur) 80 proof.

Great Britain Is Great Britain a wine country? Not exactly, not since the Roman vineyards declined in time, yet it does produce a small amount of wine, albeit its climate is not suitable for vineyards. The previously British-held island of Cyprus produced in 1939 more than all of the United Kingdom. Britain holds a peculiar place in the wine field. It produces nothing to speak of, it consumes little, yet it serves importantly as importer and distributor. Since the 15th century, it has regularly imported wine, and its cultured tastes have influenced wine-growing practices in exporting countries.

Britain maintains huge cellars where wine is blended and bottled for export around the world. The Port Wine of Portugal was developed to British taste and largely by Britons. It was Britain who bottled Port and carried it abroad to world markets. Queen Elizabeth I loved her Sherry, and her subjects—including Sir Walter Raleigh, Ben Jonson, William Shakespeare—often drank Sherry in the Mermaid Tavern of London. Sherry, in fact, was the English mispronunciation of the Spanish town Jerez.

The connection of the George G. Sandeman Sons & Co. establishment with Port and Sherry Wine dates back to 1790 when the house was founded by the Scot George Sandeman. The founder's father had lent him £300 with which he purchased a small wine vault. He had no idea, of course, that his modest undertaking would eventually expand to worldwide proportions with vast Port Wine lodges in Oporto, Portugal, and extensive Sherry bodegas at Jerez in Spain (the bodegas are Spanish wine-storage rooms usually above the ground).

Portuguese Douro Wine soon became a favorite with the English. In 1790, Vintage Port was introduced; George Sandeman had shipped to England a sample of it at its best. At first he did his office work in Tom's Coffee House in Birchin Lane, Cornhill, where he met other importers and merchants like himself. Later, he began to travel both in Portugal and Spain, enlarging his activities. By 1805, he leased the building at 20 St. Swithins Lane, with adjoining premises, and lived there with his family. He wore knee breeches, top boots and a white wig; people called him "Old Cauliflower." After his death in Brussels in 1841, his nephew, George Glas Sandeman, took charge of the company until his own death in 1868. The company purchased its own clipper ship *Hoopoe* to run between Oporto and England's east-coast ports. Family loyalty and devotion built a fine business enterprise. In 1928, the firm acquired the company's now universally known Spanish trademark, the black-cloaked figure with the Spanish hat and raised glass over the blocked letters of SANDEMAN PORT. They banked on one thing: the temperament of the Briton is suitable to Port because of the raw English climate.

The simple premise became the foundation of a respected house that today features great Ports: One Star Ruby, One Star White, Three Star Tawny, Partners and Imperial. Vintage Ports come from the vintage years of 1927, 1934, 1935, 1942, 1943, 1945, 1947, 1950, 1955, 1958, 1960 and 1963. In time, 1960 should really be outstanding. The foregoing Ports and the following Sherries constitute Sandeman's current list for export to the United States: Three Star

Medium Dry Amontillado, Fine Rich Cream, Fine Cocktail and Cream Sherry—all wonderful wine with a wonderful history.

Responding to a gracious invitation from the Sandemans to lunch at their London headquarters, we passed through the cobble-stone courtyard at 20 St. Swithins Lane and once up a narrow flight of back stairs, we were ushered into a bright, elegantly appointed room. A great oval table was spread with white linen and glistening crystal stemware. A massive stone fireplace sent forth a rosy glow from a crackling fire, which warmed the wooden-paneled room and locked out the late-August chill of a rain-soaked outdoors.

Handsome, blond young David Sandeman welcomed us into the coterie of his company's officers. Company chief since his father, Patrick's, death in June 1960, David had continued to correspond with us across the Atlantic when we had in preparation our manuscript on the Sandeman story for our previous book on haute cuisine.

Spending much of his time in Spain in pursuit of the family's wine business, David Sandeman met and married Teresa Valdespino of Jerez de la Frontera in 1952, and brought his Spanish wife to England. At the time we were in England, there were six children. David assured us Teresa had long ago inducted him into the mysteries of many of her own best Spanish dishes. The superb boiled salmon of the luncheon at Sandeman's was accompanied by an array of excellent Sandeman wine of Spain, with English wit for spice and much merry laughter.

Canada   The vineyard district of Canada is in the Niagara Peninsula between the Erie and Ontario lakes. About four-fifths or more of Canadian wine is made from native grapes, varieties of the Vitis Labrusca. It is lower in sugar content but hardier than the Vitis Vinifera of Europe. The wines made from the Concord, Catawba, Fredonia, Niagara and Delaware resemble those of New York made from these grapes. Experiments with French hybrids since World War II have given interesting and encouraging results for better quality.

The history of Canadian wine goes back to the 17th century. Father Le Jeune, a Jesuit priest, wrote of his visit in 1636 to the shores of Lake Ontario: "In some places there are many wild vines loaded with grapes. Some have made wine from them. Through curiosity I tasted it and it seemed to me very good."

The early French settlers in Canada made wine as they had in France. In 1811, John Schiller of Cooksville, Ontario, produced and sold wine in a small way. The Canadians as a whole are not a wine-drinking people, and the Canadian wineries have had a struggle to establish themselves.

In British Columbia, about 10 percent of Canadian wine is produced from imported grapes. Fermented beverages are also made from loganberries, cherries and apples. The results, strictly speaking, are not wine. The chief wine producers in Canada are: T. G. Bright, Ltd., founded in 1874, with its plant at Niagara Falls and a bottling plant in Lachine, Quebec (Bright's 5 President wines—from the Niagara Peninsula—are available only in Ontario: Muscatel, Canadian Port and Canadian Sherry). Jordan-Danforth Wines, Ltd., has two wineries at St. Catherines and a modern bottling plant at New Toronto. Château-Gai Wines, Ltd., at Niagara Falls, has pioneered in producing white and red table wine.

Canadian wine is known according to its type: Sherry, Port, Burgundy, Champagne. All are blended like Sherry and Madeira, and therefore always have the same quality. In most provinces, wine is permitted to be sold only in government local stores. In some provinces, bottling is under the Liquor Control Board and the winery is limited in activity to bulk deliveries. The Canadian Wine Institute encourages Canadians to drink their native wine, but the wine industry is hampered by governmental regulations on advertising. This, however, does not prevent hotels and restaurants from showing pictures of vineyards and wineries on their wine lists and from fully describing the merits of wine they offer to the guest.

The French National Touring Office in Montreal advises us of a remarkable rise of French influence in Canada within the past decade. Canada now ranks second among the buyers of French books, immediately following Belgium, whereas once it ranked only sixth. The Canadians traveling to France return with the inclination to follow French ways and to consume more French wine while living in Canada. The importation of French wine into French-speaking Canada as well as into the Anglo-Saxon provinces is a welcome sign of a growing appreciation of the importance in cultural enjoyment of fine French wine and gastronomy.

Australia

Production in Australia, begun over a century ago with European grapecuttings, is concentrated in the south: in New South Wales, Victoria, West Australia and Queensland. There is an Australian Claret, Burgundy, Hock, Sauternes and Port for home consumption.

India and China

India does not include wine in its national life because of the traditional religious prohibition against it. Nevertheless, two wineries opened in India within a year. The pioneer in the field, Mr. Gerhardt M. Jacoby, a German, came to India from Dresden, and after a 30-year residence became a naturalized Indian citizen. It took a special act of the Mysore State Assembly to grant a permit in 1967 to produce wine in Bangalore, a southern Indian state. The handsome rolling country has long produced grapes delicious for eating.

Mr. Jacoby imported the necessary equipment from Germany in

1960, and his first experimental efforts were based on German and Swiss textbooks on wine making. Finally, when he was granted a permit, he brought over a Swiss wine expert to assist him in production. He began with a winery in a small bungalow with six employees, but by 1968 had drawn plans for a modern plant. Mr. Jacoby advertises his Capri Port as "sweet and mellow and a wonderful after-dinner drink." He predicts his wine will improve as better grapes are cultivated in Bangalore, and, of course, as he himself becomes more expert at making wine. Mr. Jacoby deliberately makes his wine taste like tonic, i.e., sufficiently unpleasant to be acceptable to a large number of Indians who "don't think they should drink for pleasure." He calls his wine Juvenea to suggest its promise of rejuvenation. The only other winery extant in India, as far as we could learn, was opened at Hyderabad in 1967.

In China, wine was allegedly discovered by I-Ty several centuries before Christ, but its use was subsequently prohibited by a Chinese emperor who had the vines uprooted.

It is a long, long trek on the wine trail around the globe from Noah's first vineyard on Mount Ararat in Armenia where his legendary ark came to rest after the Flood. The fruit of the vine has devotees whose languages are as many as the Tower of Babel.

*Wine is the child of sun and earth, the
collaboration of art, patience, time and
care, the triple communion: Firstly with
the soil into which it sinks its roots
and from which it receives soul and body.
Secondly, communion with ourselves. It
educates our taste, training us to turn
our attention inwards, frees the mind and
illuminates the intelligence. Lastly, wine
is a symbol and the means of social communion . . .
around a table all guests are at the same level
as the cup goes round . . .*

PAUL CLAUDEL

Chapter 7 # Wine Of France

FRENCH wine is made, aged and bottled with great and loving care
by people who place their pride in it. To a Frenchman, a bottle of
good wine is an achievement on the part of the vintner and an art to
be enjoyed. The countries surrounding the Mediterranean have
made wine for thousands of years, but in France, especially, winemaking has been considered important for at least 2,000 years. The growing of vines and appreciation of wine have become part of France's
civilization, art and culture. Julius Caesar and his legions brought
to Gaul in the second century the cuttings of vines as well as the
cultivation of medicinal and culinary of herbs. Before Caesar's time,
vines were nurtured in Marseilles as early as the beginning of the
sixth century B.C. The people of this seaport were familiar with the
pruning of the vines, which makes the difference between wild and
cultivated wine-producing grapes. The whole science of vine growing
depended on pruning the vines until as late as 1869, when new
improvements were made through grafting, which has been practiced
in France ever since.

By the first century B.C., wine making was carried on all over Gaul. During this early period, vines to resist harsh weather were invented. A vine grown in the Rhone Valley was nurtured to be resistant to cold, and another vine in the Bordeaux region was cultivated to be resistant to rains and storms. The Roman historian Tacitus (55 to c.120 A.D.) wrote of the commerce of wine between Gaul and Ireland. By the end of the first century, Gaul exported wine to Greece and Italy and to all of the then known world. By the fourth century, the wine of ancient Gaul was famed far beyond its own borders. The Latin poet Marcus Ausonius, who owned a vineyard in Bordeaux, tells of his travels to see his customers in Germany. At the time there was a "negotiator Brittanicus" who had a central buying agency in Bordeaux for exporting wine to the British Isles.

The long history of wine making in France proves that the French knew how to treat their vines and how to produce wine from the harvest. It is more than this, however, that makes French wine so unique. The difference lies in the fact that in France all of the conditions—geographical, geological and climatic—necessary to the vineyards happen to be ideal. It is the nature of the vine that it is dependent on the conditions of the soil, climate and exposure to the sun. Thus the wine of one region or district cannot be duplicated in another. The harvest and the aging of the wine are often fraught with the threat of failure, much of which has eventually been corrected by science in overcoming conditions that brought damage.

Since the wine of one region or district cannot be duplicated in another, the exact place of origin is the most important fact to know when buying a bottle. It provides an idea of the probable qualities of the wine. That is why the name of the producer, shipper or importer on the label tells the exact story of what the wine represents. French wines are subject to the strict control of the governmental agency of Appellations Contrôlées. A wine may *not* bear the name of a region (such as Bordeaux), a district (such as Médoc) or township (such as St. Julien) unless it has been made in the area of the same name, in strict compliance with the official regulations. Such a wine is always bottled under a label bearing the words "Appellation Contrôlée" and the name of the exact area from which it comes.

"Appellation Contrôlée" refers to French law covering the deed of title to the estate, its size, what vines may be planted, how much wine the owner may make from them and forbidding his use of grapes brought in from outside of his property.

The term "Appellation d'Origine" refers to the character of a wine, which depends on the place where it is produced: soil, subsoil, climate and its local variations, orientation, microflora, all playing a part in giving the wine its peculiar quality. If any one of these factors changes, the wine also changes. These natural factors are not the only ones involved. The vigneron plays a decisive role in choosing the varieties of vines, the methods of cultivation and winemaking and in deciding how to keep the wine. Thus the combination of both natural and human factors give the wine its own original quality.

There is a tremendous number and variety of French wine, different vintages, difficult-to-pronounce names. There is at least one red wine from Bordeaux (Atlantic seaport region) on every good wine list. The name *Claret* is applied to Bordeaux dry red wines. The best Clarets are expensive and often difficult to obtain, but the effort is worthwhile. To understand the better Clarets, it is necessary to understand the stature the vineyard has in French viticulture. The vineyards, definite geographic locations, make their own wine and label them in the following manner:

1. Name of the château around which the vineyard is situated

2. The owner's name

3. The village name in which the vineyard is situated

4. The vintage year

5. The phrase "Appellation Contrôlée"

6. The phrase "Mise en bouteilles au château"
(placed in bottles at the château)

The owner, who may or may not actually live at the château, makes the wine from grapes he has grown. If results are good, he places his name on the bottle, informing you of same and telling you he has bottled the product himself. Here is the information from a sample label that contains all six requirements:

1. Château Ausone

2. Edouard Dubois-Challon, Propriétaire à Saint-Emilion

3. Saint-Emilion

4. 1953

5. Appellation Saint-Emilion Contrôlée

6. Mise en bouteilles au château

What does V.D.Q.S. on the label signify? It means that although the wine is not the greatest, it is still of an excellent quality (Vins Délimités de Qualité Supériéure). Thus the title V.D.Q.S. on the label is not a trademark. It is a guarantee by which the groups of wine makers certify that they have complied with the strict rules for producing their wine of quality and have given the origin of their wine. Such wine has enjoyed a good reputation for centuries in different

French provinces. The letters are awarded for use on the label only if the wine fulfills certain conditions set forth in a decree of the Ministry of Agriculture, with particular reference to:

1. *Area of production*

2. *The wine*

3. *The methods of vine growing and wine making*

4. *The alcohol content and yield*

The V.D.Q.S. category covers more than 60 regional or local types, including a complete range of red, Rosé and white table wine.

The key to understanding the wine of France is to have some knowledge of the wine regions of origin, into which the country is divided.

Bordeaux The Bordeaux region, which spreads along both banks of the Garonne River in the southern part of France, is by far the most important wine region on earth. The vastness of land planted in vineyards —some 300,000 acres—staggers the imagination. In an average year, Bordeaux produces about 500 million bottles of wine. France produces half of the world's quality wine, and half of that quality wine comes from Bordeaux. No other region can match it in quantity and variety of wine. The spectrum of Bordeaux wine is complete: light, elegant reds as well as full, burly ones, Rosés and sparkling whites.

Most of the Bordeaux countryside presents a scraggly appearance. From the Saint Emilion area come the famous Clarets: Rosé wine and dry, medium-dry, sweet and very sweet white wine.

The city of Bordeaux, the greatest seaport in the southwestern part of France, is 13 miles up the confluence of the Garonne and Dordogne rivers, its harbor bustling with ships from the Middle and Far East, Africa, the Baltic, England, the Antilles and America. It is reached from Paris by air, road or rail, on the direct route between Paris and Biarritz. Some of the fastest trains in the world link Bordeaux with Paris—400 miles distant—in five hours; one run is a nonstop express.

Bordeaux, 2000 years ago, was already a port of Celtic Gaul when the Romans took it over in 55 B.C. and called it Burdigala. It boasted a population of 60,000 when it was made a capital of the Roman Province of Aquitania, famed as a center of arts, architecture and law.

The Latin poet Marcus Ausonius, tutor of the Emperor Gratian and a native Bordelais, often paid tribute in his poems to the virtues of the wine of Bordeaux. He traveled throughout the Roman Empire with the court, but returned to retire in his native *pays* to cultivate his vines and garden. His vineyard in Saint Emilion was located near where the massive Château Ausone perpetuates his name and owns vast vineyards. Here the finest Saint-Emilion wine is produced. Situated on the crest of one of the hills, the famous château is said to have been built on the site of the poet's country house. Beneath the Château Ausone are enormous wine storage chambers.

A matter of love changed the fortunes of Bordeaux in the 12th century. The beautiful and wealthy Eleanor, Duchess of Aquitaine, who owned as her feudal fiefs all of the southwest of France from the Spanish frontier to the Loire River, was disappointed in her marriage to King Louis VII of France, yet she remained his queen for 13 years (1137-1150). All Christendom was scandalized when Eleanor had her childless marriage annulled and promptly married her waiting lover, the wealthy and powerful Henry Plantagenet, Duke of Normandy and Count of Anjou, who controlled all of northwest France from the Loire to the English Channel. In this fruitful union, she bore Henry three daughters and five sons, one becoming England's King Richard the Lion-Hearted.

The marriage set off a lethal political rivalry between Louis VII, Eleanor's rejected husband, and his two most powerful nobles. Eleanor and Henry together controlled half of Louis' kingdom. In 1154, Henry became King of England and ushered in three centuries of warfare as the successive kings of France tried to regain their kingdoms from England. It was three good centuries, however, in the Middle Ages for the English-controlled Bordelais. Their chief city, Bordeaux, was fully recognized by the English as a city of culture. Civil liberties were encouraged, while their parliament, the powerful Jurade, based its political success upon the production and trade of Bordeaux wine. The English initiated the important wine trade, calling the red wines of Bordeaux, Clarets. English rule of Bordeaux ended in 1453 when John Talbot, first Earl of Shrewsbury, marshall of the king's armies and Constable of Aquitaine, was killed at the battle of Castillon, 25 miles east of the city. It also ended the Hundred Years' War between France and England. When Charles VII, King of France, regained control of Bordeaux, it became known as the great "Gironde wine country," taking its name from the River Gironde.

The French, however, treated the inhabitants of the city as occupants of a defeated city, erecting two forts. One, the Château Trompette, lives in the name of the Château Trompette Restaurant at 5 Rue Château-Trompette. It is located in an elegant old townhouse and is renowned for its fantastic gourmet food and lengthy wine list. The French victory of 1453 was a disaster for the city of Bordeaux. It was cursorily deprived of its great wine market (it had been the wine storeroom of England, its only and faithful client). Bordeaux fell into economic distress because it did not possess its own mercantile marine and English merchant ships no longer entered its harbor. Aid came, however, when King Louis XI authorized Flemish shipowners to undertake the export of wine from Bordeaux.

The Chartrons District became the nucleus of the trading settlement. As the markets moved away from Bordeaux, some Dutchmen, Danes, Germans, Irishmen, Scotsmen and even a few Englishmen settled in Chartrons and opened up the harbor of Bordeaux to the ships of their native countries. Beyond question, Les Chartrons District, the city within the city of Bordeaux, owes its birth to the maritime economy. As a whole, the city of Bordeaux still retains an English atmosphere, and to this day many of the great châteaux and exporting wine firms are owned by the British and their descendants.

Where are the vineyards? To the north of Bordeaux are the vineyards of Bourg and Blaye, to the east those of Pomerol and Saint Emilion, to the southeast Entre-Deux-Mers and the Premieres Côtes de Bordeaux, to the south Sauternes and Barsac, to the southwest and west Graves and to the northwest the Médoc and the Haut-Médoc.

The vineyards of the Médoc are situated on a peninsula between the Garonne River and the Atlantic Ocean. The vines grow from pebbly soil once part of the riverbed. Gigantic storage cellars cannot be dug near swamplands, so barrels of wine rest on tracks on stone floors in sheds built in a raised position from the ground. Modern vine-growing Médoc dates from an edict of King Henry IV (February, 1607) that granted privileges to foreigners to dry up the Médoc marshes. Many Dutch nationals arrived, skilled in the art of polders. A Bordeaux firm founded in 1620 by a Dutchman, G. Beyermann, still exists today and is operated by a direct descendant of the founder.

Alexis Lichine, President of Hedges & Butler Imports, Ltd., New York City, in that firm's house organ, *The Grape and the Grain,* tells of the Château Lafite and its neighbor, the Château Mouton-Rothschild, owned by rival branches of the Rothschild family. The Château Lafite is a jumble of architectural styles, several towers rising above a great balustraded terrace near the dramatic cellars. These house one of the world's most extensive wine collections, with 80,000 bottles containing vintages going back to 1797. From the vineyards of this château, the great light wine, famed for finesse, is produced in nearly every good year. In 1953, Lafite was supreme in this vintage, and 1952 and 1955 are considered exceptionally good. As in the case of so many other top vineyards, writes Mr. Lichine, the soil is often more important than vintage years. A wine from a great vineyard of a small year is often better than a small wine from indifferent soil in a great year.

The Château Mouton-Rothschild nearby, which has been in the Rothschild family since 1868, is a series of low Spanish-looking buildings. The new wine is kept in a long, low *chai.* Underneath are cellars lit with hanging wrought-iron hoops holding clusters of tiny electric candles. Philip de Rothschild, who deserves credit for having been the first promoter of the Médoc, in 1962 opened a wine museum of great interest to all visitors to the Médoc.

Wine is known by the districts in Bordeaux that produce them. Here are the principal ones:

Médoc: Some of the famous parishes of Médoc are Saint-Estèphe, Pauillac, Saint-Julien, Moulis and Margaux. The wines of Médoc are red, light-bodied and unique for their elegant fragrance, mellowness and delicate and lasting taste.

Saint Emilion: The wine of this district is red, full-bodied and robust, having a strong bouquet and a distinctive taste.

Pomerol: This is a very small district, yet its red wine is elegant— a little lighter than the Saint-Emilions, with which they share most of the same characteristics in bouquet and taste.

Graves: Graves produces both red and white wine, the whites being either dry or medium-dry, well-balanced, elegant wine with delicate bouquet and a fruity flavor.

Sauternes: This is the name of a district that includes the township of Barsac, which produces the greatest naturally sweet wine in the world. Sauternes have a lovely deep golden color; they are mellow, very fruity, and with a long-lasting, rich flavor.

The greatest wine of Bordeaux comes from Médoc, Saint Emilion, Pomerol, Graves, Sauternes and Barsac, but excellent wine is also produced in other districts within the region of Bordeaux. Among them are: Cérons, Sainte-Croix-Dumont, Loupiac, Côtes de Bordeaux-Sainte Macaire, Premieres Côtes de Bordeaux, Sainte-Foix, Entre-Deux-Mers, Graves de Vayres, Canon Fronsac and Côtes de Canon-Fronsac.

Most of the wine may be drunk when young, but it ages well, especially the red wine from Médoc, Graves, Pomerol, and Saint Emilion. They may be kept for several years. Some of the greatest red Bordeaux may reach their peak between 10 and 20 years; some have been known to last for half a century.

White wine matures more quickly than reds. The dry white Bordeaux are drunk when young, although they keep well for several years. The rich Sauternes are slower in reaching their peak and age very well.

There are two principal types of bottled Bordeaux: regional bottlings and château bottlings. Château (meaning castle) is the Bor-

Château, Regional and Parish Wine

deaux term for vineyard estate, some of which do have real castles on them. A château-bottled wine is one that has been bottled at the vineyard where the grapes were grown and, therefore, the wine will have come from that specific place.

Regional and parish bottlings also come from a specified place, except that meanings have changed. Instead of an individual vineyard, the place is the district or "Appellation d'Origine Contrôlée." There is a fine distinction drawn: Whereas the château wine stands or falls with the reputation of the owner of the vineyard, regional bottlings are guaranteed by the reputation of the shipper.

This is how it works in practice: Wine is brought from the different vineyards of a district called after the region from where they come: "Saint-Julien," "Barsac," "Saint-Emilion," and so on. They are matured in the cellar of the shipper in Bordeaux, and it is the shipper's name one sees on the label. If a wine happens to be the special choice of the shipper or "monopole," it will be so identified.

Reading labels yields a great deal of information about a wine. The name of the shipper indicates that the wine is one of quality, because reliable shippers will only sell under their own label wine that will be sure to maintain their good reputation.

In France, there is no more serious subject than that of wine. Politics takes second place, which may well be why the country has gone through so many different governments. One can therefore be sure that French custom with regard to wine is strictly enforced.

The great reference book on Bordeaux wines is the book *Bordeaux et Ses Vins* now in its twelfth edition. The ninth edition published in 1898 contained 858 pages. The twelfth edition of 1969 has grown to 1744 pages. It is considered the bible of Bordeaux wine and gives details of the history, ownership, soil and production of all the vineyards in this world-renowned area. Included are detailed maps and 1000 illustrations of château labels. It is published by Feret et Fils, 9 Rue de Grassi in Bordeaux, France.

The earliest Bordeaux labels used the name of a château and were adorned with a picture representing a genuine castle. This reflected the taste prevailing at the beginning of the 19th century when those castles generally were built. Most are reminiscent of neo-Gothic style fostered by Sir Walter Scott's novels. However, when the glory of Architect Viollet-le-Duc declined—he was renowned for the restoration of medieval French buildings—it became quite the thing to despise the neo-Gothic style. Nevertheless the Médoc châteaux have grown old and charming, taking on a century-old patina.

Every Médoc castle, architectural facts of the Romantic age, are also commercial facts. The châteaux were actually the frame of the classification of wine, and they made the Bordeaux wine famous around the world. Every quality vintage desired a château label, even if the grower lived in a tiny village house. Some deliberately built castles for economic reasons. Imagine how many castles rose in Médoc, a strip of land 50 miles in length and six to nine miles wide. The idea of a château being a definite building was provided by the Civil Court of Bordeaux on May 8, 1939. It stipulated the word *château* as a possible designation of a well-defined estate. A decree was finally issued on September 30, 1949, laying down the following conditions:

> *1. The wine must have an Appellation of Origin.*
>
> *2. The wine must originate in the estate, or vineyard, designated by the name of the château or its counterparts, which must really exist as an agricultural estate, and which must be duly described by these words.*
>
> *3. The name château, or its counterparts, is limited to the yield or production of the estate duly qualified.*

It must not be assumed that Bordeaux châteaux have been recently constructed to fulfill the law, or that they exist by virtue of their official registration. Noble mansions, manor houses and châteaux are numerous and, often as not, encompassed by a more or less famous vineyard.

In late September, the air of all Bordeaux is heavy and intoxicating, reeking of a vast winery as the fumes rise of grapes fermenting in the vats of hundreds upon hundreds of châteaux from the regal Haut-Brion to the house of a small-vineyard farmer. In the *chai,* or wine-storage room, of Château Beychevelle, harvest ceremonies are held by La Commanderie du Bontemps du Médoc et des Graves. Likewise, members of La Jurade de Saint-Emilion stroll in full regalia to their initiation ritual in an underground Benedictine church. Many dinners are given before the grapes ferment. Mme. Achille-Fould recently presided over a gastronomic luncheon in the *cuverie* (cellar) of her castle, Château Beychevelle. The elegant meal celebrated the beginning of the harvest, when expectations ran high and the empty vats awaited the infusion of the exalting wine of Bordeaux. The most famous château of the Bordeaux region is probably the Château d'Yquem, owned by the Marquis de Lur-Salluce at Sauternes. Here the well-known musical festival takes place during the month of May.

As of April 1970 there were more than 4,000 registrations of a château name in the Bordeaux region. There are 38 localities that have the right to put their names on labels, such as Montagne-Saint-Emilion or Pauillac. There are also three major systems of classifications of châteaux according to quality in the Médoc, Sauternes and Saint-Emilion regions. The nine top châteaux send 80 percent of their wine to the United States, but Bordeaux is losing a market of connoisseurs in Britain and Western Europe because they cannot pay the high prices.

There are five Premiers Grands Crus (outstanding first growths) rated in the general classification of 1855, which has not yet been amended, although continuously but thus far (1971) ineffectually protested. They are the châteaux of Lafite-Rothschild, Latour and Margaux in the Médoc; Haut-Brion in the Graves and Yquem in the Sauternes. The ratings were awarded in a competition in the Paris Exposition of 1855 only after some bitter infighting in which Latour and Haut-Brion sought separate honors. It was not until 1954 that an official classification brought a little order to the hundreds of Saint-Emilion châteaux that since 1855 had endowed themselves with unofficial premier ratings. The market has made its own classification: Château Beychevelle, a fourth growth, now sells dearer than some second growths. Mouton, which is now Mouton-Rothschild, has achieved parity in price with the top five, along with Ausone in Saint-Emilion and Petrus in Pomerol.

Burgundy A gastronome's and wine lover's paradise, Burgundy (Bourgogne) has been famous for hundreds of years. Half of its wine bears some of the most renowned names of all French wine. The outstanding characteristics of Burgundy wine are their warmth and strong bouquet, full-bodied and mellow. The whites are very dry.

Lying south in almost the center of France, the northern tip of this lush region is only 70 miles from Paris. In going from Paris to the Riviera, it is amiss not to plan to stop off for a couple of days in Burgundy.

A straight road brings the traveler to Vézelay, a beautiful village. Its great cathedral, built eight centuries ago, has a massive doorway of carved stone that is a masterpiece of Romanesque art. Luncheon in Vézelay is a delight: Escargots, Coq au Vin and Bresse Bleu with fruit, accompanied by Chablis and Musigny, with its faint aroma of violets and truffles, suggests some of the culinary splendors of Burgundy.

Ten miles farther south from Vézelay is Avalon, a hill-top town whose imposing ramparts overlook a sea of vineyards. At Avalon, dinner might comprise such specialties as quenelles of lobster, charollais steak, a tart and wines: Meursault and Chambertin, the favorite of Napoleon. The following morning, it is a 60-mile drive to Dijon, capital of Burgundy, medieval town of art and gastronomy, synonymous with Dijon mustard and fanciful gingerbreads. Here the ancient palace of the dukes of Burgundy is now a museum rich in paintings, tapestries, sculptures, ivories, enamels and armor.

Fascinating Dijon! In the spring of 1515, when King Francis I rode toward Italy (and what would be his victory at Marignano), he stopped his steed at the height of Talant, which looks down over the vast plain extending to the region of the Jura and on to the Swiss Alps. Before the monarch lay Dijon, nestled behind the ramparts, its watchtower rising majestically from the center of the town. Behind the walls rose the slender silhouettes of a vast number of church spires, bell towers and turrets, their airiness contrasting with the massiveness of the château built by King Louis XI to defend Dijon. Francis exclaimed in wonder: "What a beautiful city, a city of a hundred steeples!" Many of the delicate spires have long since disappeared, but Dijon remains a great book of stone in which can be traced the entire development of French art.

In Dijon, the local aperitif is called Kir, named for the friendly priest who was once mayor of Dijon. It is a white Burgundy spiced with Black-currant Liqueur. Gougère, a local cheese tart, makes a substantial summer luncheon when followed by broiled trout and a dessert of divine wild strawberries. For wine—Pouilly Fuissé and a Fleurie. In the autumn, when the grapes are harvested, hundreds of people flock to Dijon for the annual Gastronomic Fair.

Continuing southward on Route des Grand Crus, we arrived at the Clos de Vougeot in the Côte de Nuits, the only vineyard in France that receives a salute from passing regiments of the French army. "Present arms and sound the general salute," ordered a colonel of Napoleon, and to this day a passing French army continues to pay its tribute to the great red wine. The vineyards grow right up to the walls of the 15th-century, three-story bluff château, Clos de Vougeot. It is now owned by the Confrérie des Chevaliers du Tastevin and used as headquarters for this famous food and wine society.

Another mile south, toward the southern extremity of Burgundy, you will note the wall-enclosed vineyard comprising only four acres called La Romanée-Conti. It produces the monarch of all Burgundies, and a single bottle may cost as much as $19 in New York City (1971).

National Highway 74 from Dijon to Chagny in the south runs through, or passes by, many small towns whose names are universally recognized on labels of famous wines: Gevrey-Chambertin, Morey-Saint-Denis (a modest village from whose vineyards come great red wines), Clos de Tart and Les Bonnes Mares, Saint-Georges, Aloxe-Corton, Beaune, Pommard, Volnay, Meursault, Puligny and Chassagne-Montrachet (the district of those choice blackberries from which Dijon extracts a delectable liqueur).

On to Beaune in time for dinner and a night's lodging. In the fall, wine merchants from all over the world gather for the wine auction held at the Hospice de Beaune for the benefit of the almshouse, a refuge for the indigent since 1443. The sale has been held annually since 1863 and has become the after-harvest occasion for three days of ritual, festival, promotion and trading. The ancient spits of the Renaissance Hospital still turn for roasting meats, and attendant nuns still wear the habits designed for them in the 15th century. At a restaurant in Beaune, dinner might comprise a terrine of duck, crayfish à la creme, poulet au Chambertin, accompanied by wine—the sublime Le Montrachet and the lordly Chambertin. Of Montrachet, Alexandre Dumas said in awe, "You should drink Montrachet on your knees."

The Regions of Burgundy

1. In the North   The small town of Chablis, located northeast of the town of Burgundy and of Dijon, produces Chablis, a very dry white wine, light, heady, inimitable, with a subtle bouquet and a characteristic yellow color with slightly greenish overtones.

2. In the Center   "A little more than a rather ugly and dried up small mountain," wrote Stendhal of Côte d'Or, "but every moment one runs across an immortal name." The finest red Burgundies come from the Côte d'Or, that Golden Slope, a 30-mile strip of hills less than half a mile in width along National Highway 74 from Dijon to Chagny. Passengers of the Paris-Riviera express can see the names of the vineyards displayed on billboards along the railroad route. The lower slopes of the hills, planted in vineyards, are overshadowed by hills crowned with woods. From the crest, you can see the plain of Burgundy and look toward the hills of the Jura, and in the distance rise the Swiss Alps.

The Côte d'Or, largest wine-producing district of Burgundy, stretching from Dijon southward to Santenay, is divided into two parts: the Côte de Nuits to the north and the Côte de Beaune to the south.

A. THE CÔTE DE NUITS   A scant 10 miles long, the Côte de Nuits is the northern half of a southeastward-facing slope of long, low hills known as the Côte d'Or. Côte de Nuits is named for the town of Nuits-Saint-Georges near its southern end. The greatest vineyards are Chambertin to the north, Musigny in the middle, and Romanée-Conti to the southward. Around each of these superlative vineyards are other excellent vineyards that share the characteristics of the region's three leaders.

Good wine is produced for laying down. Rough when young, these noble wines improve by being kept for a long time. Here are the names of some of the greatest, which are full-bodied and generous with a remarkable bouquet:

Fixin (a tiny village two miles south of Marsannay with five good vineyards), Gevrey-Chambertin, Morey-Saint-Denis, Chambolle-

Musigny, Clos de Vougeot, Flagey-Échézeaux, Vosne-Romanée and Nuits-Saint-Georges, Romanée (Vosne) and Richebourg (Vosne).

A well-known French sparkling wine, Chauvenet Red Cap, is matured in the century-old cellars of F. Chauvenet in Nuits, Burgundy. It is fruity and elegant, a sparkling wine of deep red ruby color, made as Champagne is made, carefully developed in bottle. Its companion piece is Pink Cap, a sparkling rosé wine of the same high quality and acceptance. F. Chauvenet also ship a variety of very good Burgundy still wine, their Pouilly Fuissé, a fresh, crisp, white wine; Beaujolais; and Pommard. Munson G. Shaw Co. of New York City, their sole United States representatives, tell us that F. Chauvenet owns some choice vineyards in the Nuits-Saint-Georges area.

Gevrey-Chambertin is the town that claims the king of wines, with eight vineyards producing Chambertin. A century ago, Gevrey added the famous name to its own, as other towns did on the Côte d'Or. The thing to remember is that a wine labeled Gevrey-Chambertin is never more than average, sometimes good but never with any distinction, and nothing at all like the noble wines that are called Chambertin or Chambertin-Clos-de-Bèze.

By stringently respected law, the wine of Burgundy is made from the grape varietal, the glorious Pinot, small grapes in tight little packs. It takes a kilo (2 1/2 pounds) to make one bottle of wine. The great reds come from the Pinot Noir; the few whites from the Pinot Chardonnay or Pinot Blanc, just as the red wines of Bordeaux are almost inevitably of several grape varieties. The nature of the soil is another factor in the production of the wines of the Côte de Nuits —a mixture of clay, silica and some limestone, enriched for 1,500 years by a compost made solely from the mulch of the leaves and cuttings of the vines. The position of the vineyards on the hill slopes plays an important part in catching the desired angle of the sun's rays.

B. THE CÔTE DE BEAUNE TO THE SOUTH   From Ladoix to Chagny, red and white wine of distinction is produced. The red wine matures more quickly than that of the Côte de Nuits. It is smooth, velvety and full—Corton and Pommard, for example. With its ramparts and the Hôtel Dieu dating from the 15th century, Beaune is the commercial center for the wine of Burgundy. The wine is a little lighter than that of the Côte de Nuits, but has a strong bouquet, delicate and smooth. Soft reds of Beaune may become drinkable in half the time of the Côte de Nuits to the north. The full white are ready to drink in three years from the southern strip of Côte de Beaune. The white wine, Meursalt and the various Montrachets are dry, fruity and rank among the very finest. The principal townships are: Aloxe-Corton, Pernand-Vergelesses, Beaune, Pommard, Volnay, Meursault, Chassagne and Puligny-Montrachet.

Wine made from the Chardonnay grapes are conspicuous for their powerful and supremely elegant bouquet. The district of Mercurey or Chalonnaise is a continuation of the Côte de Beaune; its red wine is rich and fragrant. Its white wine, Rully and Montagny, leave you "with a fresh mouth and a clear head."

The 1970 vineyards were marvels. The wine made in 1970 will be exceptional. Plenty of wine was in production. In the harvest weeks of November 1970, a glorious smell filled the air in each town, a green odor like early spring, an aroma of fruits and flowers. It is what you taste in the young wine that is meant to be enjoyed soon after the vintage, the white wine and the reds. Only the greatest will last beyond this decade, but in 1975, Le Chambertin of 1970 will be enchanting.

3. In the South   Southern Burgundy refers to Chalon, Macon and Beaujolais.

A. CHALON   Chalon produces the well-known wine of Mercurey, Rully, Givry and Montagny. The 30 miles of the Côte d'Or reach an end at Chagny, where the Chalonnaise begins along Motor Route National 6.

B. MACON   From Tournus to Creches is a region of splendid vineyards rich in agricultural treasures and beautiful landscapes. The Maconnais produce red and white wine, both very fine, the most famous being Pouilly-Fuissé, a dry, fruity, heady, white wine made from white Pinot Chardonnay grapes. This is the wine so familiarly requested as an accompaniment to fish dishes. Macon Blanc and its companions, Pouilly-Vinzelles and Pouilly-Loché complete the group.

On the chalky soil in the north of the Macon region, the black Gamay grape with white juice is used in making the sprightly Macon Rouge and Macon Rosé wine.

C. BEAUJOLAIS   Along the Saône as far as the city of Lyon, the region of Beaujolais basks in a hotter sun. A series of pleasant vineyards produce the Beaujolais-Villages wine, each bearing the name of the village it comes from—for example, Beaujolais-Quincie. On the granite ridges to the north are nine great vineyards surrounding as many villages: Saint Amour, Juliénas, Chénas, Moulin-à-Vent, Fleurie, Chiroubles, Morgon and Brouilly.

These are the fresh, light, lively, fruity wines with an earthy flavor and bouquet, younger and cooler than the great Burgundies. Visitors are welcome to the cellars to sample them. Beaujolais is said to be the democracy of winedom, since most of the vignerons either own or have an interest in the vineyards they work. This makes for a jovial independence and good humor that transfers itself to the wine, which reflects the pleasantness of life. The people are generous, kind and hospitable. Lyon itself is renowned for gastronomy. Charolles is the home of the white Charolais beef cattle. Across the river Saône, the province of Bresse is rich in eggs, cream, butter and that Gorgonzola-like blue cheese made from cow's milk called Bresse Bleu. Beaujolais makes good, tart, white cheese from goat's milk called Chèvres or Chevretons. From the Saône, the eastern boundary of Beaujolais, come freshwater fish including eels, crayfish, perch and carp, all of which are combined into a delicious fish stew called Pochouse. The pike or brochet is used to make Quenelle de Brochet, a subtly poached croquette.

Not far from Romanèche-Thorins on the northern boundary of Beaujolais is the village of Chenas, one of the most famous vineyard centers. The local specialty—Poularde de Bresse, capon cooked in red wine—is a splendid dish offered in a little country inn called Relais des Grands Crus Monsieur Robin, where local wines are on the table. (It is a short distance outside of Chenas on the scenic Route de Beaujolais, road number D 68.) In Belleville on the banks of the Saône, the Hôtel-Restaurant Beaujolais serves Ecrevisses à la creme, crayfish in cream sauce, accompanied by a dry white wine of Pouilly-Fuissé.

Smoothness and fruitiness are the characteristics of a Beaujolais wine, a gay, happy companion. At every famous vineyard there is a tasting shed where motorists are welcomed. On the wine route, we are now not far from Lyon, third largest city of France, renowned for its culinary excellence and wine lists.

Champagne

Champagne is a country and it is a wine. This section is herewith joyously presented in behalf of Champagne because the grape harvest in the fall of 1970 from the nearly 25,000 acres of vineyards was at an all-time record high. So much was gathered that major producers brought in all kinds of temporary containers to hold the must, or juice, through the first period of fermentation. Complete tanker car trains were parked on railroad sidings around Reims and Epernay to handle the great overflow. The firm of Moët & Chandon towed in five giant wine-tanker barges up the Marne River to accommodate the bumper harvest. The 12,000 vineyard owners were jubilant, and this feeling will spread around the world years from now when the long-awaited vintage of 1970 begins to be shipped out.

The grapes destined for the press houses of each vineyard town are weighed and heaped into the square or round presses about 12 feet across. A great lid comes down on the mound of grapes and they are lightly pressed. The sweet, pinkish juice is pumped into vats or distributed to the Champagne firms, where the juice ferments into wine. Around Christmas 1970 or January 1971, the first fermentation was complete. The wine from the various vineyards was then blended, the result called a cuvée or a vatting.

The traditional blend is from the black Pinot Noir grapes grown around the mountain of Reims. Wine from the white Chardonnay grapes from the southern ridge are called Côte des Blancs. Taittinger makes Champagne only from the white grapes, calling it Blanc des Blancs. The wine rests for a period of three years before being shipped.

The sparkling wine of pleasure and lightheartedness is the wine for every hour and occasion. Champagne has been called the "exquisite ambassador of French perfection," a must in celebrating a success, announcing an engagement, entertaining at a wedding, christening a child—or a ship. Champagne is the most famous of all of the great wine regions of France. No other wine has had the worshipful respect and joyous welcome of Champagne. It never varies in popularity, except to grow even more welcome as time goes on.

By French law, only wine made from grapes grown in the Champagne region may be called Champagne. The process of making Champagne, termed "Champagnization," is widely used in other parts of France as well as in other countries for the making of better sparkling wine. Yet even the best of the sparklers are not Champagne, because only in that region is there the combination of soil and climate that makes the unique quality of the wine.

Champagne is not a large area, yet it is the most concentrated vine district of France. It lies about 80 miles east of Paris on the way to Germany, a wide plain of cultivated land from which the world-famous city of Reims rises. To the south, the Montagne de Reims stretches in a series of long, wooded hills. On the slopes lie some of the finest wine districts of Champagne. On the southern side of the Montagne de Reims runs the Marne River, with wine areas on both banks. Chief among these is Ay, classed as one of the very best, and Epernay, the principal and renowned town of this section; still farther south and across the Marne River is the Côte des Blancs, then Cramant and Avize.

Nowhere in the world can be found such a favored combination of soil, climate, geological and geographical conditions to make up the exact factors needed for producing the original Champagne. The annual average daily temperature is 50° F., precisely right for bringing the grapes to maturity. The vines are well sheltered from the north wind; the slight altitude above plain level sufficient in most cases to preserve them from spring frosts.

The work of the vinegrower, nevertheless, is intense and never-ending as he battles insects, disease, occasional frosts and storms, any of which may bring disaster to the crop.

In the prehistoric Second Epoch, an inland sea covered the vast Champagne district. In the course of thousands of years, the sea withdrew, leaving behind large deposits of chalk that make up the soil. Chalky soil reflects the sun's rays and provides the maximum heat and light needed by the vines. Nearby forests hold and regulate the variations of moisture; the lime and calcium of the soil help to make the wine what it is.

The vineyards are a great ring of black grapes around the mountain slopes of Reims and another long curve of white grapes along a slope that runs south from a ridge that begins near the Marne. The narrow band runs midway along the slopes, 100 miles or so in length and from 4 to 1,500 yards wide.

The grapes are small, with thin skins and few seeds. The vines are kept short by pruning, so there is no waste of either heat or sap. The delicate vine demands exacting care as many dangers constantly threaten its life and health. When the harvest comes, the grape bunches are minutely examined and selected, the spoiled grapes eliminated. It takes four tons of grapes to yield 444 gallons of must, which begins the life of the wine. Each of the districts produces wine with special characteristics, and the successful blending of these make what we know as Champagne.

In the country of Champagne are deep cellars 100 feet below the ground, dug out of the waterproof chalk foundations. They are everywhere, stretching for more than 120 miles. Millions of bottles remain resting in these cellars in a cool and even temperature before they go forth to grace the festive boards of the world.

In 1690, Dom Perignon, the blind cellarkeeper of the Abbey of Hautvillers in the Benedictine Abbey of Epernay, accidentally discovered how to control fermentation—i.e., the secret of a second fermentation, the chemical action that puts the bubbles into Champagne. Wine would be obtained that kept both its limpidity and sparkle. At the moment of his find, the excited monk rushed from his cellar crying exultantly, "Come quickly, I am drinking the stars!" Later he produced the cuvées by blending wine of different growths, which gave the wine a richer bouquet. His artistry was greater than that ever before used in developing Champagne.

The most festive and extraordinary of wine went directly to the tables of royalty. Each European court drank Champagne at its celebrations, following the examples of Louis XIV, Louis XV, the king of Prussia and the English Court. The coronation of the kings of France took place at the ancient Cathedral of Reims, and Champagne was the drink in toasting: "Vive le roi! Vive la France!"

Improvements in production, with special bottles being manufactured with the right power of resistance and new ways found for making use of the cork stopper, came during the reign of Napoleon Bonaparte. The emperor himself encouraged Champagne making during a visit to Champagne in July 1807, when he was received at Epernay by the Moët & Chandon people.

It was during the French Revolution that Champagne was divided into four departments: Aisne, Aube, Haut-Marne, Marne. The plains run along rolling hills, the big river, woods, forests, but very few of the charming little villages and towns you expect to find in France. In the summer it rains frequently. In the spring, the country is lush and beautiful from all of the rains. Vintage time is the long-awaited sunny season. There is a strange luminosity or dazzle as the bits of chalk dust in the fields reflect the light. There are about 24 large Champagne producers and some 16,000 people who now sell their grapes to the producers at fair prices.

Times were not always good. During the past two centuries, Champagne has been invaded time and again. Russians, Prussians, English and Americans have all trampled over the fields and through the vineyards. After Napoleon's defeat at the Battle of Leipzig—when he was compelled to abdicate and retire to the island of Elba—the Russians invaded France. Again Champagne was occupied by the troops of the Czar. They helped themselves to the thousands of bottles stored in the great cellars, slaking a heroic thirst. A criminal amount of Champagne thus went down the Cossack throats.

To know the history of the Champagne country is to touch the heartbeat of France. Hardly a region is more closely associated with great events. In 57 B.C., Julius Caesar was confronted at Reims by a Belgic tribe. Having an affinity for Latin civilization, they wisely offered Caesar their alliance rather than pitting their strength against his legions, who would only destroy whatever they had built up. Caesar made the town of the Belgians a fine Gallo-Roman city, calling it Durocortorum. It became the capital of the province of Belgae the Second, the crossroads of eight main highways, famed for its magnificent monuments. At the time Durocortorum, the forebear of Reims, was a bustling city with statues and fine roads, Paris was still only an obscure village on an island in the Seine known as Lutetia Parisorum.

When the Roman Empire collapsed, early in the fifth century, and was overrun by Goths and Vandals, Reims was destroyed by fire. Epernay and Chalons shared a similar fate. However, even in the confusion of destruction, the Archbishops of Reims asserted their authority and prestige. In 496, Saint Remi baptized—in the presence of King Clovis—the Frankish monarchy in the Cathedral of Reims, thereby inaugurating the long tradition of coronations that made Reims the holy city of France.

This is important to the history of Champagne because the successors of Saint Remi, who later frequently intervened in the affairs of the kingdom, were given the title of Counts, then elevated to that of Ducs de Reims, the first peers of France. Under the feudal system, they were temporal lords, quite independent of the Counts of Champagne, and governed as sovereign rulers. This applied as well to the Count and Bishop of Chalons; Epernay, several times claimed by the Counts of Champagne, also came under the domination of the royalty of the Church.

In the course of time, out of so many seignorial estates (comprising vast areas of land and skillfully cultivated vineyards) regions were founded with an intellectual life: Saint-Rémi de Reims, Saint-Thierry, Hautvillers, Verzy, Orbais, and others. The 12th century marked the first crusade to the Holy Land in which the Champenois enthusiastically participated. In the shady glades at Chalons, Saint Bernard preached Christianity in 1147. In an era of economic prosperity, Champagne Fairs were held which attracted world travelers. Population movements increased circulation of merchandise and money, and the building of magnificent Romanesque churches began. The churches were the true fruits of an artistic genius developed so remarkably in the 12th century in the erection of the awe-inspiring Champenois cathedrals: Reims, Troyes, Chalons and Soissons. They manifested in the highest degree the marvels of Remois sculpture, and all of the beauty arose out of the gratitude of the human spirit to a beneficent God who gave them the gifts, the bountiful gifts, of the vines.

The northern part of Champagne was in a dangerous location. It was the line of march during the One Hundred Years War with England, trampled upon, then ravaged by rival factions of the Armagnacs and the Anglo-Burdunians. Ramparts were built at Reims, making it possible to repel the assault made upon the city in 1359 by King Edward III of England. Edward was determined to be crowned king at Reims, but so well protected was the city he was unable to gain entry. The less well-protected town of Epernay was lost and retaken, burned, ransacked and ruined no less than 22 times. But days of consolation were to come. July 17, 1429, marked the coronation of Charles VII as King of France, escorted to Reims with superhuman tenacity by Joan of Arc.

The Three Separate Districts in Champagne

Montagne de Reims: Gueux, Villedommange, Ecueil, Rilly-la-Montagne, Sillery, Chigny-les-Roses, Ludes, Mailly, Champagne, Verzenay, Verzy, Villers, Louvois, Bouzy.

Marne Valley and Epernay: Ay, Mareuil, Dizy, Cumieres, Hautvillers, Binson, Chatillon, Vaudières, Vincelles.

Côte des Blancs (South of the Marne): Cramant, Pierry, Avize, Oger, Le Mesnil-sur-Oger, Vertus, Bergères.

The wine of Champagne is fruity, light, sparkling. Generally it is pale yellow, although some pink Champagne is also produced. Each great Champagne producer has its own standard in blending, and the reputation of the Champagne producer is the best guarantee of quality. Nonvintage wine from a reputable firm often equals or even surpassas a vintage wine from an obscure house. Champagnes are labeled according to the degree of dryness. The quantity of sugar and old wine added in the blending determines whether it will be:

Brut—the driest

Extra Dry—fairly dry

Sec (dry)—sweet

Demi-Sec (medium dry)—very sweet

This is the only region in which the word "sec" (dry) has such meaning.

Small oak casks are used by Bollinger for the first fermentation rather than enormous vats. Mme. Jacques Bollinger, known as Tante Lily, and often seen on her trusty bicycle, continues the family tradition begun in 1829. She personally supervises all processes including the making of the cuvée, and blending, a very sensitive task in producing a properly balanced Champagne. The secondary fermentation takes place in the bottle, where pressure builds up to 110 pounds per square inch, so the bottle must be sturdy. The cellar cork must be adequate. A bad cellar cork or bottle cap can ruin Champagne during aging because it may not seal properly. Bollinger uses only fresh, firm Spanish and Portuguese cork from trees at least 50 years old. The whole process takes place underground. Once bottled, the wine is stored in chalky subcellars where the temperature never varies from 50° F. Bollinger's cellars spread out under the entire town of Ay.

In France, law decrees Vintage Champagne must age at least three years. Bollinger keeps their vintage wine in their cellars at least five years before marketing them. During the aging process, natural sediment forms. Each bottle is turned clockwise one-eighth of a turn by hand every two or three days during the last three months of aging; a good worker can thus riddle 30,000 bottles in a day. Special racks hold the bottles vertically, necks down. Sediment settles in the neck against the cork.

It is a tricky process to disgorge the sediment. After riddling, the neck of each bottle is frozen. The cellar cork is released and takes the frozen sediment with it. The shipping cork is secured, with the familiar wire-retaining cage. All of this is done very quickly so no sparkle is lost. Before shipping, Bollinger Champagne is permitted to rest from the strain of disgorging by aging further, then it is labeled and shipped. Julius Wile is the sole importer to the United States.

The Abbey at Hautvillers where Dom Pérignon discovered the

delicate process for making the fine sparkling wine, we call Champagne, is part of the famous Maison Moët & Chandon, the world's largest producer of fine Champagnes. Founded on the site by Claude Moët in 1743, he was succeeded by his son Nicolas-Claude and his grandson Jean-Rémy Moët. The latter, who was well educated, traveled to the great capitals of Europe and was many times the mayor of Epernay. Members of the imperial family of France and Napoleon himself visited his estate. The Emperor decorated him personally in 1814. In 1832, Jean-Rémy Moët released the active control of the business to his son, Victor Moët, and to his son-in-law, Pierre-Gabriel Chandon. Henceforth, the firm was known as Moët & Chandon and has ever since remained in the hands of descendants of the two families involved.

From its fabulous 16-mile cellar that holds 20 million bottles in reserve come the distinctive Moët Champagnes: White Seal (nonvintage), Brut Imperial (nonvintage), Dry Imperial and Dry Imperial Rosé (vintage) and the incomparable Dom Pérignon (vintage). White Seal is available in half-bottles (13 ounces), bottles (26 ounces), magnums (52 ounces). Brut Imperial is available in splits (6 ½ ounces), Rehoboams (156 ounces), Methuselahs (208 ounces). Dry Imperial is available in half-bottles (13 ounces), bottles (26 ounces), magnums (52 ounces), Jeroboams (104 ounces). Dom Pérignon and Dry Imperial Rosé come only in bottles (26 ounces)—exclusively imported by Schieffelin & Co., New York City.

Taittinger Champagne is made in Reims, France, with every resource to produce the best. Their long, deep wine cellars reach far into the chalk earth, actually those of the most famous Abbey of Reims, the Abbey of Sainte-Nicaise, whose buildings were destroyed during the French Revolution. More than 150,000 visitors from all over the world annually visit these cellars, which were excavated in Gallo-Roman times. Taittinger Champagne is made from grapes grown in vineyards exclusively owned by the family, and the vines are located in what are called "les plus grands crus" of Avize, Ambonnay, Mailly and others. Great care is taken in picking the grapes, and only the first pressing is used. The pressing plants are located at Rilly-la-Montagne, Mailly, Ambonnay, Hautvillers, Avize and Pierry.

The ancient house of Fourneaux, Forest et Succrs, founded in 1734, was the predecessor of the Taittinger family. Pierre Taittinger, a director of Fourneaux, acquired the company in 1936 and with it the Château de La Marquetterie in the village of Pierry, where monks formerly practiced the art of making Champagne. In the cellars of La Marquetterie toward the end of the 17th century, Frère Jean Oudart, contemporaneously with Dom Pérignon of Hautvillers, discovered the secret of second fermentation that causes Champagne to sparkle.

Dating from the 18th century, La Marquetterie is situated in the heart of one of the largest vineyard holdings of the Taittinger family.

During the Battle of the Marne it served as headquarters of Marshal Joffre, but today is more happily used for the reception of distinguished visitors to the Taittinger vineyards. In Reims, Taittinger owns two other historical monuments of France, the former home of the Comtes de Champagne, Thibault IV, and the Maison de Musiciens, both dating from the 13th century. Taittinger named its finest cuvée Comtes de Champagne, Blanc des Blancs, Thibault IV in honor of this aristocrat.

One of the principal reasons for the high quality of Taittinger Champagne is that it has been produced under the supervision of the gifted and personable Monsieur Roger Lenique, whose family members have been "chefs de caves" for eight generations. In the medieval mansion of Count Thibault IV, glittering candelight receptions are given in honor of visitors to the city of Reims.

Originally from Lorraine, the Taittinger family established themselves in Paris in 1870 when the Germans took Lorraine. At the present time, this Champagne family controls the Hôtel Le Crillon, Hôtel du Louvre, Hôtel du Palais d'Orsay, Hôtel Lutetia and the Hôtel Terminus Saint-Lazare, as well as Le Poccardi, the celebrated Italian restaurant in Paris. Claude Taittinger, one of Pierre's sons, supervises the export sale and distribution of Taittinger Champagne in world markets. In the United States, the special representative for Taittinger is gracious Prince Ivan P. Obolensky, who has with great dedication successfully introduced Taittinger for use in connection with distinguished social events in the United States. He has promoted Taittinger Champagne continuously since its introduction in 1945, imported by Kobrand Corporation, New York City.

There is much nobility of family in the Champagne country and what may justly be called an aristocracy of the wine. Monsieur Emile Moreau of Pol Roger Champagne is the supreme authority on all that is Champagne—soil, vine, grape, taste and bouquet. He has been a wine taster since 1912, and for years was president of the Champagne Producers League.

Count Bertrans de Vogue, an ex-mayor of Reims, now heads the Syndicat des Grandes Marques and is a director and president of Veuve Clicquot, whose cellars were built in Roman times. The Lanson dynasty is represented by Victor Lanson and his son François, whose Lanson's Black Label is one of the choicest nonvintage Champagnes, much appreciated as an aperitif by those who know. They have awe-inspiring, mammoth, ultramodern cuvées or vats used in processing their Champagne.

Other notables known to the Champagne world are Monsieur Snozzi, director-general and president of Mumm, and Monsieur Couvreur, managing director of cellars and bottling plants for Cordon Rouge. Count Raoul Chandon-Moët is administrator of Moët &

Chandon, whose family château of Saran is surrounded up to the walls by lush vineyards. Count Robert Jean du Vogue is the debonair president of Moët & Chandon. Few Champagnes enjoy a better reputation than those bottled in this area of Epernay. The Marquis d'Aulan, young and handsome, directs Piper-Heidsieck. Piper-Heidsieck is not connected with another great brand of Champagne, Charles Heidsieck, whose wife, Odette, and three children bring beauty and youth to Champagne making. The family château of Pol Roger is located at Epernay, where Mme. Jacques Pol Roger is a social leader. Winston Churchill named his pet racing horse Pol Roger.

Each house produces Champagne suitable to special tastes, which depend on the consumer. Champagne flavors range from the delicate, light and flowery—Pol Roger, Perrier-Jouet and perhaps Taittinger—to the full wine such as Veuve Clicquot and Krug. Lanson's Black Label promotes a nonvintage wine. The skill is in choosing such wine, for all vintage wine not more than 10 years old will be good. Mercier and Moët & Chandon are the largest producers. There are three firms that dispute the succession of the 18th-century Florens-Louis Heidsieck—Heidsieck Dry Monopole, Piper-Heidsieck and Charles Heidsieck—which seem to resemble each other. There is a long list for your pleasure—Mumm, Irroy, Ruinart (oldest of all), Bollinger, Pommery, Roederer and more.

Côtes du Rhone

The vineyards of this area extend for 120 miles between Lyon and Avignon on both banks of the Rhone River, which flows southward to the Mediterranean. There are two wine regions, separated from each other by a zone of some 40 miles where there are no vineyards. In the northern section, which stretches from Vienne down to Valence, the land rises steeply from the river valley and the vines grow on the terraced hillsides. The vineyards are protected by rough-hewn stone walls similar to those in the Provence region. There are great variations in soil, climate, exposures and types of vine all contributing to the variety of the wines produced. The wines are warm and full-bodied, vigorous, with a rich bouquet and luscious taste.

The principal wines come from Côte Rôtie, Condrieu, Hermitage, Cornas, Saint Péray, Lirac, Tavel and Châteauneuf-du-Pape.

White Wine (few)

From the North: Condrieu, Château Grillet, White Saint-Joseph, Hermitage and Crozes-Hermitage and Saint Péray, among others.

From the South: Southern Côtes du Rhone wine is of a notable finesse and elegance only when it comes from the light, sandy soils like Laudin and Lirac. Small quantities of white Châteauneuf-du-Pape recall the wine served for Mass in the Papal Palace when Avignon was the seat of the Catholic Church from 1305 to 1377. The

Papacy at that time was occupied by men of French birth, who maintained the Holy See at Avignon. The first of the Avignon Popes was Clement V, a native of Bordeaux and its Archbishop. Familiar with viticulture, he left as a legacy the wonderful wine Graves Claret, Château Pape Clement. When he built a château, truly a fortress, just outside of the town, this building was promptly dubbed "the new château of the Pope"—Châteauneuf-du-Pape. This is probably the most well-known wine of the Côtes du Rhone, the 1955 vintage especially precious and scarce. The palace itself is a vast labyrinth that goes from magnificence to monasticism to whimsey. The white wine is to be drunk when young, going perfectly with fish dishes and other seafoods.

Rosé Wine   Chusclan, Lirac and especially Tavel, with its beautiful light, ruby color and golden gleam, were highly coveted by Louis XIV. Vaucluse Rosé wine is finding more and more favor with visitors who have an opportunity to taste these rosés. Tavel is justly famous as one of the best rosés produced anywhere. The town of Tavel, situated across the river from Avignon, gives its name to this clean, fresh, dry, fruity wine. It is always served chilled like a white wine, and consumed when about five years old.

Red Wine   These "children of the sun" are all robust, generous, high in alcoholic content. Their warmth and fullness vary according to the condition of the soil, orientation, and the variety of vines. In the north, the Syrah and Viognier vines in the Côte Rôtie near Ampius produce fine, vigorous wine with a rich bouquet that age well. Red Hermitage and Crozes-Hermitage wine from the granitelike soil near Tournon are deep in color, delicate and mellow, achieving with age the glory of the great Burgundies. The deep red Cornas is an elegant wine; Saint-Joseph, an unassuming, modest wine. Côte Rôtie, one of the most famous and oldest of all of the Côte du Rhone red wine, comes from the vineyards almost opposite Vienne, on the other bank of the river. It has been favored down through the ages for its richness and aroma. South of Lyon, near the ancient Roman city of Vienne and across the river from Condrieu, lie the vineyards that produce Côte Rôtie. In Roman times, they were highly praised by Pliny, Plutarch and Columella. Côte Rôtie wine is 12 to 15 years old before it is considered ready to drink.

In the south, the light red wine (when young, too high in alcohol) is supple, fine, well balanced, reaching its peak at the end of the first year. The fuller-bodied red wine is warm, heady, with a noticeable tannin content. It keeps well, has a good aroma and a lusty bouquet. To mention a few: wine from Cairanne, Gigondas, Vacqueras and Vinsobres (here Rosés are also produced).

Between Orange and Avignon, where the pebbly soil is thoroughly sun-baked, are the vineyards that produce the noble red Châteauneuf-du-Pape, a specially good companion for venison and game.

Rasteau produces a sweet, natural wine. Beames-de-Venise produces Muscatel aperitif or dessert wine. Saint Péray produces a sparkling, heady, fruity wine. These are only an aristocratic sampling suggested by the French Government. The Côtes du Rhone district proudly encompasses 140 wine-producing communes.

Special Wine

From the Rhone River to the Pyrenees spreads the region of Languedoc Province called Midi, the South, where much good table wine is produced. The superior ones bear the V.D.Q.S. label. We have traveled 120 miles from Dijon through the greatest of the world's vineyards, up and down hill and dale among the cheerful, hardworking French vineyard people, whose friend and adversary is nature itself. To enjoy the privilege of tastings and cellar visits in Burgundy, you may contact:

> *In Beaune: Négociants en Vins fins de Bourgogne*
>
> *In Macon: Comité Interprofessionnel des Vins de Bourgogne, B.P. No. 113, Macon, France*
>
> *In Belleville: Maison de Beaujolais, Saint-Jean d'Ardières*

The Côtes de Provence (Côte d'Azur) produces some lovely wine, of which the reds are full-bodied and full-flavored, the rosés light, fresh and fruity. The whites are dry and full-bodied, sometimes slightly sparkling. They go perfectly with fish and shellfish. Such wine is to be drunk when young. The sun-drenched region bordering on the Mediterranean offers wine that is natural for Mediterranean-type foods.

Côtes de Provence

There is an array of wine—red, rosé, white—produced from Marseilles to Nice, from Aix-en-Provence to Toulon and Draguignan along the Côte d'Azur and on the slopes of the Maures from Sainte-Victoire to Sainte-Beaume. Among these under Appellation Contrôlée are Cassis, Bandol, Bellet de Nice and Palette d'Aix. Full-bodied red wine of Puget-Ville, Taradeau, Pierre-a-feu, and so on go well with Provençal venison dishes.

Aix-en-Provence is one of the most beautiful cities in France. Its superb old houses are reminiscent of the days when there were more of nobility than commoners inhabiting them. Many have courtyards and fountains. In Aix is held the annual Music Festival. Many of the concerts take place in the inner courtyard of the old Archbishop's Palace. Tickets are at a premium to be booked in advance by one's travel agent or by the concierge at the Hôtel Roy René. Over a century ago, a great cache of 18th-century tapestries of Beauvais weaving was discovered in one of the dust-covered palace attics, hidden away from the ravages of the French Revolution. They are presently on display in the Museum of Tapestries on the ground floor of the palace. Many have a motif of the grape and vineyards.

Cézanne lived and painted in Aix, where his little house is now preserved. Around it is one Cézanne living landscape after another —wheatfields, gnarled cypresses that surround Arles not far away, like a vast painting by Van Gogh. Arles is the bullfighting center of Provence, the bullring situated in the ancient Roman arena. Surrounded by vineyards, Arles is full of picturesque ruins, including a theater left over from Roman times, and much saffron-colored pottery for sale. Up the road from Arles is Avignon, with its famous bridge and renowned Palais des Papes, that great tangle of corridors, rooms, chapels, oratories and reminders of much lusty dining and drinking. For instance, we found La Chambre au Cerf to be frescoed with scenes of hunting, hawking and fishing, comissioned by a Pope who reveals himself as a mighty hunter, a bon vivant with an earthy sense of humor.

Alsace   The Alsatian vineyards are situated on the eastern slopes of the Vosges Mountains opposite the Black Forest of Germany. They cover the acres along the French side of the Rhine from Strasbourg to Thann. In Julius Caesar's time, Alsace-Lorraine was part of Gaul, bounded on the west by France and on the north by the Grand Duchy of Luxembourg and Germany, on the east by Germany and on the south by Switzerland. The name was combined when Germany took it in the War of 1870. It was returned to France after World War I, but again taken by Germany in World War II until liberated by the Allies in 1945. It is divided into three departments: Moselle, Bas-Rhin and Haut-Rhin.

Strasbourg is the chief city of Alsace, more prominent than Mulhouse and Colmar. Metz, on the Moselle River, is the chief city of Lorraine. The Rhine separates Alsace from Germany. The Ill, an affluent of the Rhine, flows through the country, and the Moselle and its affluent flows through the Saar. Alsace is a broad plain bounded on one side by the Rhine and on the other by the Vosges Mountains. Lorraine is more hilly than mountainous. Together, Alsace-Lorraine comprises one of the richest sections of France, known to gourmets for its excellent cuisine, especially the delicacy Foie Gras—and its famous white wine.

Originally a part of ancient Gaul, it was later included within the Empire of Charlemagne, then fell to the Germans, who had this section for seven centuries. It was at the home of Baron Philippe-Frederic de Dietrich, Mayor of Strasbourg, that the "Marseillaise" was sung for the first time in 1792.

Alsace is very German in appearance, the towns and villages bearing German names, the people speaking a German dialect. The wine is made from the same grapes, Sylvaner, Traminer and Riesling, as the best wine of Germany. Yet, the Alsatians feel intensely French. The Route du Vin d'Alsace runs from Thann, just to the west of Mulhouse, northward for 60 miles through Colmar and almost to Strasbourg, passing as many villages, the houses with ironwork balconies ablaze with flowers. Some villages have no more than 500 or 600 people, all connected with the vineyards. There are 440 communes with some 30,000 people involved with the grapes and making of the wine.

The wine is not named from the geographical locations of the vineyards, but after the grapes from which they are made:

LIGHT RED GRAPES: Traminer, a smooth, full-bodied wine, dry and luscious Gewürztraminer, a choice Traminer, has all of the same characteristics to the highest degree. Both may be served throughout the meal, perfect accompaniments to highly seasoned dishes and pungent cheeses, as well as to sweet desserts.

WHITE GRAPES: Pinot Gris (or known as Tokay d'Alsace), a dry, white wine, full-bodied and heady. It acquires a magnificent richness in very good years, but still retains a pleasing freshness. This wine enhances all rich food, particularly juicy roast meats and Foie Gras.

Riesling, a proud, elegant wine with a distinguished bouquet and exquisite flavor that complements the finest food, superb with fish and shellfish.

Muscat d'Alsace, a fruity, dry, noble wine, with a characteristic bouquet that gives the drinker a sensation of biting into freshly picked grapes. It is delicious as an aperitif wine.

Pinot Blanc (or Clevner), a dry, white wine, supple and virile, round and vigorous, with a pleasing freshness, a clean-cut wine that can be drunk whenever a dry, white wine is proper.

Sylvaner, a fine wine, dry, white, light-bodied, delicate and fresh, soft, fruity. It goes well with fish, shellfish and white meat, delightful as an aperitif.

Every August for more than two decades, there has been a Wine Fair held in Colmar to promote Alsatian wines and increase their imports by other countries. The Association of Wines of Alsace was set up in 1911, and within a year, 3,800 members joined the Association. The vineyards affected by the deadly phylloxera were destroyed and new vines planted, grafting adopted, Alsatian wines improved. New vicissitudes seriously imperiled this promising revival. The damage wrought by World War I was so serious that by 1918 the vineyards were destroyed once again for many reasons—the shortage of labor; children, women and old people trying to tend the vineyards during the war; a lack of copper sulphate used to combat mildew. World War II brought its destruction of parishes and towns. This was rectified by the setting up of cooperative societies from 1945 to 1958, enabling wine growers to enlarge their properties.

Near the great cathedral in Strasbourg is the Maison Kammerzell, a restaurant established in a house built in 1472, which belongs to a group of Alsatian wine growers. Here can be enjoyed the array of Alsatian wines—the light, dry Pinot and the fruitier Sylvaner, the delicate Riesling, the full-bodied Traminer, accompanying the classic cuisine from the royal Paté de Foie Gras de Strasbourg to the peasant dish of Choucroute. There are Alsatian Brandies, too, and the Liqueurs: Kirsch distilled from cherries; Mirabelle or Quetsch from different varieties of plums; Fraise from strawberries and Framboise from wild raspberries.

The Jura   Between Burgundy and Alsace along the eastern part of Burgundy stretch the wine-growing areas of Franche-Comté from Arbois, Poligny and Château Chalon to Lons-le-Saunier. The vineyards, which produce good wine for laying down, are situated at the foot of steep limestone slopes. Among the famous names of the Côtes du Jura are Arbois, l'Etoile, Château-Chalon, Seyssel, Vin Jaune, Pupillin, Montigny-les-Arsures, Menetru-le-Vignoble, Quintigny, Cesancey, Saint-Laurent, La Roche, Château d'Arlay.

Rosé wine (from Poulsard grapes) is lively and fresh, gradually acquiring a bronze gleam known as "onion-skin."

White wine of the Jura (from grapes called Melon) is pale gold in color, well-balanced, fruity, delicate.

Sparkling wine of the Jura, such as Etoile, is called "straightforward and fine."

Yellow wine of the Jura (from Savagnin grapes) is allowed to mature slowly in casks that for at least six years are not filled up as the level drops from evaporation. The process is similar to that used for Johannisberg wine and Sherry, the wine being protected from the air by a layer of yeast. This yellow wine, which will keep for a century in its special bottle (clavelin), is rare and consequently expensive.

"Straw wine" (Vin de Paille) is made from grapes that are allowed to dry for a long time and then pressed on straw mats. This wine has a high alcoholic content (16 percent) but is still deliciously sweet.

Louis Pasteur, born in Arbois, is the famous son of the Jura whose experiments on alcohol fermentation (1866) are well known in viniculture. He paid high tribute to the qualities of wine: "Wine can with justice be regarded as the healthiest and most hygienic beverage there is."

Savoy   This area, lying below Lyon, includes the mountainous area around Grenoble toward the eastern border of France and Switzerland. The fresh aroma of Savoy wine has the tang of its native mountain air.

  White wine, excellent with river and lake trout, includes some notable names: Crépy, Seyssel, Apremont, Chautagne, Marignan Savoy Roussettes, which come from Frangy, Marestel, Monthoux, Monterminod and Ayse. Red and rosé wine includes Montmelian, Arbin, Cruet and Saint-Jean-de-la-Porte.

The Loire

The Loire, France's greatest river, runs 600 miles from its mouth near the city of Nantes (where the famous Muscadet Wine is produced) to its source, swinging in an enormous curve through the larger area of France from the Atlantic coast into the low, ranging hills called the Cévennes almost into Provence a scant 80 miles north of the Mediterranean. From there the Loire winds its way northwest through several of France's great medieval provinces: Languedoc, Lyonnais, Bourbonnais, Burgundy, Nivernais, Berry, Orléanais, Touraine, Anjou and Brittany. Its tributaries fan out to include Poitou (summer home of Cardinal de Richelieu), Angoumois, Limousin, Marche, Auvergne, Maine and even Normandy. In the Middle Ages, when the bulk of heavy commerce was moved by barges, this net of waterways made the Loire Valley the main highway of the country.

  Roanne, Nevers, Bourges, Orléans, Blois, Saumur, Angers and Nantes were all medieval centers of importance; Tours, the Loire's most well-known city, outshone Paris for several centuries as a center of commerce and culture. Tours was an advanced city right after the collapse of the Roman Empire, a factor in the creation of the entity known as France. The valley of the Loire is still considered the area where the purest French is spoken. From the ninth century onward, the Vikings and Vandals came out of the north into the interior to pillage, rob, burn and rape. Although Tours was 150 miles from the sea, the dragon ships came up and sacked her of her wealth. As Tours declined, Paris rose to prominence, protected by its situation in the middle of a winding stream, on whose every bend stood a defending fortress against attackers.

  The highest point of the Loire's history came during the reign of François I. He was the contemporary of Henry VIII of England and Charles V of Germany and Spain. Under François, the Loire flourished to new heights, attracting the finest artists and craftsmen— Leonardo da Vinci and Benvenuto Cellini. Catherine de'Medici, wife of Henry II, son of François, brought in her Florentine chefs, classic recipes and the fork. Literary lights such as Joachim Du Bellay, François Rabelais and Pierre de Ronsard sculpted the French language into its elegantly subtle form.

  Touraine is blessed with fruits and vegetables. From the mouth of the river at Le Croisic come some of the world's most delicious oysters. The Loire's waters offer salmon, shad, eel, pike, trout, carp. The best ducks, it is said, come from Nantes (some say from Rouen).

The forests are replete with game and fowl. Berry and Auvergne have made famous lamb, fine beef from Charolais and an abundance of cheeses.

The refreshing wine of the Loire comes from vineyards stretching for some 300 miles along the river's banks. Most is white wine, ranging from very dry to medium sweet. There are also reds, rosés and sparkling wine. The upper reaches of the Loire and its tributary, the Cher, produce full, dry white wine at Pouilly, Sancerre, Quincy and Reuilly. The center of the Loire Valley produces reds, whites and rosés of Anjou and Amboise; the pale reds of Bourgeuil and Chinon; whites of Vouvray and Montlouis; and the very wonderful sparkling wine of Saumur.

The greatest vineyards of the Loire Valley are located in the provinces of Anjou and Touraine in the 100 miles of the river valley between Angers and Blois. All the moderately priced wine of the Loire have a clean, refreshing taste, suitable for luncheons and even picnics. They mature early and so are the wine of youth—charming and light. They rarely age well.

The upper Loire, like the rest of the river, produces all sorts of wine, red as well as white. It makes excellent dry white wine, the best from a grape native to Bordeaux called the Sauvignon Blanc, but here called the Blanc-Fumé. Sauvignon Blanc is grown in four major vineyard areas:

Around the little village of Pouilly, just north of Nevers: This is not to be confused with Pouilly Fuissé, Pouilly-Loché and Pouilly-Vinzelles of southern Burgundy. This is full, dry, white wine, but there is no further resemblance. The best wine of Pouilly-sur-Loire is made from the Fumé grape and is called Pouilly-Fumé. Secondary wines are made from the Chasselas and are named Pouilly-sur-Loire after the village. The Burgundian Pouillys are made from Pinot Chardonnay, which gives them a different flavor entirely. Pouilly-sur-Loire, the wine from the Chasselas, is a good wine with a somewhat heavier aftertaste than the dry, white wine Pouilly-Fumé. Both go well with all fish dishes as well as Blanquette de Veau, ham, pork, creamed fowl, sweetbreads and brains.

The village of Pouilly-sur-Loire has 1800 inhabitants, either vintners or culinary artists. Eight of its restaurants are listed in the Michelin Guide.

The region of Sancerre is downriver on the western shore, opposite Pouilly. The hilltop village has the quiet charm of winding streets, towers and ramparts as well as a Roman ruin. Its old-fashioned family hotel is owned and operated by the gracious Monsieur Sylvain. The region of Sancerre produces two types of wine: a white made from the Blanc-Fumé and a refreshing rosé made from the Burgundian red wine grape, the Pinot Noir. There is very little Rosé produced, so when Sancerre is mentioned, it usually refers to the white wine. Sancerre Wine is pleasant, good in hot weather for light luncheons. It is fruity, dry enough, with a zest and freshness. Only about 100,000 cases are produced each year, and almost all of it is sold in Paris; hardly any at all is exported.

About 35 miles from Sancerre, to the west of Sancerre and Pouilly near the medieval city of Bourges, are the vineyards of Quincy and Reuilly, whose white wine resembles that of Pouilly and Sancerre. Quincy is on the River Cher, at this point only a stream that flows by the 17th-century Château de Quincy.

The sweet white wine of Anjou is very smooth and delicate. Especially worthy of note are the names Coteaux du Layon, Aubance, Bonnezeaux, Savennières and Quart de Chaume. The light red wine of Touraine has a bouquet reminiscent of violets and raspberries: Chinon, Bourgueil and St. Nicolas. The sparkling and semisparkling wine of Vouvray are smooth, soft and fine: Montlouis, Saumur and Touraine. The dry white wine from the vineyards surrounding Nantes: Muscadet, gay and sprightly, and the wine from the large vineyards of the Coteaux d'Ancenis. The rosé wine of Touraine and Anjou are made from Cabernet grapes. The wine from Nivernais and Berry are Sancerre, Pouilly-Fumé, Menetou-Salon (the only wine made from Sauvignon grapes), Pouilly-sur-Loire (from Chasselas grapes) and further upstream, Saint-Pourçain-sur-Sioule (V.D.Q.S. wine).

Languedoc's Simple Table Wine

The French people drink everyday wine with family meals that are simple, healthy and refreshing. The presence of wine, whether red, white or rosé, turns the plainest meal into a festive occasion. They cheer the worker in field and factory with their sunshine. They are either drunk just as they come from the cellars of the wine cooperatives or they are blended with other wine to ensure a standard quality. All the wine-making areas of France, even the most famous, share in producing this simple type wine. However, Languedoc is best able to market this wine to advantage. Languedoc stretches in a sunny, scented heathland from the Rhone to the province of Rousillon.

Abundant wine is made in the departments of Herault, Aude and Gard, and there is also a variety of A.O.C. (wines of contrôlée origin and quality) and V.D.Q.S. (local wines of superior quality) that enjoy an established reputation:

The Dry White Wine: Languedoc Clairettes and Bellegarde.

The Red Wine: Corbières, Minervois, Fitou, Saint-Chinian, Saint-Georges-d'Orques, Costières, and so on.

The Sparkling Wine: Blanquette de Limoux.

Come, thou monarch of the vine
Plumpy Bacchus with pink eyes
In thy fats our cares be drowned
With thy grapes our hours be crowned
Cup us, till the world go round
Cup us, till the world go round!
SHAKESPEARE'S *Antony and Cleopatra*

Wine Of Italy

Chapter **8**

ENDOWED by nature and geography, Italy has always been the vine-yard of the world. Cradled in the north by the Alpine range, which protects it from icy northern winds, the vineyards are nurtured by vintners through bitter winters, in summers basking luxuriantly in the sunny climate of the Mediterranean Sea. Tradition, soil and vari-etal grapevines have made Italy a natural wine-producing country. Now it is considered equal to that of France in wine production and in notable varietal wines.

Cultivated by vine devotees on the steep terraced slopes of the Alps, all the way to the volcanic terrain of Sicily, the vines spread their roots expansively. In essence, they are the surviving beauty, virtue and poetry of their ancient vinous ancestors. From the Swiss, French and Austrian borders of the north, down to the Strait of Messina, and over to Sicily and Sardinia, Italy is one sprawling vineyard.

Many have written about wine journeys through Italy. The most authoritative, perhaps, was Hans Barth, the able German journalist who lived in Italy for many years at the beginning of this century.

When his *Italian Journal* was translated into Italian, the poet Gabriele D'Annunzio wrote the preface for him. Many since Barth's time have written about Italian wine. In this chapter, we shall mainly confine ourselves to the wine about whose authenticity there can be no shadow of doubt.

Even before the legendary founding of Rome by wolf-nurtured Romulus and Remus (in 753 B.C.), vineyards were cultivated in what became the country of Italy, where wine has always been recognized as the perfect refreshment—a nutrient, a medicine, a spiritual ritual, a way of enjoying life. Since not all well water was considered palatable or safe, bottled mineral and spring waters and wine have been the customary beverages in Italy from time immemorial.

Julius Caesar and his legions brought vine cuttings to France, Portugal and Germany, but the vineyards in these countries have always required far more cultivating and selection of varieties, because the soil and climate are less hospitable than that of Italy. This favored land has enjoyed the soil and climate devised for it by the gods. Italians are born with a taste for wine, for the most part. Wine is the natural beverage—inexpensive, available, nutritious, advantageous, safe. It is sunshine captured in the grapes and converted magically into liquid warmth, which soothes body and soul.

Italian wine is named either after the grape from which it is produced or for the place where it originates. It is generally conceded that northern wine is superior to central and southern wine. Italy exports to many countries: the United States, Switzerland, Germany, France, Belgium, England, Canada. Exports include bottled wine, bulk wine for processing, must and grape juice. Germany, Switzerland and Holland are markets for wines for processing, as well as for the must and grape juice. Much Italian wine does not travel well. Therefore, the best way to enjoy it is in or near the localities where it is produced, or in nearby countries.

In 1906, the Italian government passed laws governing the manufacture and sale of wine and spirits. In 1924, they were revised and made more stringent. In 1927, the Italian Vintners' Guild was organized. It is known as INE, Instituto Nazionale per l'Esportazione. Before a vintner is permitted to manufacture and sell wine he must meet the requirements of membership in this Guild. The Guild regulates areas, wine types, minimum standards of quality, crop and vintage and vine disease control.

However, many factors since 1927 have prevented implementation, particularly the period of the Fascist regime and World War II, preceding Italy's formation of a Republic in 1946. Not until 1963 was it possible for the subject of wine production to receive proper attention. On February 3, 1963, a law was enacted for the most comprehensive labeling and control of origin, so that the variety of grapes that can be grown in a specific region or place, as well as quality control, are under governmental regulation.

Government certificates of origin now cover: Simple denomination of region, controlled denomination of origin and controlled and guaranteed denomination of origin. The red seal of the Vintners' Guild on every bottle exported guarantees to the buyer that the wine contained therein has met the minimum standards of Italian regulations.

There has been a revolutionary change in transportation between France and Italy in recent years, making access to either country far more amenable than ever before. For instance, the 2 1/2-hour, 7 1/2-mile trip from Chamonix, France, to Courmayeur, Italy, has been drastically cut to 30 minutes by the Mont Blanc Tunnel. It can be traversed year-round at a cost of about $5 one way. The completion in 1967 of the 32-mile Quincinetto-Aosta Turnpike has eased motor traffic from the major highways to Milan and the Italian Riviera.

The arduous passage through the Alps, with which all travelers have been so long familiar, has been likewise ameliorated. There is the great Saint Bernard Tunnel, 3 1/2 miles long, that passes through the mountains from France to Martigny, Switzerland, in the Rhone Valley. This reduces the previously formidable journey to a few miles. The access road to the tunnel begins at Saint Themy. It climbs an additional 180 feet to an altitude of 6,200 feet. Then it enters the tunnel. This is an all-weather passage through the Alps, the longest road tunnel in the world. Even the access roads are roofed against avalanches. Tolls are calculated according to the size of your automobile engine. The eight-mile Frejus Tunnel, now completed, runs from Modane, France, to Bardonecchia in the Upper Susa Valley in Piedmont.

There has been increased promotion of wine products in Italy in recent years. It is only natural that large firms, well-known brands, wine-growing associations and wine producers desire to make themselves known precisely on motorways. Several Italian vineyards—as in Alsace, Burgundy and Languedoc in France—have their Route du Vin or Wine Road. Italy's wine motorway runs from Turin to Piacenza via Alessandria, through the famous vineyards of Piedmont, Asti, Cuneo, Alessandria, Pavia and Piacenza. All along this motorway, travelers are reminded of the well-known growths produced nearby and even along the road: Barolo, Barbarresco, Grignolino, Asti, Barbera de Monferatto, Asti Spumante, Cortese de l'Alessandria, Frecciarossa, Oltro, Pavese, and so on. Advertisements emphasize the virtues of native products.

Until fairly recently, the regions around Asti, Pavia and Alessandria, felt forgotten and isolated to tourists. Not only did production decrease, but slow, expensive and complicated means of transport considerably increased prices. The motorway now enables carriage costs to be lowered by at least 40 percent.

It is best to see the vineyards during late summer and especially at harvest time. Summertime in Italy is an enchanting canvas of aquamarine skies and cobalt-blue areas, grayish mountains and green hills, yellow sunshine and a dazzling palette of blooming flowers and shrubs.

The wine regions of Italy do not fall into the convenient regional patterns as do those of France. On this type of classification there is a dearth of source material available to the writer. We have decided, therefore, on the following presentation as being the most illuminating to the reader interested in identifying the wine and their grapes as well as the important fact of their place of origin.

The North Across the border from France into Italy lies the province of Pied-
Piedmont mont, where I, Peter Robotti, was born in the village of Fubine, a suburb of Piedmont's Alessandria, in the valley surrounded by rolling hills whose every inch is covered with vineyards. In any one year, Piedmont produces as much wine as the combined vineyards of the whole United States. Although Italy is far smaller than California, it produces, in all, seven times as much wine as the United States . . . some one billion gallons a year. Most of this vast flow of delight is *vin ordinaire* made to be enjoyed within a year, yet Italy still has more than its share of notable wines.

Considering good table wine and also special wine drunk before or after a meal, or at any other time of the day, Piedmont is perhaps the richest wine-producing area of all Italy, both in variety and quality. All sections of Piedmont, aside from the plains, or the villages and towns, are wine-producing. As we descend the Italian Alps, which encircle the area like a bastion, it is obvious that vineyards on the steep mountain slopes of the high Valle di Susa Pass or in the Val d'Aosta, for instance, have much less favorable growing conditions than those on the broad, rolling hillsides. However, brief mention is made of the famous Carema that comes from a narrow strip of country between the Val d'Aosta and the northernmost part of Turin Province. Produced on a small scale, Carema is one of the great red wines of Piedmont, known to wine growers and gourmets alike as the wine for roast meats. Wine of this type accompanies robust foods such as red meats and game. In Piedmont, it is served with hare "au civet," pheasant, or even with a tasty braised beef dish.

Barolo: The most famous of this wine for meats comes from the vine stock Nebbiolo, dating back to the 14th century. From Turin, we travel southward and climb the range of hills known as the Langhe.

They stretch as far as Liguria. On this journey we find Barolo, "king of wines and the wine of kings." Good Barolo ranks among the highest of the wine aristocracy. Only about 660,000 gallons of this precious wine is produced each year.

Barolo takes its name from the locality in which it is produced, not far from Alba, the site of the ancient castle belonging to the Marquis of Barolo since 1200 A.D. In the town of Barolo, perched on top of an extinct volcano, the house of Borgogno et Figli has established the reputation as the foremost estate, bottling superb Piedmontese wine. Since 1847, their extensive cellars have sent forth vintage Barolo to crown the tables of Italy's most deluxe restaurants and hotels.

Close by are other important Barolo wine cellars; Fontanafredda d'Alba is one. There are also cellars in the surrounding districts of La Morra, Castiglion Faletto, Serralunga d'Alba, Casteletto, Monforte, Perno, Grinzane and Verduno.

Barolo is a dry, full-bodied wine, 13.6 percent alcohol. Strong, hearty and health-giving, Barolo is aged in wooden barrels for at least three years. It is even better after two years in the bottle. Only then does it develop its full, fragrant bouquet reminiscent of violets, of tar, and more noticeably of faded roses.

This bright, ruby-red aristocrat—rich, velvety, and even—is exquisite with roasts, red meats and game. It should be drunk at a temperature of not less than 68° F. It should be uncorked for a while before serving.

The ancient Faletti family, the Marchesi of Barolo, were the forebears of the company that now owns and operates the vineyards of Barolo. The charitable activities of the last Marchessa, who devoted much of her time and money to the poor, were spoken of as Opera Pia Barolo. Upon her death in 1864, a committee was formed to perpetuate the kindnesses of the Barolos through the present wine company.

Barbaresco: This is known as Barolo's younger brother, also coming from the famous Nebbiolo grape. Softer and a little less austere, about 150,000 gallons of it are produced annually. It takes its name from a small, picturesque village over which rises an old Roman red brick tower above the Tamaro River. On the vine slopes of this region, and in the neighboring villages of Treiso and Neive, grow the Nebbiolo grapes for this great wine. Barbaresco is mature and perfect at three years, a little less time than that required for Barolo. As its age increases, the color changes from a beautiful ruby red to garnet. Borgogno estate-bottles this dry, red wine, which blends well with fowl.

Barbera: This is a half-brother to Barolo, a dry, red and beautiful wine, on the type of Burgundy. Produced from the Barbera grape, it comes to as much as 14 percent alcohol. Warm and hearty, Barbera is pleasing with all red meats and cheeses.

Not so fine as Barolo or Barbaresco, Barbera dominates the field because such a lot of it is produced. Barbera comes from Asti, getting its name from a locality in the region, as well as from the area bounded by Alessandria on the Monferrato hills, and from a small zone in the province of Cuneo. Cuneo Barbera is especially famous for its excellent quality. It is darkish ruby red in color, has full vinous bouquet with a persistent aroma, full-bodied, inclined to be a little sharp particularly when young. Suitably aged, it is excellent with rich roast meats and spicy local dishes.

Nebbiolo: The same vine stock and the same province (Cuneo) also produce the group of three pleasant wines known simply as Nebbiolo, not so robust and strong as Barolo or Barbaresco. They are paler in color, sometimes sweet and sparkling. These are good even after the first year, but it is customary to age them a little longer.

There are several other "roast meat" wines of superior quality having much in common with Barolo, although not so powerful or full-bodied, that are produced from the Nebbiolo grape, locally known as Spanna, mixed with other varieties such as Croatina. These wines usually go under the name of Gattinara, named after the main town of the Vercelli province lying at the foot of the hills that stretch toward Biella in the west and Ticino in the east, ending in the province of Novara.

Gattinara: This is a dry, red wine of Piedmont, made from the Nebbiolo grape grown near Vercelli. It has a pleasant flavor with a slightly bitter undertone.

Cortese: This is a light-bodied, straw-colored white wine with green undertone. It has a delicate aroma. It is produced from the Cortese Bianco grape grown in Piedmont and in Liguria, which borders it on the south, whose capital is Genoa.

Malvasia Bianco: Malvasia Bianco grapes grown in Piedmont, Tuscany, Marche, Abruzzi and Sicily yield the harvest for Malvasia Bianco, rare, white, fruity, delicious dessert wine. The grapes are good for eating. Very little Malvasia Bianco is produced.

Freisa: This is a red, younger edition of Barbera, produced for the most part between Chieri and Asti, also on the slopes of Basso Monferrato. It is not quite as strong as Barbera, is drunk after moderate aging, has a delicious scent of violets and strawberries. One type is dry and initially somewhat rough, but becomes smoother and softer as it ages. The other type is soft to the palate, sparkling and sweetish. This wine goes well with fruit.

Grignolino: This very fine, red, Piedmontese wine comes from a small area near Asti and from the Monferrato terraces. It is clear, ruby red in color, smelling of roses, dry, light-bodied, becomes superior in the second year and at its best when three years old. Only a small quantity of it is produced, and it is therefore scarce. It is Piedmont's desired table wine.

Dolcetto: Originating in the Langhe region, Dolcetto is produced in large quantities. Much of it comes from Alba and the slopes that surround the spa of Acqui Terme. A pleasant wine, it is a favorite among visitors of all nationalities who come to take the mud-bath cures, renowned for their therapeutic virtues since the days of the Roman Empire. Hans Barth, the German journalist, was so enthusiastic, he wrote that to take the mud baths and to drink a "couple of bottles of Dolcetto and Barbera" could enable a man to throw away his crutches and run and jump with joyous health. Clear and bright red, this very dry Dolcetto goes well with light meals. There is only an underlying, lingering, subtle sweetness. Well-rounded, full of flavor, a pleasant perfume, it has an 11 to 13 percent alcoholic content.

Sparkling Spumanti: From the red table wine, we come to the special white wine produced in Piedmont. The vineyards around Asti, the ancient village in the center of the Muscat grape-growing region, produce the sparkling white wine Asti Spumante, Moscato Spumante and the dry, white, sparkling Lacrima Christi. Asti Spumante is justly famous. The name denotes a special type of Muscat "spumante," produced by using the same techniques employed for the great French sparkling wine. Asti Spumante differs from the Muscat of Asti in its characteristics. The basic vine stock is the white Muscat grape also known as the Canelli Muscat, from the town of Canelli at the center of this branch of the wine industry. The most treasured Moscato grapes are grown in the vineyards along the banks of the Belbo River around Canelli. Near Acqui and Alessandria are grown the Brachetto vines for a light wine that is brilliantly red in color and delicate in flavor. Brachetto is a palatable Rosé, aromatic and sweet, made from Brachetto grapes.

Asti Spumante, to which sugar is never added since the natural sugar in the must is left unfermented, retains its fresh taste and the fragrance of the grapes. Quantities of other nonaromatic white wine (Pinot, Riesling) are blended into the Asti in order to mitigate the smell of the Muscat grape, sometimes too pronounced. Asti Spumante is an excellent choice for entertainment at receptions, parties and celebrations, a perfect wine with cakes and other desserts. It is a favorite at Panettone and Spumante parties, at Christmas, when the wine is served with the traditional breadlike cake.

Spumanti may range from brut to extra dry, from dry to demi-sec. It is made from several varieties of Pino grapes with perhaps a little Riesling added, according to the classic Champagne-blending method.

Passito di Caluso: This is an exquisite, Liqueur-type wine made from the white Erbaluce grape, cultivated in the countryside from Turin to the Val d'Aosta. Passito di Moscato wine comes from the same area as Moscato d'Asti.

Turin Vermouth: This, from the sophisticated Turin of my Italian youth, is the true star of Piedmont wine. First produced in 1786 by a Turinese vintner, an energetic herbalist, who is said to have re-created the fragrant wine beloved of the ancient Romans, who called it Absinthianum Vinum. Originally the Turin Vermouth was made from Muscat Wine, but increasing demand has made it necessary to substitute good white wine from Sicily and Apulia for Muscat Wine. However, this has not affected the high standards, because a good Vermouth is tested by its aromatic qualities and its artistic balance into a good white wine flavored with fragrant herbs and spices from a secret formula. Turin Vermouth is *the* aperitif in Italy, served neat, or with Soda Water, or over ice cubes during hot weather. It also is a good mixer and serves as the base for many cocktails.

Lake Garda   East from Lake Garda, up to, around and beyond Verona, are grown the Corvino, Molinara, Roassar and Negrara grapes along the eastern slopes of Lake Garda for the ruby red Valpolicella Wine with its slightly bitter tang, softness and delicate bouquet. Another notable wine from Lake Garda is the Lugana. Bordolino, a light, red wine, comes from vineyards farther east and around turreted Verona. Beyond ancient Verona (remembered for Romeo and Juliet), the Garganega and Trebbiano grapes produce the very aptly called Soave Bolla, a good, pleasant, dry, white wine, velvety in texture and with a haunting bouquet. Vineyards surround the walled city of Soave near Verona, with its impressive medieval battlements and old castle of the Scaligeri family.

Venetia   Some fine red table wine comes from the vineyards cultivated in the long, narrow Valpolicella Valley. The Corvino, Molinara and Negrara grapes, and some other varieties are used for making Valpolicella, once favored in the 11th century by Pope Gregory VII. From the Venetian shore of Lake Garda, we continue on to the three Venetos: Veneto, Trentino-Alto Adige and Friuli-Venezia Giulia. Alto Adige was the province of South Tyrol until the end of World War I. Valpolicella and Valpantena take their names from the valleys on whose steep, enclosing sides the vines grow. This wine should be aged two to three years at the most, when it is of a superior quality.

Recioto Nobile de la Valpolicello is a good, garnet red, sparkling dessert wine. (*Recioto* means "ear" in Italian. The upper part of the grape cluster, as it hangs heavily on the vine, has the appearance of ears.) These ripen earlier than the rest of the bunch. By the time the whole cluster has ripened, the ears are overripe and a mold has developed. The Recioto grapes are gathered and pressed separately to produce, by Champagne methods, a richly perfumed, delightful wine. Some will remember when it was turned into a Liqueur, but today it is usually a sparkler, Spumante. Deep red in color with a strong bouquet, it is full, harmonious and velvety.

Gambellara, a pale, straw-colored wine strongly resembling Soave, is found farther east on the Vicenza border. Both Soave and Gambellara have the distinctive flavor of almonds, are dry and refreshing, excellent with soups, hors d'oeuvres, egg and seafood dishes.

Moscato Dei Colli is a delicious dessert wine made from white Muscat grapes and given the spumante treatment. It comes from the vineyards in the Euganean Hills a few miles from Padua, where the soil reflects its volcanic origin. This area also produces good red and white table wine.

Tocai or Tocai Friulano is an exquisite, dry wine (no relationship to the Hungarian Tokay). It has a slightly bitter aftertaste, but the wine is mellow when it is mature. It has a clear yellow color tending toward lemon, and has a delicate, slightly flowery aroma.

Conegliano and Valdobbiadene are white wines from Treviso, where impressive villas dot the landscape. Made for the most part from the Prosecco grape, they are excellent dry wines for accompanying fish dishes. There are also some Spumante varieties.

The Portofino Bianco and Portofino Rosé, as well as the precious Cinque Terre wine, are available through the Banfi Products Corporation, New York City. Since 1919, two generations of the Mariani family have selected the finest estate-bottled wines of Italy for American consumption. (They will send you a catalogue upon request.)

Lombardy

Leaving behind the enchanting Côte d'Azur and the shimmering blue Tyrrhenian Sea, we drive among the vineyards of Lombardy, still in northern Italy. This fertile farming country is one of the richest in the land, but the wine is not comparable to Piedmont's.

Oltrepo Pavese produces from its tangle of hillside vines mainly red wine. However, there are some whites of fairly good quality. Most of it finds a market in nearby industrial Milan as everyday table wine.

Sangue di Guide (Blood of Judas) is a robust local wine intensely red in color.

Sassella is red and dry.

Barbacarlo (Buttafuoco, "scatters like fire," in the local dialect), Clastidio and Monte Napoleone. These robust wines, rich in color and of fairly strong alcoholic content, 14 to 15 proof, are refined by an aging process involving a mixture of grapes from Croattina, Ughetta, Uva Rara and Barbera.

White Wine of the Val Versa, the largest town near Pavia, is mostly dry, made from Riesling, Cortese, Malvasia and Pinot grapes. This is subtle wine that goes well with fish dishes. There is also some sweet wine with good bouquet made from white Muscats of the fragrant Malvasia grape. This is often treated to make it effervescent. Santa Maria Della Versa is a delicious example of this Spumante type.

A large part of the Pinot grape harvest gathered around Oltrepo in Lombardy goes into making the famous dry Spumanti of Piedmont. The vineyards are endless in passing from Milan to the Valtellina, famous for their classic red wine. Much backbreaking toil goes into the cultivation of the Valtellina vineyards in the Alpine region north of Lake Como. How can you ever forget such a superb sight as that which unfolds as you take the road parallel with the River Adda from Sondrio as far as the Swiss border?

The pattern of the tightly packed vines leaning on their sticks on the mountain slopes is like a great wave of the sea. Here and there are rocks that could not be removed. Sometimes the soil has been carried up on a man's back from the plain below, a feat incredible in our machine age. It is the achievement of determination and self-sacrifice. The feeling of awe persists, and the mystic realization that Dionysus and Bacchus are not dead. They are worshiped as fervently as they ever were. Here nature's savagery has had to bow to man's strength of will.

In Lombardy, they call the Nebbiolo grape by the name of Chiavennasca, and, as in Piedmont, the wine made from it is sharp and rough when young, growing more mellow with age, so that it goes well with roast meats. Names vary with the locality: Sassella, Grumello, Interno and Valgella. A translation of Leonardo da Vinci's lines on Valtellina wines: "Valtellina produces powerful wines—and how!"

From the Italian northeastern frontier we enter the Friuli-Venezia Giulia region famous for its tenacious, courageous, hard-working people, who have seen their beloved vineyards trampled upon and destroyed by the ravages of marching armies of two world wars. With loving, painstaking care, they replanted their vines, increasing and improving their stock so that now they have some quarter million acres under cultivation.

Verduzzo, Pinot, Riesling and Tokai are the dry whites.

Cabernet, dry with a scent of raspberries, and Merlot, dry, tangy, mellow, are the fine reds that are good with roasts.

Piccolit of Friuli is an outstanding fruity liqueur, very scarce, prized by those who can enjoy it.

As we return to the valleys of the Trentino-Alto Adige Alps, those harsh, high mountains, we find on the slopes many flourishing vineyards.

Marzemino is a clear, soft, ruby-colored red table wine.

Teroldego is a stronger, more alcoholic wine with a characteristic violet color. Its celestial bouquet recalls almonds, violets and raspberries. Teroldego is the leading wine of Trentino, good with entrées. It ages well until it becomes a fine companion for white meat roasts.

Traminer has a faint vanilla perfume. This white wine is served with fish or desserts. It is velvety, slightly bitterish, but warm and strong.

Pinot Bianco and Riesling are good white fish wines.

Our final stop on this wine tour in the northern area is at Bolzano (Bozen), the German-Italian city of the Dolomites, those strange, sky-piercing rock formations. This is the chief city of Upper Adige Province. Not as inaccessible as in former years, it now has its own airport for planes of the lighter type.

Terlano, a white wine, is clear, pale, straw-colored with greenish reflections when young. When aged, it becomes golden amber. This color change is natural to many white wines in this part of the country.

Santa Maddalena, a superior red wine, matures at one year, but is perfect at two. It is dark ruby red, subtle and velvety.

Lago di Caldaro, a superior white wine, is perfect with white meat roasts: full-bodied, soft and smooth.

Rosé Lagarino Rosato, pink in color, with a distinct scent of vanilla, is a fresh and slightly sparkling wine.

Emilia Romagna In the rich region of the Po Valley in Emilia, the Trebbiano grape grows on the hills around ancient Bologna. This is one of the largest wine-producing areas of Italy, with 72 qualities of wine. In general, these wines are best enjoyed where you find them, to accompany the rather heavy, but delicious, local cuisine, served in gargantuan portions. Elaborate wine would not be in harmony in such rustic settings.

Lambrusco di Sorbara, a lively, violet-perfumed wine suitable for moderate aging, has a bright ruby color and a vivid red froth. Lambrusco, very good with a stew of lentils or a dish of pasta, is exquisite with river trout prepared with butter and sage.

Bianco di Scandiano is sometimes dry, sometimes a bit bitter. There is also a sparkling version of this wine.

Albana di Bertinoro, from nearby Forli, is a golden-yellow wine, palatable, sometimes sweet and sparkling, suitable for fish or dessert.

Sangiovese, a dry, vivid ruby red wine, rather robust and tannic, becomes more subtle with age. Then it goes well with red meat roasts.

Trebbiano, Certosino and Malvasia are other well-known white wines.

Liguria, the Italian Riviera In winter it is preferable to enter Italy from France by driving along the Tyrrhenian coast rather than through the Alpine passes, along that marvelous curve known as the Côte d'Azur and the breathtaking Riviera of the flowers. In the center is San Remo, festival city. If you arrive by sea, docking at Genoa or Savona, you find yourself in the midst of Liguria. It is not a wine-producing area in the real sense, but it does have some wine well worth knowing about. The dry white wine is more important than the red ones from the Vermentino, an old vine stock that grows throughout this region. They are correctly served cold to accompany the famous seafood dishes of Liguria. This is the land that winter has forgotten, surely one of the most beautiful spots in the world. Near the picturesque resort of Portofino, Cantine Massucco estate-bottles the brilliant and vivacious wines called Portofino Bianco. It is very old, being mentioned by Pliny and praised by Petrarch in 97 A.D. It is a full-bodied, dry white wine with a delicate golden color. Rosé Portofino is a fruity and light dry wine with a bouquet of freshness and a pinkish color most pleasing to the eye.

These enchanting, soft, harmonious wines are served with distinction in the finest hotels and restaurants of Italy.

Cinque Terre (Five Lands), surrounding La Spezia, comprises five wine-producing communes whose mountainous territory runs down to the very edge of the sea. This short stretch of coastline, east of the Côte d'Azur, has vineyards, walled from the Alpine winds and carved into layer-cake mountains, that date back to the days of the Roman Empire. At that period, the Ligurians hauled soil on their backs up the rocky slopes and anchored it with stone walls. Then they planted their vines. Even now, men must let themselves down by ropes to reach the steepest vineyards. Some actually hang precipitously over the sea, and are so inaccessible that the grapes are brought in small boats to Cantine Massucco for processing.

The Italian Riviera, rhapsodized by poets and painters, is popular with visitors because of its attractive coastline, mild climate, flowers and the ever-fascinating vineyards. This craggy region produces a rare wine, almost a Liqueur called Sciacchetra, golden in color. The white grapes are hung in the sun for 15 days before hand pressing, so this raisinlike wine is sweet and heady. After four or five years of aging, it becomes pure nectar to be served in Liqueur glasses with dessert or on its own. Liguria's output of wine is mainly white, but near the coast town of Imperia and along the French border toward Ventimiglia, red wine is to the fore.

Rossese di Dolce Aqua, (very red sweet water), is often almost a rosé. Ready for the table after one year, it improves if aged to two or three. It is softer and more gentle than the great and powerful Piedmontese dinner wine.

Monterosso, estate-bottled by Cantine Massucco, is a luscious red wine, mellow and dry.

Bianco is a soft, mellow, white wine with a pale golden color and fresh-fruit taste.

Several pleasant wines come from the western shores of Lake Garda in Lombardy, known by the generic name of Riviera del Garda. In this group are the Valtenesi wines, ruby-red in color, intensely aromatic, fresh, with a definite aftertaste, and Chiaretto di Moniga, a rosé. Made by a mixture of grapes, they are ready to be consumed during the same year, and should never be drunk after more than two years.

Lugana, an excellent, dry, white wine from the part of Lake Garda that borders the town limits of Sirmione, is very good with fish dishes.

Central Italy Tuscany Tuscany is full of treasures, the natural beauties of rolling, wooded landscapes, priceless art collections. It is crowned by Florence, a jewel of a city with its traditional handicrafts. The trademark of Tuscany is its Chianti in the straw-covered bottles.

Chianti is a blend of 70 percent Sangiovese grapes with the balance of Canaiolo Nero, Trebbiano, Malvasia and, in several great vineyards, some Cabernet and Malbec grapes. Chianti marked for aging is bottled in regular Claret bottles because straw tends to deteriorate. From the time of bottling, Chiantis in *fiasci* (straws) are intended to be drunk within five or six years, at the most. The problem of the territorial limits of the true Chianti zone has finally been solved. Apart from the tiny area of historic Chianti production that has the right to call itself Chianti Classico, there are at this time six other districts, more or less adjoining, that can legitimately call their wine Chianti. These are qualified by the names of the hillsides on which they are produced:

> *Chianti Dei Colli Fiorentini (Chianti of the Florentine Hills)*
>
> *Chianti Dei Colli Aretini (of the Arezzo hills)*
>
> *Chianti di Montalbano (of Mount Albano, near the Tuscan town of Pistoia)*
>
> *Chianti Delle Colline Pisane (of the Pisan slopes)*
>
> *Chianti Rufina*

Chianti Classico is limited to a special area. Its characteristics are established by the Consorzio per la Difesa del Vino Tipico Dei Chianti. It is estate-bottled in Castellina in Chianti, the heart of the renowned but delimited Chianti Classico region. Suali is a true vintage wine with a superbly clean taste and velvety softness. An aristocratic wine, its great charm is its suitability with red meat roasts, game and all Italian dishes. Such wine is entitled to the use of an emblem picturing a black rooster on a golden background. Each of the seals is numbered and its issue controlled. The Chianti Classico region lies between Florence and Siena. It includes the parishes of Radda in Chianti, Castellina in Chianti, Greve, San Casciano and part of Castelnuovo—Berardenga.

This wine has an unmistakable aroma of fruit and a smooth, well-balanced taste with a light frothiness. The ruby-red color changes to garnet with maturity. The alcoholic content is moderate, between 11 and 12 percent. It should be served at a temperature of 70° F. in round crystal glasses to evoke the quality of both the bouquet (violets and irises) and the color (vivid ruby changing to brick-red with age).

Many fine houses market Chianti. The House of Ruffino, established in 1877, which purveys to the Holy See of the Vatican, has large cellars and bottling plants at Pontassieve in Chianti.

Ruffino Red Capsule, the traditional Chianti, lively, ruby red, with a warm and brisk taste, naturally matured.

Ruffino Blue Capsule, long-matured wine with balanced roundness and rich refinement.

Ruffino White Capsule, a white vintage wine, limpid, a brilliant color, delicate bouquet, delicious when served chilled.

Rosatello Ruffino, Rosé wine from the must of choice grapes made by a special system of vinification. Its distinctive bottle, pyramid-shaped, is patented and has a wickered basket flask to protect it.

Ruffino Orvieto, a white vintage wine from the Orvietan vineyards, matured in cellars at close-by Pontassieve. The shape of its flask is known as "pulcianella." The wine is velvety smooth and springtime fresh.

There are other wines worth including from Tuscany, such as Spumante dell'Elba; wines of the Pistoria Hills and Brolio; Vin Santo Toscano, dry, golden in color, and the following:

Vin Nobile di Montepulciano, a good red wine, is to be drunk after fairly lengthy aging.

Brunello di Montalcino, another red wine for roasts, matures in five years. It becomes truly magnificent at a ripe old age, sometimes up to 50. It is very scarce.

Bianco di Pitigliano, a light yellow, dry wine, is among the good white Tuscans.

Vernaccia di San Gimignano, a great golden-yellow wine, is dry and slightly bitter. This wine and Bianco di Pitigliano are good with fish dishes. San Gimignano is a little town of 13 towers set in a soft fold of hills on the way from Florence to Siena.

Tuscany also has several good dessert wines: Moscatello di Montalcino, Moscato Dell'Elba, Aleatico di Portoferrato and the golden-amber Vinsanti (Holy wines), all of them sweet, velvety, generous Liqueurs.

Umbria From the rolling hills of Umbria comes the white wine of Orvieto. Like Chiantis, they go to the marketplace in straw-covered *fiasci*. Orvieto comes *secco* (dry) and *abbocato* (sweet), straw-colored, with a fruity freshness. Orvieto is produced on the terraced slopes encircling the ancient Etruscan town of the same name. Of superior quality, it is straw-colored, dancing with golden lights. The dry version is deliciously refreshing and is preferred today to the sweet Orvieto. This white wine cannot travel well, but when consumed locally, it has charm, freshness and fruitiness.

The Marches On the Adriatic side of the Apennines, in the region known as the Marches, with its capital town Ancona situated high above the Adriatic, is the home of the white Verdicchio dei Castelli di Jesi. This white wine is gaining recognition in Italy and abroad as an accompaniment to fish dishes. The pestilential Pontine Marshes, polluted for aeons by city dwellers, encompassed the City of Rome, stretching to the west and to the south. These were deadly wastelands where malaria prevailed for many centuries since the end of the Lower Roman Empire. Thousands of these uncultivated acres were an eyesore of desolation.

After the Fascists came to power, Il Duce, Benito Mussolini, turned his attention to national improvements. The city of Littorio was born in the very middle of the Maccarese Province, obliterating for all time the muddy lands, feeders of rushes and mosquitoes. The Marshes were finally drained, ploughed, sowed and planted, so that by 1932 the acres yielded every kind of fruit, especially grapes in abundance. Baskets of great red and white bunches came to the table, and there were other grapes for the vat to make wine with a heady bouquet. Maccarese became a luxuriant and fortunate islet, a symbol of the new forces of another Renaissance in Italy in these vineyards newly born out of wastelands.

Verdicchio is a very old wine, with many legends attached to its historic past. When Hannibal crossed the Marches with his army of Gallic mercenaries and veterans of the Carthaginian wars, he was in danger of seeing his whole army inebriated with Verdicchio and consequently at the mercy of the Roman soldiers. Only with the strictest discipline could he keep the men from the charms of this wine. It is light, straw-colored, crystal clear, slightly bitter, fresh and well-balanced.

Vernaccia a white wine of Serrapeliona, is one of the wines from Piceno Hills; Moscato is the white wine of Metauro.

Latium Latium, the region with provincial and eternal Rome as its capital, is rich in white wine. Most of the grapes that produce the famous white wine of Latium are grown on a range of volcanic hills rising gently south of Rome. These are the Castelli, and each locality has its wine: Frascati, Marino, Grottaferrata, Albano, Genzano, Lanuvio, Velletri and others.

The people of Rome find it very diverting to visit any of these villages in early evening, when couples may be seen enjoying their porchetta, slices of roast pork cut from a whole roast suckling pig crackling away on an open fire in the square . . . wrapped in crusty country bread . . . and enjoying sample glassfuls of mellow golden wine from the cool, grottolike shops lined with giant barrels and rustic, unpainted tables. This wine, usually dry (although some have a definitely sweet flavor), is slightly tannic, with a pleasantly bitter touch, well-perfumed and of moderate alcholic content (12 percent on the average) and extremely good from the first year.

Latium, the home of the Roman poet Horace, has some good red table wine, particularly from the Cesanese vine, and some specials such as Aleatico di Gradoli of Viterbo and a good Muscat Wine from the dessert grape Moscato di Terracina. Horace told of the beauties of Tusculum in Latium. Over the centuries, the name of Tusculum was changed to Frascati, where Horace once contentedly cultivated his vines and cherished his fruit orchards, and wealthy Romans had their villas. Frascati is about 13 miles from Rome by bus, a convenient distance for holidays. Even today, proud villas dot its hills. Here are the many cantinas that do not serve food. Late in the afternoon, after the long siesta, people bring bread, sausages, cheese and fruit and buy wine, enjoying their refreshments picnic fashion at the long, rough-hewn wooden tables. Through the evening, as the town loses its deserted look, it becomes a living tableau of enjoyment.

The cantina is, of course, a Roman institution. Unassuming in appearance and austere of decor, it is the traditional wineshop. No wine bottles are displayed in the window and no wine barrels are visible inside the shop. Usually rough, unpainted tables and chairs are set against stark, whitewashed walls. Customers usually ask for "Un mezzo," a half-liter of wine—white wine, in particular, Frascati. White Frascati is Rome's all-purpose wine, even if it comes from Marino, Velletri or Grottaferrata.

But the real Roman wineshops are at tree-lined Trastevere on the other side of the Tiber. There it is still the Rome of the past. They sell no food, but customers buy sliced prosciuto, ham, bread, olives, mushroom caps, six to eight inches in diameter, for roasting. In an article for *The New York Times* (March 12,1967), Michael Berry reports from Rome on his experiences with drinking Frascati in the cantinas. People of all ages, children to grandparents, eat, drink and enjoy. Looking into a bakery window in Trastevere, he was startled by a display of large cookies in the shape of triple-breasted women.

He saw the same anatomical anomaly in another bakeshop and asked the saleswoman for the reason behind it. "L'abbondanza," was her enthusiastic reply. "It is the symbol of abundance, generosity, plenty . . . and these cakes are symbols of Frascati!"

"Here is the Kingdom of the God crowned with vine leaves," wrote Hans Barth about Latium. "The stakes of the vines, like innumerable pyramids of an army's guns, and like an apocalyptic fortress, surround and defend the places of grace, and the perfume of the wine and the sun spread themselves poetically all over this land." Historic vineyards are still under cultivation amidst the Castelli Romani of 14 castles of the ancient Roman nobles. The wine produced from the varietal Trebbiano and Bonvino grapes is smooth, delicate and lively, with a refreshingly dry taste. Marino, principal among these wines, is produced in the historic town of its name. Rich in tradition, the entire community prides itself on exacting standards of excellence. Their ultramodern winery is one of the finest in Europe.

Marino "Gotto d'Oro," white, red and rosé wine, light-bodied, delicate and velvety dry with a fresh, fruity taste. Enjoyed best at a young age, they are ideal beverage wines, low in sugar and tannic acids.

Marino "Extra," white and rosé wine estate-bottled from the finest vineyard, site of the Castelli Romani. These superb wines have won first-place honors annually in the Ancona Festival, the top competition for Italy's superior white wine.

Marino Frascati, popular wine from the town of Frascati, bottled by Marino. They are limpid, refreshing to the palate and delightfully dry. Both the white and red type may be served with enjoyment during all seasons and are most refreshing when poured chilled.

Est! Est!! Est!!! Golden Moscatello, a legendary dry or semi-dry wine with an elegant bouquet comes from Latium north of Rome. It is made from grapes grown around the ancient town of Montefiascone on Lake Bolsena on the highway from Florence to Rome. The story goes that 400 or 500 years ago, the German Bishop named Fuger journeyed to the Vatican to see the Pope. To assure himself of the best accommodations, he would send his servant ahead to scout out the best places for refreshment and lodging for the night, instructing him to chalk on the wall of an inn the word "est," meaning "it is," if he found the accommodations suitable. His master was prepared then to stop over when he saw his man's approbation. When the servant tasted the wines at Montefiascone, the word "est" was not enough, so he chalked on the outer wall of the inn, "Est! Est!!

Est!!!" This advance notice was very exciting to the Bishop. After sampling the food and wine, he was so delighted he tarried there without continuing on to Rome at all.

He never left Montefiascone, staying on and on until his death. The late wine authority Harold J. Grossman relates how he was so intrigued with this tale that he personally checked it out. He found the good Bishop's tomb within the entrance of the Basilica of St. Flaviano. The inscription, he reported, is hardly legible, but sure enough it reads: "Est! Est!! Est!!! et propter nimium est, Johannes De Fuger, dominus meus, mortuus est." "It is! It is!! It is!!! and through too much It Is, my master John De Fuger, dead is." The vintners of Montefiascone who profit by the fame of this wine express their gratitude on each anniversary of the Bishop's death by spilling a barrel of Est over his tomb.

The wine called Montefiascone is a Muscat type, extremely heady and exciting to the nerves, matched by its engaging aroma, a beguiler of the senses. The writer Tavernier speaks of a particular preparation of the grape drunk by a Grand Seignior in company with the women of his seraglio, believed to be this heady wine. In this connection, we found a new facet of the amusing Est story in the old book *Pleasures of the Table* (London, 1902) by George H. Ellwanger. The servant of the German Bishop, who must have been quite a fellow in his own right, remembered that a Sultan of Lahore, the capital of Punjab Province of India, had engraved an inscription on the door of his seraglio: "If there is a paradise on earth, it is here, it is here, it is here!"

Abruzzo and Molise

The Abruzzo, where the Apennines rise to their highest peak, and Molise regions are on the same latitude as Latium but farther east in the direction of the Adriatic. This area is more famous for its marvelous table grapes than for its wine, although its Rosé, Cerasuolo d'Abruzzo, with its pretty cherry red color, delicate perfume and pleasant flavor, is worth noting. Montepulciano d'Abruzzo is a ruby red, well-balanced wine which, when properly aged, becomes a worthy accompaniment to roasts. Trebbiano, golden yellow white wine, and Moscato di Capestrano, semisweet, are good wines. In the mountainous center of the Italian peninsula, the soft, rounded wine of Abruzzo is produced.

Southern Italy

As we leave Rome, driving southward, we reach Campania, a region dotted with resort names. This is the land of romantic Naples and its perfect bay, of Capri's Blue Grotto, Vesuvius, Salerno, Sorrento, the offshore islands and the beautiful Amalfi coastline that reveals one dazzling inlet after another, as well as scores of picturesque towns and villages that retain all of their old-world charm, yet provide modern comforts for the traveler. No other part of Italy is so rich in homemade wine.

Lacrima Christi: Long ago on the southern slopes of Mount Vesuvius, monks at the monastery of Jesus Christ produced a wine from carefully selected grapes, crushing them only when they showed a sugar tear, or "tears of Christ." This elegant, full-bodied, white or red wine is ripe and harmonious. Its aromatic bouquet and fragrantly dry taste is the result of vines cultivated in rich volcanic soil for superior table wine. Today the dry type is preferred to the sweet, and is excellent served with fish and shellfish dishes.

Capri, Ischia, Ravello: Local wines taken from those enchanting islands of Naples—Capri with its Blue Grotto and hillsides dotted with villas, and Ravello the tiny town nestling near Amalfi. Capri is a delicate, pale yellow, fragrant wine fresh to the palate. Capri Red is bright ruby red, with a subtle bouquet of violets and a full, mellow taste. Both are dry. Ravello, white and red, is also a superior dry wine with freshness of flavor and subtlety of perfume. All three are alive, full-bodied, occasionally a little salty, with alcoholic content not exceeding 13 percent. Of the red wines, Capri Rosso, Lacrima Christi Rosso, Gragnano and Ischia Rosso are all of fine quality and may be served with white meat roasts.

Similarly in the Campania area, Falerno is a deep red wine, somewhat austere, with a dry, harmonious taste, excellent with wild game and fowl. Strega, the spicy, chartreuse-colored Liqueur, 78 proof, comes from Benevento near Naples.

Moving inland to Avellino, Greco di Tuto stands out as a delicate white wine to drink with fish dishes, particularly appetizing with trout. Fiano has a deep, very characteristic aroma and a slightly scorched taste. Taurasi and Solopaca are refined red table wine somewhat rough when young but becoming pleasant and velvety with age. Taurasi enters the great class as it matures, even fifteen years, when it is a fitting companion to spicy game dishes, and the best wine of all to serve with wild boar.

Calabria   This is the mountainous toe of Italy where many wines are noted: Lacrima of Castrovillari, dry red; Zibibbo, dry red; Greco of Gerace, dry, white; Moscato of Cosenza, the white dessert wine. The splendid wild beauty of Calabria's countryside is contrasted by the high cliffs that rise steeply and spectacularly straight out of the blue sea. The olive groves, silvery-green with twisted, writhing shapes of anguished-looking trees, contrast with the gay gardens and luxuriant grape vineyards, the orange and lemon orchards. Greco di Gerace, a golden-amber wine with an exquisite perfume, resembles orange blossoms, with an alcoholic content of 17 percent. Moscato di Cosenza is in this class. Savuto, Pollino, Pellaro and Lacrima di Castrovillari are all fine red table wines. Properly aged, they become true wines for roast meat courses. Pollino can be served without aging, and all except vivid-pink Pellaro are dry.

This region follows the coastline of the Gulf of Taranto. Apulia is the "cellar " of Italy, a very large producer of wine and table grapes. The strong, full-bodied Apulia wine is unpretentious, genuine, sometimes sweet and sometimes sour, strong, dark, velvety, staining the lips. Much Apulian wine is shipped north, where it is cut and blended with weaker wine. Sansevero is an example of a more refined Apulian wine suitable for moderate aging, dry, a pale straw color, light and fresh. Locorotondo, another dry white wine, deserves to be noticed. Until recently it has been used to blend with other red and white wine, but when well aged, it can be a really good table wine. Others in this category are Martina Franca and Ostuni, dry-tasting, neutral. Verdes di Alberobello comes from the locality famous for its circular-type whitewashed cottages, "trulli," with their pointed roofs shaped like fir cones. Torre Giulia from Cerignola, and Castel del Monte Bianco, are good with fish dishes. Among the good red table wine of Apulia are Castel del Monte Rosso (there is also a Rosé), Santo Stefano from Cerignola, Torre Quarto and, from among the Rosés, Rosato del Salento.

Apulia and Lucania

DESSERT WINES OF APULIA: Moscato di Trani, liqueur-type (16 to 17 percent alcohol); Moscato del Salento and Aleatico di Puglia, sweet, aromatic, full, velvety.

In the neighboring region of Lucania is found Aglianico del Vulture, a superior dry table wine, good with highly flavored foods. This is vivid garnet, with a pleasant aroma of strawberries and violets. As it ages, it becomes austere, velvety, warm, full-bodied and harmonious. There are many good red and white wines in the heel of the boot: Castel del Monte, San Severo, Moscato of Trani and Malvasia of Brindisi. In Basilicata in Lucania: Malvasia, Spumante of the Vulture, both sparkling, medium dry.

We have now completed the wine tour of Italy's mainland. Two important islands remain.

There is a plane from Naples to Palermo. Sicily can be reached by Terrenia steamer, overnight, from Naples. There is a train from Naples with sleeping cars ferried across the Strait of Messina to reach Taormina by morning. That ancient, sun-drenched island with its old cities, temples and amphitheaters has a civilization 1,000 years older

Sicily

than that of northern Italy. Sicily is very hot during six months of the year. To avoid this parched period, there is a Motor Coach route since World War II, Il Nastro d'Oro (The Ribbon of Gold), operated from November 1 to April 30. The first Greek settlement in Sicily was made in 735 B.C. The island has been the home of the Greeks, the Byzantines, the Saracens and the Normans.

There is great wine in Sicily. Mamertino, golden-yellow, high in alcohol, with an intense aroma, is produced on the eastern side of the island. Faro, a red table wine smelling of oranges, mature at two years and perfect at five, comes from the district surrounding Messina. It is wonderful with red and white meat roasts, fowl and game. Etna Bianco, greenish-white with golden reflections, comes from vineyards near Mount Etna, Sicily's rumbling volcano, in the vicinity of Catania. It has a rich bouquet, dry, well-balanced and delicate. Etna Rosso is a vivid ruby red with a bright, full bouquet. This is a noble wine, dry, genuine, with a sustained quality. Etna Rosso is kept in barrels of Slavonic oak for three years before it is bottled.

Farther south, from the fertile land encircling the ancient Greek city of Syracuse, come the superior Eloro Bianco and Eloro Rosso, also the Moscato di Siracusa e di Noto dessert wine. The latter is made from the white Muscat grape. Under Sicily's scorching sun, it acquires a high sugar content and therefore produces exquisite dessert wine. The tiny Lipari Islands are grouped just north of Messina, where we find the ambrosial Malvasia di Lipari, a sweetly soft, liqueurlike wine.

Western Sicily has its prized Marsala, produced in an area specified by law. This includes the towns in the three provinces of Palermo, Trapani and Agrigento. The wine's name means "harbor of God" in Arabic. It is the warm, classic, coveted dessert wine. It became well-known at the end of the 18th century when an English tradesman living in Sicily promoted its virtues. Its fame took flight when England's Lord Nelson, at anchor with his fleet in the Mediterranean, ordered 500 casks of Marsala for his officers and crews. There are various Marsalas: the very sweet Garibaldi Brand; medium sweet SOM, Superior Old Marsala; dry or "vergine" Soleras, with an alcoholic content of not less than 18 percent; Marsala Speciale, Crema Marsala and Marsala flavored either with eggs, almonds, strawberries or coffee. The alcoholic content can be as high as 20 percent.

Banfi Products Corporation is the sole agent for the importation of the precious Marsala called Sun Drops. V.S.E.P. is a sweet nectar, especially aged, produced from the choicest grapes and Brandy, whose minimum age is 21 years. Almond Cream, a classic after-dinner drink; Creamovo, with egg taste; Coffee Cream, flavored with coffee beans, soft and mellow; Cocoa Cream, chocolate flavor; Strawberry Cream, made with crushed fresh Italian strawberries; Blackberry Cream, made with ripe Italian blackberries; Cherry Cream from fresh, ripened cherries; and Mandarino Cream from tree-ripened tangerines.

Isolated from the mainland, many local customs have remained intact in Sardinia, an island of reserved, courteous and generous people. Only recently is their wine becoming known. The most popular Sardinian wine is the amber-colored Vernaccia di Oristano, completely fermented with a minimum sugar content. Delicately perfumed with a hint of almonds, it is like a Spanish Sherry, velvety, dry, a little bitter, warm. Nasco, Moscato del Tempio di Campidano, Giro and Monica are all dessert wines, the first two being beautifully golden yellow. Nasco is flower-perfumed, warm, dry tasting and with a bitter touch. A great dessert wine, it goes particularly well with fruit. Moscato del Tempio di Campidano is sweet and velvety. Giro is ruby tending to garnet, sweetish, full-bodied, honest. *Sardinia*

Among the good Sardinian table wine is Nuragus, straw-colored, with a beautiful bouquet, dry and fresh. This is excellent with fish dishes, which are popular in Sardinian cuisine. A number of wineries have been established on the island to produce the white wine. Malvasia di Bosa, Vermentino di Gallura, Cannonau and the red Oliena, cardinal-red Anghelu Ruju. This has a cinnamon bouquet and can compete with any good Port.

Others to remember from Sardinia are: Ogliastras, dry and white, and Moscato of Cagliari, the capital of Sardinia, a sweet white dessert wine.

A New York State grape harvest.

*Therefore God give thee of the dew
of heaven, the fatness of the earth
and plenty of corn and wine.*

GENESIS 27, v. 28

Chapter 9

Wine Of The United States

LEGEND has it that when Leif Ericson and his Viking giants came to the Atlantic Coast, somewhere around the year 1000 A.D., they found great forests, an abundance of wildlife and a profusion of wild grapes. "Vineland the Good," they called their discovery, and the name Vineland appears in many of the old records in the New England archives. On Martha's Vineyard, late one summer, we saw lush growths of the wild grapes that gave the little island off the Atlantic Coast its Biblical name.

Even before the *Mayflower* brought the Pilgrims to Massachusetts in the winter of 1620, wine production in the New World was already a subject of consideration. In 1616, Lord Delaware, Governor of Virginia, proposed to the sponsoring London Company that wine making be developed on a business basis in the English settlements. Thereafter, cuttings of European vines were shipped to America, and many vine-growing and wine-making experiments ensued, but with little success. Late in the 18th century, John Dufour was successful in domesticating the wild vines native to Kentucky. This effort initiated the development of American grapevines. After that, many native vines were crossbred and domesticated. Within the brevity of its history, America was on its way to provide many wines for the enjoyment of its people. It is well known, however, that every great wine, the king of liquids, that carries the exaltation of the palate to the highest degree, is closely related to the geographical origin that produces it.

It is impossible, for example, to produce Rhone wine, Bordeaux, Burgundy, Moselle, Chianti, Asti Spumante, Jerez Sherry or Port (from that small area of Portugal) in this country. Granted the authenticity of the vine and the grape, it is not enough. The soil, the sun, the air, the orientation of situation of the vineyard—thousands of subtle factors enter into the life history of every wine. Nevertheless, the viticulturists and wine makers of America have been able to achieve in a relatively short time, as history goes, an astonishing advancement, commanding the respect of the Old World.

As wine enjoyment becomes more and more a necessary accoutrement to our culture, every American should be familiar with the basic facts of the vineyards and wine production in his own country. Before World War I, in the days of legendary private fortunes (B.I.T.—before income tax), there existed in the United States a certain aristocracy in which wine drinking was part of those traditions inherited from Great Britain, France, Germany, Spain and Portugal. Albeit this nucleus was limited, it was a serious gastronomic dedication.

In addition, French and Italian immigrants brought with them their natural taste for table wine. Prohibition put a stop to all that wonderful joyousness. Not only did it foster the evil of subversive crime in this country, but it gave Americans a taste for the stronger spirits, destroying in them the sense of refinement in the matter of drinks. So the European tradition of wine enjoyment was lost, and with alcoholic drinks forbidden, a great deal of drinking was done surreptitiously just for the sake of drinking, while the imbiber knew very well he was drinking too much and not well enough.

After two decades of this drought, a new generation emerged with no wine culture, ready to drink neat or not at all, and consuming a great variety of mixed drinks that dull the palate. To enjoy great gastronomy, spirits should properly be postponed for another occasion. Partaking of too many cocktails makes the consumption of fine food, beautifully prepared and served, of no particular importance—and as for the wine, the good wine cannot be appreciated as it should be by the offended taste buds.

In 1946, the United States did not present too bright a market for French and other foreign exporters, nor, indeed, for our own producers. The first post-war years were difficult, with some unscrupulous foreign exporters exploiting Americans' lack of wine knowledge by sending poor wine, that did not help matters. However, the situation has fortunately greatly changed. Americans travel more, read more and have become more interested than ever in other countries thanks to improved audio and visual communications with all parts of the globe. Thus the American continent has, indeed, lost the barriers of cultural isolationism. Distance is no longer an obstacle. Much provincialism and many particularly local habits are fast diminishing. Intellectual attainments have never before been held in such high esteem, and there is a more pronounced taste for the good things in life in the realm of gastronomy and wine. When not in haste, many Americans have learned to relish meals accompanied by wine. They prefer European imports, but have also learned to enjoy the wine of America.

When vintners or wine merchants speak of American wine, they mean any wine produced in the United States. However, more specifically, the term is applied to wine produced east of the Rocky Mountains, because that wine is made from grapes native to America. Furthermore, the wine grown west of the Rockies—California wine —is not native because it is made from vines originally brought from Europe. Technically, however, "United States wine" aptly describes all wine produced in the United States.

The Finger Lakes district in upper New York state produces the best known of the American wine made from grapes native to our country.

APPETIZER WINE: Pale Dry Cocktail Sherry, Extra Dry Vermouth, Sweet Vermouth

Types of American Wine (East of the Rockies)

RED TABLE WINE: Burgundy, Claret, Rosé

WHITE TABLE WINE: Sauterne, Rhine

SPARKLING WINE: Dry Champagne (Royal Quality), Brut Champagne (very dry), Sparkling Burgundy (Champagne Rouge)

DESSERT WINE   Port, Tawny Port, Sherry, Cream Sherry, White Tokay, American Muscatel

The states of California and New York are the great wine producers. California leads. The other most important wine-producing areas in the United States center in the Finger Lakes district of New York State and in the Hudson River Valley. Next is the Sandusky-Lake Erie Island region in the northern part of Ohio and in the Cincinnati district.

In the years before the Civil War, Americans drank more Bordeaux

Wine than they do today, and our leading domestic vineyards were on the banks of the Ohio River near Cincinnati; then came the Trans-Continental railway, with cheaper and better wine from California, and the end of the era. (In France, the vineyard acreage in Burgundy declined by 50 percent in the marginal vineyards almost as soon as there was a railway from Marseilles to Paris and the far less expensive Midi Wine could be shipped for a reasonable price up to the populous north of France.)

In Ohio, Meier's Wine Cellars produce a number of premium wines from the varieties of native Ohio district grapes. In the mid-19th century, John Michael Meier was one of Ohio's pioneer vintners. In 1895, his son, John C. Meier, expanded the wine and grape business of the family farm. Now the Meier Company has a winery at Silverton in the Ohio Valley and at Sandusky in the northern Ohio grape area. The large wine storage vaults at Silverton contain great old casks of white oak and modern equipment for creating the Meier table wine.

From Meier's, Cincinnati, Ohio come good quality red, white and blended Rosé; Meier's Ohio State Sherry, Isle St. George Sauterne; Lake Erie Islands Rhine and White Burgundy, after-dinner Ohio State Port; American Muscatel; Meier's Ohio State Champagne and Meier's Ohio State Sparkling Burgundy. Additional Ohio producers are Cohodas Vineyards, Geneva; Engels and Krudwig Wine Co., Sandusky; Heineman Winery, Put-in-Bay; M. Hommel Co., Sandusky; Klingshirn Winery, Avon Lake; George F. Linz, Middle Bass; Mantey Vineyards, Venice; Mon Ami Champagne Co., Port Clinton; Put-in-Bay Wine Co., Put-in-Bay; August Zimmer Winery, Cincinnati.

Other regions in the United States produce some table wine that is not too widely known, such as the Puget Sound District and the Yakima Valley in Washington State; the Willamette Valley in Oregon; the Council Bluffs area in Iowa; areas along the Missouri River in Missouri; the whole of southwest Michigan; Onslow Wine Cellars, Holly Ridge, North Carolina.

In the north-central part of New Jersey, grapes for wine production are cultivated in the Egg Harbor district. There is an area around Charlottesville, Virginia, where grapes are grown from cuttings brought from France by Thomas Jefferson, who planted the vines around his hillside home at Monticello in the Blue Ridge Mountains. Vineyards are cultivated as well in the eastern coastal plains of North Carolina. Aside from grape cultivation, many of the southeastern and northwestern portions of the country produce a wide variety of fruits for wine and Brandy. In the South-central area, there are vineyards in the Ozark Mountains in Arkansas, where we least expected to find them.

California

Northern California's wine making is a blend of ancient lore, modern technology and economics in the sun-kissed Sonoma and Napa valleys. In the rural town of Sonoma, wine and its history are inextricably mixed. The Franciscan friars arrived there in 1823. San Francisco de Solano was the last and most northerly of their great chain of missions traversing California from the Mexican border. In 1835, shortly after the missions were secularized, Mexico's governor sent out young Mariano Guadalupe Vallejo as officer of his troops, under orders to subdue the rebellious Indians and to colonize the area. Vallejo founded a settlement that he called Sonoma Pueblo, and his men staked out the eight-acre plaza that still serves in its Old-World style as the center of the town of Sonoma.

Mexican-reared to the best of food and wine at the table, Señor Vallejo energetically set about salvaging the deserted mission vineyards of the Franciscan friars. Four years after the Mexican War of 1846, Vallejo settled permanently in California. He became both legislator and vintner. In fact, it was Mariano Guadalupe Vallejo who encouraged Hungarian nobleman-adventurer Count Agaston Haraszthy to initiate vineyards in Sonoma. Vallejo planted his first vineyards in Sonoma in the year of the Gold Rush, christening his winery Buena Vista. California Governor John C. Downey was influenced by the Count to assist in sending him as a wine advocate to Europe in 1861. The following year, he brought back 100,000 cuttings of 300 grape varieties, which he distributed among the growers. In a few years, Count Haraszthy's vineyard in the Sonoma Valley had 85,000 vines from European stocks. These vines and a vast nursery of 460,000 vines became the foundation plantings in the northern California wine industry.

It is a mile's drive east of Sonoma's Plaza down Old Winery Road to Buena Vista's ivy-covered stone buildings. Towering eucalyptus trees give shade to wooden picnic tables in the pleasant courtyard with its spraying fountain. Inside the winery are the cellars that were dug out by Chinese laborers. More than any other town in California, Sonoma is evocative of old-fashioned California, especially during the annual Vintage Festival held in late September. Beside the restored mission, a Franciscan priest gives the traditional prayer of thanks for a bountiful harvest at the opening of the festival. Then, in the shadow of balconied old adobe houses that face the plaza, there are concerts, parades, dances, barbecues. The many historic buildings are open to the public.

California's wine industry had its roots in Mexico, where vine cultivation and wine production increased because Hernando Cortez (1485–1547) encouraged Mexican viticulture by stipulating that "certain holders of land grants must plant each year for five years 1,000 vines for each 100 Indians laboring on the land." The Jesuit fathers were responsible for introducing vineyards and wine making into what became California. They carried Spanish colonization up the western coast into the Mexican peninsula of Lower California, discovered by Cortez. The successors of the Jesuits, the Franciscans, advanced farther north into what is now California. As each new mission or settlement was established, vines were planted. It was one of the first steps in bringing civilization into the wilderness, the inevitable march of the indestructible cult of the vine from its inception at Mount Ararat in Persia through China, Greece, Italy, France, Portugal and Spain.

Padre Junípero Serra and his Franciscan brothers, who were soldiers and settlers, founded the mission at San Diego de Alcala in 1769. Here they planted the true *vitis vinifera* grapevines. Therefore, the early California vines were closely related to those brought into Mexico from Spain. In ensuing years, the Mexican transplants became known as "mission vines," with a character of their own drawn from the different soil and climate. The Franciscans established their chain of missions from the Mexican border to Sonoma, north of San Francisco. Wine was needed not only for the table but for the ritual of Mass. Many of the present vines are the direct descendants of these ancestral Spanish and Mexican vines.

Part of an old Franciscan winery survives at San Gabriel Mission near Los Angeles. Here is preserved the original adobe building in which Indians trod the grapes, and there are three old wine presses. Until 1824, the Franciscans were the only wine producers in the territory of California. But that year an American, Joseph Chapman, settled near Los Angeles on land suitable for the establishment of a vineyard. He set out 4000 vines. In 1831, Jean Louis Vignes, a native Frenchman, brought from Bordeaux precious vinifera cuttings. He planted them on the site of the Los Angeles Union Railway Station, and soon was able to produce some good wine and Brandy. By 1840, he shipped wine and Brandy from the El Aliso vineyards to Santa Barbara, Monterey and San Francisco.

Other California vineyards, besides El Aliso of Los Angeles, have vanished before the juggernaut of progress as shopping centers replaced many of them. There was, too, the normal march of the cities. California vineyards flourish along a strip of coastal land for 700 miles where the soil and climate are favorable. Nowhere, however, are the conditions comparable to what they are in France in Bordeaux, Champagne, Burgundy or the Rhineland, even though the frosts are a constant menace there. California has regions where the sun is too fierce, and long droughts are severe in the counties of the great central valley—Sacramento, San Joaquin, Merced, Fresno, Madera, Tulare, Kings and Kern—so that irrigation is needed as an artificial stimulant. The northern and central coastal counties encompass San Francisco Bay, Sonoma, Napa, Santa Cruz and Alameda with the famous Valley of the Moon and Livermore Valley.

Recognition of California as a wine producer came much earlier and from more widespread sources than one would guess. For instance, *Bérauds Geographical Dictionary,* published in Paris in 1853, stated that "California is immense, a territory bordered on the west by the Pacific Ocean and on the east by little-known regions with no well-fixed boundaries, inhabited by indigenous tribes. The soil is remarkable for its prodigious fertility and is susceptible to diversified cultivation. The most important products up to this time are barley, wheat, corn, olive oil and wine, the latter two of superior quality."

When European type wine was first produced in California, the red grapes were well suited to the local soil and climate. The foreign red grapes were the first to be used for the prized varietals because they tasted like the European wine. This did not apply, however, to the white wine, which still lacked distinction. But Californians persistently (and in self-delusion) kept classifying the white as Sauterne or white Burgundy even though there was faint resemblance to the European originals. A California Pinot Chardonnay was simply *not* a white Burgundy, such as a beeswax-flavored Meursault or a Puligny-Montrachet.

Since we wrote our first wine book in 1961, wine consumption in the United States has greatly increased, and many wine qualities have since then been enhanced. For instance, it *is* now possible to compare a scarce Chardonnay from Wente Brothers, Beaulieu, Krug or Mondavi with its European counterparts. A decade ago this was impossible. At this writing (January 1971), California white wine is at long last coming into its own. In 1968, for instance, for the first time two California vineyards turned out a tart, lively Beaujolais almost indistinguishable from the French prototype produced from grapes harvested on the rolling hills north of Lyon. This Beaujolais is really exciting wine when contrasted with the bottles of bland white wine previously labeled "Gamay" or "Gamay-Beaujolais."

Likewise, the quality of several other whites from California is measuring up to Pinot Chardonnay. Two are especially worthy of note:

> *1. Krug and Almadén are presently producing Alsatian-type Gewürztraminers whose subtle delicacy are winning favor. These do not even have the bitter aftertaste found in the European version.*

> *2. Inglenook (Italian Swiss Colony Wine) and Krug are producing a fantastic California counterpart of Chenin Blanc. The grape originates with the Vouvray*

> *of the Loire. If you like this wine bone dry, Louis Martini
> has it.*

Since the repeal of Prohibition, two-thirds of California wine production has been devoted to Sherry, Port, Angelica, Muscatel—fortified wine rather than table wine, whose production predominates in other wine-producing countries where home consumption is very high. Fortified wine contains 20 percent alcohol and is produced in volume for the mass market. In the past two decades, and particularly since 1960, there have been more plantings of European vines such as Cabernet, Pinot, Riesling, Semillon and others. There has been much improvement in methods and equipment, so that now the best California plants can be rated with those of France and Germany.

Most of California's 58 counties grow grapes, and there are bonded wineries in 28 of these counties. The state is divided into two major wine districts: the North Coast area around San Francisco, principally producing table wine, and the much warmer interior valley where most of the fortified wine is made.

*From
Northern
California
to Southern
California*

Wine producing centers are:

Mendocino	Alameda (Livermore Valley*)
Sonoma*	Santa Clara*
Napa*	Santa Cruz*
Contra Costa	San Benito*

(*indicates important area)

Table grapes and grapes dried for raisins are also used in making inexpensive wine fortified with Brandy. Cultivation is in the vast, irrigated, interior valleys of San Joaquin and Great Central, which comprise California's second major area:

Sacramento	Madera
San Joaquin	Fresno
Stanilaus	Tulare, Kings and Kern

A smaller area of grape cultivation is in the San Bernardino County, directly east of Los Angeles, where more than 25,000 acres of wine grapes are grown.

*California
Wine*

1. APPETIZER WINE   includes California Sherry, California Madeira, Marsala, California Vermouth

2. WHITE TABLE WINE   (alcoholic content not to exceed 14 percent) includes California Sauterne, California Sweet Sauterne, Haut-

Sauterne or Château Sauterne, California Sauvignon Blanc, Semillon, California Riesling, California Rhine Wine, Hock or Moselle, California Chablis, California White Chianti, California Folle Blanche, Pinot Blanc, Chardonnay, Ugni Blanc, Chablis-type wine, California Light Muscat

3. RED TABLE WINE   from pale pink rosé to dark red (not to exceed 14 percent alcohol), includes California Claret and California Burgundy, California Chianti, California Zinfandel, California Barbera and Barberone, California Carignan, Grignolino, Mourastel, California Charbono, Duriff, Gamay, Pinot Noir, Petite Sirah (Burgundy-type), California Aleatico and California Rosé.

4. DESSERT WINE   (usually 20 percent alcohol) includes California Sherry, California Port, California Muscatel, California Tokay, California Angelica and California Malaga.

5. CALIFORNIA SPARKLING WINE   includes California Champagne, California Pink Champagne, California Sparkling Burgundy, California Sparkling Moselle, Sauterne, Muscat.

6. CALIFORNIA BRANDY   includes California Brandy, California Muscat Brandy, California Grappa or Pomace Brandy.

Where does the industry stand today? Two warring philosophies beset West Coast wineries. Highly successful mass producers persist in making all types of wine regardless of tradition, taste or suitability of soil. High-powered promotion often assails the public with a poor product that is claimed to be very good. On the other hand, a group of small wineries operate in the age-old tradition of the vine, quietly working to select and develop the most appropriate grapes. In the production of the wine these small wineries respect Old World traditions and methods and are wise enough to realize that California, with all of its advantages, cannot honestly duplicate European wine. The growing excellence of their products, however, lays the small wineries open to invitation by the bigger producers to absorb their plants, but the Mondavis, the Souverains, the Concannons and the Wentes want to continue making it on their own. Their select production at a premium is almost always consumed by Californians themselves.

Joseph Heitz, formerly of Beaulieu Vineyard, who now owns Heitz Cellars, features red wine. Concannon Vineyards in the Livermore Valley has "Limited Bottlings" purchased by Californians. Bob Mondavi who heads Mondavi Winery in the Napa Valley, goes to Europe to visit vineyards as often as he can. His Fumé Blanc as well as the Charles Krug Chenin Blanc are wines of distinction.

California's finest quality wine is made by a handful of small wineries in the Napa and Sonoma valleys north of San Francisco, in the Livermore Valley and in a few other areas to the south. One of the most dedicated small producers in California is Fred McCrea, a retired San Francisco businessman whose modern ranchhouse and vineyards are situated halfway up a mountainside overlooking St. Helena in the Napa Valley. McCrea's beautiful Stony Hill Vineyard makes only two wines: white McCrea Pinot Chardonnay and white McCrea Gewürztraminer. Only a few hundred cases of each are produced per year.

Mr. Lee Stewart, likewise a retired San Franciscan, of Souverain Cellars at St. Helena, has produced a very dry white wine called Green Hungarian. Inadequately imitated by several others, it won gold medals at California wine exhibits every year for a decade. Stewart has three other fine wines: Zinfandel, Riesling and Cabernet Sauvignon. His winery's annual production is less than 4,000 cases.

Wente Brothers, who produce some of the finest white table wine of the country, was founded by a native of Hanover, Germany. Carl H. Wente came to California in 1880 and received his training under Charles Krug, the pioneer viticulturist of Napa Valley. In late fall of 1883, Carl Wente bought some vineyards in the Livermore Valley south of the town of Livermore, where the original Wente Winery is still located. His good quality table wine brought above-average prices for the times. He found that the Semillon and Sauvignon Blanc grapes of the Sauternes region in France could adapt themselves to the soil and climate of Livermore. Later on, he imported vines of the Pinot Chardonnay of white Burgundy and Champagne. Carl's sons, Ernest and Herman, extended the acreage and acquired the El Mocho vineyards when Louis Mel, pioneer of the Livermore Valley, retired and released his treasured property to the Wentes.

Charles Wetmore, founder of Cresta Blanca, was sent by the California Vinicultural Society to obtain choice cuttings in France. The "open sesame" was a letter of introduction from Mrs. Mel-de-Bire to the Marquis de Lur-Saluces, who owned the world-renowned Château d'Yquem in Sauternes near Bordeaux. Wetmore obtained from him choice cuttings of the Semillon, Sauvignon Blanc and Muscadelle du Bordelais vines. Some of these he gave to Louis Mel, who propagated them in his El Mocho vineyards. The tradition is perpetuated when Marquis de Lur-Saluces, proprietor of Château d'Yquem visits California and samples what the California climate and soil can produce in the way of Sauternes.

The gravelly-dry soil of the Wente Vineyards produces good crops. Much of the soil is alluvial deposit washed down from the hills to the east. The considerably heavy gravel content is well suited to the healthy growth of the finer grape varieties. Each variety of grape is picked at peak of ripeness, the juice pressed in small batches, bottled wine placed on racks in a small cooperage, then aged in oaken puncheons and finally aged again in the bottle to full maturity. Wente wine—white, red and rosé—is labeled with the Valle de Oro brand. (Valley of Gold was the romantic name given to Livermore Valley by the Spaniards who first colonized there.)

WHITE WINE: *Wente*
                                                              Wine
Dry Semillon,   similar to a French Graves, but less sweet; vintaged

Sweet Semillon,   produced from late-picked grapes to ensure maximum richness and sweetness; nonvintaged

Sauvignon Blanc,   from the grape; vintaged

Grey Riesling,   popular dry, tart, straw-colored; vintaged

Pinot Blanc and Pinot Chardonnay,   dry, Chablis type; vintaged

VALLE DE ORO WHITE WINE: Château Wente, blend of Semillon and Sauvignon Blanc grapes with the addition of a little Muscadelle du Bordelais, a sweet Sauterne

VALLE DE ORO RED WINE AND ROSÉ: Burgundy, Rosé, Claret, all obtainable locally from winery in large containers; pleasing, inexpensive, ideal wine for home bottler

The Beaulieu Vineyard at Rutherford in northern California has a   *Beaulieu*
great name. The trade designation B.V. is for its selection of red,   *Vineyard*
white, sparkling, aperitif and dessert wine. It was founded by Georges   *(B.V.)*
de Latour, who arrived in California from France at the turn of the
century. Traveling throughout the state, he searched for the ideal
location for vineyards. Finally he settled in the Rutherford area of the
Napa Valley, where today the Beaulieu estate with its Versailleslike
gardens, well-kept orchards and spreading mansion is a showplace of
the Valley. Within four decades, Latour had established a sound
reputation for Beaulieu wine throughout the United States. In 1917,
he made the proud announcement: "We are in position to supply all
those who are solicitous to secure Altar Wine of the best quality
which is absolutely pure." He also informed the clergy that the authorization to make Altar Wine, first given to Beaulieu by Archbishop
Patrick J. Riordan, had been confirmed by his successor, the Most
Reverend Edward J. Hanna, Archbishop of San Francisco. These
words from the past bring to mind the pre-Prohibition days when
California wine growing was mostly centered in the North Coastal

region with many of the important producers in Napa Valley, the home of Beaulieu Vineyard. During the Prohibition era, many vintners ripped out their vineyards, but Beaulieu's vines were not uprooted during those years. The winery was operated under governmental supervision to produce sacramental wine for the various faiths that use them in their ritual. Thus the fine art of wine making has progressed without interruption at Beaulieu since the vineyard was established at the turn of the century. Today, as ever, Beaulieu is privileged to produce and sell Altar Wine of the best quality "which is absolutely pure."

Beaulieu Wine

RED:

Georges de Latour Private Reserve, a vintage Cabernet Sauvignon from that grape, produced only in better years and considered the premier Claret of California.

Beaumont, a mild table wine principally from the Beaumont grape but with small proportions of Merlot and Petit Verdot added, as in the better Red Bordeaux of France.

Burgundy from Pinot Noir, Napa Valley Gamay and Mondeuse de Savoie.

WHITE:

Château Beaulieu, vintage sweet Sauterne from late-picked Sauvignon Blanc and Semillon grapes, with a bit of Muscadelle du Bordelais added.

Pinot Chardonnay, vintage wine from that grape, limited production.

Beauclair, vintage Johannisberger or White Riesling.

Dry Sauternes and Sweet Sauternes, both from Semillon and Sauvignon Blanc grapes.

Chablis, from Pinot Chardonnay, Chenin Blanc and Melon de Bourgogne.

Riesling from Johannisberger or White Riesling and Sylvaner.

Rosé and Beaurosé mainly from Cabernet Sauvignon.

SPARKLING WINE (bottle-fermented): The Beaulieu Champagnes, dry and medium dry in character, were first available in 1955, followed by a Sparkling Burgundy.

APERITIF AND DESSERT WINE: Pale Dry Sherry; Sherry XXX, medium sweet; Cream Sherry, sweet; Port XXX; Muscatel XXX; and Muscat de Frontignan, from the vines of that name whose cuttings were imported by George de Latour in the early part of this century for a sweet red Liqueur-type wine.

When Georges de Latour died in 1940, his widow presided over the company until her own death in 1951. In wine circles, Madame de Latour is remembered as the Grande Dame of California viticulture. With innate grace and charm in the French manner, she made her home a true château. Their daughter Helene and her husband, the knowledgeable Marquis de Pins, continued the work of upholding the de Latour tradition. He and his wife pay periodic visits to France and also maintain the Beaulieu Château and gardens. There are four Beaulieu vineyards, two at Rutherford and two at Oakville, each planted with varieties suited to the soil and location.

Paul Masson Vineyards

The Paul Masson Vineyards at Saratoga, California, were initiated in 1852. Monsieur Etienne Thée from Bordeaux planted the first vineyard on the original Narvaez land grant south of San Jose, where he pioneered in viticulture in the Santa Clara Valley. Thée was succeeded by his son-in-law, Charles Lefranc, who was in turn succeeded by his son-in-law, Paul Masson. Paul, born in 1859 at Beaune, Burgundy, of a vintner family, emigrated to California at 19, worked with Charles Lefranc, married his daughter and in the traditional pattern became the partner of his wife's father. Paul Masson built the historic stone winery at the "vineyard in the sky" on top of the Santa Cruz Mountains above Saratoga. This became the nucleus of the Paul Masson establishment. The picturesque vine-covered structure of the winery received its unusual door after 1906. The 12th-century Romanesque portal, originally brought on a wind ship around Cape Horn from Spain for St. Patrick's Church in nearby San Jose, was bought and erected in its present location by Paul Masson when the great earthquake destroyed the church in San Jose.

The stone winery had its foundations sunk deep into the hillside, thus providing a cellar where cool temperatures could be maintained for storing and aging the wine. On repeated trips to France, Paul Masson returned with cuttings of grape varieties, which he planted in his mountain vineyard. In 1892, he perfected the first Paul Masson Champagne. This along with other Paul Masson wine and Brandy, began to win awards in national and international competitions.

Paul Masson personally continued making his wine on his baron-like estate until his retirement in 1936 at the age of 77. A disastrous fire in 1940, the year of his death, swept the winery. Completely restored, the famous old stone winery was designated a California historic landmark in 1960. After passing through the hands of intermediary owners until 1945, the Paul Masson firm was acquired by Alfred Fromm and Franz Sichel, who, like its president, Otto E. Meyer, were members of European wine-producing families.

The Champagne Cellars of Paul Masson Vineyards were opened at Saratoga on June 6, 1959, with a stock of four million bottles of Champagne and still wine. The beautiful winery, costing many millions (designed by John S. Bolles), was the first in the United States built for the primary purpose of producing and aging bottle-fermented Champagne. It is open to visitors from all over the world. American wineries are, in fact, becoming increasingly cordial in their public relations, providing guided tours, as in Europe, so that people may learn first-hand and be initiated into the wonderful world of wine.

Today's gleaming Masson winery and cellars cover 17 landscaped acres off the Santa Clara-Saratoga Highway. The wine-tasting hall and reception room measures 11,000 square feet. One of the walls of glass faces a 9,000-square-foot pool. A gushing fountain symbolizes the effervescence of Champagne. The opposite wall shows 16 huge transparencies of Paul Masson wine, Champagnes, Vermouth and Brandy, each associated with the variety of the grape from which it is made. Nearby is the tasting counter.

One enters the impressive winery by ramp, devised to show on its inner face a mosaic by the Spanish-born artist José Moya del Pino depicting the history of wine making. The main building devotes 156,000 square feet to the making and aging of wine, especially Champagne, and to blend and bottle Brandies. Sightseeing is done from the mezzanine level of the five main areas: Champagne cellars, bottling and packaging departments, finished goods, storage cellars and the Brandy blending and bottling room.

One sees the glass-lined steel tanks used in Germany and France for aging wine before final aging in the bottle. In effect, the tanks are enormous bottles of 5,000-gallon capacity. In contrast to this dazzling modern magic, there are private tastings at the chalet near the original old stone winery three miles up the curving mountain road. In the oak-beamed reception room of the chalet, with its log fireplace, Paul Masson long ago, in his elegant French fashion, entertained the personalities of his day who were attracted by the amiable and knowledgeable host, the quality of his wine and the culinary excellence of his household. Good wine, good food and handsome men and women to enjoy them were the dreams on which Paul Masson built his life. Today the wall facing the Santa Clara Valley has been removed and, in true California architectural style, has been replaced with wall-to-wall windowpane so that one sits seemingly suspended in space above the valley overlooking San Jose, Sunnyvale and Mount Hamilton beyond.

Emerald Dry, reminiscent of the drier wine from the Rhine and Moselle valleys of France and Germany, is made from grapes of an improved Riesling vine developed by viticulturists at the University of California. Picked by hand at the exact moment of the grapes' prime maturity, they are pressed with care so as not to break the seeds. The wine is matured naturally in wooden casks before bottling. Emerald Dry in its tall, green Rhine bottle is the perfect companion for all light foods: fish, seafood, chicken, spring lamb and casseroles.

From Paul Masson Vineyards

Rhine Castle, the color of pale gold, with a bouquet reminiscent of spring flowers, is a California wine akin to the great, ripe Liebfraumilchs of the Rhineland. Rhine Castle is best chilled, served with fish and shellfish, light meats, fowl and omelettes.

Rubion, a red, velvety soft, dry table wine that traces its origin to the time Paul Masson brought his grape cuttings from Europe in the 19th century. It is related to Paul Masson's other family of fine wine: Cabernet Sauvignon, Gemay Beaujolais, Burgundy, Pinot Noir and Sparkling Burgundy.

Paul Masson Madeira, medium dry, has a pronounced nutty flavor from long, slow baking at controlled temperatures, a mellow bouquet from aging in small oak casks. This all-purpose wine is ideal as an aperitif or during meals, especially with or following soup. It also combines well with dessert. Excellent as an ingredient in recipes, it is no more expensive than the Masson regular Pale Dry, Cocktail, Fine and Cream Sherries, Tawny and Rich Ruby Port and Choice Muscatel.

In the past 30 years, grape-breeding research by viticulturists of the University of California has developed additional strains of Old World grapes, which now thrive in the Paul Masson Vineyards. In the past decade, two entirely original Paul Masson white table wines have been evolved, the Emerald Dry and Rhine Castle mentioned above. In 1965, Paul Masson Vineyards was presented with the United States Presidential Award for Export Achievement for its sales of wine, Champagne and Vermouth in some 30 foreign countries, small ambassadors of America's good life as exemplified in its viticulture.

For almost a century this Order has produced a superlative line of California wine. The Brothers of Christian School, popularly known as The Christian Brothers, are a Catholic Teaching Order, founded

The Christian Brothers

in Rheims, France, in 1680 by nobleman and priest St. John Baptiste de la Salle. Education is their primary responsibility and interest. "To give a Christian education to youth, especially to the poor" are the words of the founder. The first American school was opened in 1948. The western province of the Christian Brothers is responsible for the schools in the western United States. The Order has grown until today it numbers over 17,000 members in 86 countries. Approximately 760,000 students receive instruction in over 1,600 schools operated by the Christian Brothers throughout the world. Included in the figures are the 3,000 Brothers who teach 114,000 students in 192 schools in the United States, including such well-known institutions as St. Mary's College in California, Manhattan College in New York, and La Salle College in Philadelphia.

After establishing their first American community in Baltimore in 1848, the Brothers moved to California in 1868 to found their first community there, eventually opening a Novitiate (Brother's Training School) at Martinez in 1879. They planted vineyards in that year, and in 1882 began to produce wine for sacramental purposes as well as for their own table. Gradually the wine began to be sold in the neighborhood, and fame of its quality spread. Demand increased, and the Brothers found themselves in the wine business in addition to their primary work of education and religion.

The Order's western province, extending from Canada to Mexico and from the Rocky Mountains to the West Coast, required more adequate facilities than those at Martinez. In 1932, the Brothers moved into the beautiful, mission-style quarters, constructed on a large estate in the western foothills of the Napa Valley. It is here at Mont La Salle, amidst flourishing hillside vineyards, that the Brothers have continued their wine making in addition to training young men for the Brotherhood. Other wine-making locations are the Wine Aging and Champagne Cellars at St. Helene and the Reedley winery, where appetizer and dessert wine as well as the famous Christian Brothers Brandy are made.

Mont La Salle Vineyards, headquartered at Napa, California, were incorporated as a separate entity from the de La Salle Institute, the educational and religious organization. The former is entirely owned and operated by the Order and net profits are used primarily to help support the religious and educational endeavors of the latter. Mont La Salle Vineyards pays Federal income and excise taxes, state and municipal taxes, property taxes and all other applicable levies. The Brothers serve without monetary compensation whether teaching in schools or working the vineyards. Specially qualified Brothers of the Order manage and supervise all winery activities from the growing of the grapes to the making, aging and bottling of the wine. They are proud of the fact that every bottle bears on its label the statement *"Produced and bottled by The Christian Brothers."*

The vines are exclusively of European stock, costly to raise, with an average yield of only 1 ½ to 3 ½ tons of grapes to the acre in Mont La Salle's mountain vineyards, which are nonirrigated. Brother Timothy, the Cellarmaster, is acknowledged as one of California's finest enologists. His palate and knowledge of wine making have set the standards in California. Brother Justin is Assistant Cellarmaster, Brother Gregory is President of the various wineries and Brother Frederick is Assistant to the President. The wine, Champagne and Brandy of The Christian Brothers are distributed on an exclusive worldwide basis by Fromm-Sichel, Inc. Visitors are welcomed to the cellars at St. Helena, Napa County, California.

Table Wines of The Christian Brothers

Pinot St. George, a ruby-red dinner wine of deep, smoothly dry, uniquely satisfying flavor.

Burgundy, a full-bodied, dry, deep-red dinner wine, with a lovely bouquet resulting from patient aging.

Pinot Noir, a dry, red wine, the finest of the Burgundies, pressed from the sparse crop of the true Pinot Noir grape.

Cabernet Sauvignon, a truly superb dry, red table wine from Cabernet Sauvignon grapes; matured to its full flavor and bouquet, it will stay in its prime for years.

Claret, for those who prefer a red dinner wine light in body, dry and appetizingly tart with a mellow bouquet.

Napa Rosé, a medium-dry wine, rose-pink in color, with a taste of the grape's natural sweetness.

Vin Rosé, sunrise-pink, very dry, light, gay and refreshing.

Chenin Blanc, a light white wine made from the Chenin Blanc grape, a noble émigré from France.

Pinot de la Loire, made from a famous Loire Valley grape, a rich, white wine, delightful and fruity.

Rhine Wine, light, crisply refreshing, very dry.

Johannisberg Riesling, pale-gold, dry wine with a flowery bouquet, made from the peerless White Riesling.

Riesling pale-gold, dry dinner Wine.

Chablis, light, tart, pale-gold dinner wine, completely dry, with a "flinty" taste.

Pinot Chardonnay, a great white dinner wine, pressed from rare Chardonnay grapes used to make the finest of the white Burgundies.

Sauterne, golden-hued wine, medium-dry and rich in flavor.

Sweet Sauterne, fruity flavor, fragrant aroma, sweet and full.

Sauvignon Blanc, rare Sauvignon Blanc grapes are used for the spicy bouquet and natural sweetness of this rich white wine.

The Christian Brothers Brandy This Brandy has taste, quality, aroma, fine amber color. It is aged for years in small oaken casks and perfectly blended.

The Christian Brothers Port

Tinta Cream Port, made from the rare Tinta Madeira grape of Portugal, is a wine of great breed, aroma and bouquet.

Treasure Port, "Black Label," a luxury wine with majestic bouquet and natural sweetness.

Tawny Port, lighter in body and color, fully mellow.

Ruby Port, rich, ruby-red, fruity flavor of sun-ripened grapes.

The Christian Brothers Sherries

Cocktail Sherry, "Black Label" specialty, light in body, very pale, perfectly dry, subtly nutlike, smooth and mellow.

Dry Sherry, light-bodied, aperitif wine.

Golden Sherry, medium-dry with great character, mellow and very smooth.

Cream Sherry, golden-amber, creamy smooth, naturally sweet, nutlike, skillfully blended. Best served chilled.

Meloso Cream Sherry, top-quality Sherry, full-bodied, luscious.

Any-Time Wine

Muscatel, spicy, enticing in flavor, naturally sweet.

Tokay, an amber nectar, medium sweet and soft.

Chateau La Salle, golden in color, naturally sweet, smoothly balanced, distinctive bouquet. Best served well-chilled with meat, fish or fowl, with main course or dessert, over ice cream or fruit.

Sweet Vermouth, a full-bodied, Italian-style Vermouth, spicy, good in Manhattans, very pleasing as an aperitif or on the rocks. *Vermouths*

Dry Vermouth, a French-style Vermouth, very pale, very dry.

Brut Champagne, a dry, white Champagne. *Champagnes*

Extra Dry Champagne, an elegant, premium white Champagne, fuller than Brut Champagne.

Champagne Rosé, a pink Champagne, with gay luster.

Sparkling Burgundy, of brilliant cardinal red color, full-bodied, round, rich fullness, flavor from long maturing.

Extra Cold Duck, capturing all the richness of premium Champagne and Burgundy grapes.

In general, California produces a wide variety of red table wine called California Clarets, red Burgundies and some red wine of the Italian type, also the white table wine known as California Sauternes and white Burgundies; Rhine Wine, Rosé table wine and Sparkling Wine. The latter are the California Champagnes. Among these are Korbel Brut and Sec, Paul Masson Brut and Extra Dry and Cresta Blanca Brut. There are also the California Pink (Rosé) Champagnes comprising Almadén Pink, and the California Red Champagnes and Sparkling Burgundies, which include Korbel Rouge, Almadén Sparkling Burgundy and the Paul Masson Crackling Rosé.

The remaining classification includes the aperitif and dessert wine of the California Sherries, dry and sweet. Not to be overlooked are the California Ports, among which are found the Louis Martini Tawny Port and the Buena Vista Vintage Port. We visited the Louis Martini plant and winery, a fine establishment where we were warmly welcomed. Muscat Wine is chiefly from the Napa Valley (Beaulieu Muscat de Frontignan) and from the Livermore and Santa Clara valleys. Black Muscat is produced in Santa Clara and goes by the intriguing name of Novitiate of Los Gatos Black Muscat. Southern Alameda County contributes Weibel Black Muscatel and Cream of Black Muscat.

The California Wine Association was initiated in 1884 when a number of wineries joined forces. In 1929, it was reorganized as Fruit Industries, Ltd., but in 1951, it reverted to its original name. Mr. A. R. Morrow, the grand old man of California viticulture, was long the dominant figure of the Association. The Association comprises cooperative and other wineries to which more than 1,200 wine growers contribute their grapes in a well-organized system. These wineries are located in the four major wine districts: one in Sonoma, which features dry table wine; six in the Lodi-Sacramento district, mostly for Sherry, Tokay and Brandy; two in the Fresno-San Joaquin district, especially for Muscatel and Grignolino; and one in the Cucamonga district, which produces Port and other sweet wine. The Association controls production of the various types of wine with regard to regional suitability and quality. There is an enormous winery for blending, finishing, aging and bottling in San Francisco. The Association's table and dessert wine is marketed under the brands Ambassador District and Eleven Cellars, which include red wine, Zinfandel, Burgundy and Claret; white, Sauterne and Chablis; Rosé and Vin Rosé.

The southern districts of California center in Los Angeles and San Bernardino counties (Cucamonga district). California is divided into two regions. The northern coastal region includes the Sonoma-Mendocino district, Napa-Solano district, Livermore-Contra Costa district, San Francisco district, Santa-Clara–Santa-Cruz–Central coastal district, with its Santa Clara County and Valley, Santa Cruz, San Benito, Monterey and San Luis Obispo counties.

The Great Inland Valley Region comprises the Lodi-Sacramento district, the Escalon-Modesto district, Southern San Joaquin Valley district, with its Madera, Fresno, Tulare and Kern counties. There are many other wineries deserving of mention, but we can include only varieties particularly familiar to those interested in the wine of California.

Italian Swiss Colony Wine

When immigrants from northern Italy and Switzerland brought their wine making knowledge to Sonoma County in northern California in 1881, they established themselves at Asti, only 85 miles north of San Francisco in the premium vineyard country. The Winery (reached by Highway 101) welcomes visitors to its tasting room, where wine is served by men and women in picturesque costumes. Italian Swiss Colony is the second largest wine producer in the United States. E & J Gallo Winery is the largest wine producer located in Modesto.

Gold Medal Wine
(Italian Swiss Colony)

WHITE TABLE WINE includes Sauterne, dry, medium-bodied, fruity bouquet; also Haut-Sauterne, a little bit sweeter

RHINE WINE and CHABLIS, light, dry table wine

Wine of the United States

285

RED TABLE WINE   includes Burgundy, full-bodied, robust and dry; Claret, lighter in body than Burgundy, ruby-red in color; Zinfandel, named after the grape variety

COCKTAIL AND DESSERT WINE   includes Pale Dry Sherry; Sherry, a standard medium Sherry, medium sweet, with a nutlike flavor, (variation Cream Sherry), some sweeter, served chilled; Port, red, full-bodied, (variations Ruby Port and Tawny Port); White Port, pale golden, sweet wine, served chilled; Muscatel, served chilled; Tokay, sweet blend of dessert wine, served cool or chilled

TABLE WINE   includes Grenache Vin Rosé, Chianti; Rhineskeller; Napa, Sonoma and Mendocino Burgundy; Chablis and Vin Rosé

Inglenook Vineyards (owned by Italian Swiss Colony Wine)

In Scottish, "Inglenook" means a cozy corner. In 1879, a wealthy retired Finnish sea captain, Gustave Niebaum, whose hobby was wine knowledge and enjoyment and who had visited all of the wine-growing regions of the world, planted the Inglenook vineyard at Rutherford, in the heart of the Napa Valley. The original old stone winery in the Old World tradition still stands. The soil of the Valley is of a type that gives firmness and body to the grapes, and the climate provides just the right combination of warm days and cool nights. The winery was built into the side of a stone hill so that nature could help keep the temperatures in the winery consistently cool. Located about 65 miles north of San Francisco, it is easily reached from any part of the Bay area.

DISTRICT-BOTTLED VINTAGE RED WINE   includes Inglenook Vintage Burgundy, a robust red wine, properly aged; Inglenook Vintage Zinfandel, medium-bodied, red dinner wine, rich with the fragrance of the unique Zinfandel grape

DISTRICT-BOTTLED VINTAGE WHITE WINE   includes Inglenook Vintage Chablis, palest gold, blended from the aristocrats of this vineyard; Inglenook Vintage Rhine, dry, light in body

VINTAGE DESSERT WINE   includes Inglenook Vintage Sherry, Pale Dry Sherry, Cream Sherry, Tawny Port and Ruby Port

ESTATE-BOTTLED VINTAGE RED WINE   includes Inglenook Cabernet Sauvignon, Pinot Noir, Red Pinot, Charbono (a rarity in America, made from the grape that in the Italian Piedmont yields an excellent red wine); Inglenook Gamay Beaujolais, Zinfandel

ESTATE-BOTTLED VINTAGE WHITE WINE   includes Inglenook Grey

Riesling, White Pinot, Traminer, Pinot Chardonnay, Johannisberg Riesling, Chenin Blanc, Sylvaner Riesling, Dry Semillon

In addition, they produce Rosé Wine and Champagnes.

Roma Wine Company Located in Fresno, it is owned by Schenley Industries. Most of the Brandies produced here are merchandised by Brandy Distillers, a division of Associated Brands, a Schenley subsidiary. The best known of the Schenley Brandies is Coronet V.S.Q. (very special quality), 84 proof blended. Other similar Brandies are J. Bavet, Old Monastery Brand and Louis Brandies, all blended and 84 proof.

The Almadén Vineyards Located at Los Gatos it is credited with the introduction of Rosé or Vin Rosé, a wine that did not exist in this country prior to 1942. News of a pink wine was brought by travelers who had tasted it in southern France, generally Tavel. A little was imported. When the first Almadén California Rosé was judged in a fair at Sacramento in 1947, it received a gold medal. The Vin Rosés of France and Italy were not available here during the war years, so when Almadén Grenache Rosé was introduced it found much favor. A fresh, gay, pretty wine, easy to serve chilled, it goes well with all foods. Rosé does not improve after the second year. It is not a mixture of red and white wine, which is forbidden by French law, but a pink wine made from black grapes. The pigment of the grape skin is soluble in alcohol and becomes a part of the wine during fermentation. If the skins are not removed until fermentation is complete, the wine becomes red.

Almadén Vineyards were established at Los Gatos in 1852. Its name means "the mine" in Arabic, deriving from the world-famous quicksilver mine at Almadén in Spain. There are hillside vineyards, vast aging cellars and tiered soleras where Sherry is matured and blended as in Spain. Champagne is produced by the old, laborious French method. At Almadén-Paicines and Almadén-Cienega, there are vast vineyards of distinguished European origin. Almadén district lies south of San Francisco Bay, rich in history. A California State Park Commission marker designates the spot where "in 1852 Charles Lefrank made the first commercial planting of fine European wine grapes in Santa Clara County and founded Almadén Vineyards. Lefranc imported cuttings from vines in the celebrated wine districts of his native France, shipping them around Cape Horn under sail."

Almadén Champagnes are bottle-fermented as in France. White and red, dry wine is aged in vast cellars extending over four acres under one roof. There are 30,000 small oak barrels that hold 1 1/2 million gallons of mostly Cabernet Sauvignon and Pinot Noir in a temperature between 55° and 62° F. year-round. After some 25 years, Almadén wines in 1965 received attractive new labels, designed by the Grabhorn Press of San Francisco, in charge of Robert Grabhorn, the younger of the two founding brothers. The labels show a vine-yard scene encompassed by a wreath.

The Wine Advisory Board of San Francisco provides for a National Wine Week in the fall of each year, when it is stressed that California wines are all-purpose, all-year beverages, inexpensive, and always appropriate for mealtime, as well as ingredients for cooking. The Board insists that American wine must be presented as native or United States wine. But nothing is more injurious to their acceptance than being designated in print or speech as domestic. The buyer is fearful of being less than elegant if he accepts a nonimported label, flatly said to be domestic. The words "native," "United States" or "America" provide an entirely different connotation and atmosphere. However, there are still some food writers and columnists who insist upon using the word "domestic," just as there are writers seriously commenting on fine restaurants who continue to say "eating" instead of "dining." We have even seen a book entitled *The Art of Eating!* The Board also educates the dining room staffs of all restaurants in the proper presentation of United States wine.

New York

Some of the grapes used in New York in the premium wine are the same types used in Europe. Others are domestications of grapes that originally grew wild in New York State. These grapes produce wine with a fruity taste.

The European type *vitis vinifera* vines that grow so successfully in California cannot be commercially cultivated in New York.

For almost two centuries, viticulturists have worked to marry the European vinifera species with the American Labrusca. Out of this union, the French-American Seibel grapes have been developed. French-American hybrids and Labrusca varieties are usually more expensive than the vinifera grown elsewhere in the United States. Experimenters in this country and in Europe continually work to produce new varieties from seedlings, hybridization and crossings.

"The wines made with traditional New York State grapes have their own particular flavor," said Charles Fournier, a director of Gold Seal and a pioneer of new wines with Greyton Taylor of the Taylor Wine Company and Great Western, in an interview for *The New York Times* (October 16, 1969). "We want to keep producing them, but at the same time we want to produce wines that have a wider appeal."

Worthy of note are the experiments of Dr. Konstantin Frank, who came to Hammondsport, New York, in 1955 and now heads Vinifera Wine Cellars. By a painstaking process of grafting European vine roots onto American root stocks, Dr. Frank was able to produce wine grapes of the best European and California varieties to survive the brutal upstate winters.

New York State's grape belt comprises:

> *1. Part of the Hudson Valley, particularly the western portion bordering Lake Erie*
>
> *2. The Niagara River area*
>
> *3. The southern shores of Lake Ontario*
>
> *4. The west-central part of New York State in the Finger Lakes district*

Table grapes are grown in the Chautauqua area on Lake Erie west of Buffalo and in the Hudson Valley, but these zones produce little wine grapes.

Wine making is big business in the Finger Lakes area of New York, the largest wine region east of the Rockies. The seven wineries of the Finger Lakes Wine Growers Association, among them Taylor, (Pleasant Valley) Great Western, Widmer's (at Naples on Lake Canandaigua) and Urbana (Gold Seal), sold more than $62 million worth of wine in 1968. About 1,000 people work for the wineries full time, and another thousand help harvest the grapes in the fall from after Labor Day until the first frost comes, usually toward the end of October.

Only the areas bordering on Lakes Keuka and Canandaigua are grape growers. The other two deep blue Finger Lakes, long and narrow, which lie southeast of Rochester, are called Seneca and Cayuga.

The main Finger Lakes grapes are easily distinguishable from each other, and they vary in taste. They mature at different times during the harvest season, and are listed here in order of their ripening:

1.	Delaware	light red
2.	Elvira	white
3.	Fredonia	medium black
4.	Niagara	light green
5.	Concord	black
6.	Ives	jet black
7.	Clinton	purplish black
8.	Isabella	deep black
9.	Catawba	light purplish red

Other wine grapes include Eumlan, Iona, Dutchess, Diana, Salem, Campbell's, Early, the Diamond, Norton, Noah, Sheridan, Vergennes.

How did New York's vineyards begin in Hammondsport? The first vines were planted here in 1829 by the Reverend William Bostwick, Rector of Hammondport's St. James Episcopal Church. He obtained shoots from Hudson Valley vineyards and set them out in his rectory garden. From this humble beginning developed the great vineyards that flourish on the steep hillsides of the lakes. The clear, deep waters of the glacier-gouged lakes temper the climate. The slow-warming lakes help to retard spring growth until frost danger is past, and their warmth in the late fall blankets the last-ripening grapes on chilly nights.

Walter Taylor moved into this district in April, 1880, with his bride, Addie. He bought a seven-acre plot near Hammondsport on the western slopes, close to Lake Keuka. After growing and shipping grapes for two years, he purchased a 70-acre farm, setting out 35 acres in Delaware (white) grapes and Ives (red) grapes.

Walter Taylor then brought his parents, George and Maria Taylor, to Hammondsport, and the combined families began producing red and white table wine, which they shipped in barrels to New York City. Later they added dessert wine. From the original seven-acre vineyard of 1880, the Taylor Wine Company's holdings expanded to 550 acres.

The rows of Delaware grapes Walter Taylor set out can be seen today next to his old winery, now the Finger Lakes Wine Museum. As the business grew, Walter's three sons, Fred, Clarence and Greyton, took their places in the family enterprise. The Taylor Wine Company shipped fine, barreled wine, and until 1913, the Bully Hill acreage provided enough grapes. In that year, however, they first purchased grapes from other growers to supplement their harvest, a practice still in effect. Taylor now buys selected varieties of grapes from more than 340 growers, some of them third generation suppliers.

In 1919, the Taylor Wine Company moved down from Bully Hill into the building next to the Pleasant Valley Wine Company, constructed in 1886. Only a few firms survived the era of Prohibition. Taylor and Pleasant Valley survived by selling table grape juice as well as wine for sacramental purposes. Buildings have replaced the vineyards that once covered the hillside behind the winery, and since 1960, eight buildings have been constructed on the valley floor, with two more large buildings in process.

In 1939, Taylor installed equipment to begin the exacting and costly bottle fermentation of premium Champagne. More than 12 million bottles were aging in storage vaults in 1971. However, it was not until 1955 that Taylor changed from a partnership to a privately held corporation. At the end of 1961, Taylor acquired Great Western, and on April 17, 1962, the company made a public stock offering. The two wineries are operated as competitors. Greyton Taylor was named Director of Pleasant Valley. In 1964, Fred Taylor became Chairman of the Board of Taylor Wine, succeeded as President by

George A. Lawrence. "Mr. Fred" died in August, 1968, at the very time we had motored to Hammandsport to visit the vineyards, winery and Bully Hill, only to find the whole town hushed by the sad news.

Horses were used for much of the work in the vineyards until not too long ago. However, modern methods of weed control have eliminated the need for plowing, and mechanical harvesters have taken over 80 percent of the work on the crops. The machines remove the stems right in the vineyard and eliminate one processing step.

In 1962, Taylor installed its first 100,000-gallon fermentation tank. There are now 44 such tanks in place, and excavations are under way for a building that will eventually house 48 more, for a total of more than nine million gallons. And still the patterns of fall in the little Village of Hammondsport are much the same today as they were more than a century ago when commercial wine making began in the Finger Lakes region. At the peak of the harvesting, men work the presses in the wineries 13 hours a day. Well-kept homes crowded together along the steep streets of the village betoken the well-being of the 1,100 people who live in Hammondsport. The vineyards draw people from the surrounding area. About 1,000 people work in the wineries full time, and another thousand help with the harvest in the fall. Hammondsport is still a little wine-making town of gingerbread houses in the center of New York State, a town that spreads out from a town square that runs down to the shores of Lake Keuka.

In the vineyards, however, harvesters pick types of grapes that are new to this area, for they are the same varieties that produce the finest wine in France and Germany. There is more emphasis in the wineries on selectivity and quality, and vintners are producing more and more premium quality wine.

For many years, New York wine producers concentrated on inexpensive wine. In recent years, however, with increasing affluence and heightened wine tastes acquired by travels in Europe, the market for premium wine has been broadened. Most of New York State's wine is blended to maintain a uniformity of taste.

Be sure to pay a visit to the Finger Lakes Wine Museum—the original building of the Taylor Wine Company—Bully Hill, Road # 2, Hammondsport. It is surrounded by vineyards over 80 years old overlooking Lake Keuka. Now owned by Walter S. Taylor, the grandson, it contains an historical collection of the Taylor family. The Winemaker's Shop is nearby. It supplies finest grape juices from 40 different varieties of grapes, plus all sorts of wine making supplies and grape vines. But more important, the shop supplies the answers to any problems that may arise during the process of making wine at home. The shop will answer letters and send illustrated brochures.

On October 10, 1970, a small group of people gathered on Bully Hill, overlooking Keuka Lake and acres of vineyards, to acknowledge the official designation of the Finger Lakes area as the "Champagne District of America." There is little doubt that this area does produce Sparkling Wine of outstanding quality. The new title links it in spirit to the famous Champagne district of France.

DINNER WINE includes Rosé, Rhine, Sauterne, Lake Country White, Lake Country Pink, Lake Country Red, Burgundy and Claret

Taylor Wine

DESSERT WINE includes Port, Tawny Port, Pale Dry Sherry, Sherry, Cream Sherry, White Tokay, Muscatel (American)

VERMOUTH includes Extra Dry Vermouth (American) and Sweet Vermouth (American)

CHAMPAGNE includes Brut Champagne (very dry), Dry Champagne (royal quality), Pink Champagne, Sparkling Burgundy (Champagne Rouge).

All bear the words "Great Western" as part of their names: Great Western Extra Dry Champagne, Brut Champagne, Special Reserve Champagne, Pink Champagne, Sparkling Burgundy, Solera Port, Solera Tawny Port, Solera Sherry, Solera Cocktail Sherry, Solera Cream Sherry, Cooking Sherry, Vintage Delaware, Vintage Diamond, Dutchess Rhine, Pleasant Valley White, Chablis, Baco Noir Burgundy, Chelois, Pleasant Valley Red, Rosé, Vintage Isabella Rosé, Pink Catawba, Sweet Vermouth, Triple Dry Vermouth.

Great Western Wine

Located on Lake Canadaigua in the town of Naples, New York, they are particularly well-known for their Sherries. Their Neapolitan Sherry is an aperitif that is not too dry but is smooth, flavorsome, golden brown. Wildmer's Cocktail Sherry is a brilliant, pale Sherry, fragrant and nutty in flavor, yet very dry and excellent as an aperitif.

Widmer's Wine Cellars

This oldest winery in America in point of continuous operation (since 1839), is situated at Washingtonville, New York, in the heart of the Hudson River Valley, distinguished for historical sites such as the United States Military Academy at West Point and Washington's headquarters at Newburgh.

Brotherhood Winery

An early band of monks had previously planted the winery's first vineyards. Legend has it that there were once two blood brothers surnamed O'Brien. One was "round as an apple" and the other "skinny as a rail." The latter ministered to the spiritual needs of the Minisink Indians, who once lived on the great slopes of the highest peak visible from the site of the winery. That slope is called Skunnimunk, "a skinny monk"(?). The younger brother, who was "round" and merry, had a penchant for cooking and baking tasty dishes for the little band of monks who toiled in the wilderness. Brother O'Brien, an able organizer who planted and supervised the small monastery's vineyards is recalled in the winery's delectable aperitif called Brother O'Brien, bittersweet and garnet-colored.

In 1837, a French wine maker bought the property where Brotherhood is now situated. The wine produced from the first harvest was delivered on horseback or shipped by riverboat to the local churches for the ritual and spiritual services. As roads improved and pioneers pushed westward, Brotherhood sacramental wine was placed in many a covered wagon or stagecoach crossing the continent bound for the frontier towns of California. As more churches were established, Brotherhood Winery supplied them with sacramental altar wine. They have consistently observed the requirements of Canon Law.

For its wine, Brotherhood Winery uses the following grapes: Elvira, Catawba, Niagara, Bacchus, Dutchess, Delaware, Ives, Norton and Isabella. Its Sherries are aged in small oaken casks: Dry Cocktail Sherry, Golden Mellow Sherry, Cream Sherry.

Besides Ruby and Tawny Ports, they also provide New York State Tokay, Muscatel Wine, Angelica Wine (honey-colored and sweet), Holiday Wine (very red, bouquet from 12 herbs and spices), May Wine (pink, pressed in the spring from the previous fall's grapes and flavored with woodruff, sweetened with fresh juice of strawberries).

Dinner wine includes Sauterne (sweet), Rhine (dry), Chablis (very dry), Burgundy (red and dry), Rosé (pink and dry), Champagne and Sparkling Burgundy.

In a thoughtful letter, Mr. F.L. Farrell, Brotherhood's President, wrote (quoted in excerpts):

" . . . The history and development of our native American wines is a fascinating story. For the producers, it has been a long and hard one, with many setbacks and disappointments. Now, however, it seems as if New York State wines have found real favor. Their sales are zooming all over the country. . . .

"In the early days of our country, the wild grapes grew so prolifically that it was apparent to the first settlers that this could become a wine growing nation. However, with their taste patterns already set in Europe, and with the naivete of the newcomer, they tried to transplant the European varieties to the new land and therefore uprooted the wild native grapes to make room for them.

"Far-sighted men, like Thomas Jefferson, tried to interest the American colonists in cultivating the native grapes, but without success. Some experimentation was done with hybridizing but compared to civilization's 1,900 years spent developing vinifera, it was a drop in the bucket. Our pioneers were too busy eking out a bare survival to take up grape culture. Of the vineyards planted, one disappointment succeeded another as insects, fungus, extremes of temperature destroyed the new vines.

"As the few became well-to-do they imported their wines, at great expense, and handed their taste patterns on to their children. However, rum made from molasses and spirits from grain were more available, so our national drinking habits grew in that direction . . .

"Meanwhile the native vines struggled along. They were just getting a foothold when the wine grapes were torn out and replanted with grape juice varieties, to satisfy the requirements of Prohibition. With Prohibition, not only the vineyards went, but the scientists and chemists who tended the making of the wines. However, it is remarkable how far the industry has come in just the one generation since repeal. It is certain that it will go much further in the next generation. For, in a provincialism in reverse, Americans are finding the fruity, tangy New York State wines to their taste. The surface has only been scratched, the industry is far short of its full strength and growth. The best New York State wines have not yet been made, but we are on our way."

Brotherhood's enormous subterranean wine cellars at Washingtonville, New York, 51 miles from New York City, are open to the public. The conducted tours and wine tastings are in a spirit of traditional hospitality. (Request driving directions and hours open from Brotherhood Winery.)

United States wine deserves better treatment in restaurants. Managers of banquets honoring foreign guests should particularly feature an appropriate United States wine and thus state the fact that Americans, too, can offer good, suitable wines.

In October 1970, Walter S. Taylor, Taylor Wine Company, sent some appropriate verses on the harvest to the newsletter of the Finger Lakes Wine Museum. These epitomize the feeling of dedication toward the vineyards and wine making:

- *When the grapes are ready for picking by human hands one can feel they are trying to communicate with me in the creativity of the moment.*

- *We need to read the signals that all plants send to us and to do so, we must listen more closely.*

- *The creative value of the fruit is directly proportioned to the communication between the vineyardist and his vines.*

- *This meaningful relationship of love must be honest, practical, straightforward and with integrity.*

- *My life, and others who have committed their lives to grapes, has been enriched by this experience.*
- *From the tips of the fingers on my hand, I can visualize my friends, the grapevines growing.*
- *An everlasting friendship and communion.*

An Egyptian wall painting shows the gathering of the grapes and the pressing of the vintage. The Metropolitan Museum of Art

The ancients' exultation in the vine is captured in this German print of a satyr family.
The Metropolitan Museum of Art, Rogers Fund, 1922

La Vierge de la Grappe, by Pierre Mignard (1612–1695). Original in the Louvre.
Courtesy New York Public Library Picture Collection

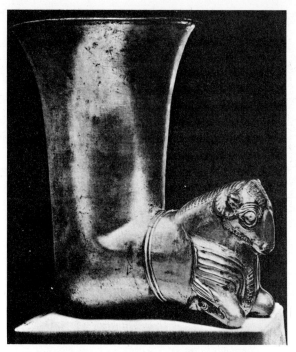

Assyrian cup with horn of silver and bull-shaped handle of beaten gold, found at the site of an ancient Hittite city.

Burgundian rock crystal tankard, late fifteenth century.

Kunsthistorisches Museum, Vienna

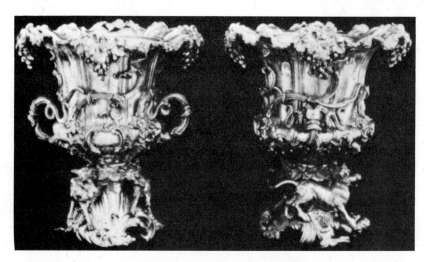

Silver wine coolers by Benjamin Smith, London, 1836. The urn-shaped pair is modeled in high relief with trailing vines, clusters of grapes, and handles formed of interlaced vines. Provided with loose silver liners.

American Art Association, 1939, Anderson Galleries

THE SAVOY LONDON

King Witlaf's drinking horn, from Henry Wadsworth Longfellow's poem about the Saxon king published in Harper's, *1857.*

Latter-day Anglo-Saxon festivities—Ronald Searle's view of the dining room of the Savoy, London.

Courtesy Savoy Hotel, London, England

This palatial building in Fécamp includes the offices, museum, and distillery where Bénédictine D.O.M and B & B Liqueur D.O.M are made.

Pierre Bergoin, Fécamp

Monsieur Jean-Remy Moet, Mayor of Epernay, welcomes Napoleon to the cellars of Moet & Chandon, July 27, 1807
By permission of Moet & Chandon

Origins of the toast: Healths have been drunk from time immemorial, but the custom of giving "toasts" dates from the seventeenth century. Pieces of toasted bread were often placed in wine in the belief that it improved the flavor. The story goes that at Bath in the days of Charles II, a celebrated beauty was immersed in the water, and an admirer dipped his goblet in the bath and drank her health. Another said he "liked not the liquor but would have the toast."

Below—hanging tavern sign in Alsace.
Courtesy F. E. Hugel et Fils, Jean Hugel Propriétaire, Viticulteur, Honorary Mayor of Riquewihr (Haut-Rhin)

An Alsatian vineyard.

Le Chateau de Saran in Epernay, home of Moet & Chandon Champagne.

Above—French monks at work in a vineyard; from a nineteenth-century engraving.
By permission of The New York Public Library

Right—corridor of gigantic vats of Moet & Chandon in Epernay.
From print by Draeger. By permission of Moet & Chandon

Below—a monk in the cellars of the Carthusian Monastery, makers of Chartreuse Liqueur. Since the Monastery is one of the vow of silence, this is presented by special permission.
Courtesy Photopress, Grenoble, France

Above—German wine country: Beilstein, Moselle, Rheinland-Pfals.

Left—a castle on the Rhine in wine country.

Below—sun-drenched vineyards surround the chapel and school of the Christian Brothers of California, Mont La Salle, Napa County, California.

Above—the nearly 100-year-old St. Helena Winery and Champagne cellars of the Christian Brothers of California at Napa, California.

Right—aging cellars of the Christian Brothers Winery, which has the largest total gallons of oak cooperage for the aging of wines in the Napa Valley.

Below—bottles "mise sur pointe" awaiting disgorgement in a cellar at Epernay. Note coating of penicillin fungi on bottles.

By permission of Moet & Chandon

Champagne cellar.

From crystal goblet quaffs the King
Of wine whereof his minstrels sing;
From earthen bowl, if it have wine
His vassal like a king doth dine.

               —A ROUNDELAY

Chapter 10 The Service And Care Of Wine And Spirits

KNOWLEDGE of the mechanics of the proper service of wine is of utmost importance if a restaurateur is to please his guests. The service principles involved are applicable as well to the gracious service of wine in the home. This chapter outlines what is expected in the way of service of the knowledgeable host and what is expected of the guest. We will discuss the importance of correct timing, the sommelier or wine steward, something about stemware, the purchase and care of wine supplies, entertaining people, keeping a cellar, the growing popularity of wine tastings, wine language and wine associations.

Entertaining guests at a restaurant is a delicate matter requiring finesse on the part of the host or hostess. In the past, fine restaurants drew most of their patronage from society, the professions and the arts. In the changing of times, growing affluence has made it possible for many to enjoy distinctive dining in well-conducted restaurants or hotel dining rooms. While the reasonable restaurateur does not expect all of his guests to be gourmets, he does expect that they should have some acquaintance with the proper ordering of food and the selection of wine and spirits. If they do not know exactly what they

The Service

295

want, they should express their wishes to the staff, who will be most happy to assist in selections.

There is a knack in ordering in a restaurant that reveals the experienced host. Fundamentally, the host should always offer the most he can to his guests. He should not repeatedly question his guests about the appetizer they desire. Some actually do not know; others may think of the cost involved and be reticent. When this happens, the host should order what he thinks is best and what his guests might enjoy to begin the dinner. To climax a festive occasion, the host should order an elaborate dessert. This will be the crowning touch of the evening. He may order Crepes Suzette for the pleasure the captain's showmanship affords, or a delicately prepared soufflé. The dramatic finale of a dinner is often Baked Alaska, arriving at the table flambéed.

Guests may be hesitant in the matter of ordering cocktails, and it is up to the host to determine *what* would be pleasing. He does not inquire *if* they wish a cocktail. He asks if they prefer an aperitif or a certain kind of cocktail.

The same holds true for wine. If a host asks pointedly whether his guests wish wine, they may decline because of the cost, and thus the opportunity passes to make the dinner a truly elegant occasion. The proper host suggests a variety of wine and, if he receives no response, proceeds to order what may prove pleasing with the meal. For two, he orders a pint; for three or four, a fifth (or $4/5$ of a quart).

Timing is of utmost importance in the service of wine. A rich accompaniment to a fine dinner can be ruined by improper timing. This can easily be avoided, however, by strict attention to detail. In the first place, wine should be ordered at the proper moment, that is, early in the visit. In patronizing a restaurant, when the party is comfortably seated, the menus should be promptly offered. Then the host may say, "We are not quite ready to order our dinner, but we would like to have a cocktail or an aperitif." From this point on, the Captain is attentive to the table until the guests are ready to order.

If the host orders wine and not cocktails or aperitifs, then the Captain should ask the host, "May I serve the wine for the appetizer or for the entrée?" This is important because sometimes people like to have the wine at the table as soon as they begin to dine. This, in fact, is habitual with European guests. Our policy as restaurateurs has always been to allow the host the privilege of inquiring for the wine list, *never* for the house to make the suggestion.

When the host has ordered the dinner as well as the wine, then the Captain or the Sommelier serves the wine promptly *before* the main course is brought to the table. Even in places of good repute, I have unfortunately observed that quite often the wine arrives simultaneously with the entrée. This creates unnecessary confusion because the guests must divide their attention between the most important dish of the dinner and the wine ritual. They must make toasts, comment on the wine *and* the entrée all at the same time. This, of course, need not be so.

Smoothness and grace may be achieved by serving the wine by itself. Toasts and comments on the wine are made leisurely and the party awaits the entrée, which must be served immediately. I have always made it a rigid rule at the Richelieu to serve wine first before the arrival of the main course. We thus avoid the indignity of having the coveted wine ceremonial ruined by the interference of bustling Captains and waiters serving entrées for several people at the very moment the wine service is in progress.

Restaurant and hotel service of wine is simple and effective, and adherence to the proper etiquette and procedure in the service of table wine adds much to the enjoyment of the meal. This applies not only to haut-cuisine restaurants but also to small rendezvous with a limited wine list. It is immaterial what wine is selected. Each bottle should be treated with deference and appreciated for the pleasure it affords. It is inconceivable that books are actually published on the mistaken premise of an ill-informed, snobbish approach to the world of wine, in effect advising people to drink only the most famous and most expensive wine because the rest are not even worth trying. Nothing could be further from the truth. This shows a complete lack of knowledge and appreciation of the infinite variety of enjoyment to be found in the varied wine available from many countries of the world.

There is actually nothing too complicated or mysterious about ordering or serving wine. It is always a delight to the knowing guest when waiters have been properly trained in the service of wine. When you order a certain wine from the wine list, you may expect to be shown the bottle with the label facing you, much in the manner a waiter or Captain will present a menu or a dish before it is served. If the bottle arrives at the table all wrapped up in a white napkin, as if it were ashamed of its label, ask that the napkin be removed. The waiter brings and presents the bottle, opens it, wipes the neck of the bottle and pours a small amount of wine into the glass of the host. This is done so that he, rather than one of his guests, will get any bits of cork that might be floating on top of the bottle. It also gives the host the opportunity to sample the wine and to approve it. Once the host nods and smiles "pleasant" or "good," the waiter continues on to the right, serving the host last. The waiter fills each glass, but only half or hardly two-thirds full. This is done to leave air space in the glass above the wine so the bouquet may be inhaled. To prevent dripping, the waiter twists the bottle slightly and wipes the lip when he has finished pouring.

It is not necessary to recork the bottle after the first pouring, nor is it necessary to keep white wine chilled in an ice bucket between servings. If thoroughly chilled when brought to the table, white wine will remain at the proper temperature throughout the dinner. I have often read releases from wine companies instructing purchasers to open red wine ahead of time, allowing for "breathing time," saying that wine in contact with the air allows for release of bouquet. There are two schools of thought on this subject of opening wine in advance. My father, William Robotti, and other vintners of Italy whose opinions as long-term viticulturists were highly respected, never agreed with the idea of opening the wine too soon. Some chemists I know feel the same way on this question. On the other hand, there are authorities in the field who maintain that it is proper to do so. This resolves into a moot problem that very likely will never be settled. We are in accord with the classic tradition and believe there is nothing to be gained by opening red wine some time before it is to be served.

An impressive wine service is achieved at our Richelieu tables in offering the entrée wine in stemmed balloon glasses: white wine in 10- to 12-ounce glasses, Bordeaux reds in 12 to 14 ounces and Burgundy in 14 to 16 ounces, the Captain or Sommelier pouring up to one-third of the glass. This presentation highlights the preciousness and beauty of the wine.

There is no greater breach of etiquette than pouring wine first into a lady's glass—unless, of course, she is the hostess without a host being present. It is proper to serve wine beginning with the appetizer. The host, rather than the hostess, serves the wine and sees to it that glasses are replenished during the meal. Once the ground rules are known, the proper etiquette of wine serving and drinking is one of informality and complete ease. Wine lovers are not at all self-conscious about their enthusiastic feelings for wine. Justly proud of offering a good wine, the host is not reticent about making comments or asking for them; guests should also feel free to remark on what they are drinking.

The alert and cultivated person never hesitates to comment on food and wine. In fact, it is a mark of the boor to partake of well-prepared food and elegantly served wine without any comment of appreciation. The possibilities of discussion of food and wine are endless in conversation. In H. Warner Allen's clever book *Through the Wine Glass,* published in London in 1954, he says that wine is, of course, not a subject uninteresting to the wine lover, but can be exceptionally boring to those who are not. While there are at least 20 golf bores, political bores, stock-exchange bores to one wine bore, it is very unlikely that a true wine enthusiast will ever waste himself on deaf ears.

There is no such thing as an uninteresting subject, only uninterested and uninteresting people. But the subject of wine is the whole world's oyster. There is no end of topics that can profitably be examined through the wine glass. The wine lover need never be a bore because he can gently observe the whole passing scene through his own wine glass. It is useful for a guest to become acquainted with the special language of wine, such as that listed under Wine Language.

The English have been, and are, connoisseurs of food and drink. *Toasting* They brought their gastronomic customs with them to America during colonial times. The first New Yorkers drank prodigious amounts of Madeira, Claret and other wine, to say nothing of beer and ale . . . and Rum. At naval and military dinners, the variety of courses was exceeded by the number of toasts drunk. The Revolution might be said to have been launched on the fruit of the grape and hops. No official dinner after Independence was complete without drinking at least thirteen toasts, one for each state, followed by toasts to popular officers and to almost any abstraction, such as love, the beauty of women, the bravery of men. While toasts were the order of the day in England and in America, they were not drunk in France until the French Revolution.

The word "toast" derives from the English. When they drank anyone's health, a piece of toast was placed at the bottom of the common beer pot. Whoever drank last got the nicely soaked toast. There have been legends of baths in Champagne and one, of course, comes out of Merrie Olde England. The story goes that Anne Boleyn, one of the most beautiful women in England, was taking her Champagne bath, a ritual witnessed by the lords of her suite. The gentlemen, very humanly courting her smiles and favor, each took a glass, dipped it in the tub and drank to the beauty's good health. All but one—a dark and handsome lord who stood apart from the others. Asked why he did not follow their example, he is said to have replied, "I am waiting for the toast!"

At an English dinner, toasts were always drunk to the ladies, extolling their charms and beauty. Well-known for his chivalry, Lord B——, a true gallant, proposed: "Gentlemen, I drink to the beautiful sex of both hemispheres."

"And I," responded the Marquis de la V——in a flash of realism, "I drink to both hemispheres of the beautiful sex."

Red wine is to be drunk at "room temperature," an old term that *Serving* does not mean exactly what it says. Centuries ago, when this phrase *Temperature* was coined by the French, dining rooms, *chambres,* were much cooler than those of today. Huge rooms were heated by a great log fire in an open fireplace, but the room was still chilly. "Room temperature" certainly does not apply to what is accepted as comfortable today in centrally heated dwellings. People now are accustomed to

70° F. in their homes, but wine's "room temperature" is fixed at a lower degree.

The right temperature for red wine is about 60° to 65° F. Regional wine may be served even a little cooler. White and Rosé wine must not be too cold, but served only slightly chilled. Rosé should be around 60°; white 50°.

Champagne and white wine generally taste better at about 50° to 55° F.; Rosé, 60° to 65°. The sweeter the wine, the colder they should be served, but overchilling will diminish the flavor. Good French Sauternes, always mellow-sweet, are dessert wines best served well chilled. Very dry Sherries should be 55° to 60°; aperitifs and Ports, about 65°.

Chilling Wine Champagne and white wine are always chilled, gradually and never suddenly. Rotate stocks to serve first those that have been in the chiller the longest. Many establishments, especially hotels, chill white wine ahead of time for long periods in refrigerators, which actually kills the wine. After 24 hours of such exposure, the bouquet suffers, as does the wine itself.

A bottle packed in ice, well-covered to the neck, with a little water, will chill to 50 degrees in 20 minutes. Champagne and sparkling wine should be allowed 25 to 30 minutes to cool in this manner. Allow two hours in a cold refrigerator. Do not place in a deep freeze, for sudden chilling can damage flavor and even break the bottle. Chilling time refers to the wine resting in the refrigerator but not in the freezing compartment.

Dry Sherry, dry Madeira	Somewhat chilled, 1/2 to 1 hour
Medium and sweet Sherries	Room temperature
Madeira and all Ports	Room temperature
White Burgundies—Chablis, Pouilly, Montrachet, Meursault	Chill 1 hour
Dry White Bordeaux—Graves, Château La Louviere, Château Olivier	
Alsatian—Traminer, Sylvaner, Riesling	
Moselles—Bernkasteler, Zeltinger	

Rhines—Johannisberger,
Rüdesheimer,
Liebfraumilch

Italian White Wine—Soave,
Orvieto, white Chianti

California Whites, New York
State Pinot Blanc, dry
Semlion, Riesling

Vin Rosés

Italian Reds—Chianti, Barolo, Freisa, Barbera	Room temperature, or cellar temperature by chilling ½ hour in refrigerator
Beaujolais and Italian Reds of light body— Bardolino, Valpolicella, Chiaretta del Garda	Room temperature, or cellar temperature
Red Bordeaux—Château Latour, Château Mouton Rothschild, Château Ausone, Château Haut-Brion	
Red Burgundies— Chambertin, Nuits-Saint-Georges, Corton, Beaune, Volnay	Traditionally served at room temperature or, in warm weather, chilled 20 to 30 minutes in refrigerator
California, New York State and Ohio Reds—Pinot Noir, Gamay, Cabernet	
Sauternes—Château d'Yquem, Barsac	Chill at least 2 hours
Champagne, Sparkling Burgundy, Sparkling Rosé	Well chilled, 2 or 3 hours

Ice Buckets

It is unfortunate that ice buckets are being used less and less except in restaurants. White wine, Rosés and Champagnes are better served in a bucket, for prechilling in the refrigerator does not serve the same purpose. Chilled White wine, Rosés and Champagnes lose their freshness as they become warm during the service of a meal, and are therefore best in a bucket, but red wine improves as it becomes warmer and thus tastes better.

Ice buckets should be large enough to hold a full-size bottle with plenty of room for cracked ice. Ice-water mixture chills a wine more rapidly than ice alone because of the complete contact with the surface of the bottle. Ice buckets made of plastic or fiber are even more effective than the traditional metal buckets because they lose the cold less rapidly. If you do not have an ice bucket, improvise by using a large pot or washbasin filled with ice and some cold water. Ornament with aluminum foil or heavy waterproof giftwrap paper to add a festive touch.

Decanting Sediment forms in a wine long in bottle. It detracts from the wine's appearance, so it should be avoided.

When wines are old or have a sediment, it is important to handle them with gentleness, so that they are not muddled. Place the bottle, as soon as it is brought from the cellar or closet, in a basket, keeping it in a horizontal position. This makes pouring possible with a minimum of sediment disturbance. After purchasing, stand the bottle upright for a day, then remove the cork gently and pour the wine into a carafe while observing it carefully against a strong light. When you reach the sediment, stop pouring. This process is known as decanting.

Decanting a wine is never mentioned in the writings of Brillat-Savarin. In England, where they cannot grow grapes successfully or produce their own wine, wine has always been something rare and special. More attention is paid to serving it and to its presentation than in France and Italy, where wine is the natural accompaniment of every meal.

A wine cradle or Burgundy-style wicker basket makes a warm and pleasing table accessory to hold the wine served. It is placed at the right of the host, together with a corkscrew. Such a cradle is also useful when wine has a sediment and the host does not care to decant the wine.

Storing Wine The foremost spoilers of finished wine are light, heat and air. Never buy a bottle that has been exposed in the shop window to sun or subjected to unusual heat.

Keep wine bottles on their sides. This will keep the cork moist and prevent the passage of air that can spoil the wine. Table and sparkling wines can be ruined by standing upright for a few weeks, thus permitting the corks to dry and to shrink. The sparkle will escape from Champagne and vinegar bacteria will attack.

Agitation hurts all wine. To get the full value from your purchase of wine, let it rest in your home at least a day, preferably longer, before serving it.

Partially filled bottles of table wine can be preserved a day or two by stoppering and putting the bottles in a cool place.

Corks are the ideal stoppers for wine because of their compressibility, strength, elasticity and resistance to decay by air or liquids. Corks are made from the bark of an evergreen oak (*Quercus Suber*) that grows in Spain and Portugal; the tree is not harmed when its outer layer of bark is peeled off after the first 15 or 20 years of growth. After the first peeling, the tree rests for another 8 or 10 years, and thereafter may be peeled for an ensuing two centuries. *Corks*

The corks are punched out of the flattened bark of the tree. The longest corks, made from the thickest part, are the most expensive. The end that will be in contact with the wine is trimmed free of any crevices containing powdery dust. When wine is stored on its side, the cork is wet and the spongy bark stays expanded, thus preventing the intrusion of air harmful to the wine.

Many inexpensive table wines in France and Italy are bottled with a plastic screw cap. It gives off no flavor and, having no cells, cannot harbor molds. A cap requires no corkscrew, is sanitary and useful for the purpose. But corks are indispensable for wine to be aged and improved in bottle. Corks permit slow evaporation and slight oxidation of the wine, which gives it the distinctive bouquet. For a wine anticipated to have a long life, a longer type cork is used. It will last longer. The great Burgundy wine needs very long corks, longer than the Beaujolais. Rhine Wine has shorter corks than a great red Bordeaux.

Champagne corks are squeezed to one-third of their normal size before being pinged and wired into the bottles. This compression is necessary to prevent the sparkle from escaping. Just before Champagne and most of the high-grade wine are shipped out by the producers, fresh corks are substituted to ensure the longest possible life to their vintages. Corks are often branded with the name of the vineyard, the vintage, the coat of arms or such to assure the buyer of the wine's authenticity.

The life of a cork is about 20 years; then it has to be replaced. The cork should be tightly fixed in the neck of the bottle to be stored correctly on its side so that the wine reaches the cork. If the cork is dry and hard to pull out, it means the bottle has been kept in a cellar or closet whose atmosphere is too dry. It is far better if the cork is moist or even black with mold.

There are four simple steps in opening a bottle of wine. The outer seal over the cork has a lead covering. Peel this away from the lip of the bottle, so that there is no chance of the wine passing over it (lead will not enhance the flavor of wine). The foil or cellulose band should be cut, not torn off. Leaving part of it on the bottle improves the appearance. The cut is made with any kind of knife, about a quarter *Opening the Bottle* of an inch below the lip of the bottle. In this way the wine will not touch the foil. Carefully wipe the mouth of the bottle before inserting the corkscrew and again after removing the cork.

Remove the cork carefully with a good, sharp-pointed corkscrew to prevent crumbling. The favorite corkscrew of waiters is the jacknife type, which uses leverage to draw the cork, because it can be carried in the pocket. This type usually has a bootlever that fits against the mouth of the bottle and aids in drawing out stubborn corks. Avoid any corkscrew with a sharp edge that could gouge out the center of the cork, leaving the rest in the bottle's neck. Use a well-made corkscrew. A cheap or poorly designed one is costly in lost time and annoyance when corks are broken. The best corkscrew has its point exactly in line with the spirals of the worm. It should have an open space down the center of the worm, and the worm edges should not be too sharp. Good bent-wire screws with a perfectly round worm work very well. To ensure effective removal, insert the screw exactly in the middle of the cork, clear through, then give an extra part turn and pull slowly.

To open a bottle of sparkling wine, first loosen the wire hood by untwisting the loop of wire there for that purpose. You can then remove the wire and the top of the foil capsule in a single motion. Hold your thumb on top of the cork to keep it from popping out unexpectedly. The cork is not supposed to go flying through the air; this is no longer considered de rigueur. Put a napkin around the bottle to keep your hands dry. Ease the cork gently before pulling, and point the neck of the bottle at the ceiling. When unduly agitated, a bottle of Champagne may occasionally act like a popgun, so take the necessary precaution. Normally all that is needed to remove the cork is to twist it slightly and let the inside pressure force it out. If it is stubborn, however, upward pressure may be applied simultaneously with the two thumbs to loosen the mushroomlike part of the cork from the neck of the bottle. While the cork is being removed, hold the bottle at a 45-degree angle. It reduces the likelihood of the wine overflowing. The cork is held tightly as it leaves the bottle to prevent it from flying out and striking someone.

Pour in two motions: first, fill the glass with foam; secondly, complete the pouring. A little over half full is about right. Pour a little into the host's glass first to make sure no bits of cork are inside. Then serve any distinguished guests present, ladies, gentlemen, and finally the host. After pouring, turn the bottle gently about a quarter turn to prevent dripping.

A napkin is not desirable in pouring Champagne—except to wipe the bottle when it is removed from the ice bucket—because it hides the label. After each pouring, the bottle is returned to the bucket to keep it cold and thus preserve the effervescence. A loud *bang* in a raucous pop of a Champagne cork indicates that the wine is insufficiently chilled, the bottle has been shaken or the cork has been removed too suddenly. Any of these faults is apt to diminish the full qualities of any sparkling wine.

On our visit to the cellars of Epernay in Champagne, France, the explosion of old Champagne bottles sounded like the bombardment by the Prussians. Glassmaking has now become so scientific that Champagne bottles rarely explode in the sparkle-developing process. (Once these losses by bottle breakage averaged 15 percent of the vintner's cellar.) To offset some of these explosions, the push-up in the bottom of Champagne bottles was devised. This reduces the pressure against the base of the bottle, but is no longer necessary. However, tradition being what it is, Champagne lovers would resent the flattened appearance of the bottom of a bottle.

The best way to open a bottle of beer is to hook the bottle cap off quickly. Open a can in two steps: a pinpoint hole to equalize the pressure, then a second's wait before you make the pouring hole. The right temperature (42° to 45° F.) is about the coldness you get by placing the beer on the bottom shelf of the refrigerator. To get a generous head, tilt the glass to a 45-degree angle and pour the beer gently down its side to about the halfway mark, then straighten the glass and upend the beer can or bottle over it. With warmer beer, do not straighten the glass. Pour in two stages, letting the premature head subside a bit before filling the glass. With colder beer, let the glass stand straight up and pour from higher above it. Consider the glass. Wash beer glasses with detergent or salt. Do not use soap because it makes a slick surface on which the head cannot get a grip. Rinse the glass before pouring because wet glasses hold the head better.

Glasses

The modern drinking glass or tumbler is identical with those of 5,000 years ago except for the materials. The first vessels were ostrich-egg shells, seashells, coconut shells and rock crystal. Later the fastidious Greeks and Romans fashioned elegant cups of gold and silver. The Greeks mixed their very thick and potent wine with water in large bowls called craters, then ladled the wine into two-handled cups called cyclices. Some were 12 inches in diameter and were passed from hand to hand around the table. The Romans also used the craters as ice buckets, packed with snow from the Alps to cool a container of wine. Mosaics of the Roman period show glasses resembling our tumblers.

The ancient Saxons, who were notorious drinkers, used golden drinking horns. The horn could not be put down until it was emptied. To stop such extravagance, Saxon King Edgar invented a new drinking cup and made a law that there be "certain cups with pins or nails set in them." Whoever drank past the mark at one draught should forfeit the equivalent of a penny. The early Christians used ceremonial drinking horns, but they were forbidden in 785 A.D. because the horns led to excessive drinking. They were replaced by wooden cups, but these were soon not used because they were porous and absorbed the wine, and were therefore impractical.

The most famous wine cup in history? The Holy Grail, the talisman of Arthurian legends and the object of the quest of the Knights of the Round Table of King Arthur's Court. The word "grail" derives from the Greek word crater (cup), from the Low Latin *cratalis* or *gradalis* and the old French *graal.* In *Parsifal,* the cup is the philosopher's stone, source of life. The Grail first mentioned in literature had miraculous powers of sustaining life through a self-renewal of physical and spiritual nourishment. Percival seeks Arthur's Court, discovers the Fisher King, presents him with the magic sword, witnesses the Grail being passed from hand to hand at the table.

In the closing years of the 12th century, Robert de Borron gave the history of the Holy Grail in his fascinating book *Joseph d'Armathie.* Joseph, a soldier of Pilate who was granted burial rights, caught the blood of the Saviour in the chalice used by the Master and His Disciples at the Last Supper of the Passover. Early in Joseph's imprisonment by the Jews, Christ appeared to him in a vision, bringing him the Grail that he, Joseph, had hidden in his house. Jesus taught Joseph the ritual of the Mass, which sustained him for the 40 years of his incarceration until he was freed by Vespasian. Upon his death, Joseph entrusted the Grail to Bron, the Fisher King, and his twelve sons, one of whom led his brothers westward perhaps to Britain. The author in this way connected the Holy Grail with King Arthur's Court.

The ritual of the Grail is traced to the fertility rites of ancient religions of the Demeter cult of Eleusis, of Adonis and of the sun myth. Christian religion identifies the Grail with the chalice containing the sacred host. Celtic religion relates it to a vessel of abundance and rejuvenation. The Grail itself is regarded as the ritual cup or vase from which springs the tree of life, containing nourishment for the initiate who becomes one with his God. Semi-pagan, semi-Christian, the Grail (or cup) in juxtaposition with the lance are the symbols of the male and female energies, the source of physical life and phallic emblems.

Glassmaking in antiquity is credited to both the early Assyrians and the Egyptians. In later times, the most famous glassmakers were the Venetians. During the 18th century, the manufacture of glassware throughout Europe reached high levels in quality and quantity. The Bohemians, who keep their method of coloring glass a secret, produced lovely wine glasses up to the end of the 19th century, and they are still popular.

The reason Rhine Wine glasses are colored is because the wines were not clear due to the ferrous deposits in the terrain of the Rhine districts, in Alsace or along the Moselle River. French wine was so golden clear by comparison that the Germans had to do something to compensate for their own wine being cloudy. So colored glasses were brought from Bohemia. Behind the deep ruby of the Bohemian glass, the opacity of the wine did not show. Now, through new and better chemical techniques, Rhine Wine is very clear, but the characteristic long-stemmed glasses have remained colored. Connoisseurs, however, prefer even their Rhine Wine glass to be clear, since the prerequisite of a fine wine glass is clarity. The second requirement is thinness. A good wine glass should be light and almost nonexistent, so to say, in order not to interfere with the pure enjoyment the gourmet derives from viewing the beauty of the wine, the sparkle of light on it and its true color as he sips it slowly and appreciatively.

For centuries, tradition prescribed different glasses for Red Bordeaux, White Bordeaux, Red Burgundy, Champagne, Alsace and Anjou. It is becoming obsolete to use so many different glasses. Experts agree that there is one perfect glass for all wine, which may be used by the homemaker not equipped for extensive wine service. This is a long-stemmed, tulip-shaped glass. The bowl is the size of a medium orange, the glass clear and thin without ornamentation. If the quality of the glass is good, clear, simple, well-suited to its purpose, it is right. The glass usually used for Burgundy or Claret has a generous bowl. The mouth is somewhat smaller so that the wine can be swiveled around without splashing it over the rim. The purpose of the narrowing lip is to concentrate the bouquet of the wine.

Wine service today favors an almost severe purity and crystal clarity. Granted the beauty of cut crystal, modern wine experts still do not advocate using it; nor do they favor the emerald or ruby colors once so desirable in German and Venetian wine glasses. The French firm of Baccarat, however, believes that cut-crystal stemware is coming back and that water goblets, all-purpose wine glasses and Champagne glasses are most in demand by their bride-customers. We recommend the traditional Champagne-type glass that has been standard for many years. Both Baccarat and Tiffany of New York City warn bride-buyers against purchasing very thin-stemmed glasses, pointing out the fragility and replacement costs. The Fostoria Glass Company, Moundsville, West Virginia, which markets hand-blown crystal wine glasses, advises a check on quality: Examine the shape and symmetry, bowls, stems and bases. To be harmonious, any ornamentation should follow the shape of the glass. Look for clarity and luster. Feel the edges for smoothness. Fine crystal has no scratchy or bumpy edges. Tap the glass with your finger and listen to the ring; it should be clear, bright and musical. Also check the signature of the maker (and possible trademark) inscribed on the bottom of the base, which ensures its authenticity and value.

Tiffany's wine glasses are justly famous. Additionally, Tiffany offers crystal barware such as 14-ounce Old-Fashioned and 14-ounce highball glass. The Pottery Barn, New York City, offers imported French crystal wine glasses of the balloon and tulip pattern, and oversized French Burgundy glasses. Most department stores across the country offer all of the popular glasses for the home: Cognac, Pousse-Café, Cocktail, Cordial, 3-ounce Brandy, Sherry, Champagne, Whiskey Sour, Red Wine, Parfait, Pilsner, 3-ounce cocktail and white wine. Commercially, Libbey Products offers a regal array of every needed stemware. Wheaton & Durand has lead-crystal stemware, plain or cut, in six sizes. Minners & Co., New York City, has a superb selection of Burgundy glasses, white wines and great Burgundies, which we have in stock for service at Richelieu.

Size and shape are important to the French master gourmets, who have devised a different size and shape for every type of wine or Brandy. Red wine, which has more aroma and bouquet than white wine, is usually served in a larger glass with more area in which to move the wine and release the bouquet. A good rule to follow is this: a delicate wine in a thin glass; a great wine in a large glass, one-third full.

Beware of serving Sherry in what is called a "Sherry glass," a stingy little inverted cone about half the size of a cocktail glass. This is no glass for that wonderfully adaptable wine. Sherry should be served as they serve it in Spain, in glasses that are both more graceful and more generous, holding at least four ounces. Even if you serve them two-thirds full, you are offering your guest not just a thimbleful drink, and Sherry has always had the reputation of being a generous wine. In Spain, Sherry glasses are of three sorts: the best is called the catavinos, or wine-taster, a slim, stemmed tulip of clear crystal, holding not far from six ounces. Less used by experts but on the whole even more popular in the bars and taverns are two others, the caña, a straight-sided, slender cylinder of glass with a heavy bottom, and the chato (which means stubby), a sort of short test tube mounted on a short stem. When you ask for a caña or a chato in Seville, you will get a glass of Sherry, not an eyecupful.

The Sommelier The Sommelier used to appear in the dining room proudly wearing the key and cup, his insignia of office, indicating that here was the fount of knowledge with regard to the correct selection of wine as an accompaniment to an excellent dinner. While some restaurants still maintain Sommeliers and a percentage of them are well versed in their profession, this picturesque addition to the dining room is often used for conjuring up a respected post for which today's Sommelier is not truly qualified. His previous eminence has been reduced to decoration because he has long since been deprived of his most important function—that of being allowed to buy the wine or even to interview or be interviewed as to his cellar needs by the wine merchants. Under such untenable circumstances, what can he do? If a diner asks questions, he knows only the price of the wine, which he quotes from the restaurant's wine list. The indication is that the higher the price, the better the wine, and that resolves the problem in a very feeble fashion indeed.

My own experience with Sommeliers is that they invariably offer the highest priced wine.* This is decidedly wrong. A lifelong familiarity with wine of many countries yields unexpected rewards. This knowledge is not to be bought. Nor does the Sommelier who does not possess wine knowledge deceive the knowing guest, gourmet or connoisseur. To them, he is just a man in costume who immediately reveals his abysmal lack of knowledge. A person who knows the reputation of a wine, its vintage and its regional source, and has a wine instinct, can go down the list offered by a merchant and select quite a number of winners.

As a matter of actual fact, I have purchased cases of wine for Richelieu's cellar which were overlooked by other restaurateurs simply because they were priced too low, and inexperienced buyers were afraid to risk a purchase. In some instances, I have found such moderately priced wine to be really finer than costly wine, but because of insufficient knowledge, they were not being made available to the dining public. Thus I have often purchased truly good wine at moderate prices, and have unhesitatingly recommended them at a fair price to patrons, with the authoritative assertion that they were indeed "excellent." This gesture of integrity is appreciated, and we may say that my judgment has been confirmed by gourmets who have received this wine with exclamations of delight.

Some distinguished Europeans visiting New York City from various countries, familiar with the cuisine and wine of world capitals, have purchased this more reasonably priced wine in our dining rooms and have been amazed at their quality. Sometimes they return to the Richelieu and inquire for this very wine, and I am sorry that even more of them are not available. My policy is: When I find a wine

*Peter Robotti, the wine expert of the two authors, is speaking here and on the following pages.—Ed. note.

above average in quality, I buy as much of the supply as possible. Diners should be cognizant of the fact that, regardless of reputation, not every wine is equal in quality from one vintage to another. Some are better than others. It is the province of nature herself. There is no monopoly on greatness by one proprietor over another in producing each year the best quality, for vineyards are subject to unstable weather conditions with more or less sunshine, wind or rain. Even a few extra hours of brilliant sunshine, or one day of overcast sky, will be reflected in the grapes, so that qualities differ from year to year.

The wine steward (formerly the Sommelier) purchases both wine and spirits. A first-class place buys the finest type of bonded Bourbon, bonded Rye, imported Gins and Scotch, in addition to those produced in the United States. At Richelieu, we order at least a case of anything the public demands, either native or imported, so as to be able to fulfill any reasonable request, even if it means having on hand a small quantity. The bartender notes requests for any brand the house does not have, and two or three bottles are purchased, even if it is only asked for once or twice a year. Restaurant and bar businesses are highly competitive. If a place does not have what is reasonably called for, the patron will go elsewhere and often take his friends with him. On the other hand, lifelong confidence is gained by a properly stocked bar and wine cellar.

Purchasing The first rule is to deal with a reliable wine and spirits merchant. In
Wine and time you will discover by actual testing what products and brands you
Spirits prefer. In regard to spirits, the brand name is important. The fact that a brand has been successfully marketed for generations or many years proves its merit and quality.

In regard to buying Brandy, never buy the large-size display bottles. Brandy evaporates quickly, and once the big bottle is opened, the quality deteriorates. It is not easy to buy good Brandy, for even the inexpensive blends usually have three stars. These are from 3 to 6 years old. Much better are the bottles marked V.O. and V.E., "very old" and "very extra," from 7 to 12 years old. The best, V.S.O.P., "very superior old pale," are over 10 years old. From there on, the safest way to buy a good Cognac is to buy a bottle that is expensive and shows the name of a world-renowned firm.

Buy wine a few days in advance of serving so it may rest. If it has any deposit, it will be stirred up in getting the bottles home and detract from the handsome appearance.

The main problem in buying wine is the confusion presented in the names on the labels. The great regions, such as Bordeaux, Burgundy or Rhineland, have many districts. After enjoying wine from a certain district, one discovers in trying to locate it again that there are also townships within the districts, and perhaps even owners of a particular vineyard are recorded on the label.

Some wine is named after grapes as well as places—for instance, the great reds: Cabernet Sauvignon, Pinot Noir, Zinfandel, Gamay. These reds vary with the producer and the year. Even Sherry, Vermouth or Port vary in taste from year to year. Wine makers have been trying to make it easier for the buying public for many years. It is quite a problem to solve since Bordeaux are marketed under the name of the châteaux where they are produced from the particular vineyards. However, there are hundreds of châteaux. Their most famous wine is expensive. The greatest wine is exorbitantly priced not only because it is exceptionally good, but also because there are so few and so little of each is produced every year. At the same time, people all over the world automatically buy them for their repute, sometimes for no better reason than because they are so famous. Such vineyards may produce 10,000 cases, sometimes a little more. It is not much when you realize that all medium-size and major cities in the world have stores, hotels, restaurants and individual consumers who demand that specific wine. As a result, demand sets the price.

Wine that takes 10 years to mature varies from vintage to vintage. The answer? Some châteaux have taken to blending some of the red wine, marketing them as nonvintage—for example, Château Margaux. Blended white wine is also offered under a brand name: Pavillon Blanc. This practice is spreading. Now many Champagnes are offered as vintage and nonvintage, i.e., a blend. Mateus Rosé from Portugal is an example, and also their widely known Lancer's Crackling Rosé in the familiar brown crockery bottle. Several kinds of German wine are sold under the label of Blue Nun. There are two California white wines justly famous: Château La Salle of the Christian Brothers, which does not vary in quality because it is blended, and Château Wente of Wente Brothers, also a nonvarying blended white wine.

Paul Masson Vineyards offer some remarkable wine that may be considered under brand names, i.e., they do not vary in taste from year to year. Therefore if you like such wine, you can return to your wine merchant and be assured you can get it and repeat your delight. Paul Masson Rubion, full-bodied, red, even, soft, is a good companion to roasts and stews. Paul Masson Baroque is a blended wine, too, excellent with fowl or fish dishes, light red, with a marked bouquet.

It is a waste of money to buy very inexpensive wine, for you get very little for your money. So many items enter into cost: bottling, shipping, handling, packing, freight, duties, tax, trucking, overhead and profit to the shipper, importer, distributor and retailer. All of this might reach a dollar, so that in a very moderately priced wine, very little is being paid for wine; mostly you are paying for the bottle, corked, labeled and delivered to the liquor store. However, the shipping, delivering and bottling are the same regardless of what the bottle contains. Therefore each increase in price is for increased quality of the wine.

It is distressing to witness an unreasoning discrimination against some wine producers or merchants by wine drinkers. For instance, in presenting a bottle of the wine ordered, to a guest in the dining room, when he catches sight of the producer's label, he immediately protests that the wine is not good without even trying it. This is probably based on a previous experience when a wine was unpleasant, which may have been the circumstances rather than the wine itself. A producer should not be unjustly maligned on such an illogical basis.

We are discussing this delicate point because, from experience over the years, we feel it is a mark of impertinence for a wine drinker to condemn a producer even though the wine is of good quality. Among many qualities of wine in any one year, it is usual to have 10 outstanding, or 5 or 6—or even 2 or 3—that are excellent. This is no reason for the producer's *entire* range of wine to be discriminated against. A wine drinker guilty of such unseemly behavior marks himself as a boor in the eyes of a connoisseur.

If we are to make a large purchase for the Richelieu Wine Cellar, we exercise every care in order to judge a wine fairly. First, I taste the wine. If it impresses me as being very favorable, I still reserve final decision until five or six hours later when I am in a relaxed frame of mind at dinner. Then I can tell if my earlier decision was correct. This is the purchasing procedure I follow. It is a fact that fatigue or nervousness affects the chemistry of the palate's taste buds, so that in such a state it is not possible to make a just decision.

Since much good wine retails for about $2 and $3 a bottle, it is obvious that millions of people are excluded from the pleasure of having such bottles on their table for meals every day. However, those who like wine are turning to the gallon jug. For years, the jug wine had a poor reputation, but this is changing. The general quality of jug wine is improving all the time. Gallons of wine have long been used in entertaining, since one jug could be relied upon for at least 8 to 10 wine-drinking guests (32 four-ounce glasses). A mere two people could easily finish off a bottle. There is a saving in buying the half gallon, but greater economy in getting the full gallon. Bottles of fifths or quart bottles can be saved, and the jug's wine can be decanted into them after chilling and opening. The price now is approximately $5 for a gallon jug, and there are some sound $3 gallons available from California.

Italy exports some quality Verona Wine made by Bertani, Bolla and Folonari in gallons available at $10. France does not bottle in gallons but only in magnums, which are double bottles, generally of their fine wine. Italy, Spain and Portugal send wicker-covered gallon bottles closed with corks. The expensive hand-wicker covering will soon be obsolete. It is impossible to store wicker-covered gallons on their sides, so their corks dry and are difficult to pull out. Occasionally they allow too much air into the bottle and the wine is spoiled.

Sometimes the shape of the jug is a straight-sided junior demijohn with a handle near the top. Chianti uses a huge bottle. Gallons of Chianti from Italy are available here at prices ranging from almost $10 for Soave, Valpolicella, Bardolino and Rosé down to about $5. Remember, the best Chianti comes from the small region between Florence and Siena where strict regulations govern grape variety, aging and other matters. This is labeled Chianti Classico and carries the black rooster seal on the neck of the bottle. Otherwise you are buying wine from Tuscany, which is labeled Chianti. Soderi Chianti Classico Superiore is an estate-bottled wine that sells at $2.49 for a 24-ounce bottle. Ruffino sells a Chianti in 24-ounce bottles at $2.57 and a gallon at $8.82. Even better is Ruffino's Chianti Riserva Ducale at $3.95 for 24-ounce bottles, no gallons.

What are really the best buys? Spain leads the world in offering wine at all price levels, from the Marqués de Murrieta Reserve 1950 at $4.59 to Torres Gran Reserva Coronas 1959 at $2.29 to Yago Burgundy at 95 cents (if you can ever find a wine merchant who will stock this bottle, on which he will only make 25 cents profit). Yago Burgundy also comes in a gallon jug for $4.85. There are some other wicker gallons from Spain that range all the way down to $3.93 for vin ordinaire. Portugal sends in bulk red wine, too.

The largest producer of jug wine is, of course, California. Christian Brothers, Inglenook and Paul Masson produce half-gallon wine at $3.65, $3.75 and $3.60 respectively. Only Christian Brothers offers full gallons, priced at $6.55. These three firms bottle Burgundy, Chablis and a Rosé. Inglenook also bottles Zinfandel. Christian Brothers and Paul Masson bottle Rhine, Sauterne and a variety of aperitif and dessert wine in gallons. Almadén and Louis Martini sell in gallon sizes, as do Italian Swiss Colony and Gallo.

Recommended jug wines: Almadén Mountain Red Claret, Charles Krug Mondavi Mountain Red Burgundy, Charles Krug Zinfandel, Christian Brothers Mountain Red Burgundy, Gallo Burgundy, Italian Swiss Colony Chianti, Louis Martini Mountain Red Wine and Light Burgundy.

Among the whites: Almadén Mountain White Chablis and their White Rhine, Gallo Sauterne, Louis Martini White Chablis.

Entertaining is an old American custom from colonial times. The ordaining of a minister in 1785 meant a jolly good time for all who attended. The records tell that in the morning before going to the

Entertaining and Etiquette

meeting, 80 people consumed 30 bowls of punch. At dinner following the ceremony, 68 persons polished off 44 bowls of punch, 18
bottles of wine, 8 bottles of Brandy and a quantity of Cherry Rum.

What is present-day etiquette? Should a dinner guest arrive with
a bottle of wine for his host and hostess? This is not de rigueur in
this country. Your hosts have either planned to serve wine with dinner, in which case they have already chilled the white or opened the
red, or they have not, in which case they will think you were fearful
about their provision for your hospitality. The hosts should be
spared the trouble of substituting your gift wine for theirs or of
resetting the table with wine glasses. Bring flowers or candy. However, it is perfectly proper to send wine or spirits to anyone who
merits this deference, or to bring Sherry, Vermouth or Cordials as
gifts.

Bar equipment is covered elsewhere in this book. However, you
will always need plenty of ice, at least a dozen cubes to a person.
Provide a large ice bucket. Have extra ice cubes in your freezer or
order a bag of it. Ice should be fresh, crystal-clear and tasteless. You
will also require cracked ice and crushed or shaved ice.

The Party   In preparing to entertain, estimate in advance the quantities of
beverages required. If the party lasts for two hours, each guest will
average two drinks; three drinks if it lasts three or four hours. Allow
an extra half drink per person to make sure there will be no shortage
of liquid refreshments.

NUMBER OF PEOPLE	COCKTAIL OR AFTER-DINNER DRINKS
4	8 to 12
6	12 to 18
8	16 to 24
12	24 to 40
20	40 to 65

DRINKS FROM A BOTTLE, BASED ON FIFTHS OR 25.6-OUNCE SIZE

Whiskey	15 highballs or 13 Manhattans or 16 Sours or 16 Old-Fashioneds
Sweet Vermouth (30-ounce bottle)	26 Manhattans or 20 drinks on the rocks
Dry Vermouth (30-ounce bottle)	60 Martinis or 20 drinks on the rocks
Gin	13 Martinis or 16 Gin and Tonics
Vodka	13 Martinis or 16 Bloody Marys

Cordials or Liqueurs	25 After-dinner drinks
Cognac or Brandy	16 Highballs or 30 Ponies
Champagne (26-ounce bottle)	8 glasses

How much Champagne for the June wedding? Plan on five cases for 100 guests. A case of 12 fifths will fill 100 glasses and allow four to five glasses of Champagne for each guest. Do not be sentimental and save Champagne. Sparkling wine has been sufficiently aged before you buy it, and it will not age any more in the bottle after the last processing. Enjoy your Champagne soon and, if you must, save the bottle.

The average serving of dinner wine or Champagne is 3 to 3 1/2 fluid ounces; of cocktail or dessert wine, 2 to 2 1/2 ounces. The following bottle sizes give these approximate servings: *How Many Servings Per Bottle?*

SIZE	OUNCES	DINNER WINE OR CHAMPAGNE	COCKTAIL OR DESSERT WINE
Fifth (4/5 quart)	25.6	8 servings	8 to 12 servings
Tenth (4/5 pint)	12.8	4 servings	4 to 6 servings
Split	6.4	2 servings	
Bottle	26	10 servings	10 to 14 servings
Pint	16	5 servings	5 to 7 servings
1/2 Gallon	64	20 servings	20 to 30 servings
Gallon	128	40 servings	40 to 60 servings

				Sizes of Champagne Bottles
Split	6 1/2 ounces	Rehoboam	156 ounces	
Half-Bottle	13 ounces	Methuselah	208 ounces	
Bottle	26 ounces	Salmanazar	312 ounces	
Magnum	52 ounces	Balthazar	416 ounces	
Jeroboam	104 ounces	Nebuchad-	520 ounces	
Tappit-hen	128 ounces	nezzar		

Tappit-hen (128 ounces), from the hen who has a topknot on her head, is an English Pewter measure for liquids. The tappit-hen, Salmanazar and Balthazar are not usually available in America; they are used mainly for display purposes abroad. The magnum equals 2 bottles, double magnum equals 4 bottles, Jeroboam equals 6 bottles, Rehoboam equals 8 bottles. The most practical sizes to buy for a party are bottles and magnums.

Portions Per Bottle of Wine and Spirits

KIND	OUNCES	SIZE OF PORTION	NUMBER OF PORTIONS
Bordeaux Wine	25.6 ounces	4 ounces	6
Burgundy Wine	26 ounces	4 ounces	6 ½
Rhine, Moselle, Alsatian Wine	26 ounces	4 ounces	6
Chianti Wine	32 ounces	4 ounces	8
Champagne	26 ounces	4 ounces	6
Madeira, Port, Sherry Wine	24 ounces	2 ounces	12
Vermouth	30 ounces	1 ounce	30 ½
Brandies, Cognacs	25.6 ounces	1 ounce	25
Irish, Scotch Whiskeys	25.6 ounces	1 ½ ounces	17
Bourbon, Rye Whiskeys	32 ounces	1 ½ ounces	21
Gins	32 ounces	1 ½ ounces	21
Rums	25.6 ounces	2 ounces	12 ½
Liqueurs, Cordials	25.6 ounces	¾ ounces	36
Ginger Ale, Soda	32 ounces	4 ounces	8

Keeping a Cellar

Even if you have only a few bottles in a closet, it means you are keeping a cellar or stock. If all you need is a supply on hand for entertaining or cooking needs, a cellar is worthwhile to prevent those last-minute trips to a liquor store. Stock it with a few bottles each of such white wine as Rhine, Riesling, Chablis, Chardonnay, Sauternes, or Semillon; such reds as Burgundy, Cabernet, Gamay Pinot Noir; dry and cream Sherries, Tawny and Ruby Ports and a bottle or two of Champagne and Sparkling Burgundy for special occasions. We keep our stock in the two lower sections of our huge breakfront in the living room.

Properly speaking, storage of wine in an apartment does not constitute a cellar; rather it is a "library," or stock of wine. The interested connoisseur may enjoy reading the labels telling about origins and, after enjoying the wine, may make a record of it for future purchases.

Wine needs a quiet, dark place free from heat or excessive vibration. Racks are required for wine bottles to keep them on their sides and to keep the bottles from rolling around. Only Yago of Spain sends wine in square bottles. If you have no racks, how can you extract a bottle from the bottom without upsetting the whole pile?

If wine will be consumed in five or six weeks, it needs not be stored on its side. Fortified wine such as Sherry, Port, Madeira and Vermouth, with more than 14 percent alcohol, may be stored in an upright position, as well as wine with screw-cap closures and, of course, all liquors. Exceptions are vintage Port and vintage Madeira, which are stored on their sides.

Many distilled spirits such as Whiskeys acquire most of their color, flavor and smoothness through aging, but *in the wood.* They do not improve after bottling. Even Napoleon Brandies bottled a century ago do not improve. A certain amount of aging can make a good Whiskey better, but all it can do for an indifferent Whiskey is to make it older. Gin and Vodka need no aging at all.

Boxes are good for storing spirits. The dark end of a clothes closet will hold some cases of wine or spirits.

Wine, an organic substance with a life of its own, is born, has its youth, maturity and old age. If not drunk in time, it becomes senile and perishes. Not until the early 1860s did chemists actually understand the miracle of the living wine. Finally Louis Pasteur, who held that wine is the most heartfelt and most hygienic of all beverages, by his ingenious researches proved that fermentation is caused by the presence of minute organisms called ferments. The gray down or bloom on the grape is a natural yeast that changes grape juice to wine. Otherwise, through boiling or freezing, it remains grape juice. Fermentation transforms the sugar into alcohol. There is a ceaseless struggle in a wine between the acids and sugar or alcohol. When these elements are well matched, the wine will live and grow mellow with age. Keeping its balance or poise, it acquires with time a more pronounced and more attractive bouquet, which varies according to the differences in the acids present in different wine.

There is danger in aging the wrong wine, unless they are the lordly Haut-Brions, Château Cheval Blanc, Lafite-Rothschild. Spanish wine, Sherry and Port, sometimes reach the century mark and even more, but this is extremely rare. French wine does not last so long, but to be really good it should be at least seven years old; 30 years is the extreme limit for drinkability. Wine aged in bottles rather than in casks runs the risk of deteriorating when the cork fails. German wine, especially from the Moselle region, matures quickly and should be drunk within four or five years.

Some wine will not improve with age. If lesser wine is kept too long, it will spoil. Table wine, which continues to age after it is bottled, can very easily grow too old.

White wine is at maturity when you buy it, so only the supply needed should be kept on hand. Rosé tends to stay about the same from the day it is bottled. Rosé should not be stored, for it loses its freshness; it is meant to be consumed when about six months old. Red wine stores better. In the voyage across the Atlantic, it ages a year and even more if it travels too close to the engine room or is left on a hot pier. Reds should not be kept through more than one summer at home. Beaujolais and Chianti, for example, although deep reds, are about as good at 18 months of age as they ever will be.

The usual error is to age the lesser wine too long and the better wine too little. Only the greatest of whites will improve after more than four or five years, and some will decline: Montrachet, Meursault and Chablis of Burgundy, finest Sauternes of Bordeaux and the classic Tokays, as well as the best of the late-gathered Rhine Wine. The longest lasting reds are the Bordeaux of Saint-Julien and Saint-Estèphe. If you ever come across a 19th-century Bordeaux, it is likely to be Cos d'Estournel or one of the Léoville vineyards. Most top-quality Bordeaux need a decade of waiting, and some can take 20 years and more before reaching their peak. However, a great deal depends on the château and the blend of grapes in the vineyard. Generally, the wine from farther north on the Côte d'Or will age longer than the others. All high-quality California red wine—Cabernet and Pinot Noir—need at least a decade and will benefit from 15 years of aging.

The True Wine Cellar

Shakespeare spoke of wine as a "familiar creature." It is not a uniform product, such as a soft drink, that makers can bottle and forget. In an uncanny way, wine has a life of its own, and unlike hard liquor which, once bottled, is "dead," wine goes on "breathing" and mellowing in the bottle as it did in the cask. Since it is alive, it always responds to outer conditions like a human being, and therefore it requires care.

For those who have aging wine in their cellar, a routine check should be made. The racks and bins must be dark, but a strong light should be available so changes in color may be checked. Seepage from the cork should be noted. Immediately drink any bottles that have been "weeping." The reds need to be decanted from time to time as sediment forms. The wine is poured from the bottle to a decanter, using a glass funnel, and the flow from the bottle should be examined for cloudiness. At the first sight of solid matter, stop pouring and bring the decanter (rather than the bottle) to the table. The bottle may be left on a sideboard so that its label can be noted.

In a charming article for *La Journée Vinicole Export*, Gaston Marchou wrote of his grandfather's era. He regrets the present disappearance of the small middle-class cellars of France. "My grandfather was a good commoner, but his cellar conferred prestige and nobility on him. A huge man, he treated in a gentle manner both precious stones and old wine. With wrinkled brow, a little telescopic eye-glass fixed in the socket, he bent his broad shoulders over the diamonds which he grasped with a doll-size pair of tongs. With the same concentrated and attentive gentleness, with a hand which didn't tremble after more than 90 years, he would decant a wine whose body and soul were as well balanced as his own. As long as he lived, he left that care to no one else. The key to his cellar never left him; it was always attached to his watch chain. This was not in any way due to miserly distrust. He was absolutely devoted to the tranquility of that place of thick vaults, all padded with venerable damp. The rights of the household ceased before the cellar door. . . . "

The ancestral wine cellar of my own Fubine boyhood was dug deep into the side of the hill in the orchard behind the sprawling house. Rows of wines from our vineyards still rest there all properly identified. Separate temperatures are not necessary for reds and for white wines. The reds were brought to table from the "cave" but the white wine bottle was lowered by a rope into the deep well in the courtyard. In this way my father chilled it, since we had no ice in those days. Foods and preserves were kept in an excavated room with its dropped natural-earth floor. The coolness was always delightful in warm weather. Both the wine cellar and this room are still in use on our Fubine homestead.

The qualities of some of the wine served at our table for festive occasions were truly phenomenal, although I had no idea of their great value until many years later when I became the proprietor of a large restaurant cellar, and after many, many years of wine experience. I recall as a youngster the presence of an American Colonel at our dinner table who exclaimed with so much delight over a white wine that he asked my father if he could not buy it in order to repeat the exquisite sensations it brought to his palate. My father replied, through an interpreter, "Sir, I am sorry but this wine you have just enjoyed is not for sale because it has no price." Actually, it was valued at about $100 a bottle because of its rarity and quality.

The temperature of a good wine cellar is nearly the same throughout the year. Double doors help to preserve this. It must be dry and be kept as clean as possible.

Some restaurateurs feel that white wine should have a different temperature in the wine cellar than red wine. This is a false premise because the wine cellars of Europe, which are natural caves dug out of the ground, provide the same degree for all wine. Red wine is served as it comes from the cellar. The whites and Champagnes are chilled before serving, but the cellar temperature is maintained at the same degree for both red and white. Where we do not have natural caves, the room designated for the wine cellar must be maintained by air-conditioning all year round at 60° to 65° F., the usual room temperature of years ago.

The wine cellar should be situated where it will not be agitated by passing traffic. To preserve the fine flavor of wine, on no account permit the presence of food such as bacon, cheese, potatoes or cider, for if there be any disagreeable stench in the wine cellar, the wine will indubitably imbibe it. Consequently, instead of the wine being fragrant and charming to the nose and palate, it will be extremely disagreeable.

The records of old New York tell of our forefathers' wine cellars in Manhattan. The élégantes such as George Washington, Alexander Hamilton and Thomas Jefferson enjoyed fine wine with their dinner. A few years ago, a news item told of the New York City Department of Parks discovering some old caves during excavations near the Manhattan side of the Brooklyn Bridge. These caves were used in Colonial times as a natural cellar for the storage of wine and rum.

Wine Tastings   More consumers are knowledgeable about wine or gaining interest in the subject than ever before in this country. Wine tastings have become a fairly common social event in many communities. In some cases they are sponsored by restaurants, aside from those sponsored by wine producers for the trade only.

A party that offers home tasting of wine should include cheese and bread—only one kind of cheese and bread—and some excellent wine, but not too many. Brother Timothy, Cellarmaster of The Christian Brothers at Mont La Salle, California, offers some expert advice on becoming a "wine taster":

APPEARANCE: Hold the glass by the stem, raise it to the light and observe the color and clarity. Good wine should be clear.

FRAGRANCE: Twirl the glass between the thumb and index finger. Now sniff for aroma and bouquet. The aroma is easy to identify—it is the grape fragrance. Bouquet is the more subtle fragrance that comes from fermenting and aging.

TASTE: Sip the wine slowly. Hold it in your mouth a moment, noting the pleasant tartness or richness, degrees of sweetness, if any; body or consistency; distinctive flavor. With a little practice, you will soon recognize delightful complexities in flavor and fragrance.

Now, swallow the wine and enjoy the aftertaste.

William Bird's classic, practical guide for the wine-butler and connoisseur, prepared for the French Government's *Comité National de Propagande en faveur du Vin of Paris,* gives a remarkable summary of wine tasting, which concludes with the statement:"We cannot expect every wine we drink to be perfect. If the good qualities outnumber the defects, let us be content. But on the day we are privileged to drink a truly aristocratic wine of a great vintage, which has been properly preserved and presented, let us rejoice, because the table affords no higher pleasure.''

There is a language of wine tasting that is used by professionals as well as amateur consumers who enjoy wine, and learning more about wine. The following glossary of terms clarifies meanings in precise relation to wine characteristics and can aid in discussing wine:

Wine Language

ACIDITY   The quality of tartness or sharpness in a wine, not to be confused with sourness, dryness or astringency. The presence of agreeable fruit acids.

APPETIZER WINE   Wine with an 18 to 20 percent alcoholic content, served before meals to stimulate the appetite in place of a cocktail. Aperitif wine (in 2 ½- to 4-ounce portions) include Sherry (dry or semidry), Vermouth, Lillet (on the rocks), Campari, Dubonnet, Byrrh, dry Port, dry Rosé.

AROMA   Fragrance of wine originating from the grapes used in its production.

ASTRINGENCY   The "puckeriness" of wine usually derived from tannin from the skins and seeds. Moderate astringency is considered desirable in most red table wine.

BALANCE   A pleasing proportion of sugar, acid and other constituents of the wine.

BODY   Consistency, thickness, substance, a mouth-filling quality. As opposed to lack of body in a "thin" wine.

BOUQUET   Fragrance that originates from the fermentation and aging of a wine. Every wine has aroma . . . bouquet is rare. Only fine and aged wine has bouquet.

BRUT   Driest type of Champagne.

CLEAR   No suspended solids in the wine, no cloudiness, a brilliant wine.

CUVÉE   An especially prepared blend of wine used in making Champagne.

DESSERT WINE   Usually sweeter than dinner wine or aperitifs, this still wine ranges between 15 and 20 percent alcohol by volume, with a wide range of choice: Cream Sherry, Port (red or white), Madeira, Marsala, Muscatel, Rosé (sweet) or fruit wine. Being sweet and full-bodied, such wine is wonderful with desserts or at the end of a meal with fresh fruit, cheese and nuts.

DRY   When the natural sugar of the grape has been consumed by fermentation, the wine is considered dry, as opposed to sweet.

FRUITY   Having fragrance and flavor of the grape, a freshness.

GENERIC   Types of wine that have similar characteristics are called by traditional, or generic, names such as Burgundy, Claret, Vermouth. When generic names are used, they are generally qualified by the wine's geographical origin.

LEES   Sediment left in vats and casks by the fermentation and storage of wine.

MATURE   Wine that has developed all of its characteristic qualities.

MELLOW   A "soft" wine, often with some sweetness. This term is usually used in reference to some red table wine.

MUST   Crushed grape pulp and juice before and during fermentation.

NATURAL WINE   No synthetic flavors are added.

NOSE   Term for the total fragrance, aroma and bouquet of a wine.

NUTTY   The characteristic pungent flavor of Sherry, applied only to this wine.

RED WINE   Any wine that has red coloring, obtained from the pigment found in the skins of certain grape varieties.

RIPE   Wine at maturity, at its best.

ROUGH   A "hard" wine, immature, not well balanced or perhaps too astringent.

SMOOTH   Having no harsh taste.

SOLERA   A continuous blending process, combining the finest of several years' Sherry or Port.

SOUND   Wine that is pleasant to look at, good smelling and tasting.

SPARKLING WINE   Wine made effervescent by a second fermentation within a closed bottle or container. Upon opening, the natural carbon dioxide gas causes the cork to pop and the wine to effervesce. Nearly half of the American output of sparkling wine or Champagne is produced in New York State. In their creation, some of the wine is married to California wine, which is brought east by tank cars. Sparkling wine includes Champagne (straw-colored or pink), Sparkling Burgundy (red) and Asti Spumante.

STILL WINE   Wine that goes through only one fermenting process.

TABLE WINE   Served in 4- to 6-ounce portions, usually dry or less sweet than dessert wine, 14 percent alcoholic content; most often served with meals. Half-bottle (12.8 ounces) for two persons; full bottle (25.6 ounces) for four. Typical table wine: Claret, Burgundy, Chablis, Sauternes, Rhone and Rhine Wine, Riesling, Chardonnay, Sauvignon, Graves, Rosé, Moselle, Bordeaux, Beaujolais.

TART   Having an agreeable fruit acidity.

VARIETAL   Wine named for the principal grape variety used in producing it. By regulation, a varietal-named wine must consist of 51 percent of the grape variety whose name it bears.

VERMOUTH   Wine flavored with herbs and other aromatic essences.

VINTAGE   Each year's harvest of grapes and the wine made therefrom.

VITICULTURE   Cultivation of the vine, or grape growing.

WINE   The naturally fermented juice of freshly gathered ripe grapes.

Wine Associations

Wine fraternities in France are the living links with the medieval and ancient past. In Bordeaux especially, many wine fraternities perpetuate the traditions of viticulture. A very famous wine fraternity is the Commanderie du Bontemps with its two branches, one in Médoc and Graves, the other in the sweet white-wine district of Sauternes and Barsac. It takes its name from the "Bontemps," the wooden bowl used to beat egg whites for clarifying wine. The headdress of the fraternity symbolizes this "Bontemps" and, in fact, the egg froth itself is symbolized by the heaped white chiffon covering the crown of the hats. The robes commemorate in dress the colors of the wine. Meetings are regular, and the ceremonies spectacular. Distinguished foreign wine lovers are accepted into the sacred order.

The Jurade of Saint-Emilion dates back to the time of Richard the Lionhearted, having received its charter from John Lackland, king of England in 1199. Four kings of France confirmed and perpetuated the order. The revived Jurade of today wear the identical robes worn at the inception of the order. In the Middle Ages, the official designated to control and supervise the wine traveling on the Garonne River was the Connétable. When the wine ships came down the Garonne to Bordeaux on their way to sea, the Connétable tasted the wine, saw that all was in order and then bestowed a cypress branch. This was a mark of approval and the official permission to carry the wine to the world. Today the white-wine fraternity of the Banks of the Garonne River is the Connétablie de Guyenne. After careful tastings, the society awards worthy wine an emblem that may be included on the bottle's label: two gauntleted hands holding out a branch of cypress. The seat of the Connétablie is on the right bank of the Garonne. It is the Château of the Dukes of Epernon at Cadillac, an enormous edifice, the most imposing perhaps of all the great châteaux of France. The Academie du Vin de Bordeaux, patterned after the Academie Française, is concerned with the cultural aspects of wine making and drinking as part of civilization. All of these wine fraternities have united into the Grand Conseil de Bordeaux, with foreign branches called the Commanderie de Bordeaux; one is in the United States.

New York City has the Sommelier Society of America, which holds regular meetings, conducts classes with lectures on wine and spirits and holds frequent tastings in which industry members participate at well-known hotels for the trade; European trips are also arranged in behalf of wine.

*My manner of living is plain: a
glass of wine and a bit of mutton
are always ready and such as are content to partake of that are always
welcome.*

GEORGE WASHINGTON (1732–1799)

Chapter 11 # The Marriage Of Food And Wine

WINE and Spirits add delightful facets to dining pleasure. In European and South American countries, wine appears on the table at
every meal even though in many cases they are vin ordinaire. This
happy European custom of serving wine at meals is rapidly becoming
an American one. Every day more Americans are discovering the
enjoyment wine brings to a luncheon or dinner party, the enhance-
ment of good food it provides, the emphasis it puts on gracious
living. Scarcely an article on recipes and menu planning in our foremost magazines fails to mention wine and spirits. The more one
knows about food and wine in their harmonious relationship to each
other, the more one may enjoy this most delectable and participatory
of arts.

Wine was the natural accompaniment of food in the lives of the
ancients. There is a running record of it preserved in the Bible, which
mentions wine no less than 165 times. It was always included in hopes
for the good life. The Prophet Amos promised that "they shall plant
vineyards and drink the wine." Jeremiah foresaw the time when "ev-

325

ery bottle shall be filled with wine." Jeremiah's idea of the perfect human state was a plentitude of provisions: wheat, wine and oil.

Most wine is consumed with food. In some countries, wine is inseparable from food, the wine bottle appearing as regularly on the table as bread. This is a healthful custom since wine promotes the appetite, well-being and digestion. The natural grape sugars in wine are readily absorbed by the body and provide a quick source of energy. Wine contains blood-building iron, Vitamins A, B and C and all of the 13 basic minerals, plus proteins and fruit acids. Wine contains the four basic elements to which our palates are sensitive: sweetness, acidity, saltiness, bitterness, balancing the same elements in solid foods. In addition, wine supplies aroma and smoothness to food that would otherwise lack these important qualities.

Alcoholic content runs about 12 percent by volume, or more. This perks up the appetite and aids digestion. For about an hour after a dinner with wine, one feels a lift of the spirits, followed by a feeling of relaxation that acts as an aid to a good night's sleep. It relieves momentary irritations, tensions and fatigue, making a person's attitude more pleasant and mild. Actually, wine is a food in its own way, one of the three basic foods made by the fermentation process; the others are bread and cheese, the world's oldest nutrients.

In March 1967, Hallmark Gallery, New York City, had one of the finest collections of wine and food lore ever displayed in the United States in its Bread and Wine Exhibit in honor of "a loaf of bread, a jug of wine and thou." "It was an awesome grouping," wrote Craig Claiborne, the erudite Food Editor of *The New York Times,* "that emphasizes the almost spiritual exaltation and adoration accorded bread and wine since the innovation of vats and ovens."

Many books have been devoted to the subject of what wine should be served with various food. The preferred combinations of wine and food are not really dictated by iron-clad rules, but are simply the combinations that have seemed best to most people over the span of years. One may safely forget the old taboos of the strict wine cult that have made so many people timid about ordering and enjoying wine at the table. The main rule is: Just drink the wine you enjoy with the food you enjoy and you can't go far wrong.

In wine-drinking countries, people instinctively use their favored red or white table wine with all food. Nevertheless, there are certain guideposts. Based on long experience, it has been found that certain wine and food naturally go together as generally recognized partnerships.

There is general agreement that a hearty dish calls for a hearty wine. Robust-flavored wine, usually dry red ones, are best with food of pronounced flavors, such as roasts and stews. Steaks, chops, game, highly seasoned dishes and pastas are also at their best with red table wine. Delicate dishes are best enjoyed with delicately-flavored wine. Seafoods, fowl and white meat harmonize well with white table wine —from dry to semisweet and sweet. Fowl with dark meat go well with either white or red table wine.

Champagne and Sparkling Burgundy are excellent with roasts, game and for all festive occasions such as baptisms, birthdays, weddings, anniversaries, graduations and, of course, Christmas and New Year's. Desserts are harmonious with sweet dessert wine, sweet table wine, sweet sparkling wine. Port and Burgundy are both wonderful with cheeses.

In France, Port, Malaga and Madeira are frequently served with soup, but they can be very pleasing as an accompaniment to cakes and sandwiches at teatime. Light still wine is intended to be enjoyed with meals. Port is especially good with nuts.

At a formal dinner party at which several kinds of wine will be served, it is usual to serve white wine first. Then a red wine with meat and Champagne with salad and dessert. White table wine and Champagne should be well chilled with ice packed around the bottle in a bucket (see Service and Care of Wine). It is heinous to put ice in the wine itself unless it is being mixed in a punch bowl. Water is never added to fine wines.

Beyond the fundamental principles, the best guide is individual preference. Many people have marked preferences and favorites in their selection of wine and spirits. To go back a bit in time, for instance, the poet John Keats was mad for Claret, as evidenced by his letter of February 18, 1819: "Now, I like Claret. Whenever I can have Claret, I must drink it. 'Tis the only palate affair that I am at all sensual in. For really 'tis fine. It fills one's mouth with a gushing freshness then goes down cool and feverless. Then you do not feel it quarreling with your liver. No 'tis rather a peacemaker, and lies as quietly as it did in the grape. Then it is as fragrant as the Queen Bee, and the more ethereal part of it mounts into the brain, not assaulting the cerebral compartments, like a bully in a bad house looking for his trull and hurrying from door to door, bouncing against the wainscot, but rather walks like Aladdin about his enchanted palace, so gently that you do not feel his step."

There are certain people who cannot drink Burgundy; others cannot drink Champagne or Port. When dining at a restaurant, it is always best for the host to inquire of his guests what they would like. If they say they "do not mind," they will be happy with Champagne. If they wish any other kind of wine, they will be specific. The psychology of this attitude is quite evident. Champagne is always expensive, so there is a natural reticence about a guest asking for it outright. Actually, other wine may be more expensive, but since it *may* be less costly as well, there is no hesitation in a guest saying he would like it. The host should suggest Champagne if he wishes to treat his guests with it.

As in other areas of human experience, there is the question of bidding for status. There are thousands of wine drinkers who mistakenly consider it a mark of discriminating taste to insist that their beverage be "dry." They imagine that dryness somehow signifies fine quality. Vintners, however, know that most people like drinks that taste sweet, so they simply make their wine sweet but label it "dry." In order to sell a rather sweet Champagne to Americans, it is labeled, of all things, demi-sec or "semidry." Since many Americans have an inclination toward sweets, vintners continue to cater to their "sweet tooth."

The French, who call the knowledge of how to drink *savoir boire,* lay down three basic rules:

> *1. Serve each wine with an appropriate dish.*

> *2. Never offer a robust and too generous wine before one that is delicate and has a bouquet, because the stronger will overwhelm the latter even if the latter is superior.*

> *3. Prepare a progression of upward quality in the succession of the served wine.*

Contrary to legend, Champagne does not solve all problems. To dine with one wine for all courses lacks elegance. To be completely proper, even with a grand wine such as Champagne, a graduation must be observed, passing according to the dishes from blanc de blanc (white of white) to blanc de rouge (white of red), from the brut to the demi-sweet. No wine is required to drink with a clear soup, but if desired, an excellent dry wine may be served. For bisques, robust soups or cream soups with a poultry or mushroom base, a fine white Graves may be preferred.

As in every art, there are degrees of refinement. It takes a knowing host and discriminating palate to choose within the narrow range of the costly, exquisite wine for the rare dinner in the true gourmet tradition. It involves a depth of knowledge and skill possessed only by the lifelong wine devotee. The carefully chosen dish of a choice dinner requires a well-selected wine just as harmonious jewels in an artist's setting. "Elegance is something more than ease, more than a freedom from awkwardness and restraint. It implies a precision, a polish and a sparkling which is spirited yet delicate," said William Hazlitt (1778–1830).

Of utmost importance in the success of any dinner is the observation of certain basic rules. Although faintly quaint when presented in our own sophisticated milieu, the principles set forth by gastronomic expert Brillat Savarin are still the eternal verities of the table.

Protocol of dining with wine from Brillat Savarin's book *Physiology of Taste,* 1825:

> *1. Number of guests should not exceed 12 so that conversation may be general.*
>
> *2. The guests should be of various analogous tastes with such points of contact that introductions are unnecessary.*
>
> *3. The dining room should be brilliantly lighted, the cloth white as snow and the temperature of the room 60° to 68° F.*
>
> *4. The men should be witty and not pedantic and the women amiable without being too coquettish.*
>
> *5. The dishes should be exquisitely choice but small in number and the wine of the first quality, each in its degree.*
>
> *6. The dishes to be served from the more substantial to the lighter and from the simpler wine to those of finer bouquet.*
>
> *7. Dining should be leisurely, the dinner being the last business of the day.*
>
> *8. The coffee should be good and hot and the liqueurs specially chosen.*
>
> *9. The signal for departure should not be before eleven.*

Wine, the living blood of the grape, is at its best when in the company of food and in the society of men and women who appreciate and love it, priming their wit, faithful in the rituals of worship and serving as a medicine for both body and spirit. When the Cardinal, Duke of Richelieu, suffered from a stomach weakness, his Bordeaux doctors prescribed Médoc. His health quickly returned for the time being (his stomach was always troublesome). He recommended Médoc to Louis XIII, who likewise found relief. In this way, the good news spread through court circles and beyond, and many sang the praises of the "Richelieu infusion."

There are four primary conditions for the enjoyment of the good table: cheerfulness, at least passably good wine, plenty of time and pleasant guests. In his *Satires* (Book II, Satire 2) the Roman poet Horace (6–8 B.C.), whose poetry is permeated with the bouquet of wine, has left us a legacy of a most comfortable if frugal supper, not destined for a potentate nor for the capture of influence, but for his friendly neighbor on a rainy day, or for the traveler who in bad weather has been obliged to seek shelter under his roof: chicken, lamb, a dessert of raisins, figs and walnuts. With these dishes, some wine of the Manlius vintage, *nate mecum Consule Manlio,* born with me during the consulship of Manlius.

We tend to look back wistfully to those rare occasions when we have dined in an atmosphere of family harmony and of friendship, spending an unhurried evening in happy talk and companionship with lovingly prepared dishes before us and with the host's eyes open to the penchants of his guests and to good wine. "What stores of sentiment in that butt of raciest Sherry! What a fund of pensive thought! What suggestions for delicious remembrance! What aids to reflection in that hock of a century old! What sparkling fancies, whirling and foaming from a stout body of thought in that full and ripe Champagne! What mild and serene philosophy in that Burgundy, ready to shed its sunset glow on society and nature" (Sir Thomas N. Talfourd, 1795–1854).

On the contrary, however choice may be the dishes and however sumptuous the accompaniments, there can be no pleasure at the table if the wine is negligible, the guests convened without discrimination, the seating unwise, the faces closed and the dinner hastily consumed. Such meals are a complete waste and an affront to the ethics of gastronomy, yet how many have we endured?

If the ancients had not proudly preserved their tributes to gastronomy as well as actual bills of fare such as in the Egyptian tombs, we would have lost an interesting insight into their personal lives and their enjoyment of the pleasures of the table. We moderns can benefit by this idea and keep what is known among epicures as a Cellar Book. This is a record in a notebook, a diary of dinners served, who the guests were, the dishes and accompanying wine; on the opposite page, paste the labels from the bottles. It is interesting and keeps the record straight.

Classification of Wine for Meals
Appetizer Wine

Ranging from fully dry to semisweet, Sherry and Vermouth, the main types, tend to sharpen the appetite before meals. Most Sherries have an alcoholic content of 15 to 20 percent by volume and vary in grape sugar content from none to 7 percent. There are two principal kinds of Vermouth: dry and pale amber (French type) and sweet and dark amber (Italian type). Each Vermouth has its own individual formula. Some contain as many as 50 different herbs, bark, leaves, flowers and seeds. Other appetizer wine is usually labeled aperitif or appetizer with the name of the producer.

White Table Wine

Traditionally served chilled, this wine—Sauternes and Rhine—vary from extremely dry and tart to sweet and mellow. During aging they clarify more equally and can be bottled earlier than reds. Sauternes are golden, full-bodied, usually semisweet, but not always. In the

United States, some "dry Sauternes" are produced containing from none to 1.5 percent net grape sugar, and there are also Sauternes with 1.5 to 4 percent grape sugar. Sweet Sauternes contain from 2.5 to 6 percent sugar. Rhine Wine, often called Hock, especially in England, is a thoroughly dry, tart, light-bodied white table wine, straw-colored or slightly greenish.

Red wine is usually dry, sometimes tart and even astringent in flavor. Alcoholic content runs from 10 to 14 percent by volume. In most countries, red table wine—in many guises and under many names— is basically Claret and Burgundy types identified by their greater body, stronger flavor, bouquet and deep color. Rosé wine of a pink-ish hue is achieved by leaving grapeskins with the must for only a fraction of the fermentation period.

Red and Rosé Table Wine

Such wine which receives its second fermentation in the bottle, in-cludes Champagne, either straw-colored or pink, and red Sparkling Burgundy.

Champagne and Sparkling Wine

In many countries, all kinds of still wine of more than 14 percent alcohol are grouped together for taxation purposes. Table wine or wine not over 14 percent receive lower tax rates. For legal purposes, appetizer wine such as Sherries and Vermouth come under Dessert Wine headings, as well as Ports and both red and white Muscatels, which generally contain about 20 percent alcohol, grape sugar being retained by adding grape Brandy to arrest fermentation of the must.

Dessert Wine

Gaston Marchou writes in French for *La Journée Vinicole Export* about the knowledge he imbibed about foods and wines from his venerable grandfather. "Concerning the harmony of wines and meats, my ancestor flattered himself on having a certain personal note. He well knew, for example, that the Sauternes are everywhere lords and in their place. He used to compare them to those greats of Spain who used the right to enter a church on horseback. With the entrées, he offered a fine white Graves and married the fillet of beef with a Médoc. For lampreys (a sort of eel), he would choose a Saint-Emilion and would reserve his Pomerol for the feathered game of strong aroma. For the Foie Gras of Landes or Perigord, there would always appear his most sumptuous Sauternes."

The noble Sauternes-Barsac of Bordeaux are at their finest with fish, crayfish, oysters, and even white meat, cheeses, fruit and des-serts (excluding those prepared with chocolate or excessively strong essences). This does not prevent them from being tasted or drunk as aperitifs. But reducing the use of Sauternes to a mere aperitif or to a wine intended for dessert time only would, indeed, be a heresy.

It is always a mark of good taste to serve a luscious white wine of unquestionable quality. All kinds of white wine may accompany shellfish dishes. All Bordeaux dry or demi-sec white wine goes well with fish dishes. Port, which is a fortified wine, is not recommended *before* the entrée. The experienced Englishman enjoys a really good Port *after* the meal, preferably while he smokes. The French do not permit either tobacco or Port at table.

Which wine must be presented at the side of white meats, chicken, rabbits? The finest red Bordeaux, Médoc, several Graves. Serve Pomerols, Saint-Emilion with red meat, duck, pigeon, guineahen. Pomerol should be remembered when serving game and venison. Serve white wine with fresh white mushroom dishes. As for cheeses —in France there are 400 varieties—they take a grand red wine. Port Salut marries well with white dry or demi-sec wine.

Although taste in wine is an individual matter, wine experts, wine lovers and generations of gourmets have agreed upon the union of certain foods with a variety of wine that seems pleasant to everyone. When in doubt, serve the wine listed on the right with the foods given on the left:

FOOD	WINE
Hors d'oeuvres, oysters, fish and white meat	White wine, light and dry
White meat and poultry	Dry white wine, light red wine
Red meat, game, cheese	Red wine
Pungent cheese, all cheeses	All wine, except sweet ones
With all foods and at all times	Champagne and Rosé
Desserts and sweet dishes	Madeira or full-bodied Sherry Sweet white wine Sweet or dry Champagne Sparkling Burgundy Rosé Natural sweet wine
Fruit	Dry Champagne, Sauterne, the fine sweet and mellow wine
Coffee, espresso	Cognac, Liqueur

FOOD	TEMPERATURE	WINE	
Beef and veal	Room Temperature	Bordeaux Rouge	*Suggested*
Lamb and pork	60° to 65° F.	Saint-Emilion	*by the*
Game and poultry	60° to 65° F.	Pomerol Médoc	*Bordeaux*
Cheese	60° to 65° F.	Red Graves	*Wine*
Veal, lamb, pork, poultry, fish, shellfish cheese	Chilled	Dry Bordeaux Blanc Dry white Graves Bordeaux Rouge	*Information Bureau*
Desserts	Chilled	Sweet Sauterne and Barsac	
All kinds of food	Chilled	Bordeaux Rosé	

FOOD	WINE	
Oysters	Sauterne, slightly cold	*More*
Soup	Sherry, slightly cold	*Suggestions*
Fish	Rhine, slightly cold	
Entrée	Claret, slightly cold	
Poultry and meats	Champagne, very cold	
Salad	Champagne, very cold Burgundy, less than room temperature	
Game	Burgundy, room temperature	
Desserts	Port, wine-cellar temperature Madeira, room temperature Champagne, chilled	
Coffee	Cordial, Brandy, room temperature	

When wine is used in the preparation of a sauce, it is politic to serve the same wine with the dish. For dishes with cream or other sauces (with the exception of those being made of vinegar), serve a white mellow wine.

On the matter of wine with salad, nobody familiar with gastronomy would serve Château Latour with assorted greens, or Romanée-Conti with watercress. However, there are substantial salads such as Chef's Salad, Chicken Salad, Lobster Salad; with these, a chilled Sylvaner, which may very well be an Almadén Sylvaner or a Grenache Rosé, is perfectly in order. Naturally, if a dinner is being served and a tossed green salad appears with French dressing between the meat course and the cheese, the proper thing to do is to drink the wine in your glass. The thing to remember is with great wine—no salad. This leaves a lot of latitude since available great wine is rare.

Wine should always be welcomed on the table. The Germans look forward in the summer to their *Spargel,* early tender asparagus. They dress it with Hollandaise or Mayonnaise and consume it with Rhine Wine. The Romans serve raw vegetables dressed with olive oil and vinegar, then their *abbacchio,* youngest of spring lamb—all with their young, fresh, local wine. The best solution is to use wine vinegar for the dressing of the salad if one has qualms, but wine should be enjoyed as much as possible in salad time.

The most renowned wine of some countries does not necessarily go with the cuisine of those countries. The Portuguese certainly do not consume Port with their meals. Spain, which exports its Sherry, produces 45 gallons of table wine to every gallon of Sherry. However, French wine goes with French food, and Italian wine is a good companion to Italian cuisine. Our experience in traveling in Germany proved that while it is possible to eat well in Germany, once one becomes reconciled to the large portions of potatoes, sauerkraut, pork and pickled dishes, very few kinds of wine go well with such food. Native dishes are happier with beer or some of the common wines of Württemberg and Baden.

In Alsace, Knipperlé or a Zwicker went well with hors d'oeuvres. Edelzwicker or Sylvaner went well with entrées, especially fish. The principal course, roasts and game called for Riesling, Traminer or a Gewürztraminer, Grande Reserve or special cuvée. There the famous sauerkraut was greatly improved when accompanied by a good Riesling, Sylvaner or Traminer. Sylvaner, Muscat and Riesling are excellent aperitifs, and for the afternoon, a good Traminer or a rich Gewürztraminer accompanies the luscious Alsatian pastries.

Usually, German wine is served by itself with no food at all. They are best enjoyed between meals, as a treat in the evening after dinner or in the afternoon in pleasant weather on the terraces. Exceptions are made when special dishes are presented at table such as trout from the Black Forest, the Eifel crayfish or salmon from the Rhine. The sequence is that a sweet wine should not be served before a red wine.

When German wine comes from the cellar at 60° F., it is just right. In America, it may seem better served a bit colder. Since our ice buckets are short, a German wine is chilled with its long neck down; the Moselles and Rhines are served in clear, thin-stemmed glasses.

In the course of time, the cuisine of a nation tends to conform to the national beverages. For instance, the gemütlichkeit of the Germans may be traced to the national beverages and the alimentation with which they harmonize. The dispensation of beer in the Wirthshaus, Gasthof, restaurants and beergardens are done on a colossal scale to sell as much of the output as possible of the vast breweries of Munich. The preeminence of the sausage in its many forms was fashioned with a special view to its harmonious combination with beer: Gerstensaft of Nürnberg, Amber Pilsener of Austria, Weiss beer of Berlin, malt extracts of Württemberg, Bockwurst, veal and pork used with Bock beer, for which it was especially designed. The regal beer of Munich reaches its apotheosis in the Café and Garten of the Hotel Royal of industrial Stuttgart, with its splendid wine cellar. One summer evening when we stopped there for dinner, we found the food and service of this wholesome place a gastronomic delight. The cuisine offered was French, but the featured wine was the best Germany and Austria had to offer.

In any discussion of combining foods with wine and spirits, it is only fair to denote the caloric content of the alcoholic beverages. Like sugar, butter, potatoes and bread, alcohol is fattening only if it gives you calories your body does not need. An ounce of whiskey lends 75 calories of energy, about as much as 4 1/2 teaspoons of sugar, 1 1/2 pats of butter or a slice of dry toast. If a person takes in more than his requirements, i.e., more than the body can burn up for immediate use, the excess calories will be stored as fat. It is true that liquor calories cannot be stored, but they still have to be counted even though the liquor energy is used first. For every ounce of alcohol consumed from whatever source, count 150 calories into your diet.

A quart of wine containing 10 percent alcohol accounts for 850 calories. Caloric values per ounce of some kinds of California wine are:

KIND OF WINE	CALORIES PER OUNCE
Red table wine	23
White table wine	28
Champagne	28
Sherry	42
Port	49
Muscatel	49
California Tokay	36

Obviously, dry wine has fewer calories than sweet wine or Liqueurs. But there are few desserts that have so few calories as wine.

Preparation of cutlets with white wine, from the Mastery of Cooking,

Jean Knobloch, Strasbourg, 1516.

There is no spectacle on earth more appealing than that of a beautiful woman in the act of cooking dinner for someone she loves.

THOMAS WOLFE (1900–1938)

Chapter 12 Cooking With Wine And Spirits

CIVILIZED countries have for a long time used wine and spirits as ingredients in the preparation of dishes. The Roman epicure Apicius, in the time of the Emperors Augustus and Tiberius, recorded rather complicated recipes in his novel book *De Re Culinaria*. Only two volumes have survived to our own times. One of these rare cookbooks was on display in New York City in 1961 at the Grolier Club's Gastronomic Exhibition.

One of the cabbage recipes in the cookbook directs: "Boil and drain cabbage. Season with cummin seed, salt, old wine (made from raisins), olive oil, pepper, mint and coriander seed."

Another suggests boiling ham with figs and honey, then adding wine and serving the dish with a sweet wine cake made with cheese, flour, bay leaf and sweet wine.

In his *Banquet of the Learned,* Athenaeus has the scholarly host Laurentius give his own personal recipe for *Dish of Roses* to be prepared with wine at table. "Pound a quantity of the most fragrant roses in a mortar, the brains of pigs and birds, boiled, also yolks of eggs, olive oil, pickle juice, pepper and wine. Pound together and put into a new dish and simmer over gentle fire." As the host uncovered the finished dish, writes Athenaeus, it diffused such a sweet perfume it swept over the whole dining party.

In France and Italy, wine is as essential in the kitchen as salt and pepper. The use of wine in cooking was customary for many centuries in Europe before the early settlers brought its traditions to the American colonies. Wine cookery declined during the 19th century. There were several reasons. Most wine imported into the United States was expensive, and the American wine that was produced was not widely publicized. At this time, too, flavoring agents and extracts were introduced and widely promoted. Finally, with the beginning of Prohibition, the use of wine and spirits in cooking was negated. Happily, this European custom has been greatly revived, along with increased usage of herbs and spices. Many of our popular dishes made with wine, originally brought to this country by Swiss, French, Italian and German cooks, were introduced on the menus of the better restaurants and hotels.

Cooking with wine steps up the flavor of familiar, favorite dishes, bringing out the natural goodness of food and adding a subtle, rich savoriness.

It is true that alcohol evaporates during cooking, but the flavor remains to season the food. The aroma of the wine or spirit delightfully accentuates the food's own flavor and adds a flavor of its own to improve the texture of the dish. Granted that herbs, spices and flavor extracts enhance sauces; wine and spirits do even more for these sauces. They act as a tenderizer on meats and improve sauces for meat and fish.

Sherry is excellent in soups, shellfish dishes, sauces for meats and poultry. Burgundy and Claret are good in pasta sauces, pot roasts and stews, and also may be used as a marinade for less expensive cuts of meat. White wine, such as Chablis and Sauterne, is especially good in fish and chicken dishes.

1. Use wine when a recipe calls for a wine. Use spirits when recipe specifies spirits. They are not interchangeable.

2. Use wine and spirits of good quality, for the alcohol evaporates and the flavor remains.

3. Use wine or spirits in only one dish to be served for a meal. If wine is served with the meal, the wine used in cooking should have been sparingly introduced in order not to detract from the wine at table.

4. *Use low or moderate heat in preparing all dishes flavored with wine or spirits.*

5. *When a recipe calls for wine as an ingredient, do not use Vermouth. It contains herbs and flavoring that will elusively remain in the dish prepared with it.*

6. *Use wine with a gentle hand. No matter how little is used, its presence is recognizable.*

7. *Even several days after wine has been served, what remains in the bottle is sufficient to enhance the flavor of a dish.*

8. *For the salad when wine will be served, use wine vinegar or French dressing made with Claret Wine instead of vinegar, or mayonnaise made with white wine instead of vinegar.*

9. *With dishes prepared with wine or spirits, do not serve side dishes using vinegar, strong spices, prepared mustards, chili sauce, catsup, pickles, sweet jellies or conserves.*

10. *Use white wine in cooking white meats or fish. Use red wine for the sauces for these foods if contrast in color is desired.*

11. *Use dry red in cooking dark meats. Use white wine for fish and in making accompanying sauces.*

12. *Use white wine in poaching liquid in cooking fish.*

13. *Use dry wine such as Sherry, Graves, Chablis, Sauterne, dry Riesling, Madeira, dry Bordeaux, red Burgundy and Champagne in preparing soups, meat, poultry, sauces, game, vegetables, egg, cheese and fish dishes.*

14. *Add three or four tablespoons of Sherry at the last moment to a sauce, stew, casserole, meat loaf. Add Sherry to each portion of soup just before serving, especially to consommé, pea soup, bean soups and soups containing stock.*

15. *Use about 1/4 cup of Sherry for basting roast pork and ham dishes. Sprinkle 2 tablespoons of Sherry over a ham steak during broiling. It will complement its naturally sweet flavor and add to the nuttiness of the ham.*

16. *Add 1/2 cup of brown Sherry to a thick cream sauce to be used with chicken.*

17. Use wine as part of pan sauce to help deglaze pan in which meat is roasted or sautéed. This will dissolve juices clinging to the pan. Just before serving, strengthen the sauce with Brandy.

18. Use wine (does not have to be top quality) as a marinade with herbs and spices to tenderize meat before braising.

19. Use Sauterne, Chablis or Rhine Wine as a baste for roast lamb. Add 1 cup to fat in roasting pan; or before roasting, marinate lamb several hours in California Rosé with chopped onion, then baste with this mixture.

20. Madeira is excellent for cooking because it contains volatile acid. The same dish prepared at different times with Madeira, Sherry and Marsala will be best with Madeira because it is far higher in volatile acid than Sherry or Marsala. The French rarely use water in cooking when they can use wine. This is the reason why you will note so many dishes on a French menu à Madère. Italians are partial to Marsala; the Spaniards to Sherry.

21. In preparing sautéed sweetbreads, when the dish is finished, place Cognac in a heavy glass container, insert into hot water (or bain-marie) to heat it and then pour it over the sweetbreads and serve. If you do not have Cognac or Brandy, you may substitute dry white wine.

22. Be careful in placing pots or pans lined with tinfoil directly under broiler flame as it may ignite. Do not put tinfoil in an electric broiler.

23. For flambéed dishes, use Cognac, Brandy, Liqueurs, Cordials, Rum, Whiskey. Since they are high in alcoholic content, a small amount is sufficient to spread the ineffable essence of the liquid throughout a dish. A tablespoonful can flambé an omelette or bring out the freshness of fruit. One-half or 1/3 of a cup will crown a dessert soufflé with blue flame or put a delectable glaze on a ham or duck.

24. Use sweet wine such as Claret, Tokay, Muscatel, Port, sweet Sherry and Marsala in preparing fruit cocktails, sweet dessert sauces, cookies, cakes.

25. Use Liqueurs, Cordials, Brandy, sweet Sherry, light or dark Rum or Marsala, in preparing sweet desserts, sauces, candies, cake fillings and cake icings.

26. Flavor finished fruitcakes with Madeira, Sherry or Brandy.

27. Remove core and chill a sectioned grapefruit. In the center of each half, add 1 1/2 teaspoons of sugar and 1 tablespoon of Dubonnet or dry Sherry. Chill 1 hour longer in refrigerator before serving.

28. Add 2 teaspoons of sweet Sherry (brown or cream) to each cup of heavy cream before whipping. Sprinkle a tablespoon of cream Sherry on freshly baked cake. Add 2 tablespoons sweet Sherry to the batter of cakes or cookies that contain fruit, molasses, chocolate or brown sugar.

29. Liqueurs are sweet and therefore should not be used indiscriminately. Use in dishes such as ham, pork, poultry, desserts and fruit in sufficient quantity to point up but not to dominate the flavor of the food.

Some Liqueurs have natural affinities for certain foods. The freshness of Crème de Menthe is a superb complement to a chocolate roll or soufflé. The anise flavor of Pernod is good for seafood. Orange-flavored Liqueurs are good in the sauce accompanying duck, Curaçao with Crepes Suzette. Try stocking six or even a dozen of the fairly inexpensive Liqueurs in miniature. Try Kirsch, Maraschino or Curaçao on fresh fruits. Ice cream is better when a little Crème de Cacao is poured over it. Enhance custard with a dash of Bénédictine. Use Apricot Liqueur or Anisette in the cream filling for cakes and tartlets.

Defined as "spirits that have been sweetened, flavored and occasionally colored," Liqueurs owe their distinctive taste to subtle extracts of ingredients (caraway and aniseed, orange and mint, coffee and cocoa are only a few). The Liqueurs most commonly used for cooking are classified in three categories: (1) those with fruit base—Grand Marnier, Apry, Cherry Heering, Crème de Cassis and others; (2) those that take their tang from aromatic herbs and spices (such as Strega, Chartreuse, Kümmel, Crème de Menthe); and (3) the coffee and chocolate Liqueurs (Kahlúa, Tia Maria, Crème de Cacao). Europe prefers Anisette flavor above all others. America's first choice is Crème de Menthe.

To add red to a dish, the most popular Cordials may be counted on: Cherry Heering, Cherry Marnier, Marie Brizard, Garnier, deKuyper, Leroux.

Besides the deep emerald green of Crème de Menthe, there is the lighter green of green Chartreuse and the yellow-green of yellow Chartreuse. Crème de Banane may be relied on for a yellow color.

For orange color there are Peach and Apricot Liqueurs. Apry is the wonderful Marie Brizard Liqueur made from the superb apricots of the Rousillon. Oddly enough, orange-flavored Liqueurs such as Curaçao, Triple Sec and Cointreau are all colorless.

Potato Salad With Almonds
Molded Shrimp and Crabmeat
    Salad
Vegetable Salad

Dressings
(Begin on p. 372)

Mayonnaise With Sauterne
Roquefort Salad Dressing

Cheese and Eggs

Cheese
(Begin on p. 372)

Champagned Cheese on Toast
Cheddar Cheese Surprise
Cheese With Port
Cheese With Sherry or
    Madeira
Edam Cheese With Chablis
Cream Cheese–Sherry Spread
Fondue Gruyère
Swiss Cheese Fondue
Swiss Cheese With
    Kirschwasser

Eggs
(Begin on p. 374)

Eggs Benedict With
    Hollandaise Wine Sauce
Mushroom-Stuffed Eggs
    Madeira
Omelette Flambé
Omelette Grand Marnier
Poached Eggs in White Wine
Rum Raisin Sauce

Desserts
(Begin on p. 377)

Anisette Soufflé
Apple Slices Muscatel
Baba au Rhum With
    Strawberries
Bavarian Cream
Cherry Jubilee

Crème de Menthe Whip
Crepes Suzette
Fruits With Cointreau
Liqueurs and Fruits
Marquise au Champagne
Mousse Anisette
Baked Oranges Sauterne
Brandied Peaches
Peach Delights
Peaches Flambé
Pears Flambé
Pears Rosé
Sherry–Almond Custard
Chilled Sherry Soufflé
Soufflé with Cointreau

Pastries
(Begin on p. 386)

Champagne Cookies
Cherry Pie Marnier With Sauce
Chocolate Cream Rum Pie
Strawberry Chiffon Pie
Flavored Whipped Cream

Miscellaneous
(Begin on p. 388)

Walnuts and Wine
Zabaglione

Beverages
(Begin on p. 389)

Café Chantilly
Café Charente
Café Diable
Café Grappa or Anisette
Café Royale
Chocolate or Cocoa Royal
Holiday Chocolate
Inspired Milk Shake
Beef Tea Pick-Up
Imperial Tea
Liqueur Tea
Russian Rum Tea
Tea Bracer
Tea Toddy

Appetizers Spreads are popular for canapés as party hors d'oeuvres. Refrigerate until the moment of serving. Use on wedges of toast, unsweetened crackers, rusks, melba toast, bread sticks or slices of party bread rounds.

Almond-Chicken Spread

1 cup cooked chicken, finely ground
1 onion, finely ground
1/4 pound soft, snappy Cheddar

1/2 teaspoon salt
1/4 teaspoon pepper
1/2 cup Sauterne Wine
1 cup salted almonds, coarsely chopped

In a mixing bowl, combine chicken, onion, Cheddar, salt and pepper. Moisten with Sauterne. Shape into balls and roll in nuts. Yields about 3 1/2 dozen balls.

Avocado-Cream Cheese Spread

1 avocado
3-oz. package cream cheese
1 teaspoon lemon juice

1 teaspoon onion juice
1/4 cup dry Sherry

Mix avocado meat, cream cheese, lemon and onion juices. Moisten with Sherry. Yields sufficient to spread 24 canapés.

Bourbon Pâté

1 pound fresh chicken livers, cut into small pieces
1 small onion, minced
1 pound butter
2 tablespoons Marsala
1/2 teaspoon paprika
1/8 teaspoon allspice
1/2 teaspoon salt

1/8 teaspoon Tabasco sauce
1 clove garlic, minced
1 1/2 cups clear chicken consommé
1/3 cup straight Bourbon
1 cup walnuts, chopped
1 envelope unflavored gelatine

Sauté livers and onion in 1/2 pound butter. Lower flame and cook for 10 minutes, stirring occasionally. Add Marsala, paprika, allspice, salt, Tabasco sauce, garlic and 1/2 of chicken consommé. Cook for 5 minutes more. Place in electric blender. Gradually add balance of butter (melted), and Bourbon. Blend until smooth. Stir in walnuts. In a saucepan, sprinkle gelatin over remaining chicken consommé. Heat and stir until gelatin is dissolved. Pour part of gelatine-consommé into mold. Chill mold for 10 minutes. Fill mold with chicken liver mixture and top with remaining consommé. Keep in refrigerator for at least 6 hours before unmolding and serving. Eight to 10 servings.

Crabmeat Canapés

1 can (16 1/2 ozs.)
   crabmeat, flaked
1 teaspoon horseradish
   sauce
1/4 teaspoon prepared
   mustard

1/2 cup mayonnaise
1/4 teaspoon Worcestershire
   sauce
1 tablespoon dry Sherry

Combine all ingredients. Chill well. Yields sufficient to spread 24 canapés.

Liverwurst Spread

1/2 pound fine liverwurst
1 onion, finely chopped
1 green pepper, finely
   chopped

1/4 teaspoon Tabasco sauce
2 tablespoons Burgundy
   Wine

Combine all ingredients. Yields sufficient to spread about 48 canapés.

Lobster Canapés

1 can (16 1/2 ozs.) lobster
   meat
1 teaspoon mayonnaise

1 tablespoon dry Sherry
1/4 teaspoon salt

Drain lobster meat and flake very fine with fork. Add mayonnaise, Sherry and salt. Blend into paste. Store several hours or overnight in refrigerator. Yields sufficient to spread about 24 canapés.

Mushroom Savory

1 2-oz. bottle mushrooms,
   parboiled, chopped
1 onion, finely chopped
2 tablespoons butter
2 tablespoons lemon juice

2 hard-boiled eggs, finely
   chopped
1/4 teaspoon garlic salt
1/4 cup Christian Brothers
   Burgundy Wine

Place mushrooms and onion in pan with butter. Sauté until limp. Add lemon juice, eggs, garlic salt and wine. Cook on very low flame 25 minutes. Set aside to cool. Spread. Yields about 48 canapés.

New Orleans Shrimp Topping

2 cups minced cooked or
   canned shrimp
1 cup chopped cucumber
2 teaspoons minced onion

1 cup mayonnaise
1/4 cup Sauterne Wine
1/4 teaspoon salt

Combine all ingredients. Yields sufficient to spread 48 canapés.

Roquefort Cheese Spread

1 pound Roquefort cheese   *1/2 pound cream cheese*
3 tablespoons butter   *1/4 cup Hennessy*

Mash Roquefort very well. Cream with butter and cream cheese until spread is smooth. Beating all the while, add Hennessy. Serve on thin strips of toast or crackers. Yields sufficient to spread 48 canapés.

Sardine-Chablis Spread

1 can (6 or 8 ozs.) sardines in oil   *1 teaspoon grated onion*
    1/4 teaspoon Tabasco sauce
1 package (3 ozs.) cream cheese   *4 tablespoons Christian Brothers Chablis Wine*

Drain oil from sardines. Combine all ingredients. Yields sufficient to spread about 24 canapés.

Tuna Burgundy Tops

3 1/2 ozs. canned tuna, drained and minced   *1/4 teaspoon salt*
    1/4 teaspoon pepper
4 tablespoons onion, finely chopped   *2 tablespoons Christian Brothers Burgundy Wine*
4 tablespoons fine bread crumbs   *48 mushroom caps*

Combine tuna, onion, bread crumbs, salt, pepper and wine. Stuff mushroom caps. Place in oiled cake pan and bake in preheated oven (375° F.) for 15 minutes. Serve very hot. Yields 48.

Soups   Steaming hot soup laced liberally with wine is good for warming the stomach and lifting the spirits on a cold winter day, but the addition of wine need not be overlooked in other seasons of the year. Add half a cup of red or white dinner wine to a quart of hot soup, be it creamy or clear, to enhance taste and strengthen the nutrition of the soup. Favorite soup-and-wine flavors include Sherry with clear or cream soups; Rhine Wine, Sauterne, Vin Blanc Sec or any white dinner wine in consommé or chowder; Burgundy, Vin Rouge, Claret or any red wine in clear, tomato, meat or vegetable soups. The alcoholic content of the wine vanishes quickly when the soup begins to simmer. But alcoholic strength remains if wine is added as the soup is being consumed, and this is the traditional way the townsmen of Fubine add their red wine—at the table.

The Captain's Chowder

2 pounds haddock or cod, fresh or frozen
1 quart salted water
1 cup salt pork, cut small
1 large onion, finely cubed
5 medium potatoes, cut into 1/4-inch cubes
1 quart milk
1 cup light cream
1/3 cup Christian Brothers Sauterne or Chablis Wine
2 teaspoons salt
1/4 teaspoon pepper

Cover fish with 1 quart salted water and simmer gently for about 10 minutes. Strain, debone and skin fish, saving stock for later use. Fry salt pork in large cooking pot until bits are lightly browned. Remove crisp bits to absorbent paper. Sauté onion in hot fat until golden brown. Add potatoes, fish and reserved fish stock. Simmer covered for 10 minutes. Add milk, cream and wine. Reheat without boiling. Season with salt and pepper. Serve piping hot, sprinkling salt pork cracklings on top. Six servings.

Chicken and Vermouth

4 cups chicken broth
1 tablespoonful thin, very fine strips of orange peel
1/3 cup dry Vermouth

Combine broth and orange peel in a saucepan. Place over moderate heat and bring to a boil. Add Vermouth. Heat 1 minute. Ladle into bouillon cups or small bowls. Four servings.

Chicken Soup Parmesan

2 cups chicken broth
2 cups cream of chicken soup
1 cup cream
1/2 cup Sauterne Wine
1/2 cup grated Parmesan cheese

In a saucepan combine broth, cream of chicken soup and cream. Add wine and cheese, stirring over low heat until cheese melts. Serve at once in heated soup bowls. Four to six servings.

Clam and Shrimp Chowder

1 can (6 1/2 ozs.) shrimp
2 cups (or 1 10 1/2 oz. can)
    New England-style clam
    chowder
1 cup milk

1/2 cup Sauterne or dry
    white wine
1 teaspoon A-1 sauce
Pinch of chervil
Pinch of thyme

Clean shrimp and break into pieces. Add shrimp to clam chowder in saucepan. Add all other ingredients. Heat but do not boil. Four servings.

Consommé Burgundy

4 cups clear, rich broth
    (chicken, beef or veal)
1/2 cup boiling water
1 small carrot, cut into
    strips and halved

1 small onion, thinly sliced
1/4 cup Christian Brothers
    Burgundy Wine
1 teaspoon chopped parsley

Pour broth into saucepan and add boiling water, carrot and onion. Simmer for 3 minutes. Add wine. Heat but do not boil. Serve garnished with chopped parsley. Four servings.

Cream of Chicken Bisque

4 tablespoons butter
4 tablespoons flour
1 1/4 cups chicken
    consommé
1/2 teaspoon salt
1 onion, cut into halves
1 stalk celery, in pieces
3 cups milk
1/4 teaspoon powdered
    garlic

3/4 cup cooked chicken,
    minced
1 egg yolk
1/3 cup Christian Brothers
    Dry Sherry
1/2 cup heavy cream,
    whipped

Mix butter and flour over low heat until it bubbles. Add consommé, salt, onion and celery. Stir until creamy. Cover and cook over low heat 15 minutes, stirring as necessary to prevent lumping. Strain liquid into pot. Add milk, minced chicken and garlic. Cook until smooth. In a separate bowl, thin egg yolk with a little hot soup. Stir into soup pot. Add Sherry. (Never boil after addition of egg yolk and wine.) Crest servings with whipped cream. Four to six servings.

Jellied Rosé Consommé

4 1/2 cups beef consommé
2 envelopes unflavored
  gelatin
1/2 cup water
1 teaspoon sugar
1 cup Rosé
1/4 teaspoon salt

1/8 teaspoon white pepper
1/4 teaspoon lemon juice
1 tablespoon chopped
  onion
1/2 teaspoon chopped
  parsley

Bring consommé to a boil. Stir in gelatin that has been soft-ened in 1/2 cup water. Add sugar and wine. Season with salt, pepper and lemon juice. Remove and cool. Place in refrigera-tor to chill until soup sets. Whip lightly with a fork and serve it in chilled soup cups. Top with combination of onion and parsley. Four servings.

Madeira Citrus Soup

4 1/2 cups strong beef
  bouillon
1 1/2 tablespoons thinly
  sliced green onions with
  part of green tops
4 thin orange slices
1 1/2 tablespoons fresh
  lemon juice

1/8 teaspoon crumbled,
  dried thyme leaves
  (optional)
4 tablespoons medium-dry
  Madeira Wine

Combine bouillon, onions, orange slices, lemon juice and thyme in a saucepan. Place over moderate heat and bring to a boil. Ladle into 4 small soup bowls, putting an orange slice in each. Add 1 tablespoon Madeira to each. Serve immedi-ately. Four servings.

Onion Soup au Gratin

6 medium-size onions,
  thinly sliced
6 tablespoons butter
2 tablespoons flour
6 cups bouillon broth

1 cup red wine
Salt to taste
6 slices thin, dry toast
6 tablespoons freshly grated
  Parmesan cheese

Sauté onions in butter until golden brown. Add flour and stir until smooth. Add bouillon and wine. Simmer 25 minutes. Add salt. Pour into individual soup casseroles. On top of each serving place a slice of toast sprinkled with grated cheese. Place casseroles in oven (400° F.) until cheese melts and is golden brown. Serve immediately. Six servings.

Oxtail Soup
Madeira

2 oxtails, separated into
    sections
2 tablespoons olive oil
1 1/2 cups sliced onions
3/4 cup thinly sliced carrots
2 quarts cold water
2 teaspoons salt

1/4 teaspoon pepper
1 cup whole canned
    tomatoes
1/4 cup raw rice
3 tablespoons flour
2 tablespoons cold water
1/2 cup Madeira Wine

Brown oxtail pieces in oil in pan. Remove to soup kettle. Sauté onions and carrots in oil in pan. Add onions and carrots to oxtail pieces in kettle. Pour in water, salt, pepper and tomatoes. Bring to boil. Cover and simmer until meat is almost tender, about 2 hours. Add rice and continue to simmer for half an hour longer. Meanwhile, make paste of flour and cold water and add to soup, stirring well. Add wine and serve. Four servings.

Meat

Beef Stew With
Sauterne

2 pounds stewing beef, cut
    into serving pieces
1/4 cup flour
1 teaspoon salt
1/4 teaspoon pepper
4 tablespoons bacon fat
1 onion, chopped
1 carrot, sliced
1 bay leaf
1 stalk celery, cut into
    1-inch pieces

2 cloves garlic, chopped
2 tablespoons chopped
    parsley
1/2 teaspoon fennel seeds
2 cups beef consommé,
    heated
2 cloves
4 peeled tomatoes, sliced
1 cup Sauterne Wine

Roll beef pieces in flour to which salt and pepper have been added. Coat pan with fat by heating bacon fat in pan, then draining fat from pan. Sauté together onion, carrot, bay leaf and celery. Add beef pieces, garlic, parsley, fennel. Cook until meat is browned. Add hot consommé, cloves and tomatoes. Simmer for 5 minutes. Pour in Sauterne. Cook gently for 2 hours. Four to six servings.

Boeuf à la Mode
Italienne

This tasty dish is suggested by the Meier Wine Company of Ohio, who sent us the recipe.

3 to 4 pounds beef, top or
    bottom round
4 cloves garlic
1 1/2 teaspoons salt
1/2 teaspoon pepper
1 teaspoon crushed thyme
1 teaspoon rosemary
8 strips salt pork
2 onions, sliced

1 1/2 cups tomato purée
1 cup Meier's Domaine
    Claret
4 large carrots, quartered
2 large turnips, quartered
1 orange peel strip, finely
    chopped
1 lemon peel strip, finely
    chopped

With a sharp-pointed knife, make small incisions in round of beef. Fill slits with garlic, cut into slivers. Rub meat with salt, pepper, thyme and rosemary. Wrap strips of pork fat around meat and tie in place with butcher's string. Brown meat on all sides in a deep baking casserole. Add onions, tomato purée, and Claret. Cover casserole and put it on an asbestos pad over very low heat. Simmer meat very slowly for about 5 hours. After 4 hours, add carrots and turnips. Sauce will be very thick and meat tender when done. Remove string. Serve carrots and turnips separately, sprinkled with lemon and orange peel. Six or more servings.

Boeuf Bourguignonne
(Braised Beef in Burgundy Sauce)

1/2 pound bacon, diced
4 pounds beef (chuck or
    round), cut into 2-inch
    cubes
1/2 cup plus 1 tablespoon
    flour
2 cloves garlic, mashed
3 carrots, sliced
3 cups sliced onion
1/4 cup Cognac or Brandy
1/2 teaspoon salt

1/4 teaspoon pepper
1 bay leaf
1/4 teaspoon thyme,
    crushed
3 1/2 cups Burgundy Wine
1 pound fresh mushrooms,
    sliced
3 tablespoons butter
1 can (16 ozs.) small white
    peeled onions
1/4 cup chopped parsley

Cook bacon until crisp and brown. Remove bacon to paper towel and reserve. Roll beef cubes in 1/2 cup of flour, shaking off excess. Brown beef in bacon fat in pan, then remove and transfer to Dutch oven or large ovenproof casserole. Sauté garlic, carrots and onion slices in bacon fat until limp and lightly browned. Warm Cognac or Brandy and ignite over meat. When flame subsides, add garlic, carrots, onion slices, salt, pepper, bay leaf, thyme and 3 cups Burgundy. Cover and cook over moderate heat 2 to 2 1/2 hours, or until meat is tender.

Meanwhile, sauté mushrooms in 2 tablespoons butter in skillet. Remove and keep warm. Sauté small white onions until golden brown, adding more butter if needed. Add 1/2 cup Burgundy to skillet. Cover. Simmer onions 15 minutes. When beef is done, skim any excess fat. Thicken sauce by blending 1 tablespoon flour and 1 tablespoon butter and stirring slowly into hot wine liquid in Dutch oven. Add reserved bacon, mushrooms, small white onions and any sauce in the skillet. Cook 5 minutes. Sprinkle with parsley. Six to eight servings.

Club Steaks With Wine Sauce

6 club steaks
6 tablespoons melted butter

1 1/2 cups Wine Sauce
(recipe follows)

Brush steaks with butter and broil 3 to 5 minutes on each side. Place on heated individual serving plates and cover with Wine Sauce. Six servings.

Wine Sauce
(For above recipe)

2/3 cup finely chopped
 scallions
1/2 cup butter
1 cup Claret Wine
1 cup beef consommé

1 tablespoon Cognac
Juice of 1 lemon
1/2 cup finely chopped
 parsley

Sauté scallions in butter until golden. Add Claret wine and simmer until liquid is reduced to half its original volume. Add consommé, Cognac and lemon juice. Blend sauce thoroughly. Remove sauce from heat and add parsley. Keep sauce warm until serving time.

Ham Slice Baked With Citrus

The salting and smoking of pork to produce ham is of French origin. The ancient Gauls were devotees of pig meat, and their methods were renowned for salting, smoking and curing various cuts of pork. Until 1813, the Faire du Lard (Bacon Fair) was held in the square in front of Notre Dame Cathedral in Paris during the three days before Good Friday. From 1813 until 1832, it was held on the Quai des Grands-Augustine. Then it kept changing locations until the end of the Second Empire when it moved to Boulevard Richard-Lenois, where it is still held today.

1 center-cut ham slice 1 1/2
  inches thick
1 tablespoon instant minced
  onion, or 1/4 cup finely
  chopped raw onion
2 medium oranges, peeled
  and sliced

1/4 cup brown sugar,
  packed
1 medium lemon, thinly
  sliced
1/2 cup California Sauterne,
  Chablis or other white
  dinner wine

Score ham fat edge to prevent curling. Place in baking dish and sprinkle onion over ham. Peel oranges and cut into medium-thick slices. Arrange on top of ham. Sprinkle with brown sugar. Top with thin slices of lemon. Pour wine over all. Bake in preheated oven (375° F.) until ham is tender, 45 minutes to 1 hour. Four servings.

Ham With Marsala Wine

1/2 cup Marsala Wine
2 tablespoons flour
1/2 teaspoon salt
1/4 teaspoon pepper

8 slices lean ham
1 (4-oz.) jar maraschino
  cherries with its liquid

In a pan, make roux with 1 tablespoon Marsala wine and flour. Add 1/4 teaspoon salt and 1/8 teaspoon pepper and dilute with balance of Marsala. Cook gently. Add ham slices to this thin sauce and cook over low heat for 15 minutes. Drain cherries, reserving liquor. Just before serving, add cherries, 1/4 teaspoon salt and 1/8 teaspoon pepper, plus some of the cherry juice. Serve piping hot. Four servings.

Ham Steak Grand Marnier

1 center-cut ham slice 1 1/2
  inches thick
2 tablespoons brown sugar
1 1/2 teaspoons dry mustard
1 1/2 tablespoons orange
  juice

4 thin orange slices
1 tablespoon sugar
4 tablespoons Grand
  Marnier Cognac,
  warmed

Slash fat around edges of ham. Place ham slice in a shallow, flameproof serving dish. Combine brown sugar, dry mustard and orange juice to form a paste. Spread half of this on top of the ham. Broil until brown and glazed on top, approximately 10 minutes. Turn ham steak. Spread balance of paste on other side and continue broiling for 5 minutes. Arrange slices of orange on top of ham steak and sprinkle lightly with sugar. Place under broiler, brown and glaze. Just before serving, pour warmed Grand Marnier over ham and ignite. Bring to the table blazing. Four servings.

Ham in Port   This recipe is suggested by The Christian Brothers of California, who recommend using their Ruby Port for mouthwatering results.

2 to 2 1/2 pounds smoked ham slice, 1-inch thick	*2 tablespoons currant jelly or cherry preserves*
2 tablespoons light brown sugar	*4 whole cloves*
	1 cup Ruby Port

Remove rind from ham and discard. Trim off outer rim of fat, leaving a neat edge. Cut fat into fine pieces. Combine pieces of fat, sugar and jelly. Mix well. Place ham in shallow baking dish. Spread with prepared fat. Stud with cloves. Pour Ruby Port around the ham, not over it. Bake 1 hour at 300 to 325° F. Four to five servings.

Lamb in White Wine

3 pounds boneless lamb shoulder, cut in pieces, trimmed of excess fat	*1 1/2 teaspoons dried rosemary*
1 1/2 teaspoons salt	*1/2 teaspoon Tabasco sauce*
1/2 teaspoon pepper	*1/2 cup chicken consommé*
2 garlic cloves, chopped	*3 eggs*
3 tablespoons olive oil	*1 tablespoon grated lemon rind*
1 cup dry white wine	*1 teaspoon chopped parsley*

Season lamb with salt and pepper. Sauté garlic in hot oil until golden. Add lamb pieces and brown over medium heat. Add wine, rosemary and Tabasco sauce. Cover and simmer over low heat for 1 hour. Baste with consommé occasionally. Beat eggs in a bowl. Remove lamb pieces to heated dish. Add eggs, lemon rind and parsley to pot juices. Heat through but do not allow to boil. Pour sauce over lamb and serve immediately. Four to six servings.

Breaded Pork Chops   Dip pork chops in Sherry Wine before breading with flour, egg and breadcrumbs.

Wine-Braised Pork Chops

6 thick pork chops, loin or
    shoulder
2 teaspoons prepared
    mustard
1/2 teaspoon salt
1/4 teaspoon pepper
1/2 teaspoon dried sage

2 tablespoons brown sugar
6 thin slices lemon
1 cup California Sauterne
    or Chablis Wine
1 tablespoon cornstarch
    mixed with a little water

Trim fat from chops and use to grease skillet. Brown chops slowly on both sides. Drain off any excess fat. Spread chops with mustard, salt, pepper and sage. Sprinkle with brown sugar. Top each chop with a lemon slice. Pour wine over chops. Cover dish and cook very slowly until tender, 50 to 60 minutes. Remove to hot plate. Skim any fat from drippings and thicken drippings slightly with a little cornstarch mixed with cold water. Spoon pan sauce over chops. Six servings.

Spareribs Glazed With Cherry Liqueur

5 pounds spareribs
4 cloves garlic, halved
1 teaspoon salt
1/4 teaspoon pepper
1 cup soy sauce

1 cup tomato catsup
1/2 cup Cherry Liqueur
1/2 cup honey
1 teaspoon Tabasco sauce

Roast the spareribs in a flat pan in 350° F. oven for 1 hour. In the meantime, sprinkle halved garlic cloves with salt and pepper and press them with flat side of a knife until they become mashed. Combine garlic with soy sauce, catsup, Cherry Liqueur, honey and Tabasco sauce in a pan. Heat gently. When the spareribs have been in the oven for 45 minutes, brush them with the mixture. Bake 10 minutes longer, then repeat coating. Bake final 5 minutes. Cut spareribs into serving-size pieces and serve with remaining glaze as a sauce. Six servings.

Steak au Poivre

Press coarse black pepper into club or porterhouse steak. Sauté peppered steak in a little butter very quickly, searing it on both sides first and then letting it cook until it is done as desired. Remove steak to a hot platter. Add 1/2 cup Cognac to pan and rinse. Pour over steak and flambée. Servings according to appetite.

Tournedos With Amontillado Sherry	4 fillets of beef, 1 1/2 inches thick 1 teaspoon salt 1/4 teaspoon pepper 3/4 cup dry Amontillado Sherry	4 tablespoons butter 1 large mushroom, finely chopped 1/4 teaspoon Worcestershire sauce 2 tablespoons heavy cream

Season fillets with salt and pepper and marinate for 2 hours in Sherry. Turn from time to time. Drain fillets and dry with clean cloth. Sauté fillets in butter to desired doneness. Remove and keep hot. To the pan juices, add mushroom, Worcestershire sauce and heavy cream. Pour over beef.

Veal Amandine Flambé

Dip veal scallops in flour seasoned with salt, garlic powder and crushed basil. Sauté quickly in ample butter. Add blanched almonds—1/2 cup almonds for 1 pound of veal—and shake pan well. At the last minute, add 1/3 cup heated Cognac and ignite. Serve with buttered noodles.

Veal Scallopini Sauterne	2 pounds scalloped veal 1/4 pound plus 2 tablespoons butter 2/3 cup Sauterne Wine	1 teaspoon chopped chives 1 teaspoon chopped tarragon 1 teaspoon chopped parsley

Sauté veal slices in 1/4 pound butter. Remove meat to heated platter. Add Sauterne to butter remaining in pan. Cook over high heat until wine is reduced to half its original volume. Add chives, tarragon and parsley. Swirl in 2 tablespoons butter until it is just melted. Pour this sauce over veal scallops. Four to six servings.

Poultry

Wine works its own magic with poultry, accenting and enriching the natural flavors of chicken, duck, turkey. Goose becomes noble when basted with Burgundy, as the French have long known. Chablis, Rhine Wine and Sauterne are natural accents for poultry. Sherry, too, imparts a nutlike flavor of its own.

Baked Chicken

2 broiling chickens, halved
1/2 cup butter
1/2 cup Sauterne or Chablis
  Wine
1 teaspoon salt

1/4 teaspoon pepper
1/2 teaspoon dried tarragon
2 tablespoons cornstarch
1 small can button
  mushrooms, halved

Place chicken in shallow baking pan, skin side up. Melt butter. Add to it the wine, salt, pepper and tarragon. Spoon a little over chicken. Bake in preheated oven (325° F.) about 1 to 1 1/4 hours, basting often with the sauce. When chicken is tender and brown, pour off sauce and heat it in a saucepan to boiling. Stir in cornstarch mixed with a little cold water. Boil 1 to 2 minutes, stirring. Add mushrooms and spoon over chicken parts. Four servings.

───────────────────────────────

Chicken Breasts in Wine Sauce

3 whole chicken breasts,
  split, boned and skinned
1 small carrot, sliced
1 medium-size onion, thinly
  sliced
1/4 to 1/2 cup dry white
  wine
1 pinch dried tarragon
  leaves
3/4 teaspoon salt
Few grains pepper

2 cups water
1/2 teaspoon vegetable oil
1/4 pound fresh
  mushrooms, thinly sliced
1 tablespoon cornstarch
1/4 teaspoon curry powder
2 tablespoons chopped
  parsley
Cooked rice (about 3/4 cup
  uncooked)

Place chicken, carrot, onion, wine, tarragon, salt and pepper in a large skillet. Add water to barely cover chicken. Cover and place over moderately low heat. Cook 25 to 30 minutes, or until chicken is tender to fork test. Remove chicken to a warm platter. Measure juices in pan. If more than 1 cup, place over moderate heat and boil until reduced to 1 cup liquid. Skim off fat. Heat a skillet over moderate heat. Brush with the vegetable oil. To the skillet add mushrooms and cook until lightly browned, stirring frequently. Combine cornstarch and curry. Gradually add the 1 cup of pan juices. Mix until blended. Pour into skillet with mushrooms. Cook over moderate heat, stirring constantly until sauce is thickened. Strain sauce over chicken breasts and garnish with parsley. Serve with hot rice. Four to six servings.

Chicken Livers With Wine

6 slices bacon
1 pound chicken livers
1/2 teaspoon salt
1/4 teaspoon pepper
1/2 cup flour, sifted

1/2 cup California Sauterne,
  or Riesling
1 tablespoon finely chopped
  parsley

Fry bacon until crisp, then drain on paper towel. Measure drippings, returning 1/4 cup to skillet. Dredge chicken livers in mixture of salt, pepper and flour. Brown lightly in hot bacon fat. Turn heat low and add wine. Cover and steam for 5 minutes, or until livers are cooked when pierced with fork. Crumble bacon and sprinkle with parsley over livers. Serve over hot rice or noodles, or on crisp toast. Four to six servings.

Chicken of Normandy Calvados

4 tablespoons butter
1 broiler-fryer (2 1/2 to 3
  pounds), quartered
1 tablespoon flour
1 cup dry white wine
1 onion, studded with a
  clove
1 teaspoon salt

1/4 teaspoon pepper
2 sprigs parsley
1 small bay leaf
1/3 cup Calvados
2 apples, peeled, cored, cut
  crosswise into thirds
1 cup heavy cream

Melt the butter in a heavy skillet. Brown chicken until lightly golden on both sides, about 5 minutes per side. (Brown skin side first.) Sprinkle with flour. Add wine, onion, salt, pepper, parsley and bay leaf. Cover and simmer gently for 40 minutes, or until chicken is tender. Remove bay leaf, parsley and onion. Pour Calvados over the chicken. Ignite. Meanwhile, simmer apples until soft in a covered saucepan. Remove chicken to a hot platter and keep warm. Pour liquid from apples into skillet and cook about 5 minutes until sauce is reduced to half its volume. Mix in cream. Cook 5 minutes more, stirring constantly until sauce is slightly thickened. Spoon over chicken and garnish with apples. Four servings.

Chicken Rosé

4 large pieces frying chicken
1/4 teaspoon garlic salt
1/4 teaspoon paprika
1 tablespoon flour
3 tablespoons butter
1/4 teaspoon dried
  rosemary

1/4 teaspoon dried basil
1/2 cup Rosé Wine
1 1/2 tablespoons cornstarch
1/2 cup sour cream
1 tablespoon water

Dredge chicken with mixed garlic salt, paprika and flour. In skillet, brown chicken on both sides in butter. Sprinkle with rosemary and basil. Add wine. Cover and cook slowly until tender, about 25 minutes. Remove chicken from pan. Skim any excess fat from pan liquid. Thicken liquid with cornstarch mixed with water. Stir in sour cream. Spoon over chicken and serve. Four servings.

Duck L'Orange
Grand Marnier

1 Long Island duck about 4 lbs.
1 teaspoon salt
1/4 teaspoon pepper
1 1/2 oranges
2 sprigs parsley
1/2 cup Grand Marnier
1 cup boiled rice, hot

Prepare duck and rub salt and pepper all over it, reserving some to season the interior. Place 1/2 orange and 2 sprigs parsley in cavity. Roast in preheated oven (325° F.) for 1 1/4 hours for rare or pink duck, 1 1/2 hours for medium, longer for well done. During the cooking, baste with pan juices. For last 15 to 20 minutes, place under medium broiler flame to get brown crust. Remove duck to hot platter. Garnish with slices of 1 orange, placing around edge of platter. Heat Grand Marnier slightly and pour over duck, igniting it just as you bring it to the table. Serve with hot rice. Four servings.

Duckling Flambé
Curaçao

1 4-pound, ready-to-cook duckling
3 oranges
1/2 cup water
1 tablespoon sugar
1 teaspoon currant jelly
2 tablespoons Curaçao
1 teaspoon cornstarch
1/4 cup Triple Sec

Roast duckling for 10 minutes in 450° F. preheated oven. Reduce temperature to 400° F. and roast for about 30 minutes (more for well done). Meanwhile, remove peel from 1 orange and cut into thin or julienne strips. Place strips in saucepan and add water to cover; boil until tender, about 15 minutes. Drain. Squeeze juice of peeled orange over drained, cooked peel. When duck is roasted, discard fat. Cut duckling in half lengthwise, removing breastbone. Add water and breastbone to pan juices in roasting pan and simmer for 5 minutes. Strain. In another saucepan, caramelize sugar. Add strained breastbone stock, orange juice, currant jelly, orange strips. Add Curaçao and stir in cornstarch. Cook a few minutes, stirring until thickened. Peel and section remaining 2 oranges. Arrange duckling halves on a heated ovenproof platter. Garnish edges with orange sections. Place in 250° F. oven until heated through. Place orange sauce in sauceboat. Pour Triple Sec over duckling and ignite. Bring to table and serve with the hot orange sauce. Two servings.

Roast Turkey Rosé

Allow 20 minutes to the pound in roasting turkey. Serve with gravy made from pan juices or with Alternate Almond-Rum Gravy.

12- to 15-pound turkey, dressed, seasoned inside and out with salt	1/2 cup Rosé Wine
	2 tablespoons flour
	2 cups hot beef broth
Almond Stuffing (recipe follows)	Salt
	Pepper
1/4 pound butter	Alternate Almond-Rum
1/2 cup chicken broth, heated	Gravy (recipe follows)

Stuff turkey with Almond Stuffing (recipe follows) and truss. Butter entire surface well. Sear in very hot oven (500° F.) for 20 minutes. Add hot chicken broth and wine to pan. Reduce oven temperature to 350° F. Continue to roast turkey until bird is thoroughly done, basting frequently with pan juices. Transfer to hot platter. Skim off all but 2 tablespoons of fat from liquid in pan. Stir flour into pan juices. Remove to saucepan or place roasting pan on top of stove, stirring in all the brown bits from the bottom and sides of roasting pan. Stir in beef broth and cook gravy for 5 minutes, stirring constantly. Correct seasoning with salt and pepper. Strain gravy through a fine sieve. Six to eight servings.

Almond Stuffing
(For above recipe)

1/2 cup currants	1 teaspoon salt
3/4 cup Rosé Wine	1/4 teaspoon pepper
2 onions, finely chopped	1/2 cup minced parsley
1/4 cup celery, finely chopped	3/4 cup slivered, toasted almonds
1/2 cup butter	1 teaspoon rosemary
8 cups bread crumbs	1/2 cup melted butter

Cover currants with 1/2 cup wine and set aside for several hours until currants are plump. Sauté onions and celery in 1/2 cup butter for 10 minutes. In a bowl place bread crumbs, salt, pepper, parsley, almonds and rosemary. Stir. Add onion and celery mixture. Add 1/2 cup melted butter and 1/4 cup wine. Yields about 6 cups stuffing.

Alternate Almond-Rum Gravy	Pan juices from turkey 2 cups chicken consommé 3 tablespoons flour 1/4 cup Rum	1/4 cup blanched, sliced almonds Salt Pepper

Pour turkey drippings into a skillet. Add consommé. Blend flour and Rum and add to skillet. Cook and stir over moderate heat until mixture begins to bubble. Add almonds, salt and pepper. Simmer an additional few minutes until gravy is thick and well blended. Serve with carved turkey.

Fish and Seafood The classic and simple way to enhance broiled fish is to baste the dish during preparation with a combination of wine and butter. Mix equal parts of butter and Rosé Wine or a white dinner wine such as Chablis or Sauterne. Add a squeeze of lemon or lime and a pinch of a favorite herb. Heat basting liquid in a small saucepan and brush often over fish while it is cooking. Also see suggestions listed under "Basic Rules for Cooking With Wine and Spirits" in this chapter.

Fish

Fisherman Fillets	1-pound package frozen
	  fillets
	1/2 teaspoon salt
	1/4 teaspoon pepper
	1 cup fine bread crumbs
		2 tablespoons butter
		1 onion, thinly sliced
		1 cup Rhine Wine or
		  Chablis Wine

Allow fish fillets to thaw and separate them. Season with salt and pepper and cover with bread crumbs. Place side by side in a shallow baking dish. Dot with butter and cover with onion slices. Bake in 350° F. oven for 10 minutes. Pour wine around but *not* over fillets and bake 30 to 40 minutes more until cooked through and brown on top. Three to four servings.

Baked Salmon Supreme	4 or 5 slices salmon 1/2 teaspoon salt 1/4 teaspoon pepper 3 tablespoons flour 1/4 cup butter 1 cup Riesling or Chablis	1 cup sour cream 1/8 teaspoon dried dill 1/4 cup chopped onion 1 canned green chili, chopped

Season salmon with salt and pepper. Dredge lightly in flour. Melt butter in skillet and brown salmon quickly on both sides. Add 1/2 cup wine to skillet. Cover and bake in 400° F. oven for 10 minutes. Blend 1/2 cup Riesling or Chablis, sour cream, dill, onion and chili. Top salmon with sour-cream mixture. Continue baking, uncovered, until fish is done and topping glazed, about 15 minutes. Four servings.

Salmon on Seashells   Use natural shells if available, or china baking shells.

1-pound can salmon   *3/4 cup hot milk*
2 dozen oyster crackers   *1/4 cup dry Sherry*
1/2 teaspoon capers   *2 tablespoons butter*
1/8 teaspoon Tabasco sauce

Flake salmon. Break oyster crackers coarsely and add to salmon. Add capers, Tabasco sauce, milk and Sherry. Stir well. Fill six large seashells, dotting tops with butter. Bake at 350° F. for 1/2 hour until heated through and brown on top. Six servings.

Trout With Sherry Sauce

4 trout, heads and tails on, washed and dried   *5 tablespoons brown sugar*
1/2 pound blanched almonds   *3/4 cup dry Sherry*
4 tablespoons butter   *2 tablespoons chopped parsley*

Wipe trout. Cut almonds into slivers and sauté in 2 tablespoons butter until golden brown. In a wide pan, fry trout in remaining 2 tablespoons butter until well done and golden brown, about 10 minutes. Meanwhile, prepare sauce: Add brown sugar to almonds and butter and let simmer 4 to 5 minutes, stirring occasionally. Add Sherry and simmer for an additional 2 to 3 minutes. Place cooked trout on a hot platter or serving plates, cover with sauce and sprinkle with chopped parsley. Four servings.

Seafood

Crab Newburg   This easily prepared dish is suggested by Brotherhood Winery of Washingtonville, New York. It is equally good with the substitution of lobster, shrimp or salmon. Serve by itself or in pastry shells.

2 6 1/2 -oz. cans crabmeat
1/4 cup Brotherhood Sherry
    Wine
1/2 stick butter (2 ozs.)
2 tablespoons flour
1/4 teaspoon salt
1/8 teaspoon white pepper
1/8 teaspoon grated nutmeg
1/8 teaspoon paprika

2 egg yolks, beaten
1 1/2 cups light cream
1 teaspoon lemon juice
1/2 teaspoon Worcestershire
    sauce
4 slices toast, crusts
    removed
4 tiny sprigs parsley

Drain crabmeat. Place in bowl and add Sherry. Meanwhile, prepare sauce: Melt butter in top of double boiler. Stir in flour, salt, white pepper, nutmeg and paprika. Cook over boiling water until mixture thickens. Blend egg yolks with cream and add to mixture in top of double boiler. Stir until sauce is thick and creamy. Add crabmeat and Sherry Wine, lemon juice, Worcestershire sauce. Heat through. Serve on slices of toast. Garnish with parsley. Four servings.

Fricassee of Frogs' Legs

2 pounds frogs' legs, ready
    for cooking
2 cups milk
3/4 teaspoon salt
1/2 teaspoon white pepper
1/2 cup flour
1/4 cup plus 1 tablespoon
    butter
1 onion, finely chopped
1 clove garlic
1 cup small mushrooms,
    sliced

1 cup Sauterne Wine
2 cups chicken consommé
2 bay leaves
1/2 teaspoon rosemary
1 tablespoon grated lemon
    rind
1/2 cup Marsala Wine
3 tablespoons light cream
1 tablespoon chopped
    parsley
1 cup croutons

Wipe frogs' legs with damp cloth. Dip in milk. Sprinkle with 1/2 teaspoon salt and 1/4 teaspoon pepper, then lightly dust with flour. Heat 1/4 cup butter. Sauté onion, garlic, mushrooms and frogs' legs until pale golden. Add Sauterne Wine and simmer for 5 minutes. Add chicken consommé, bay leaves, rosemary, 1/4 teaspoon salt, 1/4 teaspoon pepper and lemon rind. Cook for 10 minutes (meat will be very tender). Remove legs from pan to heated dish and keep hot. Add to pan Marsala Wine and cream. Stir. Top frogs' legs with pan sauce, sprinkle with parsley and garnish with croutons browned in 1 tablespoon butter. Four to five servings.

Lobster Newburg

2 cups lobster meat
1 1/2 cups Sherry Wine
1/4 cup butter
3/4 cup light cream
2 egg yolks, beaten

1/2 teaspoon salt
1/8 teaspoon cayenne
   pepper
4 slices toast

Marinate lobster meat for 1 1/2 hours in 1/4 cup Sherry, then drain off all of the Sherry. To make the Newburg sauce, melt butter, add cream slowly and gradually stir in beaten egg yolks. Do not hasten this process or mixture will curdle. Season with salt and cayenne pepper. Fold drained lobster meat into Newburg sauce. Allow to stand for 10 minutes, then heat through well. Just before serving, add remaining 1 1/4 cups Sherry, folding twice. Serve on toast. Four servings.

Scallops Supreme

The small Long Island scallops, mollusks, from the eastern coastal bays are about 3/4 -inch thick and pinkish white, in season from September through April. The larger white deep-sea scallop in season all year may be as large as 2 inches in diameter. The small scallops are considered to have the sweetest flavor. This recipe, which calls for the use of sea scallops and Rhine Wine, results in an intriguingly flavored dish, suggested by Greyton H. Taylor of the Taylor Wine Company, New York.

2 pounds fresh sea scallops
1/4 cup Rhine Wine
2 teaspoons lemon juice
1 teaspoon instant minced
   onion
1/4 cup finely chopped
   green pepper

1/2 teaspoon rosemary
1/2 teaspoon salt
1/4 teaspoon pepper
1/2 cup light cream
1/3 cup soft bread crumbs
2 tablespoons butter

Place scallops in single layer in shallow baking dish. Combine Rhine Wine, lemon juice, onion, green pepper, rosemary, salt and pepper. Pour over scallops. Pour cream evenly over all and sprinkle with bread crumbs. Dot with butter. Bake at 450° F. 15 to 20 minutes, then briefly place under broiler for further browning. Six servings.

Scalloped Oysters Chablis

1 1/2 cups cracker crumbs
1/3 cup melted butter
1 pint oysters, well drained
1/2 teaspoon salt
1/4 teaspoon pepper

1/3 cup Chablis Wine
1/2 cup light cream
1 cup grated Cheddar
   cheese

Mix crumbs and melted butter and spread a layer over bottom of shallow baking dish (10" x 6" x 2"). Cover with half the oysters and season with salt and pepper. Repeat layers of crumbs, oysters and seasoning, topping with crumbs. Pour wine over all. Add cream and sprinkle grated cheese on top. Bake at 425° F. about 20 minutes. Three or four servings.

───────────────────────

Vegetables

There are many ways to enhance the natural goodness of vegetables. Sherry in a cream sauce combines well with cooked carrots. For a delicious celery dish, cut celery in short lengths; cook until tender in equal parts of beef bouillon and Chablis, Rhine Wine or Sauterne; and serve dotted with butter. You may also combine Sherry with melted butter and beat into cooked squash, sweet potatoes or yams.

───────────────────────

Asparagus With Butter–Wine Sauce

2 pounds asparagus
1 1/2 quarts boiling water
1/2 teaspoon salt
1/2 teaspoon sugar

1 1/4 cup Butter-Wine Sauce (recipe follows)
1/2 teaspoon lemon juice

Trim asparagus, cutting off tough root ends. Wash twice in tepid water to remove sand. Tie stalks together and stand upright in deep kettle. Pour in 1 1/2 quarts boiling water. Add salt and sugar. Cover tightly and boil 25 minutes. The steam from the boiling water will cook the asparagus. Drain, cut string, add lemon juice, and serve with Butter-Wine Sauce.

───────────────────────

Butter-Wine Sauce
(For above recipe)

This is an excellent sauce to serve not only with asparagus but with cauliflower, broccoli, artichokes or boiled fish.

4 egg yolks
1/2 cup cold water
1/4 cup dry white wine
1 tablespoon lemon juice

1/2 teaspoon onion juice
1/8 teaspoon salt
1/2 cup butter

Beat egg yolks until light. Add to top of double boiler with water, wine, lemon juice, onion juice and salt. Cook, stirring until thick and creamy. Add butter, a teaspoon at a time, beating well after each addition. Yields 1 1/4 cups.

Brussels Sprouts Sauterne

1 quart Brussels sprouts
1 quart cold water
2 teaspoons salt
1 quart boiling water
4 tablespoons butter

1 cup beef consommé
2 eggs, beaten lightly
1/2 teaspoon flour
3 tablespoons Sauterne Wine

Choose crisp, solid, bright-green sprouts. Remove soiled outer leaves and cut a thin slice from stem ends to remove all discoloration. Wash well and soak for 20 minutes in 1 quart cold water with 1 teaspoon salt. Drain. Add 1 teaspoon salt to 1 quart boiling water in uncovered saucepan and boil Brussels sprouts vigorously until just tender, 12 to 15 minutes depending on size of sprouts. Drain. Remove to heated dish. Melt butter in a pan, add sprouts and sauté for 10 minutes, turning. In another saucepan, warm beef consommé. Whisk eggs and flour together until smooth, then add to pan with consommé. Simmer gently until mixture thickens. Add Sauterne. Whip again and pour sauce over sprouts. Four servings.

Cabbage Cooked in Sauterne

1 large white cabbage
1 quart cold water
2 1/2 teaspoons salt
2 tablespoons cooking oil
1 onion, chopped

1 cup boiling water
1/2 teaspoon sugar
1 cup Sauterne
1 tablespoon capers

Trim and wash cabbage and cut into quarters. Soak 30 minutes in 1 quart cold water with 2 teaspoons salt. Drain and cut into thin strips. Heat oil in saucepan and sauté onion until golden. Add cabbage, boiling water, 1/2 teaspoon salt and sugar. Toss gently. Add Sauterne and capers. Stir ingredients. Cover pan and cook slowly about 20 minutes until cabbage is tender. Drain cabbage (although most of moisture will be reduced). Four servings.

Mushrooms Sautéed With Sherry

When mushrooms are first picked and packed, the veil is closed around the stem. The mushrooms are firm and dry-moist. Mushrooms are perfectly good when they have brown spots on them. Do not let mushrooms remain unrefrigerated too long because they will become dry and toughened. However, if left too long and too closely covered in the refrigerator, they will take on a slick, too-moist quality.

2 cups thinly sliced mushrooms	*2 tablespoons dry Sherry*
3 tablespoons butter	*1 tablespoon dill, finely chopped*

Sauté mushrooms in butter for 3 minutes, stirring frequently. Stir in Sherry and dill and serve hot. Four servings.

Creamed Onions

This dish is excellent with lamb or mutton.

1 can (16 oz.) cooked, whole onions	*1/4 teaspoon pepper*
1/2 cup water	*1 tablespoon flour*
1/4 teaspoon salt	*1/2 cup Sauterne Wine*
	1/4 teaspoon grated nutmeg

Drain onions and reserve liquid. Place all onion liquid except 2 tablespoons in saucepan and add water, salt and pepper. Heat through. Add paste made of flour and remaining 2 tablespoons onion liquid. Cook over low flame about 5 minutes, stirring until sauce thickens. Add Sauterne and nutmeg. Stir well. Add onions. Heat and continue to cook gently about 8 minutes. Four servings.

Sherried Onions au Gratin

The ancient humble onion appreciates the addition of Sherry in the preparation of this tasty dish, which we have adapted from the original suggestion made by Brotherhood Winery, Washingtonville, New York.

6 medium onions, sliced	*1/4 teaspoon salt*
2 cups cold water	*1/8 teaspoon white pepper*
1/3 cup light cream	*2 tablespoons butter*
3 tablespoons Brotherhood Sherry Wine	*3 tablespoons grated Parmesan cheese*

Parboil onions in 2 cups water until tender, about 10 minutes. Drain, reserving 2 tablespoons liquid. Turn onions into greased baking dish. Mix cream, 2 tablespoons onion liquid, Sherry, salt and pepper. Pour over onions. Dot with butter and sprinkle with Parmesan cheese. Cover dish and bake at 375° F. about 30 minutes. Four servings.

Salads and Dressings

Substitute wine for vinegar to lend special interest to salads and their dressings.

Salads

Avocado With Wine Vinaigrette

The avocado, a member of the laurel family, was discovered in Mexico and South America by early Spanish explorers. Technically a fruit, in culinary literature it is treated as a vegetable and purchased in the vegetable section. Buy fully ripe avocados soft to the touch, or ripen at room temperature.

2/3 cup Rosé Wine
2/3 cup olive oil
1 tablespoon lemon juice
1 teaspoon salt
1 teaspoon chopped parsley

1/4 teaspoon white pepper
1/4 teaspoon capers
1/4 teaspoon chopped dill
3 fully ripe avocados, chilled

In a bowl, combine wine, olive oil, 1/4 tablespoon lemon juice, salt, parsley, white pepper, capers and dill to make Wine Vinaigrette. Place in refrigerator to chill several hours or overnight. When ready to serve, cut avocados lengthwise. Insert a sharp knife directly into seeds and twist gently to lift out. Brush surfaces with remaining lemon juice. Serve half shells with chilled Wine Vinaigrette. Six servings.

Fillings

Fill hollow with cottage cheese, crabmeat or cooked shrimp, chopped up. Serve with Wine Vinaigrette. Four servings.

Chicken Salad With Sherry

2 cups chicken, cooked and cubed
1/4 cup chopped celery
2 tablespooons onion, finely chopped
1/2 cup sour cream

2 tablespoons dry Sherry
1/4 teaspoon salt
1/4 teaspoon dry mustard
1/2 bunch watercress, trimmed and washed
1 lemon, quartered

In bowl combine chicken, celery and onion. Place in refrigerator to chill. Meanwhile, prepare dressing by mixing sour cream, dry Sherry, salt and dry mustard. Fold this dressing into chicken mixture and serve on bed of watercress with lemon wedges as garnish. Four servings.

Green Salad With Wine Dressing

1/2 head Boston lettuce
1/4 pound spinach, trimmed and washed well
1/4 pound chicory, trimmed and washed well

1 clove garlic
1 tomato, quartered
Wine Dressing (recipe follows)

When greens have been washed, place in a clean towel. Gather ends of towel together and shake so that extra moisture is absorbed by towel. Place greens in wooden bowl rubbed with garlic. Add quartered tomato. Serve with Wine Dressing. Four servings.

Wine Dressing
(For above recipe)

2 tablespoons olive oil
1 tablespoon lemon juice
2 tablespoons dry Rhine
    Wine or Sauterne

1/4 teaspoon salt
1/4 teaspoon pepper
1/2 teaspoon capers

Combine olive oil and lemon juice in a bowl. Add remaining ingredients and stir well. Chill and serve with salad. Yields 1/4 cup.

Potato Salad With Almonds

6 large potatoes
2 tablespoons white wine
    vinegar
3/4 cup dry Sauterne
1/4 cup scallions, minced
2 tablespoons parsley,
    minced
1/4 cup melted butter

1/2 cup olive oil
2 pimientos, cut in small
    pieces
1/2 cup blanced, halved,
    toasted almonds
1/4 teaspoon white pepper
1/2 teaspoon salt

Boil potatoes in jackets for 30 minutes, or until tender to fork test. Cool a bit, peel and slice. Add wine vinegar to Sauterne. While potatoes are still warm, combine with scallions, parsley, melted butter, Sauterne-vinegar mixture, olive oil, pimientos, almonds, pepper and salt. Let salad stand in a cool place for several hours before serving, or serve while it is still warm. Eight to ten servings.

Molded Shrimp and Crabmeat Salad

This recipe was suggested by Martini & Rossi since their extra dry Vermouth gives the subtle flavor of herbs and can be substituted for a dry white wine.

2 envelopes unflavored
  gelatin
2 1/4 cups chicken broth
3/4 cup Martini & Rossi
  extra dry Vermouth
1 cup mayonnaise
2 tablespoons parsley, finely
  chopped
3 tablespoons chives, finely
  chopped

1 tablespoon Worcestershire
  sauce
1/2 teaspoon salt
1/4 teaspoon pepper
1 cup shrimp, cooked or
  canned
1 cup cooked crabmeat,
  fresh or canned
1 cup celery, finely chopped

Soak gelatin in broth and heat until dissolved. Add Vermouth and stir into mayonnaise. Add parsley, chives, Worcestershire sauce, salt and pepper. Chill until thickened. Add shrimp, crabmeat and celery. Pour into 6-cup mold and chill until firm. Six servings.

Vegetable Salad

4 stalks cooked celery, cut
  into 2-inch pieces
1/2 pound whole green
  beans, cooked
8 canned asparagus spears
1/4 French dressing
1/4 Claret or Rosé Wine

1/2 head Boston lettuce
1 small Bermuda onion,
  sliced
8 strips pimiento
2 hard-boiled eggs,
  quartered
Juice of 1/2 lemon

On a flat dish or oval plate, place celery, green beans and asparagus spears side by side. Marinate by combining French dressing and wine and pouring over vegetables. Refrigerate for at least 1 hour. Serve vegetables on bed of lettuce leaves. Garnish with onion rings, pimiento and hard-boiled eggs. Squeeze a little lemon juice over all. Four servings.

Dressings

Mayonnaise With Sauterne

The combination of mayonnaise and Sauterne or Rhine Wine provides a tasty dressing for any green salad or for use on fish or cold cuts.

3 tablespoons Sauterne
1/2 tablespoon lemon juice

1 cup mayonnaise

Add the Sauterne and lemon juice to mayonnaise and stir well. Yields over 1 cup.

Roquefort Salad Dressing

This perfect dressing for serving over a salad of mixed greens or over sliced tomatoes is suggested by Brotherhood Winery, Washingtonville, New York.

1/4 pound Roquefort cheese
3 tablespoons mayonnaise
3 tablespoons salad oil
1/8 teaspoon coarse black pepper
1/2 teaspoon Worcestershire sauce

1 clove garlic, crushed
2 tablespoons Brotherhood Burgundy Wine
2 tablespoons red wine vinegar
1/4 teaspoon salt

Mash cheese with fork and beat in mayonnaise and oil. Combine remaining ingredients in a bowl. Stir well, then add to cheese mixture. Cover and chill for several hours in refrigerator to blend the flavors. Yields 1 cup.

Cheese and Eggs

A little imagination in the use of wine can add interest to cheese dishes. Wine greatly improves the taste of eggs, and a handsomely flamed omelette has the gourmet touch.

Cheese

Champagned Cheese on Toast

2 tablespoons butter
3/4 pound grated Cheddar cheese

1/4 cup Champagne
1/4 teaspoon salt
4 slices crustless toast

Melt butter in the blazer of a chafing dish over hot water. Add cheese and, as it melts, gradually stir in Champagne. Season with salt and serve. Four servings.

Cheddar Cheese Surprise

1 tablespoon butter
2 tablespoons Sherry
2 tablespoons dry mustard
1 cup Cheddar cheese, diced
2 tablespoons anchovy paste

1/8 teaspoon cayenne pepper
1/8 teaspoon powdered tarragon
3 slices crustless toast

Melt butter in saucepan. Add Sherry, dry mustard, cheese, anchovy paste, cayenne pepper and tarragon. Stir until well blended. Cut toast in strips. Place on heated plates and pour on melted cheese mixture. Two or more servings.

Cheese With Port   Put a Stilton or Blue cheese in a crock. Punch holes in cheese with an ice pick and fill with Port. Set aside for 7 to 10 days in refrigerator. Cheese will be smooth to spread.

Cheese With Sherry or Madeira   Follow recipe for Cheese with Port, using Cheddar cheese with Sherry or Madeira.

Edam Cheese With Chablis   Cut off top of Edam cheese and reserve. Remove enough cheese in center to form a shallow crater about 2 inches deep. Punch holes with ice pick and fill hollow with Chablis. Replace top and allow to stand in refrigerator about a week until cheese can be scooped with a spoon.

Cream Cheese–Sherry Spread

3 3-oz. packages cream cheese	1 tablespoon minced onion
1 3-oz. can deviled ham	1 teaspoon Worcestershire sauce
1/2 cup Sherry Wine	1/4 teaspoon dry mustard
2 tablespoons sweet pickle relish, well drained	1/4 teaspoon garlic powder
	1/4 teaspoon salt

Mash cheese with a fork and blend in ham and wine. Beat until smooth. Add remaining ingredients. Six servings.

Fondue Gruyère   This preparation makes an admirable sauce for cooked broccoli, cauliflower or green beans. It can also be used as a dip for the cocktail hour or served as a delicious fondue.

1/2 pound Gruyère cheese, grated	1/2 teaspoon salt
1 tablespoon butter	1/4 teaspoon white pepper
3/4 cup dry Sherry Wine	2 egg yolks, beaten
	6 half slices toast

Melt cheese in saucepan or top of double boiler over hot water. Add butter and Sherry. Stir and season with salt and pepper. When very hot, remove from heat and beat in egg yolks. Serve immediately on toast. Two servings.

Swiss Cheese Fondue   Use a brown pottery casserole dish with a stubby handle. When serving, place casserole dish over alcohol table burner or electric unit. Traditionally this fondue is intimately shared, the diners using long-handled forks to spear their bread pieces and dipping the bread in a stirring motion. Each diner takes his turn. Serve Kirschwasser or Cognac as an accompaniment with this dish or a cup of hot tea or coffee. Stir fondue from time to time while it is being eaten to maintain consistency. A brown crust will form at bottom of casserole when most of the fondue has been enjoyed. It can be lifted out with the fork as a choice tidbit.

Swiss Cheese With Kirschwasser
(This is a variation of Fondue.)

Take a pound of Swiss cheese and soften it by allowing to stand in a warm place on stove, but do not allow it to melt. When soft, place in a crock, punch holes and fill with Kirschwasser. Let stand until saturated, about 2 days in refrigerator.

1 clove garlic
2 cups Riesling or Chablis Wine
1 pound Swiss cheese, coarsely grated
2 tablespoons flour
1/8 teaspoon nutmeg

1/2 teaspoon salt
1/4 teaspoon pepper
6 tablespoons Kirschwasser or Cognac
1 loaf French bread or 8 crispy hard rolls

Rub casserole with garlic. Pour in wine and place over low heat. When air bubbles form, stir with fork. Combine cheese and flour and stir in by tablespoonsful. When cheese dissolves, add more, stirring in same direction. Add nutmeg, salt and pepper. Stir in Kirschwasser or Cognac. Remove from heat and immediately set casserole on alcohol burner on table. Pierce pieces of bread or roll with fork and dip into the fondue. Four servings.

Eggs

Eggs Benedict With Hollandaise Wine Sauce

1 teaspoon butter
6 4-inch diameter round pieces of ham
1 tablespoon Madeira Wine
6 eggs

3 English muffins, halved
3 sprigs parsley
1 teaspoon capers
Hollandaise Wine Sauce (recipe follows)

Melt butter in heated frying pan. Add ham pieces. When they begin to brown, turn with spatula and add wine. Meanwhile, poach the eggs by dropping into boiling water or lowering in individual poacher receptacles into water and cooking for 2 1/2 minutes. Toast and butter the muffin halves. Prepare Hollandaise Wine Sauce and have hot and ready. Arrange 2 toasted muffin halves on each plate. Cover each muffin half with 2 pieces ham. Top serving with a poached egg. Spread lightly with Hollandaise Wine Sauce. Garnish with parsley and capers.

Hollandaise Wine Sauce
(For above recipe)

This is excellent with asparagus, broccoli, green vegetables, broiled or poached fish, Eggs Benedict. The flour is added to keep sauce from separating.

1/2 cup soft butter	*4 egg yolks*
1/3 teaspon salt	*1 1/2 teaspoons lemon juice*
1/8 teaspoon paprika	*1/3 cup dry Sauterne Wine*
1 teaspoon flour	

Put butter into top of small double boiler and stir until creamy. Stir in salt, paprika and flour. Gradually stir in egg yolks, one at a time. Then add lemon juice and wine. Stir rapidly with wire whisk over hot water 3 to 5 minutes. Sauce will become thick and creamy. Yields 1 cup.

Mushroom-Stuffed Eggs Madeira

6 hard-boiled eggs, shelled	*1/4 teaspoon pepper*
6 large mushrooms	*1 tablespoon Madeira Wine*
1 small onion	*1/4 cup bread crumbs*
1 teaspoon chopped parsley	*12 rounds of toast*
1 tablespoon butter	*1/4 teaspoon paprika*
1/4 teaspoon salt	

Cut eggs in half and remove yolks preparatory to stuffing. Chop mushrooms with onion and add parsley. Mix in yolks. In a saucepan, melt 1 tablespoon butter. Add mushroom-onion-egg mixture. Season with salt and pepper. Add Madeira and cook together until mushrooms and onions are tender, about 10 minutes. Stuff egg whites with mixture. Sprinkle with bread crumbs. Place a portion on each round of toast. Dab little butter on each. Sprinkle with paprika and brown quickly under broiler. Yields 12 stuffed eggs.

Omelette Flambé

4 eggs	*1 1/3 teaspoons sugar*
1/8 teaspoon salt	*1/4 cup Curaçao*
1 tablespoon butter	

Beat eggs and add salt. Heat butter in pan and add eggs to pan. When underside is done after 3 minutes, turn with spatula and fry for 3 more minutes. Remove to a very hot service dish. Sprinkle with sugar. Warm Curaçao and pour over omelette. Ignite and serve immediately. Two servings.

Omelette Grand Marnier

2 eggs, separated
2 teaspoons water
1 teaspoon sugar
2 teaspoons butter
1 tablespoon powdered sugar

1/4 cup Grand Marnier
2 tablespoons heated Cognac

Beat egg yolks and reserve. Beat whites. Add water, combining both yolks and whites. Add sugar. Heat butter in a pan and pour in egg mixture. When set on one side, about 3 minutes, turn over with spatula and cook on other side. When omelette is ready, place in preheated dish and sprinkle with powdered sugar. Pour Grand Marnier over omelette and heated Cognac. Ignite and baste omelette with the Liqueur. Two servings.

Poached Eggs in White Wine

The beauty of a poached egg is that it is neat and whole. If you use an egg poacher, brush egg compartments with butter and sprinkle with salt. Break in eggs and dot each with butter. Then place over boiling water, cover and poach. In this recipe the eggs are poached in wine.

2 tablespoons sweet butter
1/2 cup dry white wine
6 large eggs
1/4 teaspoon salt

1/8 teaspoon white pepper
3 slices toast, decrusted and buttered

Melt butter in pan, being careful not to brown. Add wine and heat through. Carefully break in eggs and poach until each is firm, about 7 minutes, basting occasionally with butter-wine mixture. Season with salt and pepper. Remove eggs carefully with perforated spoon so eggs will not break and eggs will drain. Place on buttered toast. Spoon remaining sauce over them. Three servings.

Rum Raisin Sauce

This is a superb sauce for omelettes and wonderful also with sliced smoked tongue, baked ham or roast pork. Suggested by Meyer's Rum, Jamaican Rum, 84 proof.

1 can beef gravy	2 tablespoons currant jelly
1/2 cup washed raisins	1 tablespoon vinegar
1 tablespoon instant minced	1/2 bay leaf, crumbled
onion	1 teaspoon black pepper,
3 tablespoons Meyer's Rum	freshly ground

Place all of the ingredients in a saucepan and simmer gently for about 10 minutes. Serve over omelette or other dish desired.

Desserts   Wine and spirits evoke the true flavors of fruits, enhancing a pudding or a sauce to pour over plain cake or ice cream. Spirits are marvelous in soufflés.

Anisette Soufflé

2 1/4 cups milk	1/4 cup Anisette Liqueur
2 tablespoons sugar	1/4 teaspoon vanilla extract
1/4 cup butter	1 tablespoon powdered
1/2 cup flour	sugar
5 eggs, separated	

Combine milk and sugar. Scald. In a bowl, melt butter and add the flour, mixing well. Gradually stir in hot milk mixture. Cook over low heat, stirring for 5 minutes or until thickened. Remove from heat. Beat egg yolks until light and fluffy. Stir into hot mixture. Add Anisette and vanilla. Cool slightly. Beat egg whites until stiff but not dry. Fold into thickened milk mixture. Turn into a well-greased 2-quart soufflé dish. Bake at 325° F. for 1 hour. Serve immediately. Eight servings.

Apple Slices Muscatel   The simple secret of successfully whipping cream called for in this recipe is to have all the utensils very cold. Pour heavy cream into a chilled bowl and set bowl in a pan of cracked ice. Beat cream in a slow, even fashion with a chilled rotary beater until it begins to hold a soft shape. When sugar is added, sprinkle it gradually over the surface of the cream and beat the cream slowly until it holds a definite shape when the beater is lifted.

3 large apples	1/2 cup whipping cream
3 tablespoons butter	1/8 teaspoon cinnamon
1/4 cup sugar	1/8 teaspoon salt
1/4 California Muscatel	
Wine	

Pare and core apples and cut into thin slices. Place in skillet with butter, sprinkling with 2 tablespoons sugar. Cover and sauté over moderate heat about 5 minutes. Turn apples once or twice. Add Muscatel. Cover again and simmer until tender, about 15 minutes. Do not overcook. Whip cream with remaining 2 tablespoons sugar, cinnamon and salt. Serve apples warm topped with cinnamon whipped cream. Four or five servings.

————————————————————————————

Baba au Rhum With Strawberries

The invention of this cake is credited to the Polish King Stanislas Leczinski. He really invented a new way to eat kugelhopf, which had been made in Lemberg, Lvow, since 1609 simply by sprinkling the kugelhopf with Rum and setting it on fire. The Polish kugelhopf enjoyed a wonderful success at the court of Lorraine in France, where it was customarily served with a sauce of sweetened and spiced Malaga Wine. King Stanislas named his favorite sweet after Ali Baba, one of the heroes in his favorite Arabian book *The Thousand and One Nights*. A pastry cook named Sthorer brought the king's cake to Paris at the beginning of the 19th century. It became the specialty of his pastry shop in the Rue Montorgueil. He made the babas in advance, then moistened them with a brush dipped in Rum just before selling them. Later the babas were immersed in a rum-flavored syrup before being served.

1 yeast cake
1/2 cup lukewarm milk
3 cups all-purpose flour
3 eggs
3 tablespoons powdered sugar
1/2 cup melted butter
2 tablespoons fine bread crumbs

1/4 teaspoon salt
3/4 cup sugar
1 cup water
1/2 teaspoon lemon juice
1/2 cup dark Rum
1 quart whole strawberries, washed and hulled

Dissolve yeast cake in lukewarm milk. Sift flour into large bowl. Make a well in center of flour and drop in eggs, powdered sugar, melted butter (reserving a little) and the dissolved yeast. Mix well. Butter a ring mold and sift bread crumbs into it, shaking out all crumbs that do not adhere to buttered surface. Sprinkle with salt. Fill mold 3/4 full of dough and let it rise until it reaches the top. Place in hot oven (450° F.) and bake for 35 minutes.

Meanwhile, make the syrup by mixing sugar, water and lemon juice in a saucepan. Boil 2 or 3 minutes, then cool.

Pour two-thirds of this syrup into a bowl, and set aside one-third for final sauce. Remove baba cake and allow to cool. Demold.

To two-thirds portion of syrup, add Rum and pour this mixture over the cake until all sauce is absorbed. Let saturated cake stand several hours. Before serving, place strawberries in and around cake. Add Rum to the reserved one-third portion of the syrup and pour over baba and strawberries, occasionally basting both with the syrup until time to serve.

Bavarian Cream Serve with crushed raspberries, blackberries or strawberries, or as a dessert by itself.

1 1/2 tablespoons unflavored gelatin	*1 1/2 cups milk, scalded*
1/4 cup cold water	*1 tablespoon Southern Comfort*
6 egg yolks	*1 1/2 cups heavy cream*
2/3 cup sugar	*1 quart crushed strawberries*
1/4 teaspoon salt	

Soak gelatin in water. Place egg yolks in large saucepan and beat until light and pale. Add sugar and salt, beating constantly. Stir scalded milk into egg mixture. Cook over low heat, stirring constantly, until the mixture begins to thicken and will coat a spoon. Add soaked gelatin and stir until dissolved. Set custard over cold water and cool, stirring often, until fairly thick. Add Southern Comfort. In a separate bowl, whip cream until stiff but not dry. Fold carefully into custard. Turn mixture into a 2-quart decorative mold and chill for several hours. When ready to serve, dip bottom of mold in hot water, loosen edges with a spatula and invert onto a cold serving platter. Garnish with strawberries. Six servings.

Cherry Jubilee

1 can (No. 2 1/2) black cherries	*1/3 cup Grand Marnier*
2 teaspoons sugar	*1/3 cup heated Cognac*

Pour off 3/4 of the cherry juice. Place cherries and remaining juice in a chafing dish or in a shallow skillet or crepe pan. Sprinkle with sugar and heat through. Add Grand Marnier and heated Cognac. Ignite and baste with flaming juice. Four servings.

Crème de Menthe Whip
(You will need a tray of ice cubes.)

2 envelopes lime-flavored pudding mix
1/8 teaspoon salt
1 cup very hot water
3/4 cup cold water
1/4 cup green Crème de Menthe
1 egg white
1 cup instant whipped dessert topping

Dissolve pudding mix and salt in hot water. Stir in cold water. Cool slightly and add Crème de Menthe. Chill until slightly thickened. Add unbeaten egg white. Place bowl of pudding in a larger bowl of ice cubes and beat with rotary beater until thick and fluffy. Fold in whipped topping. Pour into 2-quart mold and chill until firm. Unmold. Six servings.

Crepes Suzette

2 eggs
2 egg yolks
6 tablespoons flour
2 teaspoons sugar
1/2 teaspoon salt
2 cups milk
3/4 cup butter
1/4 cup Cointreau
1/2 cup orange juice
1 tablespoon grated lemon rind
1/4 cup Brandy

Beat eggs and egg yolks together lightly. Sift flour into bowl with eggs. Add sugar and salt. Add milk and beat well. Strain through a fine sieve. For each crepe, melt 1 teaspoon butter in a small skillet. Add 2 tablespoons batter and cook over high heat for 2 minutes on each side. Set crepes aside.

To serve, melt remaining 1/2 cup butter in chafing dish. Add Cointreau, orange juice and lemon rind and cook for 5 minutes, or until mixture comes to a boil. Add a few crepes and cook them for 2 or 3 minutes, basting frequently with Cointreau sauce. Fold each crepe in quarters. Push to one side of chafing dish. Repeat until all twelve crepes are used. Pour Brandy into a ladle and warm it over a match. Light the brandy and pour it over the crepes to flambé them. When the flame dies down, serve the crepes with the sauce. Two crepes to a serving. Six servings.

Fruits With Cointreau

2 oranges, deeply peeled and cut into sections
2 Bartlett pears, peeled and quartered
$1/2$ quart fresh strawberries, washed and hulled
8 mint leaves
$1/2$ fresh pineapple, peeled and cut into finger slices

4 tablespoons sugar
$1/2$ cantaloupe, in small balls
$1/2$ honeydew melon, in small balls
2 tablespoons powdered sugar
$1/2$ cup Cointreau

In the center of a large serving dish, arrange orange sections, pears and strawberries. Garnish with mint leaves. Around it, arrange pineapple slices sprinkled with sugar, cantaloupe and melon balls sprinkled with powdered sugar. Pour Cointreau over all and chill thoroughly before serving. Four or more servings.

Liqueurs and Fruits

LIQUEUR	FRUIT
Crème de Vanille, Irish Mist, Drambuie, Southern Comfort	Cooked apples, Apple Tarts, Apple Pie
Grand Marnier, Crème de Noyaux, Chartreuse Jaune, Framberry, Southern Comfort	Apricots (cooked, preserved or in tarts)
Cointreau, Apricot Liqueur, Anisette, Crème de Cacao, Grand Marnier	Baked or broiled bananas
Grand Marnier, Triple Sec, Cointreau, Irish Mist, Southern Comfort	Blueberries
Cherry Herring, Apricot Liqueur, Irish Mist, Crème de Noyaux	Cherries (cooked or canned)
B and B, Cointreau, Galliano, Chartreuse Jaune, Apricot Liqueur	Dried figs (reconstituted and preserved)
Triple Sec, Southern Comfort with brown sugar, Apricot Liqueur, Crème de Cassis	Grapes

Grand Marnier, Triple Sec	Melons
Grand Marnier, Cointreau, Apricot Liqueur, Crème de Cassis	Oranges (sliced or sectioned)
Framberry, Grand Marnier, Apricot Liqueur, Peach Liqueur, Bénédictine, B and B	Peaches (fresh, cooked, in tarts or cakes)
Cointreau, Crème de Cassis, Chartreuse, Cherry Liqueur	Pears (cooked or canned)
Grand Marnier, Chartreuse, Apricot Liqueur, Drambuie	Pineapple (fresh or canned)
Peach Liqueur, Southern Comfort Grand Marnier, Cherry Liqueur	Raspberries (fresh or cooked)

Marquise au Champagne

1 1/2 cups water	2 cups chilled Champagne
3/4 cup sugar	2 cups heavy cream, whipped
Grated rind of 1/2 orange	1/4 teaspoon almond extract
Juice of 2 lemons	1 1/2 tablespoons Brandy
Juice of 2 oranges	
1/4 teaspoon salt	

Place water in a saucepan and add sugar. Boil for 5 minutes. Add orange rind, lemon juice, orange juice and salt. Remove from heat. Cool and add Champagne. Strain mixture into a refrigerator tray and freeze. Just before serving the Marquise, stir in whipped cream to which has been added almond extract. Add Brandy. Pile Marquise into sherbert glasses. Four servings.

Mousse Anisette

3 ounces unsweetened chocolate	1/4 teaspoon salt
1 stick (4 ounces) butter	6 egg yolks, well beaten
5 tablespoons sugar	4 tablespoons Anisette Liqueur
1 1/2 cups milk	4 squares sponge cake

Melt chocolate and butter in top of double boiler over warm, not boiling, water. Add sugar, milk and salt. Cook gently for 3 or 4 minutes, stirring until smooth. Remove from stove and let cool. Add egg yolks and 2 tablespoons Anisette. Beat rapidly, or in an electric blender. Pour mixture into mold. Chill in freezer compartment of refrigerator until set (several hours). Serve on squares of sponge cake to which has been added about a teaspoon of Anisette. Four servings.

Baked Oranges Sauterne

6 small, thin-skinned oranges
1/2 cup diced, canned pineapple
6 tablespoons chopped walnuts
6 tablespoons white raisins
1/2 cup sugar
1/2 cup water
1/2 cup Sauterne Wine

Wash oranges and cut off tops. Reserve tops. Scoop out pulp. Remove seeds and white membrane. Reserve remaining pulp. Combine pineapple, walnuts and raisins with pulp. Stuff orange hollows with this mixture and replace tops. Place oranges in a casserole. Combine sugar, water and wine, mixing until sugar is dissolved. Add to casserole around oranges. Cover and bake at 375° F. until oranges are tender, about 40 minutes. Six servings.

Peach Delights

4 large canned peach halves
4 tablespoons brown sugar
4 tablespoons Sherry Wine
1 cup heavy cream, whipped
4 tablespoons confectioners' sugar
1 egg yolk

Place peaches in baking pan. Fill hollows with mixture of brown sugar and 2 tablespoons Sherry. Bake at 375° F. for 1 hour. Meanwhile, prepare sauce by adding sugar to whipped cream, egg yolk and remaining 2 tablespoons Sherry, stirring until smooth. Spoon over hot peaches and serve immediately. Four servings.

Brandied Peaches

1 pound freestone peaches, parboiled
3 cups water
1/2 pound sugar
1/2 cup Brandy

Rub skins off peaches. Boil water and sugar. Drop peaches into this syrup and cook for 25 minutes. Remove with perforated spoon and put into glass jar. Boil syrup until quite thick. Add Brandy and pour over peaches in jar. Seal with melted paraffin. Yields 1 quart peaches.

———————————————————————

Peaches Flambé This recipe calls for the use of a chafing dish. Any dish that is to be flamed should have the right balance of juices or sauces. Too much liquid will dilute the alcohol and too little will shoot flames too high. When a recipe calls for several different liqueurs, the Brandy is always poured on last; there should be no flaming until after the Brandy is poured over the dish. Never ignite with a match. Move the pan to the side and tip the corner toward the chafing dish flame, which will easily ignite the alcohol. You can create a pretty blue color by sprinkling a teaspoon of sugar into a dessert dish as it flames. It is better to flame the dessert course than the main dish if you are a beginner at this. If you do not succeed with the dessert course, nothing is lost; but if you fail to flame the main course and ruin it, the dinner gets a setback. This dish is easily prepared and flamed. It may be served with vanilla ice cream.

1 can (No. 2 1/2) peaches   *1 teaspoon sugar*
3 tablespoons butter   *2 ounces Cognac*

Warm the chafing dish pan. Put the peaches and half of the juice from the can into the pan. Add butter and sugar. Let cook for a minute to make a sauce. Pour Cognac over this and flame. Six servings.

———————————————————————

Pears Flambé   *1 tablespoon butter*   *2 tablespoons Brandy*
                 1/4 cup orange marmalade   *2 tablespoons sour cream*
                 1 can (8 1/2 oz.) pear halves

Heat butter and marmalade in a saucepan over moderately low heat until melted, stirring frequently. Add pears and heat thoroughly, basting the pears frequently with the marmalade mixture. Warm Brandy slightly in a small saucepan or double boiler (bain-marie). Just before serving, pour warmed Brandy over pears and ignite. Serve pears with marmalade sauce and a spoonful of sour cream. Two servings.

———————————————————————

Pears Rosé   *1 can (No. 303) pear halves*   *1 tablespoon fresh lemon*
                1/3 cup sugar   *juice*
                1 teaspoon grated orange   *1/2 cup California Rosé*
                   rind   *Wine*
                1 3-inch piece cinnamon

Drain syrup from pears into saucepan. Add sugar, orange rind and cinnamon. Blend in lemon juice and wine. Pour syrup over pears. Chill well. Four servings.

Sherry–Almond Custard

2 eggs
1/4 cup sugar
1/4 teaspoon salt
1/4 teaspoon almond extract

1 cup light cream
1/4 cup water
1/4 cup Sherry Wine

Beat eggs lightly. Stir in sugar, salt, almond extract, cream and water. Stir until sugar is dissolved. Blend in Sherry. Pour into custard cups and set in double boiler (bain-marie) or pan of hot water. Bake in moderate oven (350° F.) about 1 hour, or until barely set. Cool before serving. Four servings.

Chilled Sherry Soufflé

2 envelopes unflavored gelatin
1/2 cup cold water
1 1/2 cups dry Sherry Wine
5 eggs, separated

1 tablespoon lemon juice
3/4 cup sugar
10 ladyfinger cookies, split
3 or 4 mint leaves

Sprinkle gelatin over cold water. Let stand 5 minutes. Place over boiling water. Stir until gelatin is dissolved. Stir in Sherry. Chill until mixture begins to thicken (several hours). Beat egg whites until foamy. Add lemon juice and beat again until whites are stiff but not dry. Beat yolks until frothy. Add sugar to yolks and beat on high speed of electric mixer until thick and lemon-colored, about 5 minutes. Fold beaten egg whites into beaten yolks. Fold egg mixture into gelatin. Fasten a 2-inch collar of wax paper around a 7-inch soufflé dish. Stand ladyfingers around inside edge of dish. Carefully pour soufflé mixture into waiting dish. Chill at least 4 hours, or until firm. Remove wax paper and garnish with sprigs of mint leaves. Twelve servings.

Soufflé With Cointreau

1 cup milk
1/2 cup sugar
1 tablespoon flour
5 eggs, separated

1 cup Cointreau
1/2 teaspoon butter
1 tablespoon powdered sugar

Place milk in saucepan and bring to boil. In a bowl, thoroughly mix sugar, flour and yolks of eggs. Pour milk over this mixture and whip well. Return to heat, continuing to whip as it cooks for 3 to 4 minutes, when it should have a thick consistency. Stiffly beat egg whites. Stir in Cointreau and egg whites. Pour mixture into a well-buttered metal baking dish with straight sides, if possible. Sprinkle with powdered sugar. Bake 8 to 10 minutes and serve immediately. Four servings.

Pastries

Champagne Cookies

1 whole egg
2 eggs, separated
1/4 cup confectioners' sugar
1/4 teaspoon salt
1/4 cup Champagne
1 1/2 teaspoons grated orange peel

1/4 cup cake flour, sifted
1/2 cup granulated sugar
1/4 cup finely chopped walnuts

Beat together the whole egg and 2 egg yolks. Sift confectioners' sugar into mixture and beat. Add salt, Champagne and orange peel and continue beating until thick and lemon-colored. Fold in flour. Beat egg whites until foamy. Gradually add granulated sugar, beating until stiff but not dry. Fold into flour mixture. Press through a pastry tube, making round cookies about 1/4 inch in diameter. Place on a cooky sheet or flat pan about 1 inch apart. Sprinkle tops with chopped nuts. Set aside uncovered for 3 hours. Bake at 300° F. about 15 minutes. Cookies should be a Champagne color. Yields about 9 dozen tiny cookies.

Cherry Pie Marnier With Sauce

2 cups tart cherries and juice
1 tablespoon Cherry Marnier
1/2 teaspoon almond extract
2 unbaked 9-inch pie shells
3/4 cup sugar

1 1/2 tablespoons flour, sifted
1 1/2 tablespoons cornstarch
1 tablespoon butter
1 tablespoon light cream
Cherry Marnier Sauce (recipe follows)

Put cherries and juice in a bowl. Add Cherry Marnier and almond extract. Pour into 1 unbaked pie shell in its baking dish. Sprinkle sugar, flour and cornstarch over mixture in pie shell. Dot with butter. Cut steam vents in second unbaked pie shell and set atop filled shell. Flute edges by squeezing together with thumb and index finger. Brush top with light cream. Place in preheated oven (425° F.) for about 30 minutes. Top with Cherry Marnier Sauce and serve hot or cold. Eight servings.

**Cherry Marnier
Sauce**
(For above recipe)

1 can (2 pounds) pitted
   black Bing cherries, with
   liquid
1 1/2 tablespoons cornstarch

3 tablespoons sugar
2 tablespoons Cherry
   Marnier

Drain cherries and reserve cherries and juice. In a saucepan, mix cornstarch with enough cherry juice to make a smooth paste. Add remaining cherry juice and cook over low heat until juice is clear and slightly thickened. Add sugar and cook until sugar is dissolved. Remove from heat. Add cherries and Cherry Marnier. Yields 2 cups sauce.

**Chocolate Cream
Rum Pie**

White Label Rum, which is light-bodied and pale in color, with delicate aroma and flavor, is suitable for cocktails and mixed drinks. Gold Label identifies a darker color Rum of a stronger flavor and aroma. It is most appropriate where the Rum flavor is to predominate, and it is also best for flavoring cakes, pastries and candies.

1 teaspoon butter
1 9-inch unbaked pie shell
6 egg yolks
1 cup sugar
1 1/2 envelopes unflavored
   gelatin
1/2 cup cold water

1 pint heavy cream,
   whipped
1/2 cup Gold Label Rum
1/4 cup strong black coffee
1/4 cup chopped pistachio
   nuts

Butter a pie plate well and line with pie pastry. Bake at 375° F. until well done and a golden color, about 30 minutes. Allow to cool. Beat egg yolks until light. Gradually add 1 cup sugar. Soak gelatin in cold water and place both gelatin and water over a low flame. Stir until completely dissolved. Pour over egg and sugar mixture, stirring well. Fold whipped cream (reserving 1/4 cup) into first mixture. Add Gold Label Rum and black coffee. Let cool until mixture begins to set. Then pour into baked pie shell. Chill until very firm. Sprinkle top of pie with nuts and decorate edges of crust with reserved whipped cream. Prepare pie well in advance because thorough chilling greatly improves the taste. Eight servings.

Strawberry Chiffon Pie

1 10-oz. package frozen, sliced strawberries
1 envelope unflavored gelatin
1/2 cup California Rosé Wine
2 tablespoons lemon juice
2 egg whites
1/4 teaspoon salt
1/4 cup sugar
1/2 cup heavy cream
1 baked 9-inch pie shell
1 tablespoon finely crushed almonds

Thaw strawberries. Soften gelatin in Rosé Wine by dissolving in top of double boiler over hot water. Blend in lemon juice. Cool until mixture begins to jell. Add strawberries. Beat egg whites with salt until stiff but not dry. Gradually beat in sugar. With same beater, whip cream until stiff in peaks. Fold egg whites and cream into strawberry mixture. Chill a few minutes until mixture mounds on a spoon. Turn into baked, cooled pie shell. Chill at least 2 hours until firm. Sprinkle lightly with almonds. Eight servings.

Flavored Whipped Cream

Liqueurs can be used to flavor whipped cream to serve with desserts as contrasting or parallel flavors.

1 cup heavy cream
1/3 cup confectioners' sugar
1 tablespoon Curaçao
2 tablespoons grated orange rind

Beat cream until frothy. Gradually add sugar. Add Curaçao and orange rind. Continue to beat until cream is of desired consistency. Yields about 1 cup.

Variations
(For above recipe)

Use 2 tablespoons Crème de Menthe, or 2 tablespoons Framberry and 1/3 cup crushed, strained raspberries.

Miscellaneous

Walnuts and Wine

Our friends, the Diamond Walnut Growers of California, remind us that even ancient history told of the combination of wine with walnuts as being an excellent final dinner course. The once-familiar bowl of nuts with its nutcracker is making a return to dinner tables. After the table is cleared, nuts and fruit and wine, Cognacs or Brandies appear, for the most appealing and satisfying concluding course. Wine is frequently combined with walnuts in recipes such as Christmas fruit cakes and puddings.

Zabaglione 6 egg yolks   *1/8 teaspoon salt*
6 tablespoons sugar   6 tablespoons Sherry Wine

In top of double boiler, combine egg yolks, sugar and salt. Beat with rotary beater until eggs are thick and yellow. Gradually add Sherry. Place over hot water and beat 4 to 6 minutes until mixture is thick and fluffy. Remove from heat and serve immediately in sherbet glasses or over canned peaches or pear halves or over whole strawberries or raspberries. Four servings.

Beverages A number of hot beverages can be made with wine and spirits, many of them old familiars.

Café Chantilly *1 cup black coffee*   *1 teaspoon whipped cream*
2 tablespoons Cognac

To black coffee, add Cognac and float whipped cream. One serving.

Café Charente *1 cup black coffee*   *2 tablespoons Cognac*

Lace piping hot coffee with Cognac and drink it very hot. One serving.

Café Diable *6 sugar cubes*   *1 tablespoon Curaçao*
Grated rind of 1 orange   *3 tablespoons Brandy*
1/3 teaspoon ground clove   *3 cups strong after-dinner*
1/3 teaspoon ground   *coffee*
cinnamon

In a small double boiler, combine sugar, orange rind, spices, Curaçao and Brandy. Cook together until sugar has dissolved. Pour mixture into coffee and serve in demitasse cups. Six servings.

Café Grappa or Anisette Serve hot black coffee, especially espresso, laced with Grappa or Anisette.

Café Royale

1 lump sugar	1 tablespoon Cognac
1 cup black coffee	

Place sugar in a spoon and set across cup of hot, black coffee. Pour Cognac over sugar until saturated. Ignite. As blue flame rises, slide sugar into coffee. One serving.

Chocolate or Cocoa Royal

1 1/2 tablespoons cocoa or bits of chocolate	2 tablespoons Brandy
2 cups hot milk	2 tablespoons whipped cream
2 cups boiling water	1/2 teaspoon sugar
1/3 cup sugar	

Put cocoa or chocolate in top of double boiler. Add milk and water. Stir and add sugar. Stir in Brandy. Have water in bottom part of double boiler very hot. Remove from heat and serve, adding whipped cream sweetened with sugar as topping. Four servings.

Holiday Chocolate

1/2 cup semisweet chocolate bits	3 cups milk
1 cup Sherry Wine	1/2 cup light cream
1/8 teaspoon salt	1/2 cup whipped cream
1/4 teaspoon cinnamon	1/2 teaspoon cinnamon

In top of double boiler, place chocolate bits, Sherry, salt and cinnamon. Cook over hot water, stirring occasionally, until chocolate is melted. Heat milk and light cream in a saucepan to scalding point and to it add chocolate mixture. Beat well and pour into mugs or cups. Top with whipped cream and dust lightly with cinnamon. Six to eight servings.

Inspired Milk Shake

2 ounces Cointreau	1/2 cup milk
1 scoop vanilla ice cream	

Mix all ingredients in a blender or whip with a hand rotary beater or with a spoon. Makes one portion. Serve in tall glass with straws.

Beef Tea Pick-Up

1/4 teaspoon beef extract	1 cup boiling water
2 tablespoons Sherry or Brandy	1/8 teaspoon salt
	1/8 teaspoon pepper

Place beef extract in cup. Add Sherry or Brandy and pour boiling water over it. Season with salt and pepper. One serving.

Imperial Tea   Add 1 to 2 tablespoons of Rum, Brandy or Whiskey to a cup of tea.

Liqueur Tea   Stir 1 to 2 tablespoons of preferred Liqueur or Cordial into a cup of very hot tea. Two or three shelled litchi nuts give the tea a delicious flavor.

Russian Rum Tea

1 slice lemon   *1 teaspoon Rum*
1 teaspoon sugar   *1 cup hot tea*

Add lemon, sugar and Rum to hot tea in a tall glass, Russian-style.

Tea Bracer   Add an ounce or so of Cointreau to a cup of hot tea for a heart-warming reviver on a cold, wintry day. Serve with a wedge of lemon.

Tea Toddy   Prepare tea in the usual way and serve with sugar, lemon and Whiskey.

General Index

Date Due

Library Bureau Cat. No. 1137